AF689752

Python Programming

Brian Evenson

Published by Wilson Publishers, 2023.

While every precaution has been taken in the preparation of this book, the publisher assumes no responsibility for errors or omissions, or for damages resulting from the use of the information contained herein.

PYTHON PROGRAMMING

First edition. March 2, 2023.

Copyright © 2023 Brian Evenson.

Written by Brian Evenson.

PART I

BASICS

Part I of this book teaches you the basic concepts you'll need to write Python programs. Many of these concepts are common to all programming languages, so they'll be useful throughout your life as a programmer.

In **Chapter 1** you'll install Python on your computer and run your first program, which prints the message *Hello world!* to the screen.

In **Chapter 2** you'll learn to store information in variables and work with text and numerical values.

Chapters 3 and **4** introduce lists. Lists can store as much information as you want in one variable, allowing you to work with that data efficiently. You'll be able to work with hundreds, thousands, and even millions of values in just a few lines of code.

In **Chapter 5** you'll use `if` statements to write code that responds one way if certain conditions are true, and responds in a different way if those conditions are not true.

Chapter 6 shows you how to use Python's dictionaries, which let you make connections between different pieces of information. Like lists, dictionaries can contain as much information as you need to store.

In **Chapter 7** you'll learn how to accept input from users to make your programs interactive. You'll also learn about `while` loops, which run blocks of code repeatedly as long as certain conditions remain true.

In **Chapter 8** you'll write functions, which are named blocks of code that perform a specific task and can be run whenever you need them.

Chapter 9 introduces classes, which allow you to model real-world objects, such as dogs, cats, people, cars, rockets, and much more, so your code can represent anything real or abstract.

Chapter 10 shows you how to work with files and handle errors so your programs won't crash unexpectedly. You'll store data before your program closes, and read the data back in when the program runs again. You'll learn about Python's exceptions, which allow you to anticipate errors, and make your programs handle those errors gracefully.

In **Chapter 11** you'll learn to write tests for your code to check that your programs work the way you intend them to. As a result, you'll be able to expand your programs without worrying about introducing new bugs. Testing your code is one of the first skills that will help you transition from beginner to intermediate programmer.

1

GETTING STARTED

In this chapter you'll run your first Python program, *hello_world.py*. First, you'll need to check whether Python is installed on your computer; if it isn't, you'll install it. You'll also install a text editor to work with your Python programs. Text editors recognize Python code and highlight sections as you write, making it easy to understand the structure of your code.

Setting Up Your Programming Environment

Python differs slightly on different operating systems, so you'll need to keep a few considerations in mind. Here, we'll look at the two major versions of Python currently in use and outline the steps to set up Python on your system.

Python 2 and Python 3

Today, two versions of Python are available: Python 2 and the newer Python 3. Every programming language evolves as new ideas and technologies emerge, and the developers of Python have continually made the language more versatile and powerful. Most changes are incremental and hardly noticeable, but in some cases code written for Python 2 may not run properly on systems with Python 3 installed. Throughout this book I'll point out areas of significant difference between Python 2 and Python 3, so whichever version you use, you'll be able to follow the instructions.

If both versions are installed on your system or if you need to install Python, use Python 3. If Python 2 is the only version on your system and you'd rather jump into writing code instead of installing Python, you can start with Python 2. But the sooner you upgrade to using Python 3 the better, so you'll be working with the most recent version.

Running Snippets of Python Code

Python comes with an interpreter that runs in a terminal window, allowing you to try bits of Python without having to save and run an entire program.

Throughout this book, you'll see snippets that look like this:

```
❶ >>> print("Hello Python interpreter!")
Hello Python interpreter!
```

The text in bold is what you'll type in and then execute by pressing ENTER. Most of the examples in the book are small, self-contained programs that you'll run from your editor, because that's how you'll write most of your code. But sometimes basic concepts will be shown in a series of snippets run through a Python terminal session to demonstrate isolated concepts more efficiently. Any time you see the three angle brackets in a code listing ❶, you're looking at the output of a terminal session. We'll try coding in the interpreter for your system in a moment.

Hello World!

A long-held belief in the programming world has been that printing a *Hello world!* message to the screen as your first program in a new language will bring you luck.

In Python, you can write the *Hello World* program in one line:

```
print("Hello world!")
```

Such a simple program serves a very real purpose. If it runs correctly on your system, any Python program you write should work as well. We'll look at writing this program on your particular system in just a moment.

Python on Different Operating Systems

Python is a cross-platform programming language, which means it runs on all the major operating systems. Any Python program you write should run on any modern computer that has Python installed. However, the methods for setting up Python on different operating systems vary slightly.

In this section you'll learn how to set up Python and run the *Hello World* program on your own system. You'll first check whether Python is installed on your system and install it if it's not. Then you'll install a simple text editor and save an empty Python file called *hello_world.py*. Finally, you'll run the *Hello World* program and troubleshoot anything that didn't work. I'll walk you through this process for each operating system, so you'll have a beginner-friendly Python programming environment.

Python on Linux

Linux systems are designed for programming, so Python is already installed on most Linux computers. The people who write and maintain Linux expect you to do your own programming at some point and encourage you to do so. For this reason there's very little you have to install and very few settings you have to change to start programming.

Checking Your Version of Python

Open a terminal window by running the Terminal application on your system (in Ubuntu, you can press CTRL-ALT-T). To find out whether Python is installed, enter **python** with a lowercase *p*. You should see output telling you which version of Python is installed and a >>> prompt where you can start entering Python commands, like this:

```
$ python
Python 2.7.6 (default, Mar 22 2014, 22:59:38)
[GCC 4.8.2] on linux2
Type "help", "copyright", "credits" or "license" for more information.
>>>
```

This output tells you that Python 2.7.6 is currently the default version of Python installed on this computer. When you've seen this output, press CTRL-D or enter `exit()` to leave the Python prompt and return to a terminal prompt.

To check for Python 3, you might have to specify that version; so even if the output displayed Python 2.7 as the default version, try the command `python3`:

```
$ python3
Python 3.5.0 (default, Sep 17 2015, 13:05:18)
[GCC 4.8.4] on linux
Type "help", "copyright", "credits" or "license" for more information.
>>>
```

This output means you also have Python 3 installed, so you'll be able to use either version. Whenever you see the `python` command in this book, enter `python3` instead. Most Linux distributions have Python already installed, but if for some reason yours didn't or if your system came with Python 2 and you want to install Python 3, refer to Appendix A.

Installing a Text Editor

Geany is a simple text editor: it's easy to install, will let you run almost all your programs directly from the editor instead of through a terminal, uses syntax highlighting to color your code, and runs your code in a terminal window so you'll get used to using terminals. Appendix B provides information on other text editors, but I recommend using Geany unless you have a good reason to use a different editor.

You can install Geany in one line on most Linux systems:

```
$ sudo apt-get install geany
```

If this doesn't work, see the instructions at *http://geany.org/Download/ThirdPartyPackages/*.

Running the Hello World Program

To start your first program, open Geany. Press the Super key (often called the Windows key) and search for Geany on your system. Make a shortcut by dragging the icon to your taskbar or desktop. Then make a folder somewhere on your system for your projects and call it *python_work*. (It's best to use lowercase letters and underscores for spaces in file and folder names because these are Python naming conventions.) Go back to Geany and save an empty Python file (**File ▸ Save As**) called *hello_world.py* in your *python_work* folder. The extension *.py* tells Geany your file will contain a Python program. It also tells Geany how to run your program and highlight the text in a helpful way.

After you've saved your file, enter the following line:

```
print("Hello Python world!")
```

If multiple versions of Python are installed on your system, you need to make sure Geany is configured to use the correct version. Go to **Build ▸ Set Build Commands**. You should see the words *Compile* and *Execute* with a command next to each. Geany assumes the correct command for each is `python`, but if your system uses the `python3` command, you'll need to change this.

If the command `python3` worked in a terminal session, change the Compile and Execute commands so Geany will use the Python 3 interpreter. Your Compile command should look like this:

```
python3 -m py_compile "%f"
```

You need to type this command exactly as it's shown. Make sure the spaces and capitalization match what is shown here.

Your Execute command should look like this:

```
python3 "%f"
```

Again, make sure the spacing and capitalization match what is shown here. Figure 1-1 shows how these commands should look in Geany's configuration menu.

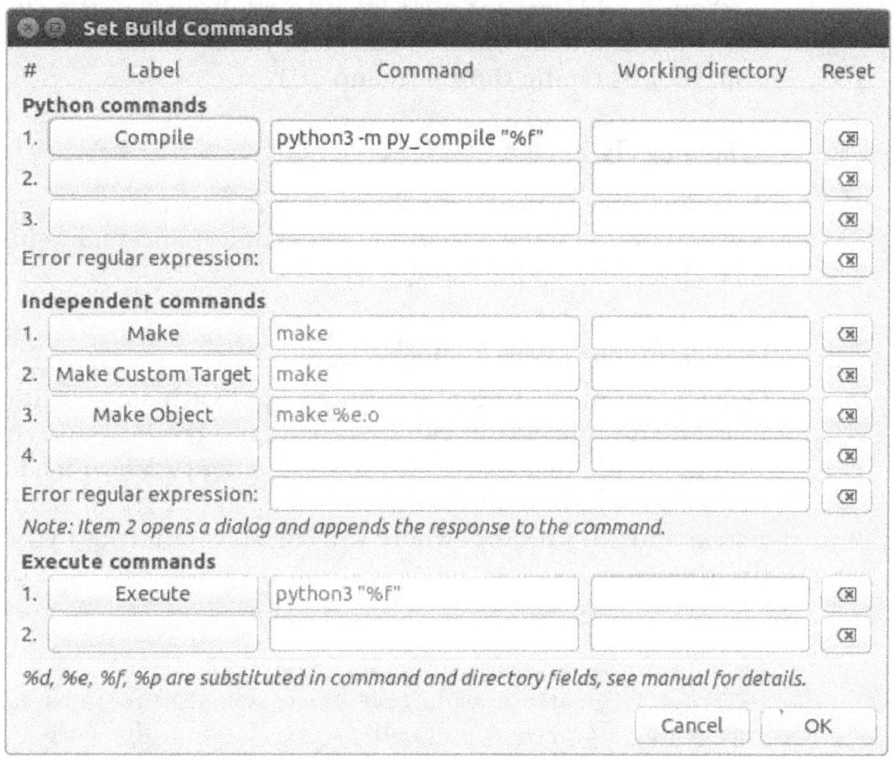

Figure 1-1: Here, Geany is configured to use Python 3 on Linux.

Now run *hello_world.py* by selecting **Build ▸ Execute** in the menu, by clicking the Execute icon (which shows a set of gears), or by pressing F5. A terminal window should pop up with the following output:

```
Hello Python world!

------------------
(program exited with code: 0)
Press return to continue
```

If you don't see this, check every character on the line you entered. Did you accidentally capitalize `print`? Did you forget one or both of the quotation marks or parentheses? Programming languages expect very specific syntax, and if you don't provide that, you'll get errors. If you can't get the program to run, see "Troubleshooting Installation Issues" on page 15.

Running Python in a Terminal Session

You can try running snippets of Python code by opening a terminal and typing python or python3, as you did when checking your version. Do this again, but this time enter the following line in the terminal session:

```
>>> print("Hello Python interpreter!")
Hello Python interpreter!
>>>
```

You should see your message printed directly in the current terminal window. Remember that you can close the Python interpreter by pressing CTRL-D or by typing the command exit().

Python on OS X

Python is already installed on most OS X systems. Once you know Python is installed, you'll need to install a text editor and make sure it's configured correctly.

Checking Whether Python Is Installed

Open a terminal window by going to **Applications ▸ Utilities ▸ Terminal**. You can also press COMMAND-spacebar, type **terminal**, and then press ENTER. To find out whether Python is installed, enter **python** with a lowercase *p*. You should see output telling you which version of Python is installed on your system and a >>> prompt where you can start entering Python commands, like this:

```
$ python
Python 2.7.5 (default, Mar  9 2014, 22:15:05)
[GCC  4.2.1 Compatible Apple LLVM 5.0 (clang-500.0.68)] on darwin
Type "help", "copyright", "credits", or "license" for more information.
>>>
```

This output tells you that Python 2.7.5 is currently the default version installed on this computer. When you've seen this output, press CTRL-D or enter exit() to leave the Python prompt and return to a terminal prompt.

To check for Python 3, try the command python3. You might get an error message, but if the output shows you have Python 3 installed, you'll be able to use Python 3 without having to install it. If python3 works on your system, whenever you see the python command in this book, make sure you use python3 instead. If for some reason your system didn't come with Python or if you only have Python 2 and you want to install Python 3 now, see Appendix A.

Running Python in a Terminal Session

You can try running snippets of Python code by opening a terminal and typing `python` or `python3`, as you did when checking your version. Do this again, but this time enter the following line in the terminal session:

```
>>> print("Hello Python interpreter!")
Hello Python interpreter!
>>>
```

You should see your message printed directly in the current terminal window. Remember that you can close the Python interpreter by pressing CTRL-D or by typing the command `exit()`.

Installing a Text Editor

Sublime Text is a simple text editor: it's easy to install on OS X, will let you run almost all of your programs directly from the editor instead of through a terminal, uses syntax highlighting to color your code, and runs your code in a terminal session embedded in the Sublime Text window to make it easy to see the output. Appendix B provides information on other text editors, but I recommend using Sublime Text unless you have a good reason to use a different editor.

You can download an installer for Sublime Text from *http://sublimetext.com/3*. Click the download link and look for an installer for OS X. Sublime Text has a very liberal licensing policy: you can use the editor for free as long as you want, but the author requests that you purchase a license if you like it and want continual use. After the installer has been downloaded, open it and then drag the Sublime Text icon into your *Applications* folder.

Configuring Sublime Text for Python 3

If you use a command other than `python` to start a Python terminal session, you'll need to configure Sublime Text so it knows where to find the correct version of Python on your system. Issue the following command to find out the full path to your Python interpreter:

```
$ type -a python3
python3 is /usr/local/bin/python3
```

Now open Sublime Text, and go to **Tools ▸ Build System ▸ New Build System**, which will open a new configuration file for you. Delete what you see and enter the following:

Python3.sublime-build

```
{
    "cmd": ["/usr/local/bin/python3", "-u", "$file"],
}
```

This code tells Sublime Text to use your system's python3 command when running the currently open file. Make sure you use the path you found when issuing the command type -a python3 in the previous step. Save the file as *Python3.sublime-build* in the default directory that Sublime Text opens when you choose Save.

Running the Hello World Program

To start your first program, launch Sublime Text by opening the *Applications* folder and double-clicking the Sublime Text icon. You can also press COMMAND-spacebar and enter **sublime text** in the search bar that pops up.

Make a folder called *python_work* somewhere on your system for your projects. (It's best to use lowercase letters and underscores for spaces in file and folder names, because these are Python naming conventions.) Save an empty Python file (**File ▸ Save As**) called *hello_world.py* in your *python_work* folder. The extension *.py* tells Sublime Text that your file will contain a Python program and tells it how to run your program and highlight the text in a helpful way.

After you've saved your file, enter the following line:

```
print("Hello Python world!")
```

If the command python works on your system, you can run your program by selecting **Tools ▸ Build** in the menu or by pressing CTRL-B. If you configured Sublime Text to use a command other than python, select **Tools ▸ Build System** and then select **Python 3**. This sets Python 3 as the default version of Python, and you'll be able to select **Tools ▸ Build** or just press COMMAND-B to run your programs from now on.

A terminal screen should appear at the bottom of the Sublime Text window, showing the following output:

```
Hello Python world!
[Finished in 0.1s]
```

If you don't see this, check every character on the line you entered. Did you accidentally capitalize print? Did you forget one or both of the quotation marks or parentheses? Programming languages expect very specific syntax, and if you don't provide that, you'll get errors. If you can't get the program to run, see "Troubleshooting Installation Issues" on page 15.

Python on Windows

Windows doesn't always come with Python, so you'll probably need to download and install it, and then download and install a text editor.

Installing Python

First, check whether Python is installed on your system. Open a command window by entering **command** into the Start menu or by holding down the SHIFT key while right-clicking on your desktop and selecting **Open command window here**. In the terminal window, enter **python** in lowercase. If you get a Python prompt (>>>), Python is installed on your system. However, you'll probably see an error message telling you that python is not a recognized command.

In that case, download a Python installer for Windows. Go to *http://python.org/downloads/*. You should see two buttons, one for downloading Python 3 and one for downloading Python 2. Click the Python 3 button, which should automatically start downloading the correct installer for your system. After you've downloaded the file, run the installer. Make sure you check the option Add Python to PATH, which will make it easier to configure your system correctly. Figure 1-2 shows this option checked.

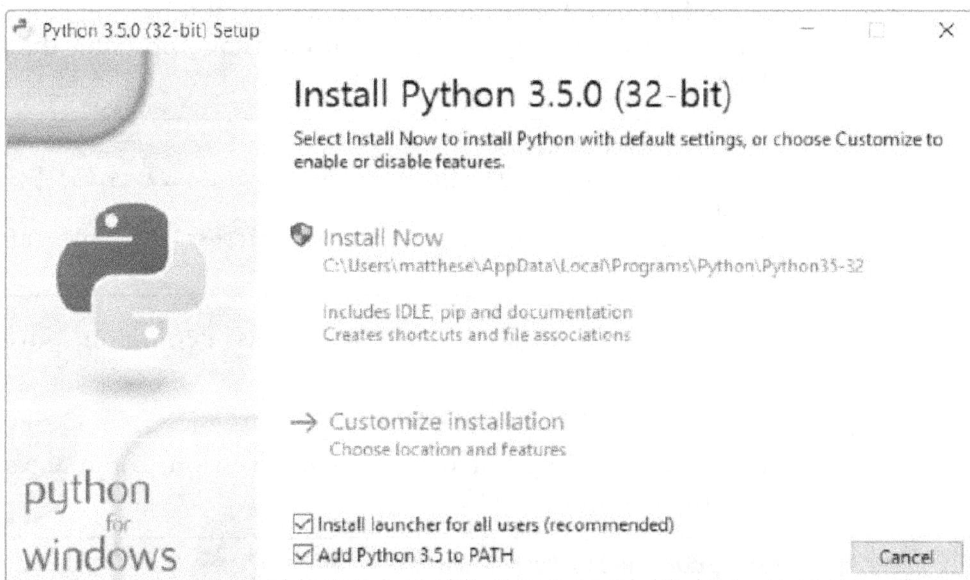

Figure 1-2: Make sure you check the box labeled Add Python to PATH.

Starting a Python Terminal Session

Setting up your text editor will be straightforward if you first set up your system to run Python in a terminal session. Open a command window and enter **python** in lowercase. If you get a Python prompt (>>>), Windows has found the version of Python you just installed:

```
C:\> python
Python 3.5.0 (v3.5.0:374f501f4567, Sep 13 2015, 22:15:05) [MSC v.1900 32 bit
(Intel)] on win32
Type "help", "copyright", "credits" or "license" for more information.
>>>
```

If this worked, you can move on to the next section, "Running Python in a Terminal Session."

However, you may see output that looks more like this:

```
C:\> python
'python' is not recognized as an internal or external command, operable
program or batch file.
```

In this case you need to tell Windows how to find the Python version you just installed. Your system's `python` command is usually saved in your *C* drive, so open Windows Explorer and open your *C* drive. Look for a folder starting with the name *Python,* open that folder, and find the *python* file (in lowercase). For example, I have a *Python35* folder with a file named *python* inside it, so the path to the `python` command on my system is *C:\Python35\python*. Otherwise, enter **python** into the search box in Windows Explorer to show you exactly where the `python` command is stored on your system.

When you think you know the path, test it by entering that path into a terminal window. Open a command window and enter the full path you just found:

```
C:\> C:\Python35\python
Python 3.5.0 (v3.5.0:374f501f4567, Sep 13 2015, 22:15:05) [MSC v.1900 32 bit
(Intel)] on win32
Type "help", "copyright", "credits" or "license" for more information.
>>>
```

If this worked, you know how to access Python on your system.

Running Python in a Terminal Session

Enter the following line in your Python session, and make sure you see the output *Hello Python world!*

```
>>> print("Hello Python world!")
Hello Python world!
>>>
```

Any time you want to run a snippet of Python code, open a command window and start a Python terminal session. To close the terminal session, press CTRL-Z and then press ENTER, or enter the command `exit()`.

Installing a Text Editor

Geany is a simple text editor: it's easy to install, will let you run almost all of your programs directly from the editor instead of through a terminal, uses syntax highlighting to color your code, and runs your code in a terminal window so you'll get used to using terminals. Appendix B provides information on other text editors, but I recommend using Geany unless you have a good reason to use a different editor.

You can download a Windows installer for Geany from *http://geany.org/*. Click **Releases** under the Download menu, and look for the *geany-1.25_setup.exe* installer or something similar. Run the installer and accept all the defaults.

To start your first program, open Geany: press the Windows key and search for Geany on your system. You should make a shortcut by dragging the icon to your taskbar or desktop. Make a folder called *python_work* somewhere on your system for your projects. (It's best to use lowercase letters and underscores for spaces in file and folder names, because these are Python naming conventions.) Go back to Geany and save an empty Python file (**File ▸ Save As**) called *hello_world.py* in your *python_work* folder. The extension *.py* tells Geany that your file will contain a Python program. It also tells Geany how to run your program and to highlight the text in a helpful way.

After you've saved your file, type the following line:

```
print("Hello Python world!")
```

If the command `python` worked on your system, you won't have to configure Geany; skip the next section and move on to "Running the Hello World Program" on page 14. If you needed to enter a path like *C:\Python35\python* to start a Python interpreter, follow the directions in the next section to configure Geany for your system.

Configuring Geany

To configure Geany, go to **Build ▸ Set Build Commands**. You should see the words *Compile* and *Execute* with a command next to each. The Compile and Execute commands start with `python` in lowercase, but Geany doesn't know where your system stored the `python` command. You need to add the path you used in the terminal session.

In the Compile and Execute commands, add the drive your `python` command is on and the folder where the `python` command is stored. Your Compile command should look something like this:

```
C:\Python35\python -m py_compile "%f"
```

Your path might be a little different, but make sure the spaces and capitalization match what is shown here.

Your Execute command should look something like this:

```
C:\Python35\python "%f"
```

Again, make sure the spacing and capitalization in your Execute command matches what is shown here. Figure 1-3 shows how these commands should look in Geany's configuration menu.

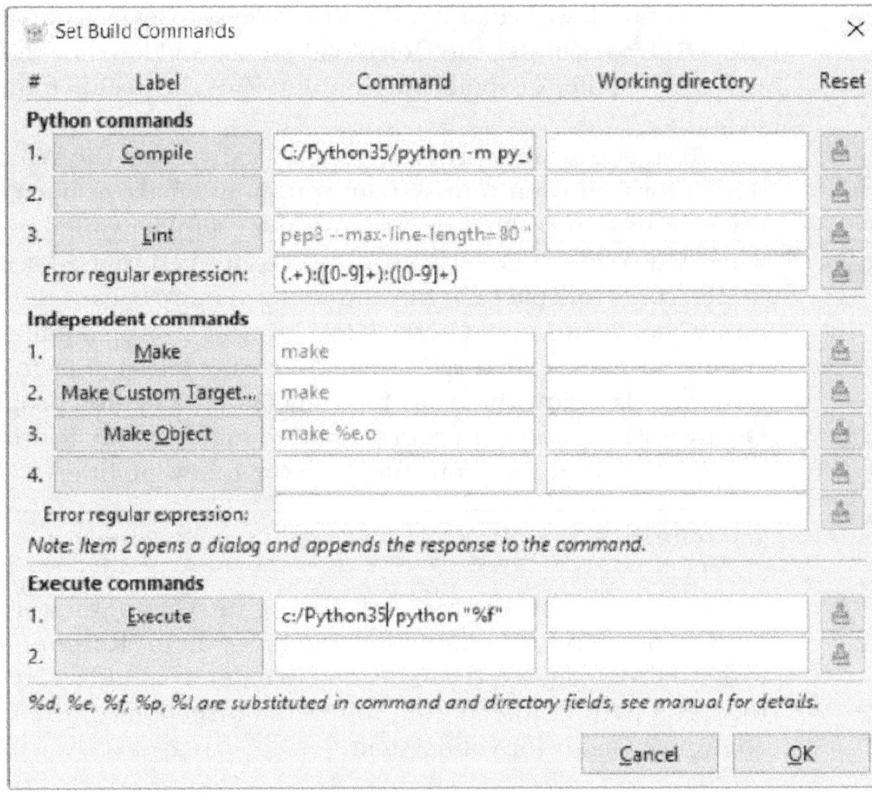

Figure 1-3: Here, Geany is configured to use Python 3 on Windows.

After you've set these commands correctly, click **OK**.

Running the Hello World Program

You should now be able to run your program successfully. Run *hello_world.py* by selecting **Build ▸ Execute** in the menu, by clicking the Execute icon (which shows a set of gears), or by pressing F5. A terminal window should pop up with the following output:

```
Hello Python world!

------------------
(program exited with code: 0)
Press return to continue
```

If you don't see this, check every character on the line you entered. Did you accidentally capitalize `print`? Did you forget one or both of the quotation marks or parentheses? Programming languages expect very specific syntax, and if you don't provide that, you'll get errors. If you can't get the program to run, see the next section for help.

Troubleshooting Installation Issues

Hopefully, setting up your programming environment was successful, but if you've been unable to run *hello_world.py*, here are a few remedies you can try:

- When a program contains a significant error, Python displays a *traceback*. Python looks through the file and tries to report the problem. The traceback might give you a clue as to what issue is preventing the program from running.
- Step away from your computer, take a short break, and then try again. Remember that syntax is very important in programming, so even a missing colon, a mismatched quotation mark, or mismatched parentheses can prevent a program from running properly. Reread the relevant parts of this chapter, look over what you've done, and see if you can find the mistake.
- Start over again. You probably don't need to uninstall anything, but it might make sense to delete your *hello_world.py* file and create it again from scratch.
- Ask someone else to follow the steps in this chapter, on your computer or a different one, and watch what they do carefully. You might have missed one small step that someone else happens to catch.
- Find someone who knows Python and ask them to help you get set up. If you ask around, you might find that you know someone who uses Python.
- The setup instructions in this chapter are also available online, through *https://www.nostarch.com/pythoncrashcourse/*. The online version of these instructions may work better for you.
- Ask for help online. Appendix C provides a number of resources and areas online, like forums and live chat sites, where you can ask for solutions from people who've already worked through the issue you're currently facing.

Don't worry about bothering experienced programmers. Every programmer has been stuck at some point, and most programmers are happy to help you set up your system correctly. As long as you can state clearly what you're trying to do, what you've already tried, and the results you're getting, there's a good chance someone will be able to help you. As mentioned in the Introduction, the Python community is very beginner friendly.

Python should run well on any modern computer, so find a way to ask for help if you're having trouble so far. Early issues can be frustrating, but they're well worth sorting out. Once you get *hello_world.py* running, you can start to learn Python, and your programming work will become more interesting and satisfying.

Running Python Programs from a Terminal

Most of the programs you write in your text editor you'll run directly from the editor, but sometimes it's useful to run programs from a terminal instead. For example, you might want to run an existing program without opening it for editing.

You can do this on any system with Python installed if you know how to access the directory where you've stored your program file. To try this, make sure you've saved the *hello_world.py* file in the *python_work* folder on your desktop.

On Linux and OS X

Running a Python program from a terminal session is the same on Linux and OS X. The terminal command `cd`, for *change directory*, is used to navigate through your file system in a terminal session. The command `ls`, for *list*, shows you all the nonhidden files that exist in the current directory.

Open a new terminal window and issue the following commands to run *hello_world.py*:

```
❶ ~$ cd Desktop/python_work/
❷ ~/Desktop/python_work$ ls
  hello_world.py
❸ ~/Desktop/python_work$ python hello_world.py
  Hello Python world!
```

At ❶ we use the `cd` command to navigate to the *python_work* folder, which is in the *Desktop* folder. Next, we use the `ls` command to make sure *hello_world.py* is in this folder ❷. Then, we run the file using the command `python hello_world.py` ❸.

It's that simple. You just use the `python` (or `python3`) command to run Python programs.

On Windows

The terminal command `cd`, for *change directory*, is used to navigate through your file system in a command window. The command `dir`, for *directory*, shows you all the files that exist in the current directory.

Open a new terminal window and issue the following commands to run *hello_world.py*:

```
❶ C:\> cd Desktop\python_work
❷ C:\Desktop\python_work> dir
  hello_world.py
❸ C:\Desktop\python_work> python hello_world.py
  Hello Python world!
```

At ❶ we use the `cd` command to navigate to the *python_work* folder, which is in the *Desktop* folder. Next, we use the `dir` command to make sure *hello_world.py* is in this folder ❷. Then, we run the file using the command `python hello_world.py` ❸.

If you haven't configured your system to use the simple command python, you may need to use the longer version of this command:

```
C:\$ cd Desktop\python_work
C:\Desktop\python_work$ dir
hello_world.py
C:\Desktop\python_work$ C:\Python35\python hello_world.py
Hello Python world!
```

Most of your programs will run fine directly from your editor, but as your work becomes more complex, you might write programs that you'll need to run from a terminal.

TRY IT YOURSELF

The exercises in this chapter are exploratory in nature. Starting in Chapter 2, the challenges you'll solve will be based on what you've learned.

1-1. python.org: Explore the Python home page (*http://python.org/*) to find topics that interest you. As you become familiar with Python, different parts of the site will be more useful to you.

1-2. Hello World Typos: Open the *hello_world.py* file you just created. Make a typo somewhere in the line and run the program again. Can you make a typo that generates an error? Can you make sense of the error message? Can you make a typo that doesn't generate an error? Why do you think it didn't make an error?

1-3. Infinite Skills: If you had infinite programming skills, what would you build? You're about to learn how to program. If you have an end goal in mind, you'll have an immediate use for your new skills; now is a great time to draft descriptions of what you'd like to create. It's a good habit to keep an "ideas" notebook that you can refer to whenever you want to start a new project. Take a few minutes now to describe three programs you'd like to create.

Summary

In this chapter you learned a bit about Python in general, and you installed Python to your system if it wasn't already there. You also installed a text editor to make it easier to write Python code. You learned to run snippets of Python code in a terminal session, and you ran your first actual program, *hello_world.py*. You probably learned a bit about troubleshooting as well.

In the next chapter you'll learn about the different kinds of data you can work with in your Python programs, and you'll learn to use variables as well.

2

VARIABLES AND SIMPLE DATA TYPES

In this chapter you'll learn about the different kinds of data you can work with in your Python programs. You'll also learn how to store your data in variables and how to use those variables in your programs.

What Really Happens When You Run hello_world.py

Let's take a closer look at what Python does when you run *hello_world.py*. As it turns out, Python does a fair amount of work, even when it runs a simple program:

hello_world.py

```
print("Hello Python world!")
```

When you run this code, you should see this output:

```
Hello Python world!
```

When you run the file *hello_world.py*, the ending *.py* indicates that the file is a Python program. Your editor then runs the file through the *Python interpreter*, which reads through the program and determines what each word in the program means. For example, when the interpreter sees the word `print`, it prints to the screen whatever is inside the parentheses.

As you write your programs, your editor highlights different parts of your program in different ways. For example, it recognizes that `print` is the name of a function and displays that word in blue. It recognizes that "Hello Python world!" is not Python code and displays that phrase in orange. This feature is called *syntax highlighting* and is quite useful as you start to write your own programs.

Variables

Let's try using a variable in *hello_world.py*. Add a new line at the beginning of the file, and modify the second line:

```
message = "Hello Python world!"
print(message)
```

Run this program to see what happens. You should see the same output you saw previously:

```
Hello Python world!
```

We've added a *variable* named `message`. Every variable holds a *value*, which is the information associated with that variable. In this case the value is the text "Hello Python world!"

Adding a variable makes a little more work for the Python interpreter. When it processes the first line, it associates the text "Hello Python world!" with the variable `message`. When it reaches the second line, it prints the value associated with `message` to the screen.

Let's expand on this program by modifying *hello_world.py* to print a second message. Add a blank line to *hello_world.py*, and then add two new lines of code:

```
message = "Hello Python world!"
print(message)

message = "Hello Python Crash Course world!"
print(message)
```

Now when you run *hello_world.py*, you should see two lines of output:

```
Hello Python world!
Hello Python Crash Course world!
```

You can change the value of a variable in your program at any time, and Python will always keep track of its current value.

Naming and Using Variables

When you're using variables in Python, you need to adhere to a few rules and guidelines. Breaking some of these rules will cause errors; other guidelines just help you write code that's easier to read and understand. Be sure to keep the following variable rules in mind:

- Variable names can contain only letters, numbers, and underscores. They can start with a letter or an underscore, but not with a number. For instance, you can call a variable *message_1* but not *1_message.*
- Spaces are not allowed in variable names, but underscores can be used to separate words in variable names. For example, *greeting_message* works, but *greeting message* will cause errors.
- Avoid using Python keywords and function names as variable names; that is, do not use words that Python has reserved for a particular programmatic purpose, such as the word `print`. (See "Python Keywords and Built-in Functions" on page 489.)
- Variable names should be short but descriptive. For example, *name* is better than *n*, *student_name* is better than *s_n*, and *name_length* is better than *length_of_persons_name.*
- Be careful when using the lowercase letter *l* and the uppercase letter *O* because they could be confused with the numbers *1* and *0*.

It can take some practice to learn how to create good variable names, especially as your programs become more interesting and complicated. As you write more programs and start to read through other people's code, you'll get better at coming up with meaningful names.

NOTE *The Python variables you're using at this point should be lowercase. You won't get errors if you use uppercase letters, but it's a good idea to avoid using them for now.*

Avoiding Name Errors When Using Variables

Every programmer makes mistakes, and most make mistakes every day. Although good programmers might create errors, they also know how to respond to those errors efficiently. Let's look at an error you're likely to make early on and learn how to fix it.

We'll write some code that generates an error on purpose. Enter the following code, including the misspelled word *mesage* shown in bold:

```
message = "Hello Python Crash Course reader!"
print(mesage)
```

When an error occurs in your program, the Python interpreter does its best to help you figure out where the problem is. The interpreter provides a traceback when a program cannot run successfully. A *traceback* is a record of where the interpreter ran into trouble when trying to execute your code. Here's an example of the traceback that Python provides after you've accidentally misspelled a variable's name:

```
  Traceback (most recent call last):
❶   File "hello_world.py", line 2, in <module>
❷     print(mesage)
❸ NameError: name 'mesage' is not defined
```

The output at ❶ reports that an error occurs in line 2 of the file *hello_world.py*. The interpreter shows this line to help us spot the error quickly ❷ and tells us what kind of error it found ❸. In this case it found a *name error* and reports that the variable being printed, `mesage`, has not been defined. Python can't identify the variable name provided. A name error usually means we either forgot to set a variable's value before using it, or we made a spelling mistake when entering the variable's name.

Of course, in this example we omitted the letter *s* in the variable name `message` in the second line. The Python interpreter doesn't spellcheck your code, but it does ensure that variable names are spelled consistently. For example, watch what happens when we spell *message* incorrectly in another place in the code as well:

```
mesage = "Hello Python Crash Course reader!"
print(mesage)
```

In this case, the program runs successfully!

```
Hello Python Crash Course reader!
```

Computers are strict, but they disregard good and bad spelling. As a result, you don't need to consider English spelling and grammar rules when you're trying to create variable names and writing code.

Many programming errors are simple, single-character typos in one line of a program. If you're spending a long time searching for one of these errors, know that you're in good company. Many experienced and talented programmers spend hours hunting down these kinds of tiny errors. Try to laugh about it and move on, knowing it will happen frequently throughout your programming life.

NOTE *The best way to understand new programming concepts is to try using them in your programs. If you get stuck while working on an exercise in this book, try doing something else for a while. If you're still stuck, review the relevant part of that chapter. If you still need help, see the suggestions in Appendix C.*

TRY IT YOURSELF

Write a separate program to accomplish each of these exercises. Save each program with a filename that follows standard Python conventions, using lowercase letters and underscores, such as *simple_message.py* and *simple_messages.py*.

2-1. Simple Message: Store a message in a variable, and then print that message.

2-2. Simple Messages: Store a message in a variable, and print that message. Then change the value of your variable to a new message, and print the new message.

Strings

Because most programs define and gather some sort of data, and then do something useful with it, it helps to classify different types of data. The first data type we'll look at is the string. Strings are quite simple at first glance, but you can use them in many different ways.

A *string* is simply a series of characters. Anything inside quotes is considered a string in Python, and you can use single or double quotes around your strings like this:

```
"This is a string."
'This is also a string.'
```

This flexibility allows you to use quotes and apostrophes within your strings:

```
'I told my friend, "Python is my favorite language!"'
"The language 'Python' is named after Monty Python, not the snake."
"One of Python's strengths is its diverse and supportive community."
```

Let's explore some of the ways you can use strings.

Changing Case in a String with Methods

One of the simplest tasks you can do with strings is change the case of the words in a string. Look at the following code, and try to determine what's happening:

name.py

```
name = "ada lovelace"
print(name.title())
```

Save this file as *name.py*, and then run it. You should see this output:

```
Ada Lovelace
```

In this example, the lowercase string `"ada lovelace"` is stored in the variable `name`. The method `title()` appears after the variable in the `print()` statement. A *method* is an action that Python can perform on a piece of data. The dot (`.`) after `name` in `name.title()` tells Python to make the `title()` method act on the variable `name`. Every method is followed by a set of parentheses, because methods often need additional information to do their work. That information is provided inside the parentheses. The `title()` function doesn't need any additional information, so its parentheses are empty.

`title()` displays each word in titlecase, where each word begins with a capital letter. This is useful because you'll often want to think of a name as a piece of information. For example, you might want your program to recognize the input values `Ada`, `ADA`, and `ada` as the same name, and display all of them as `Ada`.

Several other useful methods are available for dealing with case as well. For example, you can change a string to all uppercase or all lowercase letters like this:

```
name = "Ada Lovelace"
print(name.upper())
print(name.lower())
```

This will display the following:

```
ADA LOVELACE
ada lovelace
```

The `lower()` method is particularly useful for storing data. Many times you won't want to trust the capitalization that your users provide, so you'll convert strings to lowercase before storing them. Then when you want to display the information, you'll use the case that makes the most sense for each string.

Combining or Concatenating Strings

It's often useful to combine strings. For example, you might want to store a first name and a last name in separate variables, and then combine them when you want to display someone's full name:

```
first_name = "ada"
last_name = "lovelace"
❶ full_name = first_name + " " + last_name

print(full_name)
```

Python uses the plus symbol (+) to combine strings. In this example, we use + to create a full name by combining a `first_name`, a space, and a `last_name` ❶, giving this result:

```
ada lovelace
```

This method of combining strings is called *concatenation*. You can use concatenation to compose complete messages using the information you've stored in a variable. Let's look at an example:

```
first_name = "ada"
last_name = "lovelace"
full_name = first_name + " " + last_name

❶ print("Hello, " + full_name.title() + "!")
```

Here, the full name is used at ❶ in a sentence that greets the user, and the `title()` method is used to format the name appropriately. This code returns a simple but nicely formatted greeting:

```
Hello, Ada Lovelace!
```

You can use concatenation to compose a message and then store the entire message in a variable:

```
first_name = "ada"
last_name = "lovelace"
full_name = first_name + " " + last_name

❶ message = "Hello, " + full_name.title() + "!"
❷ print(message)
```

This code displays the message "Hello, Ada Lovelace!" as well, but storing the message in a variable at ❶ makes the final `print` statement at ❷ much simpler.

Adding Whitespace to Strings with Tabs or Newlines

In programming, *whitespace* refers to any nonprinting character, such as spaces, tabs, and end-of-line symbols. You can use whitespace to organize your output so it's easier for users to read.

To add a tab to your text, use the character combination \t as shown at ❶:

```
>>> print("Python")
Python
❶ >>> print("\tPython")
    Python
```

To add a newline in a string, use the character combination \n:

```
>>> print("Languages:\nPython\nC\nJavaScript")
Languages:
Python
C
JavaScript
```

You can also combine tabs and newlines in a single string. The string "\n\t" tells Python to move to a new line, and start the next line with a tab. The following example shows how you can use a one-line string to generate four lines of output:

```
>>> print("Languages:\n\tPython\n\tC\n\tJavaScript")
Languages:
    Python
    C
    JavaScript
```

Newlines and tabs will be very useful in the next two chapters when you start to produce many lines of output from just a few lines of code.

Stripping Whitespace

Extra whitespace can be confusing in your programs. To programmers 'python' and 'python ' look pretty much the same. But to a program, they are two different strings. Python detects the extra space in 'python ' and considers it significant unless you tell it otherwise.

It's important to think about whitespace, because often you'll want to compare two strings to determine whether they are the same. For example, one important instance might involve checking people's usernames when they log in to a website. Extra whitespace can be confusing in much simpler situations as well. Fortunately, Python makes it easy to eliminate extraneous whitespace from data that people enter.

Python can look for extra whitespace on the right and left sides of a string. To ensure that no whitespace exists at the right end of a string, use the rstrip() method.

```
❶ >>> favorite_language = 'python '
❷ >>> favorite_language
  'python '
❸ >>> favorite_language.rstrip()
  'python'
❹ >>> favorite_language
  'python '
```

The value stored in favorite_language at ❶ contains extra whitespace at the end of the string. When you ask Python for this value in a terminal session, you can see the space at the end of the value ❷. When the rstrip() method acts on the variable favorite_language at ❸, this extra space is removed. However, it is only removed temporarily. If you ask for the value of favorite_language again, you can see that the string looks the same as when it was entered, including the extra whitespace ❹.

To remove the whitespace from the string permanently, you have to store the stripped value back into the variable:

```
  >>> favorite_language = 'python '
❶ >>> favorite_language = favorite_language.rstrip()
  >>> favorite_language
  'python'
```

To remove the whitespace from the string, you strip the whitespace from the right side of the string and then store that value back in the original variable, as shown at ❶. Changing a variable's value and then storing the new value back in the original variable is done often in programming. This is how a variable's value can change as a program is executed or in response to user input.

You can also strip whitespace from the left side of a string using the lstrip() method or strip whitespace from both sides at once using strip():

```
❶ >>> favorite_language = ' python '
❷ >>> favorite_language.rstrip()
  ' python'
❸ >>> favorite_language.lstrip()
  'python '
❹ >>> favorite_language.strip()
  'python'
```

In this example, we start with a value that has whitespace at the beginning and the end ❶. We then remove the extra space from the right side at ❷, from the left side at ❸, and from both sides at ❹. Experimenting with these stripping functions can help you become familiar with manipulating strings. In the real world, these stripping functions are used most often to clean up user input before it's stored in a program.

Avoiding Syntax Errors with Strings

One kind of error that you might see with some regularity is a syntax error. A *syntax error* occurs when Python doesn't recognize a section of your program as valid Python code. For example, if you use an apostrophe within single quotes, you'll produce an error. This happens because Python interprets everything between the first single quote and the apostrophe as a string. It then tries to interpret the rest of the text as Python code, which causes errors.

Here's how to use single and double quotes correctly. Save this program as *apostrophe.py* and then run it:

apostrophe.py

```
message = "One of Python's strengths is its diverse community."
print(message)
```

The apostrophe appears inside a set of double quotes, so the Python interpreter has no trouble reading the string correctly:

```
One of Python's strengths is its diverse community.
```

However, if you use single quotes, Python can't identify where the string should end:

```
message = 'One of Python's strengths is its diverse community.'
print(message)
```

You'll see the following output:

```
  File "apostrophe.py", line 1
    message = 'One of Python's strengths is its diverse community.'
                             ^❶
SyntaxError: invalid syntax
```

In the output you can see that the error occurs at ❶ right after the second single quote. This *syntax error* indicates that the interpreter doesn't recognize something in the code as valid Python code. Errors can come from a variety of sources, and I'll point out some common ones as they arise. You might see syntax errors often as you learn to write proper Python code. Syntax errors are also the least specific kind of error, so they can be difficult and frustrating to identify and correct. If you get stuck on a particularly stubborn error, see the suggestions in Appendix C.

NOTE *Your editor's syntax highlighting feature should help you spot some syntax errors quickly as you write your programs. If you see Python code highlighted as if it's English or English highlighted as if it's Python code, you probably have a mismatched quotation mark somewhere in your file.*

Printing in Python 2

The print statement has a slightly different syntax in Python 2:

```
>>> python2.7
>>> print "Hello Python 2.7 world!"
Hello Python 2.7 world!
```

Parentheses are not needed around the phrase you want to print in Python 2. Technically, print is a function in Python 3, which is why it needs parentheses. Some Python 2 print statements do include parentheses, but the behavior can be a little different than what you'll see in Python 3. Basically, when you're looking at code written in Python 2, expect to see some print statements with parentheses and some without.

TRY IT YOURSELF

Save each of the following exercises as a separate file with a name like *name_cases.py*. If you get stuck, take a break or see the suggestions in Appendix C.

2-3. Personal Message: Store a person's name in a variable, and print a message to that person. Your message should be simple, such as, "Hello Eric, would you like to learn some Python today?"

2-4. Name Cases: Store a person's name in a variable, and then print that person's name in lowercase, uppercase, and titlecase.

2-5. Famous Quote: Find a quote from a famous person you admire. Print the quote and the name of its author. Your output should look something like the following, including the quotation marks:

> *Albert Einstein once said, "A person who never made a mistake never tried anything new."*

2-6. Famous Quote 2: Repeat Exercise 2-5, but this time store the famous person's name in a variable called `famous_person`. Then compose your message and store it in a new variable called `message`. Print your message.

2-7. Stripping Names: Store a person's name, and include some whitespace characters at the beginning and end of the name. Make sure you use each character combination, `"\t"` and `"\n"`, at least once.

Print the name once, so the whitespace around the name is displayed. Then print the name using each of the three stripping functions, `lstrip()`, `rstrip()`, and `strip()`.

Numbers

Numbers are used quite often in programming to keep score in games, represent data in visualizations, store information in web applications, and so on. Python treats numbers in several different ways, depending on how they are being used. Let's first look at how Python manages integers, because they are the simplest to work with.

Integers

You can add (+), subtract (-), multiply (*), and divide (/) integers in Python.

```
>>> 2 + 3
5
>>> 3 - 2
1
>>> 2 * 3
6
>>> 3 / 2
1.5
```

In a terminal session, Python simply returns the result of the operation. Python uses two multiplication symbols to represent exponents:

```
>>> 3 ** 2
9
>>> 3 ** 3
27
>>> 10 ** 6
1000000
```

Python supports the order of operations too, so you can use multiple operations in one expression. You can also use parentheses to modify the order of operations so Python can evaluate your expression in the order you specify. For example:

```
>>> 2 + 3*4
14
>>> (2 + 3) * 4
20
```

The spacing in these examples has no effect on how Python evaluates the expressions; it simply helps you more quickly spot the operations that have priority when you're reading through the code.

Floats

Python calls any number with a decimal point a *float*. This term is used in most programming languages, and it refers to the fact that a decimal point can appear at any position in a number. Every programming language must be carefully designed to properly manage decimal numbers so numbers behave appropriately no matter where the decimal point appears.

For the most part, you can use decimals without worrying about how they behave. Simply enter the numbers you want to use, and Python will most likely do what you expect:

```
>>> 0.1 + 0.1
0.2
>>> 0.2 + 0.2
0.4
>>> 2 * 0.1
0.2
>>> 2 * 0.2
0.4
```

But be aware that you can sometimes get an arbitrary number of decimal places in your answer:

```
>>> 0.2 + 0.1
0.30000000000000004
>>> 3 * 0.1
0.30000000000000004
```

This happens in all languages and is of little concern. Python tries to find a way to represent the result as precisely as possible, which is sometimes difficult given how computers have to represent numbers internally. Just ignore the extra decimal places for now; you'll learn ways to deal with the extra places when you need to in the projects in Part II.

Avoiding Type Errors with the str() Function

Often, you'll want to use a variable's value within a message. For example, say you want to wish someone a happy birthday. You might write code like this:

birthday.py

```
age = 23
message = "Happy " + age + "rd Birthday!"

print(message)
```

You might expect this code to print the simple birthday greeting, `Happy 23rd birthday!` But if you run this code, you'll see that it generates an error:

```
Traceback (most recent call last):
  File "birthday.py", line 2, in <module>
    message = "Happy " + age + "rd Birthday!"
❶ TypeError: Can't convert 'int' object to str implicitly
```

This is a *type error*. It means Python can't recognize the kind of information you're using. In this example Python sees at ❶ that you're using a variable that has an integer value (`int`), but it's not sure how to interpret that value. Python knows that the variable could represent either the numerical value 23 or the characters *2* and *3*. When you use integers within strings like this, you need to specify explicitly that you want Python to use the integer as a string of characters. You can do this by wrapping the variable in the str() function, which tells Python to represent non-string values as strings:

```
age = 23
message = "Happy " + str(age) + "rd Birthday!"

print(message)
```

Python now knows that you want to convert the numerical value 23 to a string and display the characters 2 and 3 as part of the birthday message. Now you get the message you were expecting, without any errors:

```
Happy 23rd Birthday!
```

Working with numbers in Python is straightforward most of the time. If you're getting unexpected results, check whether Python is interpreting your numbers the way you want it to, either as a numerical value or as a string value.

Integers in Python 2

Python 2 returns a slightly different result when you divide two integers:

```
>>> python2.7
>>> 3 / 2
1
```

Instead of 1.5, Python returns 1. Division of integers in Python 2 results in an integer with the remainder truncated. Note that the result is not a rounded integer; the remainder is simply omitted.

To avoid this behavior in Python 2, make sure that at least one of the numbers is a float. By doing so, the result will be a float as well:

```
>>> 3 / 2
1
>>> 3.0 / 2
1.5
>>> 3 / 2.0
1.5
>>> 3.0 / 2.0
1.5
```

This division behavior is a common source of confusion when people who are used to Python 3 start using Python 2, or vice versa. If you use or create code that mixes integers and floats, watch out for irregular behavior.

TRY IT YOURSELF

2-8. Number Eight: Write addition, subtraction, multiplication, and division operations that each result in the number 8. Be sure to enclose your operations in `print` statements to see the results. You should create four lines that look like this:

```
print(5 + 3)
```

Your output should simply be four lines with the number 8 appearing once on each line.

2-9. Favorite Number: Store your favorite number in a variable. Then, using that variable, create a message that reveals your favorite number. Print that message.

Comments

Comments are an extremely useful feature in most programming languages. Everything you've written in your programs so far is Python code. As your programs become longer and more complicated, you should add notes within your programs that describe your overall approach to the problem you're solving. A *comment* allows you to write notes in English within your programs.

How Do You Write Comments?

In Python, the hash mark (#) indicates a comment. Anything following a hash mark in your code is ignored by the Python interpreter. For example:

comment.py

```
# Say hello to everyone.
print("Hello Python people!")
```

Python ignores the first line and executes the second line.

```
Hello Python people!
```

What Kind of Comments Should You Write?

The main reason to write comments is to explain what your code is supposed to do and how you are making it work. When you're in the middle of working on a project, you understand how all of the pieces fit together. But when you return to a project after some time away, you'll likely have forgotten some of the details. You can always study your code for a while and figure out how segments were supposed to work, but writing good comments can save you time by summarizing your overall approach in clear English.

If you want to become a professional programmer or collaborate with other programmers, you should write meaningful comments. Today, most software is written collaboratively, whether by a group of employees at one company or a group of people working together on an open source project. Skilled programmers expect to see comments in code, so it's best to start adding descriptive comments to your programs now. Writing clear, concise comments in your code is one of the most beneficial habits you can form as a new programmer.

When you're determining whether to write a comment, ask yourself if you had to consider several approaches before coming up with a reasonable way to make something work; if so, write a comment about your solution. It's much easier to delete extra comments later on than it is to go back and write comments for a sparsely commented program. From now on, I'll use comments in examples throughout this book to help explain sections of code.

TRY IT YOURSELF

2-10. Adding Comments: Choose two of the programs you've written, and add at least one comment to each. If you don't have anything specific to write because your programs are too simple at this point, just add your name and the current date at the top of each program file. Then write one sentence describing what the program does.

The Zen of Python

For a long time, the programming language Perl was the mainstay of the Internet. Most interactive websites in the early days were powered by Perl scripts. The Perl community's motto at the time was, "There's more than one way to do it." People liked this mind-set for a while, because the flexibility written into the language made it possible to solve most problems in a variety of ways. This approach was acceptable while working on your own projects, but eventually people realized that the emphasis on flexibility made it difficult to maintain large projects over long periods of time. It was difficult, tedious, and time-consuming to review code and try to figure out what someone else was thinking when they were solving a complex problem.

Experienced Python programmers will encourage you to avoid complexity and aim for simplicity whenever possible. The Python community's philosophy is contained in "The Zen of Python" by Tim Peters. You can access this brief set of principles for writing good Python code by entering `import this` into your interpreter. I won't reproduce the entire "Zen of

Python" here, but I'll share a few lines to help you understand why they should be important to you as a beginning Python programmer.

```
>>> import this
The Zen of Python, by Tim Peters

Beautiful is better than ugly.
```

Python programmers embrace the notion that code can be beautiful and elegant. In programming, people solve problems. Programmers have always respected well-designed, efficient, and even beautiful solutions to problems. As you learn more about Python and use it to write more code, someone might look over your shoulder one day and say, "Wow, that's some beautiful code!"

```
Simple is better than complex.
```

If you have a choice between a simple and a complex solution, and both work, use the simple solution. Your code will be easier to maintain, and it will be easier for you and others to build on that code later on.

```
Complex is better than complicated.
```

Real life is messy, and sometimes a simple solution to a problem is unattainable. In that case, use the simplest solution that works.

```
Readability counts.
```

Even when your code is complex, aim to make it readable. When you're working on a project that involves complex coding, focus on writing informative comments for that code.

```
There should be one-- and preferably only one --obvious way to do it.
```

If two Python programmers are asked to solve the same problem, they should come up with fairly compatible solutions. This is not to say there's no room for creativity in programming. On the contrary! But much of programming consists of using small, common approaches to simple situations within a larger, more creative project. The nuts and bolts of your programs should make sense to other Python programmers.

```
Now is better than never.
```

You could spend the rest of your life learning all the intricacies of Python and of programming in general, but then you'd never complete any projects. Don't try to write perfect code; write code that works, and then decide whether to improve your code for that project or move on to something new.

As you continue to the next chapter and start digging into more involved topics, try to keep this philosophy of simplicity and clarity in mind. Experienced programmers will respect your code more and will be happy to give you feedback and collaborate with you on interesting projects.

> **TRY IT YOURSELF**
>
> **2-11. Zen of Python:** Enter `import this` into a Python terminal session and skim through the additional principles.

Summary

In this chapter you learned to work with variables. You learned to use descriptive variable names and how to resolve name errors and syntax errors when they arise. You learned what strings are and how to display strings using lowercase, uppercase, and titlecase. You started using whitespace to organize output neatly, and you learned to strip unneeded whitespace from different parts of a string. You started working with integers and floats, and you read about some unexpected behavior to watch out for when working with numerical data. You also learned to write explanatory comments to make your code easier for you and others to read. Finally, you read about the philosophy of keeping your code as simple as possible, whenever possible.

In Chapter 3 you'll learn to store collections of information in variables called *lists*. You'll learn to work through a list, manipulating any information in that list.

3

INTRODUCING LISTS

In this chapter and the next you'll learn what lists are and how to start working with the elements in a list. Lists allow you to store sets of information in one place, whether you have just a few items or millions of items. Lists are one of Python's most powerful features readily accessible to new programmers, and they tie together many important concepts in programming.

What Is a List?

A *list* is a collection of items in a particular order. You can make a list that includes the letters of the alphabet, the digits from 0–9, or the names of all the people in your family. You can put anything you want into a list, and the items in your list don't have to be related in any particular way. Because a list usually contains more than one element, it's a good idea to make the name of your list plural, such as `letters`, `digits`, or `names`.

In Python, square brackets (`[]`) indicate a list, and individual elements in the list are separated by commas. Here's a simple example of a list that contains a few kinds of bicycles:

bicycles.py

```
bicycles = ['trek', 'cannondale', 'redline', 'specialized']
print(bicycles)
```

If you ask Python to print a list, Python returns its representation of the list, including the square brackets:

```
['trek', 'cannondale', 'redline', 'specialized']
```

Because this isn't the output you want your users to see, let's learn how to access the individual items in a list.

Accessing Elements in a List

Lists are ordered collections, so you can access any element in a list by telling Python the position, or *index*, of the item desired. To access an element in a list, write the name of the list followed by the index of the item enclosed in square brackets.

For example, let's pull out the first bicycle in the list `bicycles`:

```
  bicycles = ['trek', 'cannondale', 'redline', 'specialized']
❶ print(bicycles[0])
```

The syntax for this is shown at ❶. When we ask for a single item from a list, Python returns just that element without square brackets or quotation marks:

```
trek
```

This is the result you want your users to see—clean, neatly formatted output.

You can also use the string methods from Chapter 2 on any element in a list. For example, you can format the element `'trek'` more neatly by using the `title()` method:

```
bicycles = ['trek', 'cannondale', 'redline', 'specialized']
print(bicycles[0].title())
```

This example produces the same output as the preceding example except `'Trek'` is capitalized.

Index Positions Start at 0, Not 1

Python considers the first item in a list to be at position 0, not position 1. This is true of most programming languages, and the reason has to do with how the list operations are implemented at a lower level. If you're receiving unexpected results, determine whether you are making a simple off-by-one error.

The second item in a list has an index of 1. Using this simple counting system, you can get any element you want from a list by subtracting one from its position in the list. For instance, to access the fourth item in a list, you request the item at index 3.

The following asks for the bicycles at index `1` and index `3`:

```
bicycles = ['trek', 'cannondale', 'redline', 'specialized']
print(bicycles[1])
print(bicycles[3])
```

This code returns the second and fourth bicycles in the list:

```
cannondale
specialized
```

Python has a special syntax for accessing the last element in a list. By asking for the item at index `-1`, Python always returns the last item in the list:

```
bicycles = ['trek', 'cannondale', 'redline', 'specialized']
print(bicycles[-1])
```

This code returns the value `'specialized'`. This syntax is quite useful, because you'll often want to access the last items in a list without knowing exactly how long the list is. This convention extends to other negative index values as well. The index `-2` returns the second item from the end of the list, the index `-3` returns the third item from the end, and so forth.

Using Individual Values from a List

You can use individual values from a list just as you would any other variable. For example, you can use concatenation to create a message based on a value from a list.

Let's try pulling the first bicycle from the list and composing a message using that value.

```
  bicycles = ['trek', 'cannondale', 'redline', 'specialized']
❶ message = "My first bicycle was a " + bicycles[0].title() + "."

  print(message)
```

At ❶, we build a sentence using the value at `bicycles[0]` and store it in the variable `message`. The output is a simple sentence about the first bicycle in the list:

```
My first bicycle was a Trek.
```

TRY IT YOURSELF

Try these short programs to get some firsthand experience with Python's lists. You might want to create a new folder for each chapter's exercises to keep them organized.

3-1. Names: Store the names of a few of your friends in a list called `names`. Print each person's name by accessing each element in the list, one at a time.

3-2. Greetings: Start with the list you used in Exercise 3-1, but instead of just printing each person's name, print a message to them. The text of each message should be the same, but each message should be personalized with the person's name.

3-3. Your Own List: Think of your favorite mode of transportation, such as a motorcycle or a car, and make a list that stores several examples. Use your list to print a series of statements about these items, such as "I would like to own a Honda motorcycle."

Changing, Adding, and Removing Elements

Most lists you create will be dynamic, meaning you'll build a list and then add and remove elements from it as your program runs its course. For example, you might create a game in which a player has to shoot aliens out of the sky. You could store the initial set of aliens in a list and then remove an alien from the list each time one is shot down. Each time a new alien appears on the screen, you add it to the list. Your list of aliens will decrease and increase in length throughout the course of the game.

Modifying Elements in a List

The syntax for modifying an element is similar to the syntax for accessing an element in a list. To change an element, use the name of the list followed by the index of the element you want to change, and then provide the new value you want that item to have.

For example, let's say we have a list of motorcycles, and the first item in the list is 'honda'. How would we change the value of this first item?

motorcycles.py

```
❶ motorcycles = ['honda', 'yamaha', 'suzuki']
  print(motorcycles)

❷ motorcycles[0] = 'ducati'
  print(motorcycles)
```

The code at ❶ defines the original list, with 'honda' as the first element. The code at ❷ changes the value of the first item to 'ducati'. The output shows that the first item has indeed been changed, and the rest of the list stays the same:

```
['honda', 'yamaha', 'suzuki']
['ducati', 'yamaha', 'suzuki']
```

You can change the value of any item in a list, not just the first item.

Adding Elements to a List

You might want to add a new element to a list for many reasons. For example, you might want to make new aliens appear in a game, add new data to a visualization, or add new registered users to a website you've built. Python provides several ways to add new data to existing lists.

Appending Elements to the End of a List

The simplest way to add a new element to a list is to *append* the item to the list. When you append an item to a list, the new element is added to the end of the list. Using the same list we had in the previous example, we'll add the new element 'ducati' to the end of the list:

```
  motorcycles = ['honda', 'yamaha', 'suzuki']
  print(motorcycles)

❶ motorcycles.append('ducati')
  print(motorcycles)
```

The append() method at ❶ adds 'ducati' to the end of the list without affecting any of the other elements in the list:

```
['honda', 'yamaha', 'suzuki']
['honda', 'yamaha', 'suzuki', 'ducati']
```

The append() method makes it easy to build lists dynamically. For example, you can start with an empty list and then add items to the list using a series of append() statements. Using an empty list, let's add the elements 'honda', 'yamaha', and 'suzuki' to the list:

```
motorcycles = []

motorcycles.append('honda')
motorcycles.append('yamaha')
motorcycles.append('suzuki')

print(motorcycles)
```

The resulting list looks exactly the same as the lists in the previous examples:

```
['honda', 'yamaha', 'suzuki']
```

Building lists this way is very common, because you often won't know the data your users want to store in a program until after the program is running. To put your users in control, start by defining an empty list that will hold the users' values. Then append each new value provided to the list you just created.

Inserting Elements into a List

You can add a new element at any position in your list by using the insert() method. You do this by specifying the index of the new element and the value of the new item.

```
  motorcycles = ['honda', 'yamaha', 'suzuki']

❶ motorcycles.insert(0, 'ducati')
  print(motorcycles)
```

In this example, the code at ❶ inserts the value 'ducati' at the beginning of the list. The insert() method opens a space at position 0 and stores the value 'ducati' at that location. This operation shifts every other value in the list one position to the right:

```
['ducati', 'honda', 'yamaha', 'suzuki']
```

Removing Elements from a List

Often, you'll want to remove an item or a set of items from a list. For example, when a player shoots down an alien from the sky, you'll most likely want to remove it from the list of active aliens. Or when a user decides to cancel their account on a web application you created, you'll want to remove that user from the list of active users. You can remove an item according to its position in the list or according to its value.

Removing an Item Using the del Statement

If you know the position of the item you want to remove from a list, you can use the `del` statement.

```
motorcycles = ['honda', 'yamaha', 'suzuki']
print(motorcycles)

❶ del motorcycles[0]
print(motorcycles)
```

The code at ❶ uses `del` to remove the first item, `'honda'`, from the list of motorcycles:

```
['honda', 'yamaha', 'suzuki']
['yamaha', 'suzuki']
```

You can remove an item from any position in a list using the `del` statement if you know its index. For example, here's how to remove the second item, `'yamaha'`, in the list:

```
motorcycles = ['honda', 'yamaha', 'suzuki']
print(motorcycles)

del motorcycles[1]
print(motorcycles)
```

The second motorcycle is deleted from the list:

```
['honda', 'yamaha', 'suzuki']
['honda', 'suzuki']
```

In both examples, you can no longer access the value that was removed from the list after the `del` statement is used.

Removing an Item Using the pop() Method

Sometimes you'll want to use the value of an item after you remove it from a list. For example, you might want to get the *x* and *y* position of an alien that was just shot down, so you can draw an explosion at that position. In a web application, you might want to remove a user from a list of active members and then add that user to a list of inactive members.

The `pop()` method removes the last item in a list, but it lets you work with that item after removing it. The term *pop* comes from thinking of a list as a stack of items and popping one item off the top of the stack. In this analogy, the top of a stack corresponds to the end of a list.

Let's pop a motorcycle from the list of motorcycles:

```
❶ motorcycles = ['honda', 'yamaha', 'suzuki']
  print(motorcycles)

❷ popped_motorcycle = motorcycles.pop()
❸ print(motorcycles)
❹ print(popped_motorcycle)
```

We start by defining and printing the list motorcycles at ❶. At ❷ we pop a value from the list and store that value in the variable popped_motorcycle. We print the list at ❸ to show that a value has been removed from the list. Then we print the popped value at ❹ to prove that we still have access to the value that was removed.

The output shows that the value 'suzuki' was removed from the end of the list and is now stored in the variable popped_motorcycle:

```
['honda', 'yamaha', 'suzuki']
['honda', 'yamaha']
suzuki
```

How might this pop() method be useful? Imagine that the motorcycles in the list are stored in chronological order according to when we owned them. If this is the case, we can use the pop() method to print a statement about the last motorcycle we bought:

```
motorcycles = ['honda', 'yamaha', 'suzuki']

last_owned = motorcycles.pop()
print("The last motorcycle I owned was a " + last_owned.title() + ".")
```

The output is a simple sentence about the most recent motorcycle we owned:

```
The last motorcycle I owned was a Suzuki.
```

Popping Items from any Position in a List

You can actually use pop() to remove an item in a list at any position by including the index of the item you want to remove in parentheses.

```
  motorcycles = ['honda', 'yamaha', 'suzuki']

❶ first_owned = motorcycles.pop(0)
❷ print('The first motorcycle I owned was a ' + first_owned.title() + '.')
```

We start by popping the first motorcycle in the list at ❶, and then we print a message about that motorcycle at ❷. The output is a simple sentence describing the first motorcycle I ever owned:

```
The first motorcycle I owned was a Honda.
```

Remember that each time you use `pop()`, the item you work with is no longer stored in the list.

If you're unsure whether to use the `del` statement or the `pop()` method, here's a simple way to decide: when you want to delete an item from a list and not use that item in any way, use the `del` statement; if you want to use an item as you remove it, use the `pop()` method.

Removing an Item by Value

Sometimes you won't know the position of the value you want to remove from a list. If you only know the value of the item you want to remove, you can use the `remove()` method.

For example, let's say we want to remove the value `'ducati'` from the list of motorcycles.

```
motorcycles = ['honda', 'yamaha', 'suzuki', 'ducati']
print(motorcycles)

❶ motorcycles.remove('ducati')
print(motorcycles)
```

The code at ❶ tells Python to figure out where `'ducati'` appears in the list and remove that element:

```
['honda', 'yamaha', 'suzuki', 'ducati']
['honda', 'yamaha', 'suzuki']
```

You can also use the `remove()` method to work with a value that's being removed from a list. Let's remove the value `'ducati'` and print a reason for removing it from the list:

```
❶ motorcycles = ['honda', 'yamaha', 'suzuki', 'ducati']
print(motorcycles)

❷ too_expensive = 'ducati'
❸ motorcycles.remove(too_expensive)
print(motorcycles)
❹ print("\nA " + too_expensive.title() + " is too expensive for me.")
```

After defining the list at ❶, we store the value `'ducati'` in a variable called `too_expensive` ❷. We then use this variable to tell Python which value to remove from the list at ❸. At ❹ the value 'ducati' has been removed from the list but is still stored in the variable too_expensive, allowing us to print a statement about why we removed 'ducati' from the list of motorcycles:

```
['honda', 'yamaha', 'suzuki', 'ducati']
['honda', 'yamaha', 'suzuki']

A Ducati is too expensive for me.
```

NOTE *The* remove() *method deletes only the first occurrence of the value you specify. If there's a possibility the value appears more than once in the list, you'll need to use a loop to determine if all occurrences of the value have been removed. You'll learn how to do this in Chapter 7.*

TRY IT YOURSELF

The following exercises are a bit more complex than those in Chapter 2, but they give you an opportunity to use lists in all of the ways described.

3-4. Guest List: If you could invite anyone, living or deceased, to dinner, who would you invite? Make a list that includes at least three people you'd like to invite to dinner. Then use your list to print a message to each person, inviting them to dinner.

3-5. Changing Guest List: You just heard that one of your guests can't make the dinner, so you need to send out a new set of invitations. You'll have to think of someone else to invite.

- Start with your program from Exercise 3-4. Add a print statement at the end of your program stating the name of the guest who can't make it.
- Modify your list, replacing the name of the guest who can't make it with the name of the new person you are inviting.
- Print a second set of invitation messages, one for each person who is still in your list.

3-6. More Guests: You just found a bigger dinner table, so now more space is available. Think of three more guests to invite to dinner.

- Start with your program from Exercise 3-4 or Exercise 3-5. Add a print statement to the end of your program informing people that you found a bigger dinner table.
- Use insert() to add one new guest to the beginning of your list.
- Use insert() to add one new guest to the middle of your list.
- Use append() to add one new guest to the end of your list.
- Print a new set of invitation messages, one for each person in your list.

> **3-7. Shrinking Guest List:** You just found out that your new dinner table won't arrive in time for the dinner, and you have space for only two guests.
>
> - Start with your program from Exercise 3-6. Add a new line that prints a message saying that you can invite only two people for dinner.
> - Use `pop()` to remove guests from your list one at a time until only two names remain in your list. Each time you pop a name from your list, print a message to that person letting them know you're sorry you can't invite them to dinner.
> - Print a message to each of the two people still on your list, letting them know they're still invited.
> - Use `del` to remove the last two names from your list, so you have an empty list. Print your list to make sure you actually have an empty list at the end of your program.

Organizing a List

Often, your lists will be created in an unpredictable order, because you can't always control the order in which your users provide their data. Although this is unavoidable in most circumstances, you'll frequently want to present your information in a particular order. Sometimes you'll want to preserve the original order of your list, and other times you'll want to change the original order. Python provides a number of different ways to organize your lists, depending on the situation.

Sorting a List Permanently with the sort() Method

Python's `sort()` method makes it relatively easy to sort a list. Imagine we have a list of cars and want to change the order of the list to store them alphabetically. To keep the task simple, let's assume that all the values in the list are lowercase.

cars.py

```
   cars = ['bmw', 'audi', 'toyota', 'subaru']
❶ cars.sort()
   print(cars)
```

The `sort()` method, shown at ❶, changes the order of the list permanently. The cars are now in alphabetical order, and we can never revert to the original order:

```
['audi', 'bmw', 'subaru', 'toyota']
```

You can also sort this list in reverse alphabetical order by passing the argument reverse=True to the sort() method. The following example sorts the list of cars in reverse alphabetical order:

```
cars = ['bmw', 'audi', 'toyota', 'subaru']
cars.sort(reverse=True)
print(cars)
```

Again, the order of the list is permanently changed:

```
['toyota', 'subaru', 'bmw', 'audi']
```

Sorting a List Temporarily with the sorted() Function

To maintain the original order of a list but present it in a sorted order, you can use the sorted() function. The sorted() function lets you display your list in a particular order but doesn't affect the actual order of the list.

Let's try this function on the list of cars.

```
cars = ['bmw', 'audi', 'toyota', 'subaru']

❶ print("Here is the original list:")
print(cars)

❷ print("\nHere is the sorted list:")
print(sorted(cars))

❸ print("\nHere is the original list again:")
print(cars)
```

We first print the list in its original order at ❶ and then in alphabetical order at ❷. After the list is displayed in the new order, we show that the list is still stored in its original order at ❸.

```
Here is the original list:
['bmw', 'audi', 'toyota', 'subaru']

Here is the sorted list:
['audi', 'bmw', 'subaru', 'toyota']

❹ Here is the original list again:
['bmw', 'audi', 'toyota', 'subaru']
```

Notice that the list still exists in its original order at ❹ after the sorted() function has been used. The sorted() function can also accept a reverse=True argument if you want to display a list in reverse alphabetical order.

NOTE *Sorting a list alphabetically is a bit more complicated when all the values are not in lowercase. There are several ways to interpret capital letters when you're deciding on a sort order, and specifying the exact order can be more complex than we want to deal with at this time. However, most approaches to sorting will build directly on what you learned in this section.*

Printing a List in Reverse Order

To reverse the original order of a list, you can use the `reverse()` method. If we originally stored the list of cars in chronological order according to when we owned them, we could easily rearrange the list into reverse chronological order:

```
cars = ['bmw', 'audi', 'toyota', 'subaru']
print(cars)

cars.reverse()
print(cars)
```

Notice that `reverse()` doesn't sort backward alphabetically; it simply reverses the order of the list:

```
['bmw', 'audi', 'toyota', 'subaru']
['subaru', 'toyota', 'audi', 'bmw']
```

The `reverse()` method changes the order of a list permanently, but you can revert to the original order anytime by applying `reverse()` to the same list a second time.

Finding the Length of a List

You can quickly find the length of a list by using the `len()` function. The list in this example has four items, so its length is `4`:

```
>>> cars = ['bmw', 'audi', 'toyota', 'subaru']
>>> len(cars)
4
```

You'll find `len()` useful when you need to identify the number of aliens that still need to be shot down in a game, determine the amount of data you have to manage in a visualization, or figure out the number of registered users on a website, among other tasks.

NOTE *Python counts the items in a list starting with one, so you shouldn't run into any off-by-one errors when determining the length of a list.*

TRY IT YOURSELF

3-8. Seeing the World: Think of at least five places in the world you'd like to visit.

- Store the locations in a list. Make sure the list is not in alphabetical order.
- Print your list in its original order. Don't worry about printing the list neatly, just print it as a raw Python list.
- Use `sorted()` to print your list in alphabetical order without modifying the actual list.
- Show that your list is still in its original order by printing it.
- Use `sorted()` to print your list in reverse alphabetical order without changing the order of the original list.
- Show that your list is still in its original order by printing it again.
- Use `reverse()` to change the order of your list. Print the list to show that its order has changed.
- Use `reverse()` to change the order of your list again. Print the list to show it's back to its original order.
- Use `sort()` to change your list so it's stored in alphabetical order. Print the list to show that its order has been changed.
- Use `sort()` to change your list so it's stored in reverse alphabetical order. Print the list to show that its order has changed.

3-9. Dinner Guests: Working with one of the programs from Exercises 3-4 through 3-7 (page 46), use `len()` to print a message indicating the number of people you are inviting to dinner.

3-10. Every Function: Think of something you could store in a list. For example, you could make a list of mountains, rivers, countries, cities, languages, or anything else you'd like. Write a program that creates a list containing these items and then uses each function introduced in this chapter at least once.

Avoiding Index Errors When Working with Lists

One type of error is common to see when you're working with lists for the first time. Let's say you have a list with three items, and you ask for the fourth item:

```
motorcycles = ['honda', 'yamaha', 'suzuki']
print(motorcycles[3])
```

This example results in an *index error*:

```
Traceback (most recent call last):
  File "motorcycles.py", line 3, in <module>
    print(motorcycles[3])
IndexError: list index out of range
```

Python attempts to give you the item at index 3. But when it searches the list, no item in motorcycles has an index of 3. Because of the off-by-one nature of indexing in lists, this error is typical. People think the third item is item number 3, because they start counting at 1. But in Python the third item is number 2, because it starts indexing at 0.

An index error means Python can't figure out the index you requested. If an index error occurs in your program, try adjusting the index you're asking for by one. Then run the program again to see if the results are correct.

Keep in mind that whenever you want to access the last item in a list you use the index -1. This will always work, even if your list has changed size since the last time you accessed it:

```
motorcycles = ['honda', 'yamaha', 'suzuki']
print(motorcycles[-1])
```

The index -1 always returns the last item in a list, in this case the value 'suzuki':

```
'suzuki'
```

The only time this approach will cause an error is when you request the last item from an empty list:

```
motorcycles = []
print(motorcycles[-1])
```

No items are in motorcycles, so Python returns another index error:

```
Traceback (most recent call last):
  File "motorcyles.py", line 3, in <module>
    print(motorcycles[-1])
IndexError: list index out of range
```

NOTE *If an index error occurs and you can't figure out how to resolve it, try printing your list or just printing the length of your list. Your list might look much different than you thought it did, especially if it has been managed dynamically by your program. Seeing the actual list, or the exact number of items in your list, can help you sort out such logical errors.*

TRY IT YOURSELF

3-11. Intentional Error: If you haven't received an index error in one of your programs yet, try to make one happen. Change an index in one of your programs to produce an index error. Make sure you correct the error before closing the program.

Summary

In this chapter you learned what lists are and how to work with the individual items in a list. You learned how to define a list and how to add and remove elements. You learned to sort lists permanently and temporarily for display purposes. You also learned how to find the length of a list and how to avoid index errors when you're working with lists.

In Chapter 4 you'll learn how to work with items in a list more efficiently. By looping through each item in a list using just a few lines of code you'll be able to work efficiently, even when your list contains thousands or millions of items.

4

WORKING WITH LISTS

In Chapter 3 you learned how to make a simple list, and you learned to work with the individual elements in a list. In this chapter you'll learn how to *loop* through an entire list using just a few lines of code regardless of how long the list is. Looping allows you to take the same action, or set of actions, with every item in a list. As a result, you'll be able to work efficiently with lists of any length, including those with thousands or even millions of items.

Looping Through an Entire List

You'll often want to run through all entries in a list, performing the same task with each item. For example, in a game you might want to move every element on the screen by the same amount, or in a list of numbers you might want to perform the same statistical operation on every element. Or perhaps you'll want to display each headline from a list of articles on a website. When you want to do the same action with every item in a list, you can use Python's `for` loop.

Let's say we have a list of magicians' names, and we want to print out each name in the list. We could do this by retrieving each name from the list individually, but this approach could cause several problems. For one, it would be repetitive to do this with a long list of names. Also, we'd have to change our code each time the list's length changed. A `for` loop avoids both of these issues by letting Python manage these issues internally.

Let's use a `for` loop to print out each name in a list of magicians:

magicians.py

```
❶ magicians = ['alice', 'david', 'carolina']
❷ for magician in magicians:
❸     print(magician)
```

We begin by defining a list at ❶, just as we did in Chapter 3. At ❷, we define a `for` loop. This line tells Python to pull a name from the list `magicians`, and store it in the variable `magician`. At ❸ we tell Python to print the name that was just stored in `magician`. Python then repeats lines ❷ and ❸, once for each name in the list. It might help to read this code as "For every magician in the list of magicians, print the magician's name." The output is a simple printout of each name in the list:

```
alice
david
carolina
```

A Closer Look at Looping

The concept of looping is important because it's one of the most common ways a computer automates repetitive tasks. For example, in a simple loop like we used in *magicians.py*, Python initially reads the first line of the loop:

```
for magician in magicians:
```

This line tells Python to retrieve the first value from the list `magicians` and store it in the variable `magician`. This first value is `'alice'`. Python then reads the next line:

```
    print(magician)
```

Python prints the current value of `magician`, which is still `'alice'`. Because the list contains more values, Python returns to the first line of the loop:

```
for magician in magicians:
```

Python retrieves the next name in the list, `'david'`, and stores that value in `magician`. Python then executes the line:

```
    print(magician)
```

Python prints the current value of magician again, which is now 'david'. Python repeats the entire loop once more with the last value in the list, 'carolina'. Because no more values are in the list, Python moves on to the next line in the program. In this case nothing comes after the for loop, so the program simply ends.

When you're using loops for the first time, keep in mind that the set of steps is repeated once for each item in the list, no matter how many items are in the list. If you have a million items in your list, Python repeats these steps a million times—and usually very quickly.

Also keep in mind when writing your own for loops that you can choose any name you want for the temporary variable that holds each value in the list. However, it's helpful to choose a meaningful name that represents a single item from the list. For example, here's a good way to start a for loop for a list of cats, a list of dogs, and a general list of items:

```
for cat in cats:
for dog in dogs:
for item in list_of_items:
```

These naming conventions can help you follow the action being done on each item within a for loop. Using singular and plural names can help you identify whether a section of code is working with a single element from the list or the entire list.

Doing More Work Within a for Loop

You can do just about anything with each item in a for loop. Let's build on the previous example by printing a message to each magician, telling them that they performed a great trick:

```
magicians = ['alice', 'david', 'carolina']
for magician in magicians:
❶     print(magician.title() + ", that was a great trick!")
```

The only difference in this code is at ❶ where we compose a message to each magician, starting with that magician's name. The first time through the loop the value of magician is 'alice', so Python starts the first message with the name 'Alice'. The second time through the message will begin with 'David', and the third time through the message will begin with 'Carolina'.

The output shows a personalized message for each magician in the list:

```
Alice, that was a great trick!
David, that was a great trick!
Carolina, that was a great trick!
```

You can also write as many lines of code as you like in the for loop. Every indented line following the line for magician in magicians is considered *inside the loop*, and each indented line is executed once for each value in the list. Therefore, you can do as much work as you like with each value in the list.

Let's add a second line to our message, telling each magician that we're looking forward to their next trick:

```
magicians = ['alice', 'david', 'carolina']
for magician in magicians:
    print(magician.title() + ", that was a great trick!")
❶     print("I can't wait to see your next trick, " + magician.title() + ".\n")
```

Because we have indented both print statements, each line will be executed once for every magician in the list. The newline ("\n") in the second print statement ❶ inserts a blank line after each pass through the loop. This creates a set of messages that are neatly grouped for each person in the list:

```
Alice, that was a great trick!
I can't wait to see your next trick, Alice.

David, that was a great trick!
I can't wait to see your next trick, David.

Carolina, that was a great trick!
I can't wait to see your next trick, Carolina.
```

You can use as many lines as you like in your for loops. In practice you'll often find it useful to do a number of different operations with each item in a list when you use a for loop.

Doing Something After a for Loop

What happens once a for loop has finished executing? Usually, you'll want to summarize a block of output or move on to other work that your program must accomplish.

Any lines of code after the for loop that are not indented are executed once without repetition. Let's write a thank you to the group of magicians as a whole, thanking them for putting on an excellent show. To display this group message after all of the individual messages have been printed, we place the thank you message after the for loop without indentation:

```
magicians = ['alice', 'david', 'carolina']
for magician in magicians:
    print(magician.title() + ", that was a great trick!")
    print("I can't wait to see your next trick, " + magician.title() + ".\n")

❶ print("Thank you, everyone. That was a great magic show!")
```

The first two print statements are repeated once for each magician in the list, as you saw earlier. However, because the line at ❶ is not indented, it's printed only once:

```
Alice, that was a great trick!
I can't wait to see your next trick, Alice.

David, that was a great trick!
I can't wait to see your next trick, David.

Carolina, that was a great trick!
I can't wait to see your next trick, Carolina.

Thank you, everyone. That was a great magic show!
```

When you're processing data using a for loop, you'll find that this is a good way to summarize an operation that was performed on an entire data set. For example, you might use a for loop to initialize a game by running through a list of characters and displaying each character on the screen. You might then write an unindented block after this loop that displays a Play Now button after all the characters have been drawn to the screen.

Avoiding Indentation Errors

Python uses indentation to determine when one line of code is connected to the line above it. In the previous examples, the lines that printed messages to individual magicians were part of the for loop because they were indented. Python's use of indentation makes code very easy to read. Basically, it uses whitespace to force you to write neatly formatted code with a clear visual structure. In longer Python programs, you'll notice blocks of code indented at a few different levels. These indentation levels help you gain a general sense of the overall program's organization.

As you begin to write code that relies on proper indentation, you'll need to watch for a few common *indentation errors*. For example, people sometimes indent blocks of code that don't need to be indented or forget to indent blocks that need to be indented. Seeing examples of these errors now will help you avoid them in the future and correct them when they do appear in your own programs.

Let's examine some of the more common indentation errors.

Forgetting to Indent

Always indent the line after the for statement in a loop. If you forget, Python will remind you:

magicians.py

```
  magicians = ['alice', 'david', 'carolina']
  for magician in magicians:
❶ print(magician)
```

The print statement at ❶ should be indented, but it's not. When Python expects an indented block and doesn't find one, it lets you know which line it had a problem with.

```
  File "magicians.py", line 3
    print(magician)
        ^
IndentationError: expected an indented block
```

You can usually resolve this kind of indentation error by indenting the line or lines immediately after the for statement.

Forgetting to Indent Additional Lines

Sometimes your loop will run without any errors but won't produce the expected result. This can happen when you're trying to do several tasks in a loop and you forget to indent some of its lines.

For example, this is what happens when we forget to indent the second line in the loop that tells each magician we're looking forward to their next trick:

```
  magicians = ['alice', 'david', 'carolina']
  for magician in magicians:
      print(magician.title() + ", that was a great trick!")
❶ print("I can't wait to see your next trick, " + magician.title() + ".\n")
```

The print statement at ❶ is supposed to be indented, but because Python finds at least one indented line after the for statement, it doesn't report an error. As a result, the first print statement is executed once for each name in the list because it is indented. The second print statement is not indented, so it is executed only once after the loop has finished running. Because the final value of magician is 'carolina', she is the only one who receives the "looking forward to the next trick" message:

```
Alice, that was a great trick!
David, that was a great trick!
Carolina, that was a great trick!
I can't wait to see your next trick, Carolina.
```

This is a *logical error*. The syntax is valid Python code, but the code does not produce the desired result because a problem occurs in its logic. If you expect to see a certain action repeated once for each item in a list and it's executed only once, determine whether you need to simply indent a line or a group of lines.

Indenting Unnecessarily

If you accidentally indent a line that doesn't need to be indented, Python informs you about the unexpected indent:

hello_world.py

```
message = "Hello Python world!"
❶     print(message)
```

We don't need to indent the `print` statement at ❶, because it doesn't *belong* to the line above it; hence, Python reports that error:

```
  File "hello_world.py", line 2
    print(message)
    ^
IndentationError: unexpected indent
```

You can avoid unexpected indentation errors by indenting only when you have a specific reason to do so. In the programs you're writing at this point, the only lines you should indent are the actions you want to repeat for each item in a `for` loop.

Indenting Unnecessarily After the Loop

If you accidentally indent code that should run after a loop has finished, that code will be repeated once for each item in the list. Sometimes this prompts Python to report an error, but often you'll receive a simple logical error.

For example, let's see what happens when we accidentally indent the line that thanked the magicians as a group for putting on a good show:

```
magicians = ['alice', 'david', 'carolina']
for magician in magicians:
    print(magician.title() + ", that was a great trick!")
    print("I can't wait to see your next trick, " + magician.title() + ".\n")

❶     print("Thank you everyone, that was a great magic show!")
```

Because the line at ❶ is indented, it's printed once for each person in the list, as you can see at ❷:

```
Alice, that was a great trick!
I can't wait to see your next trick, Alice.

❷ Thank you everyone, that was a great magic show!
David, that was a great trick!
I can't wait to see your next trick, David.

❷ Thank you everyone, that was a great magic show!
Carolina, that was a great trick!
I can't wait to see your next trick, Carolina.

❷ Thank you everyone, that was a great magic show!
```

This is another logical error, similar to the one in "Forgetting to Indent Additional Lines" on page 58. Because Python doesn't know what you're trying to accomplish with your code, it will run all code that is written in valid syntax. If an action is repeated many times when it should be executed only once, determine whether you just need to unindent the code for that action.

Forgetting the Colon

The colon at the end of a `for` statement tells Python to interpret the next line as the start of a loop.

```
magicians = ['alice', 'david', 'carolina']
❶ for magician in magicians
    print(magician)
```

If you accidentally forget the colon, as shown at ❶, you'll get a syntax error because Python doesn't know what you're trying to do. Although this is an easy error to fix, it's not always an easy error to find. You'd be surprised by the amount of time programmers spend hunting down single-character errors like this. Such errors are difficult to find because we often just see what we expect to see.

TRY IT YOURSELF

4-1. Pizzas: Think of at least three kinds of your favorite pizza. Store these pizza names in a list, and then use a `for` loop to print the name of each pizza.

- Modify your `for` loop to print a sentence using the name of the pizza instead of printing just the name of the pizza. For each pizza you should have one line of output containing a simple statement like *I like pepperoni pizza*.
- Add a line at the end of your program, outside the `for` loop, that states how much you like pizza. The output should consist of three or more lines about the kinds of pizza you like and then an additional sentence, such as *I really love pizza!*

4-2. Animals: Think of at least three different animals that have a common characteristic. Store the names of these animals in a list, and then use a `for` loop to print out the name of each animal.

- Modify your program to print a statement about each animal, such as *A dog would make a great pet.*
- Add a line at the end of your program stating what these animals have in common. You could print a sentence such as *Any of these animals would make a great pet!*

Making Numerical Lists

Many reasons exist to store a set of numbers. For example, you'll need to keep track of the positions of each character in a game, and you might want to keep track of a player's high scores as well. In data visualizations, you'll almost always work with sets of numbers, such as temperatures, distances, population sizes, or latitude and longitude values, among other types of numerical sets.

Lists are ideal for storing sets of numbers, and Python provides a number of tools to help you work efficiently with lists of numbers. Once you understand how to use these tools effectively, your code will work well even when your lists contain millions of items.

Using the range() Function

Python's `range()` function makes it easy to generate a series of numbers. For example, you can use the `range()` function to print a series of numbers like this:

numbers.py

```
for value in range(1,5):
    print(value)
```

Although this code looks like it should print the numbers from 1 to 5, it doesn't print the number 5:

```
1
2
3
4
```

In this example, `range()` prints only the numbers 1 through 4. This is another result of the off-by-one behavior you'll see often in programming languages. The `range()` function causes Python to start counting at the first value you give it, and it stops when it reaches the second value you provide. Because it stops at that second value, the output never contains the end value, which would have been 5 in this case.

To print the numbers from 1 to 5, you would use `range(1,6)`:

```
for value in range(1,6):
    print(value)
```

This time the output starts at 1 and ends at 5:

```
1
2
3
4
5
```

If your output is different than what you expect when you're using range(), try adjusting your end value by 1.

Using range() to Make a List of Numbers

If you want to make a list of numbers, you can convert the results of range() directly into a list using the list() function. When you wrap list() around a call to the range() function, the output will be a list of numbers.

In the example in the previous section, we simply printed out a series of numbers. We can use list() to convert that same set of numbers into a list:

```
numbers = list(range(1,6))
print(numbers)
```

And this is the result:

```
[1, 2, 3, 4, 5]
```

We can also use the range() function to tell Python to skip numbers in a given range. For example, here's how we would list the even numbers between 1 and 10:

even_numbers.py

```
even_numbers = list(range(2,11,2))
print(even_numbers)
```

In this example, the range() function starts with the value 2 and then adds 2 to that value. It adds 2 repeatedly until it reaches or passes the end value, 11, and produces this result:

```
[2, 4, 6, 8, 10]
```

You can create almost any set of numbers you want to using the range() function. For example, consider how you might make a list of the first 10 square numbers (that is, the square of each integer from 1 through 10). In Python, two asterisks (**) represent exponents. Here's how you might put the first 10 square numbers into a list:

squares.py

```
❶ squares = []
❷ for value in range(1,11):
❸     square = value**2
❹     squares.append(square)

❺ print(squares)
```

We start with an empty list called squares at ❶. At ❷, we tell Python to loop through each value from 1 to 10 using the range() function. Inside the loop, the current value is raised to the second power and stored in the variable square at ❸. At ❹, each new value of square is appended to the list squares. Finally, when the loop has finished running, the list of squares is printed at ❺:

```
[1, 4, 9, 16, 25, 36, 49, 64, 81, 100]
```

To write this code more concisely, omit the temporary variable square and append each new value directly to the list:

```
squares = []
for value in range(1,11):
❶    squares.append(value**2)

print(squares)
```

The code at ❶ does the same work as the lines at ❸ and ❹ in *squares.py*. Each value in the loop is raised to the second power and then immediately appended to the list of squares.

You can use either of these two approaches when you're making more complex lists. Sometimes using a temporary variable makes your code easier to read; other times it makes the code unnecessarily long. Focus first on writing code that you understand clearly, which does what you want it to do. Then look for more efficient approaches as you review your code.

Simple Statistics with a List of Numbers

A few Python functions are specific to lists of numbers. For example, you can easily find the minimum, maximum, and sum of a list of numbers:

```
>>> digits = [1, 2, 3, 4, 5, 6, 7, 8, 9, 0]
>>> min(digits)
0
>>> max(digits)
9
>>> sum(digits)
45
```

NOTE *The examples in this section use short lists of numbers in order to fit easily on the page. They would work just as well if your list contained a million or more numbers.*

List Comprehensions

The approach described earlier for generating the list squares consisted of using three or four lines of code. A *list comprehension* allows you to generate this same list in just one line of code. A list comprehension combines the for loop and the creation of new elements into one line, and automatically appends each new element. List comprehensions are not always presented to beginners, but I have included them here because you'll most likely see them as soon as you start looking at other people's code.

The following example builds the same list of square numbers you saw earlier but uses a list comprehension:

squares.py

```
squares = [value**2 for value in range(1,11)]
print(squares)
```

To use this syntax, begin with a descriptive name for the list, such as `squares`. Next, open a set of square brackets and define the expression for the values you want to store in the new list. In this example the expression is `value**2`, which raises the value to the second power. Then, write a `for` loop to generate the numbers you want to feed into the expression, and close the square brackets. The `for` loop in this example is `for value in range(1,11)`, which feeds the values 1 through 10 into the expression `value**2`. Notice that no colon is used at the end of the `for` statement.

The result is the same list of square numbers you saw earlier:

```
[1, 4, 9, 16, 25, 36, 49, 64, 81, 100]
```

It takes practice to write your own list comprehensions, but you'll find them worthwhile once you become comfortable creating ordinary lists. When you're writing three or four lines of code to generate lists and it begins to feel repetitive, consider writing your own list comprehensions.

TRY IT YOURSELF

4-3. Counting to Twenty: Use a `for` loop to print the numbers from 1 to 20, inclusive.

4-4. One Million: Make a list of the numbers from one to one million, and then use a `for` loop to print the numbers. (If the output is taking too long, stop it by pressing CTRL-C or by closing the output window.)

4-5. Summing a Million: Make a list of the numbers from one to one million, and then use `min()` and `max()` to make sure your list actually starts at one and ends at one million. Also, use the `sum()` function to see how quickly Python can add a million numbers.

4-6. Odd Numbers: Use the third argument of the `range()` function to make a list of the odd numbers from 1 to 20. Use a `for` loop to print each number.

4-7. Threes: Make a list of the multiples of 3 from 3 to 30. Use a `for` loop to print the numbers in your list.

4-8. Cubes: A number raised to the third power is called a *cube*. For example, the cube of 2 is written as `2**3` in Python. Make a list of the first 10 cubes (that is, the cube of each integer from 1 through 10), and use a `for` loop to print out the value of each cube.

4-9. Cube Comprehension: Use a list comprehension to generate a list of the first 10 cubes.

Working with Part of a List

In Chapter 3 you learned how to access single elements in a list, and in this chapter you've been learning how to work through all the elements in a list. You can also work with a specific group of items in a list, which Python calls a *slice*.

Slicing a List

To make a slice, you specify the index of the first and last elements you want to work with. As with the `range()` function, Python stops one item before the second index you specify. To output the first three elements in a list, you would request indices `0` through `3`, which would return elements `0`, `1`, and `2`.

The following example involves a list of players on a team:

players.py

```
players = ['charles', 'martina', 'michael', 'florence', 'eli']
❶ print(players[0:3])
```

The code at ❶ prints a slice of this list, which includes just the first three players. The output retains the structure of the list and includes the first three players in the list:

```
['charles', 'martina', 'michael']
```

You can generate any subset of a list. For example, if you want the second, third, and fourth items in a list, you would start the slice at index `1` and end at index `4`:

```
players = ['charles', 'martina', 'michael', 'florence', 'eli']
print(players[1:4])
```

This time the slice starts with `'martina'` and ends with `'florence'`:

```
['martina', 'michael', 'florence']
```

If you omit the first index in a slice, Python automatically starts your slice at the beginning of the list:

```
players = ['charles', 'martina', 'michael', 'florence', 'eli']
print(players[:4])
```

Without a starting index, Python starts at the beginning of the list:

```
['charles', 'martina', 'michael', 'florence']
```

A similar syntax works if you want a slice that includes the end of a list. For example, if you want all items from the third item through the last item, you can start with index 2 and omit the second index:

```
players = ['charles', 'martina', 'michael', 'florence', 'eli']
print(players[2:])
```

Python returns all items from the third item through the end of the list:

```
['michael', 'florence', 'eli']
```

This syntax allows you to output all of the elements from any point in your list to the end regardless of the length of the list. Recall that a negative index returns an element a certain distance from the end of a list; therefore, you can output any slice from the end of a list. For example, if we want to output the last three players on the roster, we can use the slice `players[-3:]`:

```
players = ['charles', 'martina', 'michael', 'florence', 'eli']
print(players[-3:])
```

This prints the names of the last three players and would continue to work as the list of players changes in size.

Looping Through a Slice

You can use a slice in a `for` loop if you want to loop through a subset of the elements in a list. In the next example we loop through the first three players and print their names as part of a simple roster:

```
players = ['charles', 'martina', 'michael', 'florence', 'eli']

print("Here are the first three players on my team:")
❶ for player in players[:3]:
    print(player.title())
```

Instead of looping through the entire list of players at ❶, Python loops through only the first three names:

```
Here are the first three players on my team:
Charles
Martina
Michael
```

Slices are very useful in a number of situations. For instance, when you're creating a game, you could add a player's final score to a list every time that player finishes playing. You could then get a player's top three scores by sorting the list in decreasing order and taking a slice that includes just the first three scores. When you're working with data, you can use slices to process your data in chunks of a specific size. Or, when you're building a web application, you could use slices to display information in a series of pages with an appropriate amount of information on each page.

Copying a List

Often, you'll want to start with an existing list and make an entirely new list based on the first one. Let's explore how copying a list works and examine one situation in which copying a list is useful.

To copy a list, you can make a slice that includes the entire original list by omitting the first index and the second index (`[:]`). This tells Python to make a slice that starts at the first item and ends with the last item, producing a copy of the entire list.

For example, imagine we have a list of our favorite foods and want to make a separate list of foods that a friend likes. This friend likes everything in our list so far, so we can create their list by copying ours:

foods.py

```
❶ my_foods = ['pizza', 'falafel', 'carrot cake']
❷ friend_foods = my_foods[:]

print("My favorite foods are:")
print(my_foods)

print("\nMy friend's favorite foods are:")
print(friend_foods)
```

At ❶ we make a list of the foods we like called `my_foods`. At ❷ we make a new list called `friend_foods`. We make a copy of `my_foods` by asking for a slice of `my_foods` without specifying any indices and store the copy in `friend_foods`. When we print each list, we see that they both contain the same foods:

```
My favorite foods are:
['pizza', 'falafel', 'carrot cake']

My friend's favorite foods are:
['pizza', 'falafel', 'carrot cake']
```

To prove that we actually have two separate lists, we'll add a new food to each list and show that each list keeps track of the appropriate person's favorite foods:

```
my_foods = ['pizza', 'falafel', 'carrot cake']
❶ friend_foods = my_foods[:]

❷ my_foods.append('cannoli')
❸ friend_foods.append('ice cream')

print("My favorite foods are:")
print(my_foods)
```

```
print("\nMy friend's favorite foods are:")
print(friend_foods)
```

At ❶ we copy the original items in my_foods to the new list friend_foods, as we did in the previous example. Next, we add a new food to each list: at ❷ we add 'cannoli' to my_foods, and at ❸ we add 'ice cream' to friend_foods. We then print the two lists to see whether each of these foods is in the appropriate list.

```
  My favorite foods are:
❹ ['pizza', 'falafel', 'carrot cake', 'cannoli']

  My friend's favorite foods are:
❺ ['pizza', 'falafel', 'carrot cake', 'ice cream']
```

The output at ❹ shows that 'cannoli' now appears in our list of favorite foods but 'ice cream' doesn't. At ❺ we can see that 'ice cream' now appears in our friend's list but 'cannoli' doesn't. If we had simply set friend_foods equal to my_foods, we would not produce two separate lists. For example, here's what happens when you try to copy a list without using a slice:

```
  my_foods = ['pizza', 'falafel', 'carrot cake']

  # This doesn't work:
❶ friend_foods = my_foods

  my_foods.append('cannoli')
  friend_foods.append('ice cream')

  print("My favorite foods are:")
  print(my_foods)

  print("\nMy friend's favorite foods are:")
  print(friend_foods)
```

Instead of storing a copy of my_foods in friend_foods at ❶, we set friend_foods equal to my_foods. This syntax actually tells Python to connect the new variable friend_foods to the list that is already contained in my_foods, so now both variables point to the same list. As a result, when we add 'cannoli' to my_foods, it will also appear in friend_foods. Likewise 'ice cream' will appear in both lists, even though it appears to be added only to friend_foods.

The output shows that both lists are the same now, which is not what we wanted:

```
My favorite foods are:
['pizza', 'falafel', 'carrot cake', 'cannoli', 'ice cream']

My friend's favorite foods are:
['pizza', 'falafel', 'carrot cake', 'cannoli', 'ice cream']
```

NOTE *Don't worry about the details in this example for now. Basically, if you're trying to work with a copy of a list and you see unexpected behavior, make sure you are copying the list using a slice, as we did in the first example.*

TRY IT YOURSELF

4-10. Slices: Using one of the programs you wrote in this chapter, add several lines to the end of the program that do the following:

- Print the message, *The first three items in the list are:*. Then use a slice to print the first three items from that program's list.
- Print the message, *Three items from the middle of the list are:*. Use a slice to print three items from the middle of the list.
- Print the message, *The last three items in the list are:*. Use a slice to print the last three items in the list.

4-11. My Pizzas, Your Pizzas: Start with your program from Exercise 4-1 (page 60). Make a copy of the list of pizzas, and call it `friend_pizzas`. Then, do the following:

- Add a new pizza to the original list.
- Add a different pizza to the list `friend_pizzas`.
- Prove that you have two separate lists. Print the message, *My favorite pizzas are:*, and then use a `for` loop to print the first list. Print the message, *My friend's favorite pizzas are:*, and then use a `for` loop to print the second list. Make sure each new pizza is stored in the appropriate list.

4-12. More Loops: All versions of *foods.py* in this section have avoided using `for` loops when printing to save space. Choose a version of *foods.py*, and write two `for` loops to print each list of foods.

Tuples

Lists work well for storing sets of items that can change throughout the life of a program. The ability to modify lists is particularly important when you're working with a list of users on a website or a list of characters in a game. However, sometimes you'll want to create a list of items that cannot change. Tuples allow you to do just that. Python refers to values that cannot change as *immutable*, and an immutable list is called a *tuple*.

Defining a Tuple

A tuple looks just like a list except you use parentheses instead of square brackets. Once you define a tuple, you can access individual elements by using each item's index, just as you would for a list.

For example, if we have a rectangle that should always be a certain size, we can ensure that its size doesn't change by putting the dimensions into a tuple:

dimensions.py

```
❶ dimensions = (200, 50)
❷ print(dimensions[0])
print(dimensions[1])
```

We define the tuple `dimensions` at ❶, using parentheses instead of square brackets. At ❷ we print each element in the tuple individually, using the same syntax we've been using to access elements in a list:

```
200
50
```

Let's see what happens if we try to change one of the items in the tuple `dimensions`:

```
dimensions = (200, 50)
❶ dimensions[0] = 250
```

The code at ❶ tries to change the value of the first dimension, but Python returns a type error. Basically, because we're trying to alter a tuple, which can't be done to that type of object, Python tells us we can't assign a new value to an item in a tuple:

```
Traceback (most recent call last):
  File "dimensions.py", line 3, in <module>
    dimensions[0] = 250
TypeError: 'tuple' object does not support item assignment
```

This is beneficial because we want Python to raise an error when a line of code tries to change the dimensions of the rectangle.

Looping Through All Values in a Tuple

You can loop over all the values in a tuple using a `for` loop, just as you did with a list:

```
dimensions = (200, 50)
for dimension in dimensions:
    print(dimension)
```

Python returns all the elements in the tuple, just as it would for a list:

```
200
50
```

Writing over a Tuple

Although you can't modify a tuple, you can assign a new value to a variable that holds a tuple. So if we wanted to change our dimensions, we could redefine the entire tuple:

```
❶ dimensions = (200, 50)
print("Original dimensions:")
for dimension in dimensions:
    print(dimension)

❷ dimensions = (400, 100)
❸ print("\nModified dimensions:")
for dimension in dimensions:
    print(dimension)
```

The block at ❶ defines the original tuple and prints the initial dimensions. At ❷, we store a new tuple in the variable `dimensions`. We then print the new dimensions at ❸. Python doesn't raise any errors this time, because overwriting a variable is valid:

```
Original dimensions:
200
50

Modified dimensions:
400
100
```

When compared with lists, tuples are simple data structures. Use them when you want to store a set of values that should not be changed throughout the life of a program.

TRY IT YOURSELF

4-13. Buffet: A buffet-style restaurant offers only five basic foods. Think of five simple foods, and store them in a tuple.

- Use a `for` loop to print each food the restaurant offers.
- Try to modify one of the items, and make sure that Python rejects the change.
- The restaurant changes its menu, replacing two of the items with different foods. Add a block of code that rewrites the tuple, and then use a `for` loop to print each of the items on the revised menu.

Styling Your Code

Now that you're writing longer programs, ideas about how to style your code are worthwhile to know. Take the time to make your code as easy as possible to read. Writing easy-to-read code helps you keep track of what your programs are doing and helps others understand your code as well.

Python programmers have agreed on a number of styling conventions to ensure that everyone's code is structured in roughly the same way. Once you've learned to write clean Python code, you should be able to understand the overall structure of anyone else's Python code, as long as they follow the same guidelines. If you're hoping to become a professional programmer at some point, you should begin following these guidelines as soon as possible to develop good habits.

The Style Guide

When someone wants to make a change to the Python language, they write a *Python Enhancement Proposal (PEP)*. One of the oldest PEPs is *PEP 8*, which instructs Python programmers on how to style their code. PEP 8 is fairly lengthy, but much of it relates to more complex coding structures than what you've seen so far.

The Python style guide was written with the understanding that code is read more often than it is written. You'll write your code once and then start reading it as you begin debugging. When you add features to a program, you'll spend more time reading your code. When you share your code with other programmers, they'll read your code as well.

Given the choice between writing code that's easier to write or code that's easier to read, Python programmers will almost always encourage you to write code that's easier to read. The following guidelines will help you write clear code from the start.

Indentation

PEP 8 recommends that you use four spaces per indentation level. Using four spaces improves readability while leaving room for multiple levels of indentation on each line.

In a word processing document, people often use tabs rather than spaces to indent. This works well for word processing documents, but the Python interpreter gets confused when tabs are mixed with spaces. Every text editor provides a setting that lets you use the TAB key but then converts each tab to a set number of spaces. You should definitely use your TAB key, but also make sure your editor is set to insert spaces rather than tabs into your document.

Mixing tabs and spaces in your file can cause problems that are very difficult to diagnose. If you think you have a mix of tabs and spaces, you can convert all tabs in a file to spaces in most editors.

Line Length

Many Python programmers recommend that each line should be less than 80 characters. Historically, this guideline developed because most computers could fit only 79 characters on a single line in a terminal window. Currently, people can fit much longer lines on their screens, but other reasons exist to adhere to the 79-character standard line length. Professional programmers often have several files open on the same screen, and using the standard line length allows them to see entire lines in two or three files that are open side by side onscreen. PEP 8 also recommends that you limit all of your comments to 72 characters per line, because some of the tools that generate automatic documentation for larger projects add formatting characters at the beginning of each commented line.

The PEP 8 guidelines for line length are not set in stone, and some teams prefer a 99-character limit. Don't worry too much about line length in your code as you're learning, but be aware that people who are working collaboratively almost always follow the PEP 8 guidelines. Most editors allow you to set up a visual cue, usually a vertical line on your screen, that shows you where these limits are.

NOTE *Appendix B shows you how to configure your text editor so it always inserts four spaces each time you press the* TAB *key and shows a vertical guideline to help you follow the 79-character limit.*

Blank Lines

To group parts of your program visually, use blank lines. You should use blank lines to organize your files, but don't do so excessively. By following the examples provided in this book, you should strike the right balance. For example, if you have five lines of code that build a list, and then another three lines that do something with that list, it's appropriate to place a blank line between the two sections. However, you should not place three or four blank lines between the two sections.

Blank lines won't affect how your code runs, but they will affect the readability of your code. The Python interpreter uses horizontal indentation to interpret the meaning of your code, but it disregards vertical spacing.

Other Style Guidelines

PEP 8 has many additional styling recommendations, but most of the guidelines refer to more complex programs than what you're writing at this point. As you learn more complex Python structures, I'll share the relevant parts of the PEP 8 guidelines.

> **TRY IT YOURSELF**
>
> **4-14. PEP 8:** Look through the original PEP 8 style guide at *https://python.org/dev/peps/pep-0008/*. You won't use much of it now, but it might be interesting to skim through it.
>
> **4-15. Code Review:** Choose three of the programs you've written in this chapter and modify each one to comply with PEP 8:
>
> - Use four spaces for each indentation level. Set your text editor to insert four spaces every time you press TAB, if you haven't already done so (see Appendix B for instructions on how to do this).
> - Use less than 80 characters on each line, and set your editor to show a vertical guideline at the 80th character position.
> - Don't use blank lines excessively in your program files.

Summary

In this chapter you learned how to work efficiently with the elements in a list. You learned how to work through a list using a `for` loop, how Python uses indentation to structure a program, and how to avoid some common indentation errors. You learned to make simple numerical lists, as well as a few operations you can perform on numerical lists. You learned how to slice a list to work with a subset of items and how to copy lists properly using a slice. You also learned about tuples, which provide a degree of protection to a set of values that shouldn't change, and how to style your increasingly complex code to make it easy to read.

In Chapter 5, you'll learn to respond appropriately to different conditions by using `if` statements. You'll learn to string together relatively complex sets of conditional tests to respond appropriately to exactly the kind of situation or information you're looking for. You'll also learn to use `if` statements while looping through a list to take specific actions with selected elements from a list.

5

IF STATEMENTS

Programming often involves examining a set of conditions and deciding which action to take based on those conditions. Python's `if` statement allows you to examine the current state of a program and respond appropriately to that state.

In this chapter you'll learn to write conditional tests, which allow you to check any condition of interest. You'll learn to write simple `if` statements, and you'll learn how to create a more complex series of `if` statements to identify when the exact conditions you want are present. You'll then apply this concept to lists, so you'll be able to write a `for` loop that handles most items in a list one way but handles certain items with specific values in a different way.

A Simple Example

The following short example shows how `if` tests let you respond to special situations correctly. Imagine you have a list of cars and you want to print out the name of each car. Car names are proper names, so the names of most cars should be printed in title case. However, the value `'bmw'` should be printed in all uppercase. The following code loops through a list of car names and looks for the value `'bmw'`. Whenever the value is `'bmw'`, it's printed in uppercase instead of title case:

cars.py

```
cars = ['audi', 'bmw', 'subaru', 'toyota']

for car in cars:
❶    if car == 'bmw':
        print(car.upper())
    else:
        print(car.title())
```

The loop in this example first checks if the current value of `car` is `'bmw'` ❶. If it is, the value is printed in uppercase. If the value of `car` is anything other than `'bmw'`, it's printed in title case:

```
Audi
BMW
Subaru
Toyota
```

This example combines a number of the concepts you'll learn about in this chapter. Let's begin by looking at the kinds of tests you can use to examine the conditions in your program.

Conditional Tests

At the heart of every `if` statement is an expression that can be evaluated as `True` or `False` and is called a *conditional test*. Python uses the values `True` and `False` to decide whether the code in an `if` statement should be executed. If a conditional test evaluates to `True`, Python executes the code following the `if` statement. If the test evaluates to `False`, Python ignores the code following the `if` statement.

Checking for Equality

Most conditional tests compare the current value of a variable to a specific value of interest. The simplest conditional test checks whether the value of a variable is equal to the value of interest:

```
❶ >>> car = 'bmw'
❷ >>> car == 'bmw'
True
```

The line at ❶ sets the value of car to 'bmw' using a single equal sign, as you've seen many times already. The line at ❷ checks whether the value of car is 'bmw' using a double equal sign (==). This *equality operator* returns True if the values on the left and right side of the operator match, and False if they don't match. The values in this example match, so Python returns True.

When the value of car is anything other than 'bmw', this test returns False:

```
❶ >>> car = 'audi'
❷ >>> car == 'bmw'
False
```

A single equal sign is really a statement; you might read the code at ❶ as "Set the value of car equal to 'audi'." On the other hand, a double equal sign, like the one at ❷, asks a question: "Is the value of car equal to 'bmw'?" Most programming languages use equal signs in this way.

Ignoring Case When Checking for Equality

Testing for equality is case sensitive in Python. For example, two values with different capitalization are not considered equal:

```
>>> car = 'Audi'
>>> car == 'audi'
False
```

If case matters, this behavior is advantageous. But if case doesn't matter and instead you just want to test the value of a variable, you can convert the variable's value to lowercase before doing the comparison:

```
>>> car = 'Audi'
>>> car.lower() == 'audi'
True
```

This test would return True no matter how the value 'Audi' is formatted because the test is now case insensitive. The lower() function doesn't change the value that was originally stored in car, so you can do this kind of comparison without affecting the original variable:

```
❶ >>> car = 'Audi'
❷ >>> car.lower() == 'audi'
True
❸ >>> car
'Audi'
```

At ❶ we store the capitalized string 'Audi' in the variable car. At ❷ we convert the value of car to lowercase and compare the lowercase value to the string 'audi'. The two strings match, so Python returns True. At ❸ we can see that the value stored in car has not been affected by the conditional test.

Websites enforce certain rules for the data that users enter in a manner similar to this. For example, a site might use a conditional test like this to ensure that every user has a truly unique username, not just a variation on the capitalization of another person's username. When someone submits a new username, that new username is converted to lowercase and compared to the lowercase versions of all existing usernames. During this check, a username like 'John' will be rejected if any variation of 'john' is already in use.

Checking for Inequality

When you want to determine whether two values are not equal, you can combine an exclamation point and an equal sign (!=). The exclamation point represents *not*, as it does in many programming languages.

Let's use another if statement to examine how to use the inequality operator. We'll store a requested pizza topping in a variable and then print a message if the person did not order anchovies:

toppings.py

```
requested_topping = 'mushrooms'

❶ if requested_topping != 'anchovies':
    print("Hold the anchovies!")
```

The line at ❶ compares the value of requested_topping to the value 'anchovies'. If these two values do not match, Python returns True and executes the code following the if statement. If the two values match, Python returns False and does not run the code following the if statement.

Because the value of requested_topping is not 'anchovies', the print statement is executed:

```
Hold the anchovies!
```

Most of the conditional expressions you write will test for equality, but sometimes you'll find it more efficient to test for inequality.

Numerical Comparisons

Testing numerical values is pretty straightforward. For example, the following code checks whether a person is 18 years old:

```
>>> age = 18
>>> age == 18
True
```

You can also test to see if two numbers are not equal. For example, the following code prints a message if the given answer is not correct:

magic_number.py

```
answer = 17

❶ if answer != 42:
    print("That is not the correct answer. Please try again!")
```

The conditional test at ❶ passes, because the value of `answer` (`17`) is not equal to `42`. Because the test passes, the indented code block is executed:

```
That is not the correct answer. Please try again!
```

You can include various mathematical comparisons in your conditional statements as well, such as less than, less than or equal to, greater than, and greater than or equal to:

```
>>> age = 19
>>> age < 21
True
>>> age <= 21
True
>>> age > 21
False
>>> age >= 21
False
```

Each mathematical comparison can be used as part of an `if` statement, which can help you detect the exact conditions of interest.

Checking Multiple Conditions

You may want to check multiple conditions at the same time. For example, sometimes you might need two conditions to be `True` to take an action. Other times you might be satisfied with just one condition being `True`. The keywords `and` and `or` can help you in these situations.

Using and to Check Multiple Conditions

To check whether two conditions are both `True` simultaneously, use the keyword `and` to combine the two conditional tests; if each test passes, the overall expression evaluates to `True`. If either test fails or if both tests fail, the expression evaluates to `False`.

For example, you can check whether two people are both over 21 using the following test:

```
❶ >>> age_0 = 22
  >>> age_1 = 18
❷ >>> age_0 >= 21 and age_1 >= 21
  False
```

```
❸ >>> age_1 = 22
>>> age_0 >= 21 and age_1 >= 21
True
```

At ❶ we define two ages, age_0 and age_1. At ❷ we check whether both ages are 21 or older. The test on the left passes, but the test on the right fails, so the overall conditional expression evaluates to False. At ❸ we change age_1 to 22. The value of age_1 is now greater than 21, so both individual tests pass, causing the overall conditional expression to evaluate as True.

To improve readability, you can use parentheses around the individual tests, but they are not required. If you use parentheses, your test would look like this:

```
(age_0 >= 21) and (age_1 >= 21)
```

Using or to Check Multiple Conditions

The keyword or allows you to check multiple conditions as well, but it passes when either or both of the individual tests pass. An or expression fails only when both individual tests fail.

Let's consider two ages again, but this time we'll look for only one person to be over 21:

```
❶ >>> age_0 = 22
>>> age_1 = 18
❷ >>> age_0 >= 21 or age_1 >= 21
True
❸ >>> age_0 = 18
>>> age_0 >= 21 or age_1 >= 21
False
```

We start with two age variables again at ❶. Because the test for age_0 at ❷ passes, the overall expression evaluates to True. We then lower age_0 to 18. In the test at ❸, both tests now fail and the overall expression evaluates to False.

Checking Whether a Value Is in a List

Sometimes it's important to check whether a list contains a certain value before taking an action. For example, you might want to check whether a new username already exists in a list of current usernames before completing someone's registration on a website. In a mapping project, you might want to check whether a submitted location already exists in a list of known locations.

To find out whether a particular value is already in a list, use the keyword in. Let's consider some code you might write for a pizzeria. We'll make a list of toppings a customer has requested for a pizza and then check whether certain toppings are in the list.

```
>>> requested_toppings = ['mushrooms', 'onions', 'pineapple']
❶ >>> 'mushrooms' in requested_toppings
True
❷ >>> 'pepperoni' in requested_toppings
False
```

At ❶ and ❷, the keyword `in` tells Python to check for the existence of `'mushrooms'` and `'pepperoni'` in the list `requested_toppings`. This technique is quite powerful because you can create a list of essential values, and then easily check whether the value you're testing matches one of the values in the list.

Checking Whether a Value Is Not in a List

Other times, it's important to know if a value does not appear in a list. You can use the keyword `not` in this situation. For example, consider a list of users who are banned from commenting in a forum. You can check whether a user has been banned before allowing that person to submit a comment:

banned_users.py

```
banned_users = ['andrew', 'carolina', 'david']
user = 'marie'

❶ if user not in banned_users:
    print(user.title() + ", you can post a response if you wish.")
```

The line at ❶ reads quite clearly. If the value of `user` is not in the list `banned_users`, Python returns `True` and executes the indented line.

The user `'marie'` is not in the list `banned_users`, so she sees a message inviting her to post a response:

```
Marie, you can post a response if you wish.
```

Boolean Expressions

As you learn more about programming, you'll hear the term *Boolean expression* at some point. A Boolean expression is just another name for a conditional test. A *Boolean value* is either `True` or `False`, just like the value of a conditional expression after it has been evaluated.

Boolean values are often used to keep track of certain conditions, such as whether a game is running or whether a user can edit certain content on a website:

```
game_active = True
can_edit = False
```

Boolean values provide an efficient way to track the state of a program or a particular condition that is important in your program.

TRY IT YOURSELF

5-1. Conditional Tests: Write a series of conditional tests. Print a statement describing each test and your prediction for the results of each test. Your code should look something like this:

```
car = 'subaru'
print("Is car == 'subaru'? I predict True.")
print(car == 'subaru')

print("\nIs car == 'audi'? I predict False.")
print(car == 'audi')
```

- Look closely at your results, and make sure you understand why each line evaluates to `True` or `False`.
- Create at least 10 tests. Have at least 5 tests evaluate to `True` and another 5 tests evaluate to `False`.

5-2. More Conditional Tests: You don't have to limit the number of tests you create to 10. If you want to try more comparisons, write more tests and add them to *conditional_tests.py*. Have at least one `True` and one `False` result for each of the following:

- Tests for equality and inequality with strings
- Tests using the `lower()` function
- Numerical tests involving equality and inequality, greater than and less than, greater than or equal to, and less than or equal to
- Tests using the `and` keyword and the `or` keyword
- Test whether an item is in a list
- Test whether an item is not in a list

if Statements

When you understand conditional tests, you can start writing `if` statements. Several different kinds of `if` statements exist, and your choice of which to use depends on the number of conditions you need to test. You saw several examples of `if` statements in the discussion about conditional tests, but now let's dig deeper into the topic.

Simple if Statements

The simplest kind of `if` statement has one test and one action:

```
if conditional_test:
    do something
```

You can put any conditional test in the first line and just about any action in the indented block following the test. If the conditional test evaluates to `True`, Python executes the code following the `if` statement. If the test evaluates to `False`, Python ignores the code following the `if` statement.

Let's say we have a variable representing a person's age, and we want to know if that person is old enough to vote. The following code tests whether the person can vote:

voting.py

```
  age = 19
❶ if age >= 18:
❷     print("You are old enough to vote!")
```

At ❶ Python checks to see whether the value in `age` is greater than or equal to 18. It is, so Python executes the indented `print` statement at ❷:

```
You are old enough to vote!
```

Indentation plays the same role in `if` statements as it did in `for` loops. All indented lines after an `if` statement will be executed if the test passes, and the entire block of indented lines will be ignored if the test does not pass.

You can have as many lines of code as you want in the block following the `if` statement. Let's add another line of output if the person is old enough to vote, asking if the individual has registered to vote yet:

```
age = 19
if age >= 18:
    print("You are old enough to vote!")
    print("Have you registered to vote yet?")
```

The conditional test passes, and both `print` statements are indented, so both lines are printed:

```
You are old enough to vote!
Have you registered to vote yet?
```

If the value of `age` is less than 18, this program would produce no output.

if-else Statements

Often, you'll want to take one action when a conditional test passes and a different action in all other cases. Python's `if-else` syntax makes this possible. An `if-else` block is similar to a simple `if` statement, but the `else` statement allows you to define an action or set of actions that are executed when the conditional test fails.

We'll display the same message we had previously if the person is old enough to vote, but this time we'll add a message for anyone who is not old enough to vote:

```
age = 17
❶ if age >= 18:
    print("You are old enough to vote!")
    print("Have you registered to vote yet?")
❷ else:
    print("Sorry, you are too young to vote.")
    print("Please register to vote as soon as you turn 18!")
```

If the conditional test at ❶ passes, the first block of indented `print` statements is executed. If the test evaluates to `False`, the `else` block at ❷ is executed. Because `age` is less than 18 this time, the conditional test fails and the code in the `else` block is executed:

```
Sorry, you are too young to vote.
Please register to vote as soon as you turn 18!
```

This code works because it has only two possible situations to evaluate: a person is either old enough to vote or not old enough to vote. The `if-else` structure works well in situations in which you want Python to always execute one of two possible actions. In a simple `if-else` chain like this, one of the two actions will always be executed.

The if-elif-else Chain

Often, you'll need to test more than two possible situations, and to evaluate these you can use Python's `if-elif-else` syntax. Python executes only one block in an `if-elif-else` chain. It runs each conditional test in order until one passes. When a test passes, the code following that test is executed and Python skips the rest of the tests.

Many real-world situations involve more than two possible conditions. For example, consider an amusement park that charges different rates for different age groups:

- Admission for anyone under age 4 is free.
- Admission for anyone between the ages of 4 and 18 is $5.
- Admission for anyone age 18 or older is $10.

How can we use an `if` statement to determine a person's admission rate? The following code tests for the age group of a person and then prints an admission price message:

amusement_park.py

```
age = 12

❶ if age < 4:
    print("Your admission cost is $0.")
```

```
❷ elif age < 18:
      print("Your admission cost is $5.")
❸ else:
      print("Your admission cost is $10.")
```

The `if` test at ❶ tests whether a person is under 4 years old. If the test passes, an appropriate message is printed and Python skips the rest of the tests. The `elif` line at ❷ is really another `if` test, which runs only if the previous test failed. At this point in the chain, we know the person is at least 4 years old because the first test failed. If the person is less than 18, an appropriate message is printed and Python skips the `else` block. If both the `if` and `elif` tests fail, Python runs the code in the `else` block at ❸.

In this example the test at ❶ evaluates to `False`, so its code block is not executed. However, the second test evaluates to `True` (12 is less than 18) so its code is executed. The output is one sentence, informing the user of the admission cost:

```
Your admission cost is $5.
```

Any age greater than 17 would cause the first two tests to fail. In these situations, the `else` block would be executed and the admission price would be $10.

Rather than printing the admission price within the `if-elif-else` block, it would be more concise to set just the price inside the `if-elif-else` chain and then have a simple `print` statement that runs after the chain has been evaluated:

```
age = 12

if age < 4:
❶     price = 0
elif age < 18:
❷     price = 5
else:
❸     price = 10

❹ print("Your admission cost is $" + str(price) + ".")
```

The lines at ❶, ❷, and ❸ set the value of `price` according to the person's age, as in the previous example. After the price is set by the `if-elif-else` chain, a separate unindented `print` statement ❹ uses this value to display a message reporting the person's admission price.

This code produces the same output as the previous example, but the purpose of the `if-elif-else` chain is narrower. Instead of determining a price and displaying a message, it simply determines the admission price. In addition to being more efficient, this revised code is easier to modify than the original approach. To change the text of the output message, you would need to change only one `print` statement rather than three separate `print` statements.

Using Multiple elif Blocks

You can use as many `elif` blocks in your code as you like. For example, if the amusement park were to implement a discount for seniors, you could add one more conditional test to the code to determine whether someone qualified for the senior discount. Let's say that anyone 65 or older pays half the regular admission, or $5:

```
age = 12

if age < 4:
    price = 0
elif age < 18:
    price = 5
❶ elif age < 65:
    price = 10
❷ else:
    price = 5

print("Your admission cost is $" + str(price) + ".")
```

Most of this code is unchanged. The second `elif` block at ❶ now checks to make sure a person is less than age 65 before assigning them the full admission rate of $10. Notice that the value assigned in the `else` block at ❷ needs to be changed to $5, because the only ages that make it to this block are people 65 or older.

Omitting the else Block

Python does not require an `else` block at the end of an `if-elif` chain. Sometimes an `else` block is useful; sometimes it is clearer to use an additional `elif` statement that catches the specific condition of interest:

```
age = 12

if age < 4:
    price = 0
elif age < 18:
    price = 5
elif age < 65:
    price = 10
❶ elif age >= 65:
    price = 5

print("Your admission cost is $" + str(price) + ".")
```

The extra `elif` block at ❶ assigns a price of $5 when the person is 65 or older, which is a bit clearer than the general `else` block. With this change, every block of code must pass a specific test in order to be executed.

The else block is a catchall statement. It matches any condition that wasn't matched by a specific if or elif test, and that can sometimes include invalid or even malicious data. If you have a specific final condition you are testing for, consider using a final elif block and omit the else block. As a result, you'll gain extra confidence that your code will run only under the correct conditions.

Testing Multiple Conditions

The if-elif-else chain is powerful, but it's only appropriate to use when you just need one test to pass. As soon as Python finds one test that passes, it skips the rest of the tests. This behavior is beneficial, because it's efficient and allows you to test for one specific condition.

However, sometimes it's important to check all of the conditions of interest. In this case, you should use a series of simple if statements with no elif or else blocks. This technique makes sense when more than one condition could be True, and you want to act on every condition that is True.

Let's reconsider the pizzeria example. If someone requests a two-topping pizza, you'll need to be sure to include both toppings on their pizza:

toppings.py

```
❶ requested_toppings = ['mushrooms', 'extra cheese']

❷ if 'mushrooms' in requested_toppings:
      print("Adding mushrooms.")
❸ if 'pepperoni' in requested_toppings:
      print("Adding pepperoni.")
❹ if 'extra cheese' in requested_toppings:
      print("Adding extra cheese.")

  print("\nFinished making your pizza!")
```

We start at ❶ with a list containing the requested toppings. The if statement at ❷ checks to see whether the person requested mushrooms on their pizza. If so, a message is printed confirming that topping. The test for pepperoni at ❸ is another simple if statement, not an elif or else statement, so this test is run regardless of whether the previous test passed or not. The code at ❹ checks whether extra cheese was requested regardless of the results from the first two tests. These three independent tests are executed every time this program is run.

Because every condition in this example is evaluated, both mushrooms and extra cheese are added to the pizza:

```
Adding mushrooms.
Adding extra cheese.

Finished making your pizza!
```

This code would not work properly if we used an `if-elif-else` block, because the code would stop running after only one test passes. Here's what that would look like:

```
requested_toppings = ['mushrooms', 'extra cheese']

if 'mushrooms' in requested_toppings:
    print("Adding mushrooms.")
elif 'pepperoni' in requested_toppings:
    print("Adding pepperoni.")
elif 'extra cheese' in requested_toppings:
    print("Adding extra cheese.")

print("\nFinished making your pizza!")
```

The test for `'mushrooms'` is the first test to pass, so mushrooms are added to the pizza. However, the values `'extra cheese'` and `'pepperoni'` are never checked, because Python doesn't run any tests beyond the first test that passes in an `if-elif-else` chain. The customer's first topping will be added, but all of their other toppings will be missed:

```
Adding mushrooms.

Finished making your pizza!
```

In summary, if you want only one block of code to run, use an `if-elif-else` chain. If more than one block of code needs to run, use a series of independent `if` statements.

TRY IT YOURSELF

5-3. Alien Colors #1: Imagine an alien was just shot down in a game. Create a variable called `alien_color` and assign it a value of `'green'`, `'yellow'`, or `'red'`.

- Write an `if` statement to test whether the alien's color is green. If it is, print a message that the player just earned 5 points.
- Write one version of this program that passes the `if` test and another that fails. (The version that fails will have no output.)

5-4. Alien Colors #2: Choose a color for an alien as you did in Exercise 5-3, and write an `if-else` chain.

- If the alien's color is green, print a statement that the player just earned 5 points for shooting the alien.
- If the alien's color isn't green, print a statement that the player just earned 10 points.
- Write one version of this program that runs the `if` block and another that runs the `else` block.

5-5. Alien Colors #3: Turn your `if-else` chain from Exercise 5-4 into an `if-elif-else` chain.

- If the alien is green, print a message that the player earned 5 points.
- If the alien is yellow, print a message that the player earned 10 points.
- If the alien is red, print a message that the player earned 15 points.
- Write three versions of this program, making sure each message is printed for the appropriate color alien.

5-6. Stages of Life: Write an `if-elif-else` chain that determines a person's stage of life. Set a value for the variable age, and then:

- If the person is less than 2 years old, print a message that the person is a baby.
- If the person is at least 2 years old but less than 4, print a message that the person is a toddler.
- If the person is at least 4 years old but less than 13, print a message that the person is a kid.
- If the person is at least 13 years old but less than 20, print a message that the person is a teenager.
- If the person is at least 20 years old but less than 65, print a message that the person is an adult.
- If the person is age 65 or older, print a message that the person is an elder.

5-7. Favorite Fruit: Make a list of your favorite fruits, and then write a series of independent `if` statements that check for certain fruits in your list.

- Make a list of your three favorite fruits and call it `favorite_fruits`.
- Write five `if` statements. Each should check whether a certain kind of fruit is in your list. If the fruit is in your list, the `if` block should print a statement, such as *You really like bananas!*

Using if Statements with Lists

You can do some interesting work when you combine lists and `if` statements. You can watch for special values that need to be treated differently than other values in the list. You can manage changing conditions efficiently, such as the availability of certain items in a restaurant throughout a shift. You can also begin to prove that your code works as you expect it to in all possible situations.

Checking for Special Items

This chapter began with a simple example that showed how to handle a special value like `'bmw'`, which needed to be printed in a different format than other values in the list. Now that you have a basic understanding of conditional tests and `if` statements, let's take a closer look at how you can watch for special values in a list and handle those values appropriately.

Let's continue with the pizzeria example. The pizzeria displays a message whenever a topping is added to your pizza, as it's being made. The code for this action can be written very efficiently by making a list of toppings the customer has requested and using a loop to announce each topping as it's added to the pizza:

toppings.py

```
requested_toppings = ['mushrooms', 'green peppers', 'extra cheese']

for requested_topping in requested_toppings:
    print("Adding " + requested_topping + ".")

print("\nFinished making your pizza!")
```

The output is straightforward because this code is just a simple `for` loop:

```
Adding mushrooms.
Adding green peppers.
Adding extra cheese.

Finished making your pizza!
```

But what if the pizzeria runs out of green peppers? An `if` statement inside the `for` loop can handle this situation appropriately:

```
requested_toppings = ['mushrooms', 'green peppers', 'extra cheese']

for requested_topping in requested_toppings:
❶    if requested_topping == 'green peppers':
        print("Sorry, we are out of green peppers right now.")
❷    else:
        print("Adding " + requested_topping + ".")

print("\nFinished making your pizza!")
```

This time we check each requested item before adding it to the pizza. The code at ❶ checks to see if the person requested green peppers. If so, we display a message informing them why they can't have green peppers. The `else` block at ❷ ensures that all other toppings will be added to the pizza.

The output shows that each requested topping is handled appropriately.

```
Adding mushrooms.
Sorry, we are out of green peppers right now.
Adding extra cheese.

Finished making your pizza!
```

Checking That a List Is Not Empty

We've made a simple assumption about every list we've worked with so far; we've assumed that each list has at least one item in it. Soon we'll let users provide the information that's stored in a list, so we won't be able to assume that a list has any items in it each time a loop is run. In this situation, it's useful to check whether a list is empty before running a `for` loop.

As an example, let's check whether the list of requested toppings is empty before building the pizza. If the list is empty, we'll prompt the user and make sure they want a plain pizza. If the list is not empty, we'll build the pizza just as we did in the previous examples:

```
❶ requested_toppings = []

❷ if requested_toppings:
      for requested_topping in requested_toppings:
          print("Adding " + requested_topping + ".")
      print("\nFinished making your pizza!")
❸ else:
      print("Are you sure you want a plain pizza?")
```

This time we start out with an empty list of requested toppings at ❶. Instead of jumping right into a `for` loop, we do a quick check at ❷. When the name of a list is used in an `if` statement, Python returns `True` if the list contains at least one item; an empty list evaluates to `False`. If `requested_toppings` passes the conditional test, we run the same `for` loop we used in the previous example. If the conditional test fails, we print a message asking the customer if they really want a plain pizza with no toppings ❸.

The list is empty in this case, so the output asks if the user really wants a plain pizza:

```
Are you sure you want a plain pizza?
```

If the list is not empty, the output will show each requested topping being added to the pizza.

Using Multiple Lists

People will ask for just about anything, especially when it comes to pizza toppings. What if a customer actually wants french fries on their pizza? You can use lists and `if` statements to make sure your input makes sense before you act on it.

Let's watch out for unusual topping requests before we build a pizza. The following example defines two lists. The first is a list of available toppings at the pizzeria, and the second is the list of toppings that the user has requested. This time, each item in `requested_toppings` is checked against the list of available toppings before it's added to the pizza:

```
❶ available_toppings = ['mushrooms', 'olives', 'green peppers',
                          'pepperoni', 'pineapple', 'extra cheese']

❷ requested_toppings = ['mushrooms', 'french fries', 'extra cheese']

❸ for requested_topping in requested_toppings:
❹     if requested_topping in available_toppings:
          print("Adding " + requested_topping + ".")
❺     else:
          print("Sorry, we don't have " + requested_topping + ".")

  print("\nFinished making your pizza!")
```

At ❶ we define a list of available toppings at this pizzeria. Note that this could be a tuple if the pizzeria has a stable selection of toppings. At ❷, we make a list of toppings that a customer has requested. Note the unusual request, `'french fries'`. At ❸ we loop through the list of requested toppings. Inside the loop, we first check to see if each requested topping is actually in the list of available toppings ❹. If it is, we add that topping to the pizza. If the requested topping is not in the list of available toppings, the `else` block will run ❺. The `else` block prints a message telling the user which toppings are unavailable.

This code syntax produces clean, informative output:

```
Adding mushrooms.
Sorry, we don't have french fries.
Adding extra cheese.

Finished making your pizza!
```

In just a few lines of code, we've managed a real-world situation pretty effectively!

TRY IT YOURSELF

5-8. Hello Admin: Make a list of five or more usernames, including the name `'admin'`. Imagine you are writing code that will print a greeting to each user after they log in to a website. Loop through the list, and print a greeting to each user:

- If the username is `'admin'`, print a special greeting, such as *Hello admin, would you like to see a status report?*
- Otherwise, print a generic greeting, such as *Hello Eric, thank you for logging in again.*

5-9. No Users: Add an `if` test to *hello_admin.py* to make sure the list of users is not empty.

- If the list is empty, print the message *We need to find some users!*
- Remove all of the usernames from your list, and make sure the correct message is printed.

5-10. Checking Usernames: Do the following to create a program that simulates how websites ensure that everyone has a unique username.

- Make a list of five or more usernames called `current_users`.
- Make another list of five usernames called `new_users`. Make sure one or two of the new usernames are also in the `current_users` list.
- Loop through the `new_users` list to see if each new username has already been used. If it has, print a message that the person will need to enter a new username. If a username has not been used, print a message saying that the username is available.
- Make sure your comparison is case insensitive. If `'John'` has been used, `'JOHN'` should not be accepted.

5-11. Ordinal Numbers: Ordinal numbers indicate their position in a list, such as *1st* or *2nd*. Most ordinal numbers end in *th*, except 1, 2, and 3.

- Store the numbers 1 through 9 in a list.
- Loop through the list.
- Use an `if-elif-else` chain inside the loop to print the proper ordinal ending for each number. Your output should read `"1st 2nd 3rd 4th 5th 6th 7th 8th 9th"`, and each result should be on a separate line.

Styling Your if Statements

In every example in this chapter, you've seen good styling habits. The only recommendation PEP 8 provides for styling conditional tests is to use a single space around comparison operators, such as `==`, `>=`, `<=`. For example:

```
if age < 4:
```

is better than:

```
if age<4:
```

Such spacing does not affect the way Python interprets your code; it just makes your code easier for you and others to read.

> **TRY IT YOURSELF**
>
> **5-12. Styling `if` statements:** Review the programs you wrote in this chapter, and make sure you styled your conditional tests appropriately.
>
> **5-13. Your Ideas:** At this point, you're a more capable programmer than you were when you started this book. Now that you have a better sense of how real-world situations are modeled in programs, you might be thinking of some problems you could solve with your own programs. Record any new ideas you have about problems you might want to solve as your programming skills continue to improve. Consider games you might want to write, data sets you might want to explore, and web applications you'd like to create.

Summary

In this chapter you learned how to write conditional tests, which always evaluate to `True` or `False`. You learned to write simple `if` statements, `if-else` chains, and `if-elif-else` chains. You began using these structures to identify particular conditions you needed to test and to know when those conditions have been met in your programs. You learned to handle certain items in a list differently than all other items while continuing to utilize the efficiency of a `for` loop. You also revisited Python's style recommendations to ensure that your increasingly complex programs are still relatively easy to read and understand.

In Chapter 6 you'll learn about Python's dictionaries. A dictionary is similar to a list, but it allows you to connect pieces of information. You'll learn to build dictionaries, loop through them, and use them in combination with lists and `if` statements. Learning about dictionaries will enable you to model an even wider variety of real-world situations.

6

DICTIONARIES

In this chapter you'll learn how to use Python's dictionaries, which allow you to connect pieces of related information. You'll learn how to access the information once it's in a dictionary and how to modify that information. Because dictionaries can store an almost limitless amount of information, I'll show you how to loop through the data in a dictionary. Additionally, you'll learn to nest dictionaries inside lists, lists inside dictionaries, and even dictionaries inside other dictionaries.

Understanding dictionaries allows you to model a variety of real-world objects more accurately. You'll be able to create a dictionary representing a person and then store as much information as you want about that person. You can store their name, age, location, profession, and any other aspect of a person you can describe. You'll be able to store any two kinds of information that can be matched up, such as a list of words and their meanings, a list of people's names and their favorite numbers, a list of mountains and their elevations, and so forth.

A Simple Dictionary

Consider a game featuring aliens that can have different colors and point values. This simple dictionary stores information about a particular alien:

alien.py

```
alien_0 = {'color': 'green', 'points': 5}

print(alien_0['color'])
print(alien_0['points'])
```

The dictionary `alien_0` stores the alien's color and point value. The two `print` statements access and display that information, as shown here:

```
green
5
```

As with most new programming concepts, using dictionaries takes practice. Once you've worked with dictionaries for a bit you'll soon see how effectively they can model real-world situations.

Working with Dictionaries

A *dictionary* in Python is a collection of *key-value pairs*. Each *key* is connected to a value, and you can use a key to access the value associated with that key. A key's value can be a number, a string, a list, or even another dictionary. In fact, you can use any object that you can create in Python as a value in a dictionary.

In Python, a dictionary is wrapped in braces, {}, with a series of key-value pairs inside the braces, as shown in the earlier example:

```
alien_0 = {'color': 'green', 'points': 5}
```

A *key-value pair* is a set of values associated with each other. When you provide a key, Python returns the value associated with that key. Every key is connected to its value by a colon, and individual key-value pairs are separated by commas. You can store as many key-value pairs as you want in a dictionary.

The simplest dictionary has exactly one key-value pair, as shown in this modified version of the `alien_0` dictionary:

```
alien_0 = {'color': 'green'}
```

This dictionary stores one piece of information about `alien_0`, namely the alien's color. The string `'color'` is a key in this dictionary, and its associated value is `'green'`.

Accessing Values in a Dictionary

To get the value associated with a key, give the name of the dictionary and then place the key inside a set of square brackets, as shown here:

```
alien_0 = {'color': 'green'}
print(alien_0['color'])
```

This returns the value associated with the key 'color' from the dictionary alien_0:

```
green
```

You can have an unlimited number of key-value pairs in a dictionary. For example, here's the original alien_0 dictionary with two key-value pairs:

```
alien_0 = {'color': 'green', 'points': 5}
```

Now you can access either the color or the point value of alien_0. If a player shoots down this alien, you can look up how many points they should earn using code like this:

```
alien_0 = {'color': 'green', 'points': 5}

❶ new_points = alien_0['points']
❷ print("You just earned " + str(new_points) + " points!")
```

Once the dictionary has been defined, the code at ❶ pulls the value associated with the key 'points' from the dictionary. This value is then stored in the variable new_points. The line at ❷ converts this integer value to a string and prints a statement about how many points the player just earned:

```
You just earned 5 points!
```

If you run this code every time an alien is shot down, the alien's point value will be retrieved.

Adding New Key-Value Pairs

Dictionaries are dynamic structures, and you can add new key-value pairs to a dictionary at any time. For example, to add a new key-value pair, you would give the name of the dictionary followed by the new key in square brackets along with the new value.

Let's add two new pieces of information to the alien_0 dictionary: the alien's x- and y-coordinates, which will help us display the alien in a particular position on the screen. Let's place the alien on the left edge of the screen, 25 pixels down from the top. Because screen coordinates usually start at the upper-left corner of the screen, we'll place the alien on the left edge of the screen by setting the x-coordinate to 0 and 25 pixels from the top by setting its y-coordinate to positive 25, as shown here:

```
alien_0 = {'color': 'green', 'points': 5}
print(alien_0)

❶ alien_0['x_position'] = 0
❷ alien_0['y_position'] = 25
print(alien_0)
```

We start by defining the same dictionary that we've been working with. We then print this dictionary, displaying a snapshot of its information. At ❶ we add a new key-value pair to the dictionary: key `'x_position'` and value `0`. We do the same for key `'y_position'` at ❷. When we print the modified dictionary, we see the two additional key-value pairs:

```
{'color': 'green', 'points': 5}
{'color': 'green', 'points': 5, 'y_position': 25, 'x_position': 0}
```

The final version of the dictionary contains four key-value pairs. The original two specify color and point value, and two more specify the alien's position. Notice that the order of the key-value pairs does not match the order in which we added them. Python doesn't care about the order in which you store each key-value pair; it cares only about the connection between each key and its value.

Starting with an Empty Dictionary

It's sometimes convenient, or even necessary, to start with an empty dictionary and then add each new item to it. To start filling an empty dictionary, define a dictionary with an empty set of braces and then add each key-value pair on its own line. For example, here's how to build the `alien_0` dictionary using this approach:

```
alien_0 = {}

alien_0['color'] = 'green'
alien_0['points'] = 5

print(alien_0)
```

Here we define an empty `alien_0` dictionary, and then add color and point values to it. The result is the dictionary we've been using in previous examples:

```
{'color': 'green', 'points': 5}
```

Typically, you'll use empty dictionaries when storing user-supplied data in a dictionary or when you write code that generates a large number of key-value pairs automatically.

Modifying Values in a Dictionary

To modify a value in a dictionary, give the name of the dictionary with the key in square brackets and then the new value you want associated with that key. For example, consider an alien that changes from green to yellow as a game progresses:

```
alien_0 = {'color': 'green'}
print("The alien is " + alien_0['color'] + ".")

alien_0['color'] = 'yellow'
print("The alien is now " + alien_0['color'] + ".")
```

We first define a dictionary for `alien_0` that contains only the alien's color; then we change the value associated with the key `'color'` to `'yellow'`. The output shows that the alien has indeed changed from green to yellow:

```
The alien is green.
The alien is now yellow.
```

For a more interesting example, let's track the position of an alien that can move at different speeds. We'll store a value representing the alien's current speed and then use it to determine how far to the right the alien should move:

```
alien_0 = {'x_position': 0, 'y_position': 25, 'speed': 'medium'}
print("Original x-position: " + str(alien_0['x_position']))

# Move the alien to the right.
# Determine how far to move the alien based on its current speed.
❶ if alien_0['speed'] == 'slow':
    x_increment = 1
elif alien_0['speed'] == 'medium':
    x_increment = 2
else:
    # This must be a fast alien.
    x_increment = 3

# The new position is the old position plus the increment.
❷ alien_0['x_position'] = alien_0['x_position'] + x_increment

print("New x-position: " + str(alien_0['x_position']))
```

We start by defining an alien with an initial *x* position and *y* position, and a speed of `'medium'`. We've omitted the color and point values for the sake of simplicity, but this example would work the same way if you included those key-value pairs as well. We also print the original value of `x_position` to see how far the alien moves to the right.

At ❶, an `if-elif-else` chain determines how far the alien should move to the right and stores this value in the variable `x_increment`. If the alien's speed is `'slow'`, it moves one unit to the right; if the speed is `'medium'`, it moves two units to the right; and if it's 'fast', it moves three units to the right. Once the increment has been calculated, it's added to the value of x_position at ❷, and the result is stored in the dictionary's x_position.

Because this is a medium-speed alien, its position shifts two units to the right:

```
Original x-position: 0
New x-position: 2
```

This technique is pretty cool: by changing one value in the alien's dictionary, you can change the overall behavior of the alien. For example, to turn this medium-speed alien into a fast alien, you would add the line:

```
alien_0['speed'] = fast
```

The if-elif-else block would then assign a larger value to x_increment the next time the code runs.

Removing Key-Value Pairs

When you no longer need a piece of information that's stored in a dictionary, you can use the del statement to completely remove a key-value pair. All del needs is the name of the dictionary and the key that you want to remove.

For example, let's remove the key 'points' from the alien_0 dictionary along with its value:

```
alien_0 = {'color': 'green', 'points': 5}
print(alien_0)

❶ del alien_0['points']
print(alien_0)
```

The line at ❶ tells Python to delete the key 'points' from the dictionary alien_0 and to remove the value associated with that key as well. The output shows that the key 'points' and its value of 5 are deleted from the dictionary, but the rest of the dictionary is unaffected:

```
{'color': 'green', 'points': 5}
{'color': 'green'}
```

NOTE *Be aware that the deleted key-value pair is removed permanently.*

A Dictionary of Similar Objects

The previous example involved storing different kinds of information about one object, an alien in a game. You can also use a dictionary to store one kind of information about many objects. For example, say you want to poll a number of people and ask them what their favorite programming language is. A dictionary is useful for storing the results of a simple poll, like this:

```
favorite_languages = {
    'jen': 'python',
    'sarah': 'c',
    'edward': 'ruby',
    'phil': 'python',
    }
```

As you can see, we've broken a larger dictionary into several lines. Each key is the name of a person who responded to the poll, and each value is their language choice. When you know you'll need more than one line to define a dictionary, press ENTER after the opening brace. Then indent the next line one level (four spaces), and write the first key-value pair, followed by a comma. From this point forward when you press ENTER, your text editor should automatically indent all subsequent key-value pairs to match the first key-value pair.

Once you've finished defining the dictionary, add a closing brace on a new line after the last key-value pair and indent it one level so it aligns with the keys in the dictionary. It's good practice to include a comma after the last key-value pair as well, so you're ready to add a new key-value pair on the next line.

NOTE *Most editors have some functionality that helps you format extended lists and dictionaries in a similar manner to this example. Other acceptable ways to format long dictionaries are available as well, so you may see slightly different formatting in your editor, or in other sources.*

To use this dictionary, given the name of a person who took the poll, you can easily look up their favorite language:

favorite_languages.py

```
favorite_languages = {
    'jen': 'python',
    'sarah': 'c',
    'edward': 'ruby',
    'phil': 'python',
    }

❶ print("Sarah's favorite language is " +
❷     favorite_languages['sarah'].title() +
❸     ".")
```

To see which language Sarah chose, we ask for the value at:

```
favorite_languages['sarah']
```

This syntax is used in the print statement at ❷, and the output shows Sarah's favorite language:

```
Sarah's favorite language is C.
```

This example also shows how you can break up a long print statement over several lines. The word print is shorter than most dictionary names, so it makes sense to include the first part of what you want to print right after the opening parenthesis ❶. Choose an appropriate point at which to break what's being printed, and add a concatenation operator (+) at the end of the first line ❷. Press ENTER and then press TAB to align all subsequent lines at one indentation level under the print statement. When you've finished composing your output, you can place the closing parenthesis on the last line of the print block ❸.

TRY IT YOURSELF

6-1. Person: Use a dictionary to store information about a person you know. Store their first name, last name, age, and the city in which they live. You should have keys such as first_name, last_name, age, and city. Print each piece of information stored in your dictionary.

6-2. Favorite Numbers: Use a dictionary to store people's favorite numbers. Think of five names, and use them as keys in your dictionary. Think of a favorite number for each person, and store each as a value in your dictionary. Print each person's name and their favorite number. For even more fun, poll a few friends and get some actual data for your program.

6-3. Glossary: A Python dictionary can be used to model an actual dictionary. However, to avoid confusion, let's call it a glossary.

- Think of five programming words you've learned about in the previous chapters. Use these words as the keys in your glossary, and store their meanings as values.
- Print each word and its meaning as neatly formatted output. You might print the word followed by a colon and then its meaning, or print the word on one line and then print its meaning indented on a second line. Use the newline character (\n) to insert a blank line between each word-meaning pair in your output.

Looping Through a Dictionary

A single Python dictionary can contain just a few key-value pairs or millions of pairs. Because a dictionary can contain large amounts of data, Python lets you loop through a dictionary. Dictionaries can be used to store information in a variety of ways; therefore, several different ways exist to loop through them. You can loop through all of a dictionary's key-value pairs, through its keys, or through its values.

Looping Through All Key-Value Pairs

Before we explore the different approaches to looping, let's consider a new dictionary designed to store information about a user on a website. The following dictionary would store one person's username, first name, and last name:

```
user_0 = {
    'username': 'efermi',
    'first': 'enrico',
    'last': 'fermi',
    }
```

You can access any single piece of information about `user_0` based on what you've already learned in this chapter. But what if you wanted to see everything stored in this user's dictionary? To do so, you could loop through the dictionary using a `for` loop:

user.py

```
user_0 = {
    'username': 'efermi',
    'first': 'enrico',
    'last': 'fermi',
    }

❶ for key, value in user_0.items():
❷     print("\nKey: " + key)
❸     print("Value: " + value)
```

As shown at ❶, to write a `for` loop for a dictionary, you create names for the two variables that will hold the key and value in each key-value pair. You can choose any names you want for these two variables. This code would work just as well if you had used abbreviations for the variable names, like this:

```
for k, v in user_0.items()
```

The second half of the `for` statement at ❶ includes the name of the dictionary followed by the method `items()`, which returns a list of key-value pairs. The `for` loop then stores each of these pairs in the two variables provided. In the preceding example, we use the variables to print each `key` ❷, followed by the associated `value` ❸. The `"\n"` in the first `print` statement ensures that a blank line is inserted before each key-value pair in the output:

```
Key: last
Value: fermi

Key: first
Value: enrico

Key: username
Value: efermi
```

Notice again that the key-value pairs are not returned in the order in which they were stored, even when looping through a dictionary. Python doesn't care about the order in which key-value pairs are stored; it tracks only the connections between individual keys and their values.

Looping through all key-value pairs works particularly well for dictionaries like the *favorite_languages.py* example on page 101, which stores the same kind of information for many different keys. If you loop through the favorite_languages dictionary, you get the name of each person in the dictionary and their favorite programming language. Because the keys always refer to a person's name and the value is always a language, we'll use the variables name and language in the loop instead of key and value. This will make it easier to follow what's happening inside the loop:

favorite_languages.py

```
favorite_languages = {
    'jen': 'python',
    'sarah': 'c',
    'edward': 'ruby',
    'phil': 'python',
    }

❶ for name, language in favorite_languages.items():
❷     print(name.title() + "'s favorite language is " +
          language.title() + ".")
```

The code at ❶ tells Python to loop through each key-value pair in the dictionary. As it works through each pair the key is stored in the variable name, and the value is stored in the variable language. These descriptive names make it much easier to see what the print statement at ❷ is doing.

Now, in just a few lines of code, we can display all of the information from the poll:

```
Jen's favorite language is Python.
Sarah's favorite language is C.
Phil's favorite language is Python.
Edward's favorite language is Ruby.
```

This type of looping would work just as well if our dictionary stored the results from polling a thousand or even a million people.

Looping Through All the Keys in a Dictionary

The keys() method is useful when you don't need to work with all of the values in a dictionary. Let's loop through the favorite_languages dictionary and print the names of everyone who took the poll:

```
favorite_languages = {
    'jen': 'python',
    'sarah': 'c',
    'edward': 'ruby',
    'phil': 'python',
    }
```

```
❶ for name in favorite_languages.keys():
      print(name.title())
```

The line at ❶ tells Python to pull all the keys from the dictionary favorite_languages and store them one at a time in the variable name. The output shows the names of everyone who took the poll:

```
Jen
Sarah
Phil
Edward
```

Looping through the keys is actually the default behavior when looping through a dictionary, so this code would have exactly the same output if you wrote . . .

```
for name in favorite_languages:
```

rather than . . .

```
for name in favorite_languages.keys():
```

You can choose to use the keys() method explicitly if it makes your code easier to read, or you can omit it if you wish.

You can access the value associated with any key you care about inside the loop by using the current key. Let's print a message to a couple of friends about the languages they chose. We'll loop through the names in the dictionary as we did previously, but when the name matches one of our friends, we'll display a message about their favorite language:

```
favorite_languages = {
    'jen': 'python',
    'sarah': 'c',
    'edward': 'ruby',
    'phil': 'python',
    }

❶ friends = ['phil', 'sarah']
  for name in favorite_languages.keys():
      print(name.title())

❷     if name in friends:
          print("  Hi " + name.title() +
              ", I see your favorite language is " +
❸             favorite_languages[name].title() + "!")
```

At ❶ we make a list of friends that we want to print a message to. Inside the loop, we print each person's name. Then at ❷ we check to see whether the name we are working with is in the list friends. If it is, we print a special greeting, including a reference to their language choice. To access the favorite language at ❸, we use the name of the dictionary and the current value of `name` as the key. Everyone's name is printed, but our friends receive a special message:

```
Edward
Phil
  Hi Phil, I see your favorite language is Python!
Sarah
  Hi Sarah, I see your favorite language is C!
Jen
```

You can also use the `keys()` method to find out if a particular person was polled. This time, let's find out if Erin took the poll:

```
favorite_languages = {
    'jen': 'python',
    'sarah': 'c',
    'edward': 'ruby',
    'phil': 'python',
    }

❶ if 'erin' not in favorite_languages.keys():
    print("Erin, please take our poll!")
```

The `keys()` method isn't just for looping: It actually returns a list of all the keys, and the line at ❶ simply checks if `'erin'` is in this list. Because she's not, a message is printed inviting her to take the poll:

```
Erin, please take our poll!
```

Looping Through a Dictionary's Keys in Order

A dictionary always maintains a clear connection between each key and its associated value, but you never get the items from a dictionary in any predictable order. That's not a problem, because you'll usually just want to obtain the correct value associated with each key.

One way to return items in a certain order is to sort the keys as they're returned in the `for` loop. You can use the `sorted()` function to get a copy of the keys in order:

```
favorite_languages = {
    'jen': 'python',
    'sarah': 'c',
    'edward': 'ruby',
    'phil': 'python',
    }

for name in sorted(favorite_languages.keys()):
    print(name.title() + ", thank you for taking the poll.")
```

This for statement is like other for statements except that we've wrapped the sorted() function around the dictionary.keys() method. This tells Python to list all keys in the dictionary and sort that list before looping through it. The output shows everyone who took the poll with the names displayed in order:

```
Edward, thank you for taking the poll.
Jen, thank you for taking the poll.
Phil, thank you for taking the poll.
Sarah, thank you for taking the poll.
```

Looping Through All Values in a Dictionary

If you are primarily interested in the values that a dictionary contains, you can use the values() method to return a list of values without any keys. For example, say we simply want a list of all languages chosen in our programming language poll without the name of the person who chose each language:

```
favorite_languages = {
    'jen': 'python',
    'sarah': 'c',
    'edward': 'ruby',
    'phil': 'python',
    }

print("The following languages have been mentioned:")
for language in favorite_languages.values():
    print(language.title())
```

The for statement here pulls each value from the dictionary and stores it in the variable language. When these values are printed, we get a list of all chosen languages:

```
The following languages have been mentioned:
Python
C
Python
Ruby
```

This approach pulls all the values from the dictionary without checking for repeats. That might work fine with a small number of values, but in a poll with a large number of respondents, this would result in a very repetitive list. To see each language chosen without repetition, we can use a *set*. A set is similar to a list except that each item in the set must be unique:

```
favorite_languages = {
    'jen': 'python',
    'sarah': 'c',
    'edward': 'ruby',
```

```
    'phil': 'python',
    }

print("The following languages have been mentioned:")
❶ for language in set(favorite_languages.values()):
    print(language.title())
```

When you wrap set() around a list that contains duplicate items, Python identifies the unique items in the list and builds a set from those items. At ❶ we use set() to pull out the unique languages in favorite_languages.values().

The result is a nonrepetitive list of languages that have been mentioned by people taking the poll:

```
The following languages have been mentioned:
Python
C
Ruby
```

As you continue learning about Python, you'll often find a built-in feature of the language that helps you do exactly what you want with your data.

TRY IT YOURSELF

6-4. Glossary 2: Now that you know how to loop through a dictionary, clean up the code from Exercise 6-3 (page 102) by replacing your series of print statements with a loop that runs through the dictionary's keys and values. When you're sure that your loop works, add five more Python terms to your glossary. When you run your program again, these new words and meanings should automatically be included in the output.

6-5. Rivers: Make a dictionary containing three major rivers and the country each river runs through. One key-value pair might be 'nile': 'egypt'.

- Use a loop to print a sentence about each river, such as *The Nile runs through Egypt.*
- Use a loop to print the name of each river included in the dictionary.
- Use a loop to print the name of each country included in the dictionary.

6-6. Polling: Use the code in *favorite_languages.py* (page 104).

- Make a list of people who should take the favorite languages poll. Include some names that are already in the dictionary and some that are not.
- Loop through the list of people who should take the poll. If they have already taken the poll, print a message thanking them for responding. If they have not yet taken the poll, print a message inviting them to take the poll.

Nesting

Sometimes you'll want to store a set of dictionaries in a list or a list of items as a value in a dictionary. This is called *nesting*. You can nest a set of dictionaries inside a list, a list of items inside a dictionary, or even a dictionary inside another dictionary. Nesting is a powerful feature, as the following examples will demonstrate.

A List of Dictionaries

The alien_0 dictionary contains a variety of information about one alien, but it has no room to store information about a second alien, much less a screen full of aliens. How can you manage a fleet of aliens? One way is to make a list of aliens in which each alien is a dictionary of information about that alien. For example, the following code builds a list of three aliens:

aliens.py

```
alien_0 = {'color': 'green', 'points': 5}
alien_1 = {'color': 'yellow', 'points': 10}
alien_2 = {'color': 'red', 'points': 15}

❶ aliens = [alien_0, alien_1, alien_2]

for alien in aliens:
    print(alien)
```

We first create three dictionaries, each representing a different alien. At ❶ we pack each of these dictionaries into a list called aliens. Finally, we loop through thc list and print out cach alien:

```
{'color': 'green', 'points': 5}
{'color': 'yellow', 'points': 10}
{'color': 'red', 'points': 15}
```

A more realistic example would involve more than three aliens with code that automatically generates each alien. In the following example we use range() to create a fleet of 30 aliens:

```
# Make an empty list for storing aliens.
aliens = []

# Make 30 green aliens.
❶ for alien_number in range(30):
❷     new_alien = {'color': 'green', 'points': 5, 'speed': 'slow'}
❸     aliens.append(new_alien)

# Show the first 5 aliens:
❹ for alien in aliens[:5]:
    print(alien)
print("...")

# Show how many aliens have been created.
❺ print("Total number of aliens: " + str(len(aliens)))
```

This example begins with an empty list to hold all of the aliens that will be created. At ❶ range() returns a set of numbers, which just tells Python how many times we want the loop to repeat. Each time the loop runs we create a new alien ❷ and then append each new alien to the list aliens ❸. At ❹ we use a slice to print the first five aliens, and then at ❺ we print the length of the list to prove we've actually generated the full fleet of 30 aliens:

```
{'speed': 'slow', 'color': 'green', 'points': 5}
{'speed': 'slow', 'color': 'green', 'points': 5}
{'speed': 'slow', 'color': 'green', 'points': 5}
{'speed': 'slow', 'color': 'green', 'points': 5}
{'speed': 'slow', 'color': 'green', 'points': 5}
...

Total number of aliens: 30
```

These aliens all have the same characteristics, but Python considers each one a separate object, which allows us to modify each alien individually.

How might you work with a set of aliens like this? Imagine that one aspect of a game has some aliens changing color and moving faster as the game progresses. When it's time to change colors, we can use a for loop and an if statement to change the color of aliens. For example, to change the first three aliens to yellow, medium-speed aliens worth 10 points each, we could do this:

```
# Make an empty list for storing aliens.
aliens = []

# Make 30 green aliens.
for alien_number in range (0,30):
    new_alien = {'color': 'green', 'points': 5, 'speed': 'slow'}
    aliens.append(new_alien)

for alien in aliens[0:3]:
    if alien['color'] == 'green':
        alien['color'] = 'yellow'
        alien['speed'] = 'medium'
        alien['points'] = 10

# Show the first 5 aliens:
for alien in aliens[0:5]:
    print(alien)
print("...")
```

Because we want to modify the first three aliens, we loop through a slice that includes only the first three aliens. All of the aliens are green now but that won't always be the case, so we write an if statement to make sure we're only modifying green aliens. If the alien is green, we change the color to 'yellow', the speed to 'medium', and the point value to 10, as shown in the following output:

```
{'speed': 'medium', 'color': 'yellow', 'points': 10}
{'speed': 'medium', 'color': 'yellow', 'points': 10}
{'speed': 'medium', 'color': 'yellow', 'points': 10}
{'speed': 'slow', 'color': 'green', 'points': 5}
{'speed': 'slow', 'color': 'green', 'points': 5}
...
```

You could expand this loop by adding an elif block that turns yellow aliens into red, fast-moving ones worth 15 points each. Without showing the entire program again, that loop would look like this:

```
for alien in aliens[0:3]:
    if alien['color'] == 'green':
        alien['color'] = 'yellow'
        alien['speed'] = 'medium'
        alien['points'] = 10
    elif alien['color'] == 'yellow':
        alien['color'] = 'red'
        alien['speed'] = 'fast'
        alien['points'] = 15
```

It's common to store a number of dictionaries in a list when each dictionary contains many kinds of information about one object. For example, you might create a dictionary for each user on a website, as we did in *user.py* on page 103, and store the individual dictionaries in a list called users. All of the dictionaries in the list should have an identical structure so you can loop through the list and work with each dictionary object in the same way.

A List in a Dictionary

Rather than putting a dictionary inside a list, it's sometimes useful to put a list inside a dictionary. For example, consider how you might describe a pizza that someone is ordering. If you were to use only a list, all you could really store is a list of the pizza's toppings. With a dictionary, a list of toppings can be just one aspect of the pizza you're describing.

In the following example, two kinds of information are stored for each pizza: a type of crust and a list of toppings. The list of toppings is a value associated with the key 'toppings'. To use the items in the list, we give the name of the dictionary and the key 'toppings', as we would any value in the dictionary. Instead of returning a single value, we get a list of toppings:

pizza.py

```
  # Store information about a pizza being ordered.
❶ pizza = {
      'crust': 'thick',
      'toppings': ['mushrooms', 'extra cheese'],
      }
```

```
    # Summarize the order.
❷ print("You ordered a " + pizza['crust'] + "-crust pizza " +
        "with the following toppings:")

❸ for topping in pizza['toppings']:
        print("\t" + topping)
```

We begin at ❶ with a dictionary that holds information about a pizza that has been ordered. One key in the dictionary is `'crust'`, and the associated value is the string `'thick'`. The next key, `'toppings'`, has a list as its value that stores all requested toppings. At ❷ we summarize the order before building the pizza. To print the toppings, we write a `for` loop ❸. To access the list of toppings, we use the key `'toppings'`, and Python grabs the list of toppings from the dictionary.

The following output summarizes the pizza that we plan to build:

```
You ordered a thick-crust pizza with the following toppings:
    mushrooms
    extra cheese
```

You can nest a list inside a dictionary any time you want more than one value to be associated with a single key in a dictionary. In the earlier example of favorite programming languages, if we were to store each person's responses in a list, people could choose more than one favorite language. When we loop through the dictionary, the value associated with each person would be a list of languages rather than a single language. Inside the dictionary's `for` loop, we use another `for` loop to run through the list of languages associated with each person:

favorite_languages.py

```
❶ favorite_languages = {
        'jen': ['python', 'ruby'],
        'sarah': ['c'],
        'edward': ['ruby', 'go'],
        'phil': ['python', 'haskell'],
        }

❷ for name, languages in favorite_languages.items():
        print("\n" + name.title() + "'s favorite languages are:")
❸       for language in languages:
            print("\t" + language.title())
```

As you can see at ❶ the value associated with each name is now a list. Notice that some people have one favorite language and others have multiple favorites. When we loop through the dictionary at ❷, we use the variable name `languages` to hold each value from the dictionary, because we know that each value will be a list. Inside the main dictionary loop, we use another for loop ❸ to run through each person's list of favorite languages. Now each person can list as many favorite languages as they like:

```
Jen's favorite languages are:
    Python
    Ruby

Sarah's favorite languages are:
    C

Phil's favorite languages are:
    Python
    Haskell

Edward's favorite languages are:
    Ruby
    Go
```

To refine this program even further, you could include an if statement at the beginning of the dictionary's for loop to see whether each person has more than one favorite language by examining the value of len(languages). If a person has more than one favorite, the output would stay the same. If the person has only one favorite language, you could change the wording to reflect that. For example, you could say Sarah's favorite language is C.

NOTE *You should not nest lists and dictionaries too deeply. If you're nesting items much deeper than what you see in the preceding examples or you're working with someone else's code with significant levels of nesting, most likely a simpler way to solve the problem exists.*

A Dictionary in a Dictionary

You can nest a dictionary inside another dictionary, but your code can get complicated quickly when you do. For example, if you have several users for a website, each with a unique username, you can use the usernames as the keys in a dictionary. You can then store information about each user by using a dictionary as the value associated with their username. In the following listing, we store three pieces of information about each user: their first name, last name, and location. We'll access this information by looping through the usernames and the dictionary of information associated with each username:

many_users.py

```
users = {
    'aeinstein': {
        'first': 'albert',
        'last': 'einstein',
        'location': 'princeton',
        },
```

```
    'mcurie': {
        'first': 'marie',
        'last': 'curie',
        'location': 'paris',
        },

    }

❶ for username, user_info in users.items():
❷     print("\nUsername: " + username)
❸     full_name = user_info['first'] + " " + user_info['last']
      location = user_info['location']

❹     print("\tFull name: " + full_name.title())
      print("\tLocation: " + location.title())
```

We first define a dictionary called `users` with two keys: one each for the usernames `'aeinstein'` and `'mcurie'`. The value associated with each key is a dictionary that includes each user's first name, last name, and location. At ❶ we loop through the `users` dictionary. Python stores each key in the variable `username`, and the dictionary associated with each username goes into the variable `user_info`. Once inside the main dictionary loop, we print the username at ❷.

At ❸ we start accessing the inner dictionary. The variable `user_info`, which contains the dictionary of user information, has three keys: `'first'`, `'last'`, and `'location'`. We use each key to generate a neatly formatted full name and location for each person, and then print a summary of what we know about each user ❹:

```
Username: aeinstein
    Full name: Albert Einstein
    Location: Princeton

Username: mcurie
    Full name: Marie Curie
    Location: Paris
```

Notice that the structure of each user's dictionary is identical. Although not required by Python, this structure makes nested dictionaries easier to work with. If each user's dictionary had different keys, the code inside the `for` loop would be more complicated.

TRY IT YOURSELF

6-7. People: Start with the program you wrote for Exercise 6-1 (page 102). Make two new dictionaries representing different people, and store all three dictionaries in a list called `people`. Loop through your list of people. As you loop through the list, print everything you know about each person.

6-8. Pets: Make several dictionaries, where the name of each dictionary is the name of a pet. In each dictionary, include the kind of animal and the owner's name. Store these dictionaries in a list called `pets`. Next, loop through your list and as you do print everything you know about each pet.

6-9. Favorite Places: Make a dictionary called `favorite_places`. Think of three names to use as keys in the dictionary, and store one to three favorite places for each person. To make this exercise a bit more interesting, ask some friends to name a few of their favorite places. Loop through the dictionary, and print each person's name and their favorite places.

6-10. Favorite Numbers: Modify your program from Exercise 6-2 (page 102) so each person can have more than one favorite number. Then print each person's name along with their favorite numbers.

6-11. Cities: Make a dictionary called `cities`. Use the names of three cities as keys in your dictionary. Create a dictionary of information about each city and include the country that the city is in, its approximate population, and one fact about that city. The keys for each city's dictionary should be something like `country`, `population`, and `fact`. Print the name of each city and all of the information you have stored about it.

6-12. Extensions: We're now working with examples that are complex enough that they can be extended in any number of ways. Use one of the example programs from this chapter, and extend it by adding new keys and values, changing the context of the program or improving the formatting of the output.

Summary

In this chapter you learned how to define a dictionary and how to work with the information stored in a dictionary. You learned how to access and modify individual elements in a dictionary, and how to loop through all of the information in a dictionary. You learned to loop through a dictionary's key-value pairs, its keys, and its values. You also learned how to nest multiple dictionaries in a list, nest lists in a dictionary, and nest a dictionary inside a dictionary.

In the next chapter you'll learn about `while` loops and how to accept input from people who are using your programs. This will be an exciting chapter, because you'll learn to make all of your programs interactive: they'll be able to respond to user input.

7

USER INPUT AND WHILE LOOPS

Most programs are written to solve an end user's problem. To do so, you usually need to get some information from the user. For a simple example, let's say someone wants to find out whether they're old enough to vote. If you write a program to answer this question, you need to know the user's age before you can provide an answer. The program will need to ask the user to enter, or *input*, their age; once the program has this input, it can compare it to the voting age to determine if the user is old enough and then report the result.

In this chapter you'll learn how to accept user input so your program can then work with it. When your program needs a name, you'll be able to prompt the user for a name. When your program needs a list of names, you'll be able to prompt the user for a series of names. To do this, you'll use the `input()` function.

You'll also learn how to keep programs running as long as users want them to, so they can enter as much information as they need to; then, your program can work with that information. You'll use Python's `while` loop to keep programs running as long as certain conditions remain true.

With the ability to work with user input and the ability to control how long your programs run, you'll be able to write fully interactive programs.

How the input() Function Works

The `input()` function pauses your program and waits for the user to enter some text. Once Python receives the user's input, it stores it in a variable to make it convenient for you to work with.

For example, the following program asks the user to enter some text, then displays that message back to the user:

parrot.py

```
message = input("Tell me something, and I will repeat it back to you: ")
print(message)
```

The `input()` function takes one argument: the *prompt*, or instructions, that we want to display to the user so they know what to do. In this example, when Python runs the first line, the user sees the prompt `Tell me something, and I will repeat it back to you: `. The program waits while the user enters their response and continues after the user presses ENTER. The response is stored in the variable `message`, then `print(message)` displays the input back to the user:

```
Tell me something, and I will repeat it back to you: Hello everyone!
Hello everyone!
```

NOTE *Sublime Text doesn't run programs that prompt the user for input. You can use Sublime Text to write programs that prompt for input, but you'll need to run these programs from a terminal. See "Running Python Programs from a Terminal" on page 16.*

Writing Clear Prompts

Each time you use the `input()` function, you should include a clear, easy-to-follow prompt that tells the user exactly what kind of information you're looking for. Any statement that tells the user what to enter should work. For example:

greeter.py

```
name = input("Please enter your name: ")
print("Hello, " + name + "!")
```

Add a space at the end of your prompts (after the colon in the preceding example) to separate the prompt from the user's response and to make it clear to your user where to enter their text. For example:

```
Please enter your name: Eric
Hello, Eric!
```

Sometimes you'll want to write a prompt that's longer than one line. For example, you might want to tell the user why you're asking for certain input.

You can store your prompt in a variable and pass that variable to the input() function. This allows you to build your prompt over several lines, then write a clean input() statement.

greeter.py

```
prompt = "If you tell us who you are, we can personalize the messages you see."
prompt += "\nWhat is your first name? "

name = input(prompt)
print("\nHello, " + name + "!")
```

This example shows one way to build a multi-line string. The first line stores the first part of the message in the variable prompt. In the second line, the operator += takes the string that was stored in prompt and adds the new string onto the end.

The prompt now spans two lines, again with space after the question mark for clarity:

```
If you tell us who you are, we can personalize the messages you see.
What is your first name? Eric

Hello, Eric!
```

Using int() to Accept Numerical Input

When you use the input() function, Python interprets everything the user enters as a string. Consider the following interpreter session, which asks for the user's age:

```
>>> age = input("How old are you? ")
How old are you? 21
>>> age
'21'
```

The user enters the number 21, but when we ask Python for the value of age, it returns '21', the string representation of the numerical value entered. We know Python interpreted the input as a string because the number is now enclosed in quotes. If all you want to do is print the input, this works well. But if you try to use the input as a number, you'll get an error:

```
   >>> age = input("How old are you? ")
   How old are you? 21
❶ >>> age >= 18
   Traceback (most recent call last):
     File "<stdin>", line 1, in <module>
❷ TypeError: unorderable types: str() >= int()
```

When you try to use the input to do a numerical comparison ❶, Python produces an error because it can't compare a string to an integer: the string '21' that's stored in age can't be compared to the numerical value 18 ❷.

We can resolve this issue by using the int() function, which tells Python to treat the input as a numerical value. The int() function converts a string representation of a number to a numerical representation, as shown here:

```
>>> age = input("How old are you? ")
How old are you? 21
❶ >>> age = int(age)
>>> age >= 18
True
```

In this example, when we enter 21 at the prompt, Python interprets the number as a string, but the value is then converted to a numerical representation by int() ❶. Now Python can run the conditional test: it compares age (which now contains the numerical value 21) and 18 to see if age is greater than or equal to 18. This test evaluates to True.

How do you use the int() function in an actual program? Consider a program that determines whether people are tall enough to ride a roller coaster:

rollercoaster.py

```
height = input("How tall are you, in inches? ")
height = int(height)

if height >= 36:
    print("\nYou're tall enough to ride!")
else:
    print("\nYou'll be able to ride when you're a little older.")
```

The program can compare height to 36 because height = int(height) converts the input value to a numerical representation before the comparison is made. If the number entered is greater than or equal to 36, we tell the user that they're tall enough:

```
How tall are you, in inches? 71

You're tall enough to ride!
```

When you use numerical input to do calculations and comparisons, be sure to convert the input value to a numerical representation first.

The Modulo Operator

A useful tool for working with numerical information is the *modulo operator* (%), which divides one number by another number and returns the remainder:

```
>>> 4 % 3
1
>>> 5 % 3
2
>>> 6 % 3
0
```

```
>>> 7 % 3
1
```

The modulo operator doesn't tell you how many times one number fits into another; it just tells you what the remainder is.

When one number is divisible by another number, the remainder is 0, so the modulo operator always returns 0. You can use this fact to determine if a number is even or odd:

even_or_odd.py

```
number = input("Enter a number, and I'll tell you if it's even or odd: ")
number = int(number)

if number % 2 == 0:
    print("\nThe number " + str(number) + " is even.")
else:
    print("\nThe number " + str(number) + " is odd.")
```

Even numbers are always divisible by two, so if the modulo of a number and two is zero (here, `if number % 2 == 0`) the number is even. Otherwise, it's odd.

```
Enter a number, and I'll tell you if it's even or odd: 42

The number 42 is even.
```

Accepting Input in Python 2.7

If you're using Python 2.7, you should use the `raw_input()` function when prompting for user input. This function interprets all input as a string, just as `input()` does in Python 3.

Python 2.7 has an `input()` function as well, but this function interprets the user's input as Python code and attempts to run the input. At best you'll get an error that Python doesn't understand the input; at worst you'll run code that you didn't intend to run. If you're using Python 2.7, use `raw_input()` instead of `input()`.

TRY IT YOURSELF

7-1. Rental Car: Write a program that asks the user what kind of rental car they would like. Print a message about that car, such as "Let me see if I can find you a Subaru."

7-2. Restaurant Seating: Write a program that asks the user how many people are in their dinner group. If the answer is more than eight, print a message saying they'll have to wait for a table. Otherwise, report that their table is ready.

7-3. Multiples of Ten: Ask the user for a number, and then report whether the number is a multiple of 10 or not.

Introducing while Loops

The `for` loop takes a collection of items and executes a block of code once for each item in the collection. In contrast, the `while` loop runs as long as, or *while*, a certain condition is true.

The while Loop in Action

You can use a `while` loop to count up through a series of numbers. For example, the following `while` loop counts from 1 to 5:

counting.py

```
current_number = 1
while current_number <= 5:
    print(current_number)
    current_number += 1
```

In the first line, we start counting from 1 by setting the value of `current_number` to 1. The `while` loop is then set to keep running as long as the value of `current_number` is less than or equal to 5. The code inside the loop prints the value of `current_number` and then adds 1 to that value with `current_number += 1`. (The `+=` operator is shorthand for `current_number = current_number + 1`.)

Python repeats the loop as long as the condition `current_number <= 5` is true. Because 1 is less than 5, Python prints `1` and then adds 1, making the current number `2`. Because 2 is less than 5, Python prints `2` and adds 1 again, making the current number `3`, and so on. Once the value of `current_number` is greater than 5, the loop stops running and the program ends:

```
1
2
3
4
5
```

The programs you use every day most likely contain `while` loops. For example, a game needs a `while` loop to keep running as long as you want to keep playing, and so it can stop running as soon as you ask it to quit. Programs wouldn't be fun to use if they stopped running before we told them to or kept running even after we wanted to quit, so `while` loops are quite useful.

Letting the User Choose When to Quit

We can make the *parrot.py* program run as long as the user wants by putting most of the program inside a `while` loop. We'll define a *quit value* and then keep the program running as long as the user has not entered the quit value:

parrot.py

```
❶ prompt = "\nTell me something, and I will repeat it back to you:"
prompt += "\nEnter 'quit' to end the program. "
```

```
❷ message = ""
❸ while message != 'quit':
      message = input(prompt)
      print(message)
```

At ❶, we define a prompt that tells the user their two options: entering a message or entering the quit value (in this case, 'quit'). Then we set up a variable message ❷ to store whatever value the user enters. We define message as an empty string, "", so Python has something to check the first time it reaches the while line. The first time the program runs and Python reaches the while statement, it needs to compare the value of message to 'quit', but no user input has been entered yet. If Python has nothing to compare, it won't be able to continue running the program. To solve this problem, we make sure to give message an initial value. Although it's just an empty string, it will make sense to Python and allow it to perform the comparison that makes the while loop work. This while loop ❸ runs as long as the value of message is not 'quit'.

The first time through the loop, message is just an empty string, so Python enters the loop. At message = input(prompt), Python displays the prompt and waits for the user to enter their input. Whatever they enter is stored in message and printed; then, Python reevaluates the condition in the while statement. As long as the user has not entered the word 'quit', the prompt is displayed again and Python waits for more input. When the user finally enters 'quit', Python stops executing the while loop and the program ends:

```
Tell me something, and I will repeat it back to you:
Enter 'quit' to end the program. Hello everyone!
Hello everyone!

Tell me something, and I will repeat it back to you:
Enter 'quit' to end the program. Hello again.
Hello again.

Tell me something, and I will repeat it back to you:
Enter 'quit' to end the program. quit
quit
```

This program works well, except that it prints the word 'quit' as if it were an actual message. A simple if test fixes this:

```
prompt = "\nTell me something, and I will repeat it back to you:"
prompt += "\nEnter 'quit' to end the program. "

message = ""
while message != 'quit':
    message = input(prompt)

    if message != 'quit':
        print(message)
```

Now the program makes a quick check before displaying the message and only prints the message if it does not match the quit value:

```
Tell me something, and I will repeat it back to you:
Enter 'quit' to end the program. Hello everyone!
Hello everyone!

Tell me something, and I will repeat it back to you:
Enter 'quit' to end the program. Hello again.
Hello again.

Tell me something, and I will repeat it back to you:
Enter 'quit' to end the program. quit
```

Using a Flag

In the previous example, we had the program perform certain tasks while a given condition was true. But what about more complicated programs in which many different events could cause the program to stop running?

For example, in a game, several different events can end the game. When the player runs out of ships, their time runs out, or the cities they were supposed to protect are all destroyed, the game should end. It needs to end if any one of these events happens. If many possible events might occur to stop the program, trying to test all these conditions in one `while` statement becomes complicated and difficult.

For a program that should run only as long as many conditions are true, you can define one variable that determines whether or not the entire program is active. This variable, called a *flag*, acts as a signal to the program. We can write our programs so they run while the flag is set to `True` and stop running when any of several events sets the value of the flag to `False`. As a result, our overall `while` statement needs to check only one condition: whether or not the flag is currently `True`. Then, all our other tests (to see if an event has occurred that should set the flag to `False`) can be neatly organized in the rest of the program.

Let's add a flag to *parrot.py* from the previous section. This flag, which we'll call `active` (though you can call it anything), will monitor whether or not the program should continue running:

```
prompt = "\nTell me something, and I will repeat it back to you:"
prompt += "\nEnter 'quit' to end the program. "

❶ active = True
❷ while active:
      message = input(prompt)

❸     if message == 'quit':
          active = False
❹     else:
          print(message)
```

We set the variable active to True ❶ so the program starts in an active state. Doing so makes the while statement simpler because no comparison is made in the while statement itself; the logic is taken care of in other parts of the program. As long as the active variable remains True, the loop will continue running ❷.

In the if statement inside the while loop, we check the value of message once the user enters their input. If the user enters 'quit' ❸, we set active to False, and the while loop stops. If the user enters anything other than 'quit' ❹, we print their input as a message.

This program has the same output as the previous example where we placed the conditional test directly in the while statement. But now that we have a flag to indicate whether the overall program is in an active state, it would be easy to add more tests (such as elif statements) for events that should cause active to become False. This is useful in complicated programs like games in which there may be many events that should each make the program stop running. When any of these events causes the active flag to become False, the main game loop will exit, a *Game Over* message can be displayed, and the player can be given the option to play again.

Using break to Exit a Loop

To exit a while loop immediately without running any remaining code in the loop, regardless of the results of any conditional test, use the break statement. The break statement directs the flow of your program; you can use it to control which lines of code are executed and which aren't, so the program only executes code that you want it to, when you want it to.

For example, consider a program that asks the user about places they've visited. We can stop the while loop in this program by calling break as soon as the user enters the 'quit' value:

cities.py

```
prompt = "\nPlease enter the name of a city you have visited:"
prompt += "\n(Enter 'quit' when you are finished.) "

❶ while True:
    city = input(prompt)

    if city == 'quit':
        break
    else:
        print("I'd love to go to " + city.title() + "!")
```

A loop that starts with while True ❶ will run forever unless it reaches a break statement. The loop in this program continues asking the user to enter the names of cities they've been to until they enter 'quit'. When they enter 'quit', the break statement runs, causing Python to exit the loop:

```
Please enter the name of a city you have visited:
(Enter 'quit' when you are finished.) New York
I'd love to go to New York!
```

```
Please enter the name of a city you have visited:
(Enter 'quit' when you are finished.) San Francisco
I'd love to go to San Francisco!

Please enter the name of a city you have visited:
(Enter 'quit' when you are finished.) quit
```

NOTE *You can use the* `break` *statement in any of Python's loops. For example, you could use* `break` *to quit a* `for` *loop that's working through a list or a dictionary.*

Using continue in a Loop

Rather than breaking out of a loop entirely without executing the rest of its code, you can use the `continue` statement to return to the beginning of the loop based on the result of a conditional test. For example, consider a loop that counts from 1 to 10 but prints only the odd numbers in that range:

counting.py

```
current_number = 0
while current_number < 10:
❶    current_number += 1
    if current_number % 2 == 0:
        continue

    print(current_number)
```

First we set `current_number` to 0. Because it's less than 10, Python enters the `while` loop. Once inside the loop, we increment the count by 1 at ❶, so `current_number` is 1. The `if` statement then checks the modulo of `current_number` and 2. If the modulo is 0 (which means `current_number` is divisible by 2), the `continue` statement tells Python to ignore the rest of the loop and return to the beginning. If the current number is not divisible by 2, the rest of the loop is executed and Python prints the current number:

```
1
3
5
7
9
```

Avoiding Infinite Loops

Every `while` loop needs a way to stop running so it won't continue to run forever. For example, this counting loop should count from 1 to 5:

counting.py

```
x = 1
while x <= 5:
    print(x)
    x += 1
```

But if you accidentally omit the line `x += 1` (as shown next), the loop will run forever:

```
# This loop runs forever!
x = 1
while x <= 5:
    print(x)
```

Now the value of `x` will start at `1` but never change. As a result, the conditional test `x <= 5` will always evaluate to `True` and the `while` loop will run forever, printing a series of 1s, like this:

```
1
1
1
1
--snip--
```

Every programmer accidentally writes an infinite `while` loop from time to time, especially when a program's loops have subtle exit conditions. If your program gets stuck in an infinite loop, press CTRL-C or just close the terminal window displaying your program's output.

To avoid writing infinite loops, test every `while` loop and make sure the loop stops when you expect it to. If you want your program to end when the user enters a certain input value, run the program and enter that value. If the program doesn't end, scrutinize the way your program handles the value that should cause the loop to exit. Make sure at least one part of the program can make the loop's condition `False` or cause it to reach a `break` statement.

NOTE *Some editors, such as Sublime Text, have an embedded output window. This can make it difficult to stop an infinite loop, and you might have to close the editor to end the loop.*

TRY IT YOURSELF

7-4. Pizza Toppings: Write a loop that prompts the user to enter a series of pizza toppings until they enter a `'quit'` value. As they enter each topping, print a message saying you'll add that topping to their pizza.

7-5. Movie Tickets: A movie theater charges different ticket prices depending on a person's age. If a person is under the age of 3, the ticket is free; if they are between 3 and 12, the ticket is $10; and if they are over age 12, the ticket is $15. Write a loop in which you ask users their age, and then tell them the cost of their movie ticket.

(continued)

> **7-6. Three Exits:** Write different versions of either Exercise 7-4 or Exercise 7-5 that do each of the following at least once:
>
> - Use a conditional test in the `while` statement to stop the loop.
> - Use an `active` variable to control how long the loop runs.
> - Use a `break` statement to exit the loop when the user enters a `'quit'` value.
>
> **7-7. Infinity:** Write a loop that never ends, and run it. (To end the loop, press CTRL-C or close the window displaying the output.)

Using a while Loop with Lists and Dictionaries

So far, we've worked with only one piece of user information at a time. We received the user's input and then printed the input or a response to it. The next time through the `while` loop, we'd receive another input value and respond to that. But to keep track of many users and pieces of information, we'll need to use lists and dictionaries with our `while` loops.

A `for` loop is effective for looping through a list, but you shouldn't modify a list inside a `for` loop because Python will have trouble keeping track of the items in the list. To modify a list as you work through it, use a `while` loop. Using `while` loops with lists and dictionaries allows you to collect, store, and organize lots of input to examine and report on later.

Moving Items from One List to Another

Consider a list of newly registered but unverified users of a website. After we verify these users, how can we move them to a separate list of confirmed users? One way would be to use a `while` loop to pull users from the list of unconfirmed users as we verify them and then add them to a separate list of confirmed users. Here's what that code might look like:

confirmed_users.py

```
  # Start with users that need to be verified,
  #  and an empty list to hold confirmed users.
❶ unconfirmed_users = ['alice', 'brian', 'candace']
  confirmed_users = []

  # Verify each user until there are no more unconfirmed users.
  #  Move each verified user into the list of confirmed users.
❷ while unconfirmed_users:
❸     current_user = unconfirmed_users.pop()

      print("Verifying user: " + current_user.title())
❹     confirmed_users.append(current_user)
```

```
# Display all confirmed users.
print("\nThe following users have been confirmed:")
for confirmed_user in confirmed_users:
    print(confirmed_user.title())
```

We begin with a list of unconfirmed users at ❶ (Alice, Brian, and Candace) and an empty list to hold confirmed users. The `while` loop at ❷ runs as long as the list `unconfirmed_users` is not empty. Within this loop, the `pop()` function at ❸ removes unverified users one at a time from the end of `unconfirmed_users`. Here, because Candace is last in the `unconfirmed_users` list, her name will be the first to be removed, stored in `current_user`, and added to the `confirmed_users` list at ❹. Next is Brian, then Alice.

We simulate confirming each user by printing a verification message and then adding them to the list of confirmed users. As the list of unconfirmed users shrinks, the list of confirmed users grows. When the list of unconfirmed users is empty, the loop stops and the list of confirmed users is printed:

```
Verifying user: Candace
Verifying user: Brian
Verifying user: Alice

The following users have been confirmed:
Candace
Brian
Alice
```

Removing All Instances of Specific Values from a List

In Chapter 3 we used `remove()` to remove a specific value from a list. The `remove()` function worked because the value we were interested in appeared only once in the list. But what if you want to remove all instances of a value from a list?

Say you have a list of pets with the value `'cat'` repeated several times. To remove all instances of that value, you can run a `while` loop until `'cat'` is no longer in the list, as shown here:

pets.py

```
pets = ['dog', 'cat', 'dog', 'goldfish', 'cat', 'rabbit', 'cat']
print(pets)

while 'cat' in pets:
    pets.remove('cat')

print(pets)
```

We start with a list containing multiple instances of `'cat'`. After printing the list, Python enters the `while` loop because it finds the value `'cat'` in the list at least once. Once inside the loop, Python removes the first instance of 'cat', returns to the while line, and then reenters the loop when it finds that 'cat' is still in the list. It removes each instance of 'cat' until the value is no longer in the list, at which point Python exits the loop and prints the list again:

```
['dog', 'cat', 'dog', 'goldfish', 'cat', 'rabbit', 'cat']
['dog', 'dog', 'goldfish', 'rabbit']
```

Filling a Dictionary with User Input

You can prompt for as much input as you need in each pass through a while loop. Let's make a polling program in which each pass through the loop prompts for the participant's name and response. We'll store the data we gather in a dictionary, because we want to connect each response with a particular user:

mountain_poll.py

```
responses = {}

# Set a flag to indicate that polling is active.
polling_active = True

while polling_active:
    # Prompt for the person's name and response.
❶    name = input("\nWhat is your name? ")
    response = input("Which mountain would you like to climb someday? ")

    # Store the response in the dictionary:
❷    responses[name] = response

    # Find out if anyone else is going to take the poll.
❸    repeat = input("Would you like to let another person respond? (yes/ no) ")
    if repeat == 'no':
        polling_active = False

# Polling is complete. Show the results.
print("\n--- Poll Results ---")
❹ for name, response in responses.items():
    print(name + " would like to climb " + response + ".")
```

The program first defines an empty dictionary (responses) and sets a flag (polling_active) to indicate that polling is active. As long as polling_active is True, Python will run the code in the while loop.

Within the loop, the user is prompted to enter their username and a mountain they'd like to climb ❶. That information is stored in the responses dictionary ❷, and the user is asked whether or not to keep the poll running ❸. If they enter yes, the program enters the while loop again. If they enter no, the polling_active flag is set to False, the while loop stops running, and the final code block at ❹ displays the results of the poll.

If you run this program and enter sample responses, you should see output like this:

```
What is your name? Eric
Which mountain would you like to climb someday? Denali
Would you like to let another person respond? (yes/ no) yes

What is your name? Lynn
Which mountain would you like to climb someday? Devil's Thumb
Would you like to let another person respond? (yes/ no) no

--- Poll Results ---
Lynn would like to climb Devil's Thumb.
Eric would like to climb Denali.
```

TRY IT YOURSELF

7-8. Deli: Make a list called `sandwich_orders` and fill it with the names of various sandwiches. Then make an empty list called `finished_sandwiches`. Loop through the list of sandwich orders and print a message for each order, such as `I made your tuna sandwich`. As each sandwich is made, move it to the list of finished sandwiches. After all the sandwiches have been made, print a message listing each sandwich that was made.

7-9. No Pastrami: Using the list `sandwich_orders` from Exercise 7-8, make sure the sandwich `'pastrami'` appears in the list at least three times. Add code near the beginning of your program to print a message saying the deli has run out of pastrami, and then use a `while` loop to remove all occurrences of `'pastrami'` from `sandwich_orders`. Make sure no pastrami sandwiches end up in `finished_sandwiches`.

7-10. Dream Vacation: Write a program that polls users about their dream vacation. Write a prompt similar to *If you could visit one place in the world, where would you go?* Include a block of code that prints the results of the poll.

Summary

In this chapter you learned how to use `input()` to allow users to provide their own information in your programs. You learned to work with both text and numerical input and how to use `while` loops to make your programs run as long as your users want them to. You saw several ways to control the flow of a `while` loop by setting an `active` flag, using the `break` statement, and using the `continue` statement. You learned how to use a `while` loop to move items from one list to another and how to remove all instances of a value from a list. You also learned how `while` loops can be used with dictionaries.

In Chapter 8 you'll learn about *functions*. Functions allow you to break your programs into small parts, each of which does one specific job. You can call a function as many times as you want, and you can store your functions in separate files. By using functions, you'll be able to write more efficient code that's easier to troubleshoot and maintain and that can be reused in many different programs.

8

FUNCTIONS

In this chapter you'll learn to write *functions*, which are named blocks of code that are designed to do one specific job. When you want to perform a particular task that you've defined in a function, you *call* the name of the function responsible for it. If you need to perform that task multiple times throughout your program, you don't need to type all the code for the same task again and again; you just call the function dedicated to handling that task, and the call tells Python to run the code inside the function. You'll find that using functions makes your programs easier to write, read, test, and fix.

In this chapter you'll also learn ways to pass information to functions. You'll learn how to write certain functions whose primary job is to display information and other functions designed to process data and return a value or set of values. Finally, you'll learn to store functions in separate files called *modules* to help organize your main program files.

Defining a Function

Here's a simple function named greet_user() that prints a greeting:

greeter.py

```
❶ def greet_user():
❷     """Display a simple greeting."""
❸     print("Hello!")

❹ greet_user()
```

This example shows the simplest structure of a function. The line at ❶ uses the keyword def to inform Python that you're defining a function. This is the *function definition*, which tells Python the name of the function and, if applicable, what kind of information the function needs to do its job. The parentheses hold that information. In this case, the name of the function is greet_user(), and it needs no information to do its job, so its parentheses are empty. (Even so, the parentheses are required.) Finally, the definition ends in a colon.

Any indented lines that follow def greet_user(): make up the *body* of the function. The text at ❷ is a comment called a *docstring*, which describes what the function does. Docstrings are enclosed in triple quotes, which Python looks for when it generates documentation for the functions in your programs.

The line print("Hello!") ❸ is the only line of actual code in the body of this function, so greet_user() has just one job: print("Hello!").

When you want to use this function, you call it. A *function call* tells Python to execute the code in the function. To *call* a function, you write the name of the function, followed by any necessary information in parentheses, as shown at ❹. Because no information is needed here, calling our function is as simple as entering greet_user(). As expected, it prints Hello!:

```
Hello!
```

Passing Information to a Function

Modified slightly, the function greet_user() can not only tell the user Hello! but also greet them by name. For the function to do this, you enter username in the parentheses of the function's definition at def greet_user(). By adding username here you allow the function to accept any value of username you specify. The function now expects you to provide a value for username each time you call it. When you call greet_user(), you can pass it a name, such as 'jesse', inside the parentheses:

```
def greet_user(username):
    """Display a simple greeting."""
    print("Hello, " + username.title() + "!")

greet_user('jesse')
```

Entering greet_user('jesse') calls greet_user() and gives the function the information it needs to execute the print statement. The function accepts the name you passed it and displays the greeting for that name:

```
Hello, Jesse!
```

Likewise, entering greet_user('sarah') calls greet_user(), passes it 'sarah', and prints Hello, Sarah! You can call greet_user() as often as you want and pass it any name you want to produce a predictable output every time.

Arguments and Parameters

In the preceding greet_user() function, we defined greet_user() to require a value for the variable username. Once we called the function and gave it the information (a person's name), it printed the right greeting.

The variable username in the definition of greet_user() is an example of a *parameter*, a piece of information the function needs to do its job. The value 'jesse' in greet_user('jesse') is an example of an *argument*. An argument is a piece of information that is passed from a function call to a function. When we call the function, we place the value we want the function to work with in parentheses. In this case the argument 'jesse' was passed to the function greet_user(), and the value was stored in the parameter username.

NOTE *People sometimes speak of arguments and parameters interchangeably. Don't be surprised if you see the variables in a function definition referred to as arguments or the variables in a function call referred to as parameters.*

TRY IT YOURSELF

8-1. Message: Write a function called display_message() that prints one sentence telling everyone what you are learning about in this chapter. Call the function, and make sure the message displays correctly.

8-2. Favorite Book: Write a function called favorite_book() that accepts one parameter, title. The function should print a message, such as One of my favorite books is Alice in Wonderland. Call the function, making sure to include a book title as an argument in the function call.

Passing Arguments

Because a function definition can have multiple parameters, a function call may need multiple arguments. You can pass arguments to your functions in a number of ways. You can use *positional arguments*, which need to be in the same order the parameters were written; *keyword arguments*, where each argument consists of a variable name and a value; and lists and dictionaries of values. Let's look at each of these in turn.

Positional Arguments

When you call a function, Python must match each argument in the function call with a parameter in the function definition. The simplest way to do this is based on the order of the arguments provided. Values matched up this way are called *positional arguments*.

To see how this works, consider a function that displays information about pets. The function tells us what kind of animal each pet is and the pet's name, as shown here:

pets.py

```
❶ def describe_pet(animal_type, pet_name):
      """Display information about a pet."""
      print("\nI have a " + animal_type + ".")
      print("My " + animal_type + "'s name is " + pet_name.title() + ".")

❷ describe_pet('hamster', 'harry')
```

The definition shows that this function needs a type of animal and the animal's name ❶. When we call `describe_pet()`, we need to provide an animal type and a name, in that order. For example, in the function call, the argument `'hamster'` is stored in the parameter `animal_type` and the argument `'harry'` is stored in the parameter `pet_name` ❷. In the function body, these two parameters are used to display information about the pet being described.

The output describes a hamster named Harry:

```
I have a hamster.
My hamster's name is Harry.
```

Multiple Function Calls

You can call a function as many times as needed. Describing a second, different pet requires just one more call to `describe_pet()`:

```
def describe_pet(animal_type, pet_name):
    """Display information about a pet."""
    print("\nI have a " + animal_type + ".")
    print("My " + animal_type + "'s name is " + pet_name.title() + ".")

describe_pet('hamster', 'harry')
describe_pet('dog', 'willie')
```

In this second function call, we pass `describe_pet()` the arguments `'dog'` and `'willie'`. As with the previous set of arguments we used, Python matches `'dog'` with the parameter `animal_type` and `'willie'` with the parameter `pet_name`.

As before, the function does its job, but this time it prints values for a dog named Willie. Now we have a hamster named Harry and a dog named Willie:

```
I have a hamster.
My hamster's name is Harry.

I have a dog.
My dog's name is Willie.
```

Calling a function multiple times is a very efficient way to work. The code describing a pet is written once in the function. Then, anytime you want to describe a new pet, you call the function with the new pet's information. Even if the code for describing a pet were to expand to ten lines, you could still describe a new pet in just one line by calling the function again.

You can use as many positional arguments as you need in your functions. Python works through the arguments you provide when calling the function and matches each one with the corresponding parameter in the function's definition.

Order Matters in Positional Arguments

You can get unexpected results if you mix up the order of the arguments in a function call when using positional arguments:

```
def describe_pet(animal_type, pet_name):
    """Display information about a pet."""
    print("\nI have a " + animal_type + ".")
    print("My " + animal_type + "'s name is " + pet_name.title() + ".")

describe_pet('harry', 'hamster')
```

In this function call we list the name first and the type of animal second. Because the argument `'harry'` is listed first this time, that value is stored in the parameter `animal_type`. Likewise, `'hamster'` is stored in `pet_name`. Now we have a "harry" named "Hamster":

```
I have a harry.
My harry's name is Hamster.
```

If you get funny results like this, check to make sure the order of the arguments in your function call matches the order of the parameters in the function's definition.

Keyword Arguments

A *keyword argument* is a name-value pair that you pass to a function. You directly associate the name and the value within the argument, so when you pass the argument to the function, there's no confusion (you won't end up with a harry named Hamster). Keyword arguments free you from having to worry about correctly ordering your arguments in the function call, and they clarify the role of each value in the function call.

Let's rewrite *pets.py* using keyword arguments to call `describe_pet()`:

```
def describe_pet(animal_type, pet_name):
    """Display information about a pet."""
    print("\nI have a " + animal_type + ".")
    print("My " + animal_type + "'s name is " + pet_name.title() + ".")

describe_pet(animal_type='hamster', pet_name='harry')
```

The function `describe_pet()` hasn't changed. But when we call the function, we explicitly tell Python which parameter each argument should be matched with. When Python reads the function call, it knows to store the argument `'hamster'` in the parameter `animal_type` and the argument `'harry'` in `pet_name`. The output correctly shows that we have a hamster named Harry.

The order of keyword arguments doesn't matter because Python knows where each value should go. The following two function calls are equivalent:

```
describe_pet(animal_type='hamster', pet_name='harry')
describe_pet(pet_name='harry', animal_type='hamster')
```

NOTE *When you use keyword arguments, be sure to use the exact names of the parameters in the function's definition.*

Default Values

When writing a function, you can define a *default value* for each parameter. If an argument for a parameter is provided in the function call, Python uses the argument value. If not, it uses the parameter's default value. So when you define a default value for a parameter, you can exclude the corresponding argument you'd usually write in the function call. Using default values can simplify your function calls and clarify the ways in which your functions are typically used.

For example, if you notice that most of the calls to `describe_pet()` are being used to describe dogs, you can set the default value of `animal_type` to `'dog'`. Now anyone calling `describe_pet()` for a dog can omit that information:

```
def describe_pet(pet_name, animal_type='dog'):
    """Display information about a pet."""
    print("\nI have a " + animal_type + ".")
    print("My " + animal_type + "'s name is " + pet_name.title() + ".")

describe_pet(pet_name='willie')
```

We changed the definition of `describe_pet()` to include a default value, `'dog'`, for `animal_type`. Now when the function is called with no `animal_type` specified, Python knows to use the value `'dog'` for this parameter:

```
I have a dog.
My dog's name is Willie.
```

Note that the order of the parameters in the function definition had to be changed. Because the default value makes it unnecessary to specify a type of animal as an argument, the only argument left in the function call is the pet's name. Python still interprets this as a positional argument, so if the function is called with just a pet's name, that argument will match up with the first parameter listed in the function's definition. This is the reason the first parameter needs to be `pet_name`.

The simplest way to use this function now is to provide just a dog's name in the function call:

```
describe_pet('willie')
```

This function call would have the same output as the previous example. The only argument provided is `'willie'`, so it is matched up with the first parameter in the definition, `pet_name`. Because no argument is provided for `animal_type`, Python uses the default value `'dog'`.

To describe an animal other than a dog, you could use a function call like this:

```
describe_pet(pet_name='harry', animal_type='hamster')
```

Because an explicit argument for `animal_type` is provided, Python will ignore the parameter's default value.

NOTE *When you use default values, any parameter with a default value needs to be listed after all the parameters that don't have default values. This allows Python to continue interpreting positional arguments correctly.*

Equivalent Function Calls

Because positional arguments, keyword arguments, and default values can all be used together, often you'll have several equivalent ways to call a function. Consider the following definition for `describe_pets()` with one default value provided:

```
def describe_pet(pet_name, animal_type='dog'):
```

With this definition, an argument always needs to be provided for `pet_name`, and this value can be provided using the positional or keyword format. If the animal being described is not a dog, an argument for animal_type must be included in the call, and this argument can also be specified using the positional or keyword format.

All of the following calls would work for this function:

```
# A dog named Willie.
describe_pet('willie')
describe_pet(pet_name='willie')

# A hamster named Harry.
describe_pet('harry', 'hamster')
describe_pet(pet_name='harry', animal_type='hamster')
describe_pet(animal_type='hamster', pet_name='harry')
```

Each of these function calls would have the same output as the previous examples.

NOTE *It doesn't really matter which calling style you use. As long as your function calls produce the output you want, just use the style you find easiest to understand.*

Avoiding Argument Errors

When you start to use functions, don't be surprised if you encounter errors about unmatched arguments. Unmatched arguments occur when you provide fewer or more arguments than a function needs to do its work. For example, here's what happens if we try to call describe_pet() with no arguments:

```
def describe_pet(animal_type, pet_name):
    """Display information about a pet."""
    print("\nI have a " + animal_type + ".")
    print("My " + animal_type + "'s name is " + pet_name.title() + ".")

describe_pet()
```

Python recognizes that some information is missing from the function call, and the traceback tells us that:

```
  Traceback (most recent call last):
❶   File "pets.py", line 6, in <module>
❷     describe_pet()
❸ TypeError: describe_pet() missing 2 required positional arguments: 'animal_
  type' and 'pet_name'
```

At ❶ the traceback tells us the location of the problem, allowing us to look back and see that something went wrong in our function call. At ❷ the offending function call is written out for us to see. At ❸ the traceback tells us the call is missing two arguments and reports the names of the missing arguments. If this function were in a separate file, we could probably rewrite the call correctly without having to open that file and read the function code.

Python is helpful in that it reads the function's code for us and tells us the names of the arguments we need to provide. This is another motivation for giving your variables and functions descriptive names. If you do, Python's error messages will be more useful to you and anyone else who might use your code.

If you provide too many arguments, you should get a similar traceback that can help you correctly match your function call to the function definition.

TRY IT YOURSELF

8-3. T-Shirt: Write a function called `make_shirt()` that accepts a size and the text of a message that should be printed on the shirt. The function should print a sentence summarizing the size of the shirt and the message printed on it.

Call the function once using positional arguments to make a shirt. Call the function a second time using keyword arguments.

8-4. Large Shirts: Modify the `make_shirt()` function so that shirts are large by default with a message that reads *I love Python*. Make a large shirt and a medium shirt with the default message, and a shirt of any size with a different message.

8-5. Cities: Write a function called `describe_city()` that accepts the name of a city and its country. The function should print a simple sentence, such as `Reykjavik is in Iceland`. Give the parameter for the country a default value. Call your function for three different cities, at least one of which is not in the default country.

Return Values

A function doesn't always have to display its output directly. Instead, it can process some data and then return a value or set of values. The value the function returns is called a *return value*. The `return` statement takes a value from inside a function and sends it back to the line that called the function. Return values allow you to move much of your program's grunt work into functions, which can simplify the body of your program.

Returning a Simple Value

Let's look at a function that takes a first and last name, and returns a neatly formatted full name:

formatted_name.py

```
❶ def get_formatted_name(first_name, last_name):
      """Return a full name, neatly formatted."""
❷     full_name = first_name + ' ' + last_name
❸     return full_name.title()

❹ musician = get_formatted_name('jimi', 'hendrix')
  print(musician)
```

The definition of `get_formatted_name()` takes as parameters a first and last name ❶. The function combines these two names, adds a space between them, and stores the result in `full_name` ❷. The value of `full_name` is converted to title case, and then returned to the calling line at ❸.

When you call a function that returns a value, you need to provide a variable where the return value can be stored. In this case, the returned value is stored in the variable `musician` at ❹. The output shows a neatly formatted name made up of the parts of a person's name:

```
Jimi Hendrix
```

This might seem like a lot of work to get a neatly formatted name when we could have just written:

```
print("Jimi Hendrix")
```

But when you consider working with a large program that needs to store many first and last names separately, functions like `get_formatted_name()` become very useful. You store first and last names separately and then call this function whenever you want to display a full name.

Making an Argument Optional

Sometimes it makes sense to make an argument optional so that people using the function can choose to provide extra information only if they want to. You can use default values to make an argument optional.

For example, say we want to expand `get_formatted_name()` to handle middle names as well. A first attempt to include middle names might look like this:

```
def get_formatted_name(first_name, middle_name, last_name):
    """Return a full name, neatly formatted."""
    full_name = first_name + ' ' + middle_name + ' ' + last_name
    return full_name.title()

musician = get_formatted_name('john', 'lee', 'hooker')
print(musician)
```

This function works when given a first, middle, and last name. The function takes in all three parts of a name and then builds a string out of them. The function adds spaces where appropriate and converts the full name to title case:

```
John Lee Hooker
```

But middle names aren't always needed, and this function as written would not work if you tried to call it with only a first name and a last name. To make the middle name optional, we can give the `middle_name` argument an empty default value and ignore the argument unless the user provides a value. To make `get_formatted_name()` work without a middle name, we set the default value of `middle_name` to an empty string and move it to the end of the list of parameters:

```
❶ def get_formatted_name(first_name, last_name, middle_name=''):
      """Return a full name, neatly formatted."""
❷     if middle_name:
          full_name = first_name + ' ' + middle_name + ' ' + last_name
❸     else:
          full_name = first_name + ' ' + last_name
      return full_name.title()

  musician = get_formatted_name('jimi', 'hendrix')
  print(musician)

❹ musician = get_formatted_name('john', 'hooker', 'lee')
  print(musician)
```

In this example, the name is built from three possible parts. Because there's always a first and last name, these parameters are listed first in the function's definition. The middle name is optional, so it's listed last in the definition, and its default value is an empty string ❶.

In the body of the function, we check to see if a middle name has been provided. Python interprets non-empty strings as `True`, so `if middle_name` evaluates to `True` if a middle name argument is in the function call ❷. If a middle name is provided, the first, middle, and last names are combined to form a full name. This name is then changed to title case and returned to the function call line where it's stored in the variable `musician` and printed. If no middle name is provided, the empty string fails the `if` test and the `else` block runs ❸. The full name is made with just a first and last name, and the formatted name is returned to the calling line where it's stored in `musician` and printed.

Calling this function with a first and last name is straightforward. If we're using a middle name, however, we have to make sure the middle name is the last argument passed so Python will match up the positional arguments correctly ❹.

This modified version of our function works for people with just a first and last name, and it works for people who have a middle name as well:

```
Jimi Hendrix
John Lee Hooker
```

Optional values allow functions to handle a wide range of use cases while letting function calls remain as simple as possible.

Returning a Dictionary

A function can return any kind of value you need it to, including more complicated data structures like lists and dictionaries. For example, the following function takes in parts of a name and returns a dictionary representing a person:

person.py

```
  def build_person(first_name, last_name):
      """Return a dictionary of information about a person."""
❶     person = {'first': first_name, 'last': last_name}
❷     return person

  musician = build_person('jimi', 'hendrix')
❸ print(musician)
```

The function `build_person()` takes in a first and last name, and packs these values into a dictionary at ❶. The value of `first_name` is stored with the key `'first'`, and the value of `last_name` is stored with the key `'last'`. The entire dictionary representing the person is returned at ❷. The return value is printed at ❸ with the original two pieces of textual information now stored in a dictionary:

```
{'first': 'jimi', 'last': 'hendrix'}
```

This function takes in simple textual information and puts it into a more meaningful data structure that lets you work with the information beyond just printing it. The strings `'jimi'` and `'hendrix'` are now labeled as a first name and last name. You can easily extend this function to accept optional values like a middle name, an age, an occupation, or any other information you want to store about a person. For example, the following change allows you to store a person's age as well:

```
def build_person(first_name, last_name, age=''):
    """Return a dictionary of information about a person."""
    person = {'first': first_name, 'last': last_name}
    if age:
        person['age'] = age
    return person

musician = build_person('jimi', 'hendrix', age=27)
print(musician)
```

We add a new optional parameter age to the function definition and assign the parameter an empty default value. If the function call includes a value for this parameter, the value is stored in the dictionary. This function always stores a person's name, but it can also be modified to store any other information you want about a person.

Using a Function with a while Loop

You can use functions with all the Python structures you've learned about so far. For example, let's use the `get_formatted_name()` function with a `while` loop to greet users more formally. Here's a first attempt at greeting people using their first and last names:

greeter.py

```
def get_formatted_name(first_name, last_name):
    """Return a full name, neatly formatted."""
    full_name = first_name + ' ' + last_name
    return full_name.title()

# This is an infinite loop!
while True:
❶   print("\nPlease tell me your name:")
    f_name = input("First name: ")
    l_name = input("Last name: ")

    formatted_name = get_formatted_name(f_name, l_name)
    print("\nHello, " + formatted_name + "!")
```

For this example, we use a simple version of `get_formatted_name()` that doesn't involve middle names. The `while` loop asks the user to enter their name, and we prompt for their first and last name separately ❶.

But there's one problem with this `while` loop: We haven't defined a quit condition. Where do you put a quit condition when you ask for a series of inputs? We want the user to be able to quit as easily as possible, so each prompt should offer a way to quit. The `break` statement offers a straightforward way to exit the loop at either prompt:

```
def get_formatted_name(first_name, last_name):
    """Return a full name, neatly formatted."""
    full_name = first_name + ' ' + last_name
    return full_name.title()

while True:
    print("\nPlease tell me your name:")
    print("(enter 'q' at any time to quit)")

    f_name = input("First name: ")
    if f_name == 'q':
        break

    l_name = input("Last name: ")
    if l_name == 'q':
        break
```

```
    formatted_name = get_formatted_name(f_name, l_name)
    print("\nHello, " + formatted_name + "!")
```

We add a message that informs the user how to quit, and then we break out of the loop if the user enters the quit value at either prompt. Now the program will continue greeting people until someone enters 'q' for either name:

```
Please tell me your name:
(enter 'q' at any time to quit)
First name: eric
Last name: matthes

Hello, Eric Matthes!

Please tell me your name:
(enter 'q' at any time to quit)
First name: q
```

TRY IT YOURSELF

8-6. City Names: Write a function called `city_country()` that takes in the name of a city and its country. The function should return a string formatted like this:

```
"Santiago, Chile"
```

Call your function with at least three city-country pairs, and print the value that's returned.

8-7. Album: Write a function called `make_album()` that builds a dictionary describing a music album. The function should take in an artist name and an album title, and it should return a dictionary containing these two pieces of information. Use the function to make three dictionaries representing different albums. Print each return value to show that the dictionaries are storing the album information correctly.

Add an optional parameter to `make_album()` that allows you to store the number of tracks on an album. If the calling line includes a value for the number of tracks, add that value to the album's dictionary. Make at least one new function call that includes the number of tracks on an album.

8-8. User Albums: Start with your program from Exercise 8-7. Write a `while` loop that allows users to enter an album's artist and title. Once you have that information, call `make_album()` with the user's input and print the dictionary that's created. Be sure to include a quit value in the `while` loop.

Passing a List

You'll often find it useful to pass a list to a function, whether it's a list of names, numbers, or more complex objects, such as dictionaries. When you pass a list to a function, the function gets direct access to the contents of the list. Let's use functions to make working with lists more efficient.

Say we have a list of users and want to print a greeting to each. The following example sends a list of names to a function called greet_users(), which greets each person in the list individually:

greet_users.py

```
def greet_users(names):
    """Print a simple greeting to each user in the list."""
    for name in names:
        msg = "Hello, " + name.title() + "!"
        print(msg)

❶ usernames = ['hannah', 'ty', 'margot']
greet_users(usernames)
```

We define greet_users() so it expects a list of names, which it stores in the parameter names. The function loops through the list it receives and prints a greeting to each user. At ❶ we define a list of users and then pass the list usernames to greet_users()in our function call:

```
Hello, Hannah!
Hello, Ty!
Hello, Margot!
```

This is the output we wanted. Every user sees a personalized greeting, and you can call the function any time you want to greet a specific set of users.

Modifying a List in a Function

When you pass a list to a function, the function can modify the list. Any changes made to the list inside the function's body are permanent, allowing you to work efficiently even when you're dealing with large amounts of data.

Consider a company that creates 3D printed models of designs that users submit. Designs that need to be printed are stored in a list, and after being printed they're moved to a separate list. The following code does this without using functions:

printing_models.py

```
# Start with some designs that need to be printed.
unprinted_designs = ['iphone case', 'robot pendant', 'dodecahedron']
completed_models = []

# Simulate printing each design, until none are left.
#  Move each design to completed_models after printing.
while unprinted_designs:
    current_design = unprinted_designs.pop()
```

```
    # Simulate creating a 3D print from the design.
    print("Printing model: " + current_design)
    completed_models.append(current_design)

# Display all completed models.
print("\nThe following models have been printed:")
for completed_model in completed_models:
    print(completed_model)
```

This program starts with a list of designs that need to be printed and an empty list called `completed_models` that each design will be moved to after it has been printed. As long as designs remain in `unprinted_designs`, the `while` loop simulates printing each design by removing a design from the end of the list, storing it in `current_design`, and displaying a message that the current design is being printed. It then adds the design to the list of completed models. When the loop is finished running, a list of the designs that have been printed is displayed:

```
Printing model: dodecahedron
Printing model: robot pendant
Printing model: iphone case

The following models have been printed:
dodecahedron
robot pendant
iphone case
```

We can reorganize this code by writing two functions, each of which does one specific job. Most of the code won't change; we're just making it more efficient. The first function will handle printing the designs, and the second will summarize the prints that have been made:

```
❶ def print_models(unprinted_designs, completed_models):
    """
    Simulate printing each design, until none are left.
    Move each design to completed_models after printing.
    """
    while unprinted_designs:
        current_design = unprinted_designs.pop()

        # Simulate creating a 3D print from the design.
        print("Printing model: " + current_design)
        completed_models.append(current_design)

❷ def show_completed_models(completed_models):
    """Show all the models that were printed."""
    print("\nThe following models have been printed:")
    for completed_model in completed_models:
        print(completed_model)

unprinted_designs = ['iphone case', 'robot pendant', 'dodecahedron']
completed_models = []
```

```
print_models(unprinted_designs, completed_models)
show_completed_models(completed_models)
```

At ❶ we define the function print_models() with two parameters: a list of designs that need to be printed and a list of completed models. Given these two lists, the function simulates printing each design by emptying the list of unprinted designs and filling up the list of completed models. At ❷ we define the function show_completed_models() with one parameter: the list of completed models. Given this list, show_completed_models() displays the name of each model that was printed.

This program has the same output as the version without functions, but the code is much more organized. The code that does most of the work has been moved to two separate functions, which makes the main part of the program easier to understand. Look at the body of the program to see how much easier it is to understand what this program is doing:

```
unprinted_designs = ['iphone case', 'robot pendant', 'dodecahedron']
completed_models = []

print_models(unprinted_designs, completed_models)
show_completed_models(completed_models)
```

We set up a list of unprinted designs and an empty list that will hold the completed models. Then, because we've already defined our two functions, all we have to do is call them and pass them the right arguments. We call print_models() and pass it the two lists it needs; as expected, print_models() simulates printing the designs. Then we call show_completed_models() and pass it the list of completed models so it can report the models that have been printed. The descriptive function names allow others to read this code and understand it, even without comments.

This program is easier to extend and maintain than the version without functions. If we need to print more designs later on, we can simply call print_models() again. If we realize the printing code needs to be modified, we can change the code once, and our changes will take place everywhere the function is called. This technique is more efficient than having to update code separately in several places in the program.

This example also demonstrates the idea that every function should have one specific job. The first function prints each design, and the second displays the completed models. This is more beneficial than using one function to do both jobs. If you're writing a function and notice the function is doing too many different tasks, try to split the code into two functions. Remember that you can always call a function from another function, which can be helpful when splitting a complex task into a series of steps.

Preventing a Function from Modifying a List

Sometimes you'll want to prevent a function from modifying a list. For example, say that you start with a list of unprinted designs and write a function to move them to a list of completed models, as in the previous example. You may decide that even though you've printed all the designs, you want to keep the original list of unprinted designs for your records. But because you moved all the design names out of `unprinted_designs`, the list is now empty, and the empty list is the only version you have; the original is gone. In this case, you can address this issue by passing the function a copy of the list, not the original. Any changes the function makes to the list will affect only the copy, leaving the original list intact.

You can send a copy of a list to a function like this:

```
function_name(list_name[:])
```

The slice notation `[:]` makes a copy of the list to send to the function. If we didn't want to empty the list of unprinted designs in *print_models.py*, we could call `print_models()` like this:

```
print_models(unprinted_designs[:], completed_models)
```

The function `print_models()` can do its work because it still receives the names of all unprinted designs. But this time it uses a copy of the original unprinted designs list, not the actual `unprinted_designs` list. The list `completed_models` will fill up with the names of printed models like it did before, but the original list of unprinted designs will be unaffected by the function.

Even though you can preserve the contents of a list by passing a copy of it to your functions, you should pass the original list to functions unless you have a specific reason to pass a copy. It's more efficient for a function to work with an existing list to avoid using the time and memory needed to make a separate copy, especially when you're working with large lists.

TRY IT YOURSELF

8-9. Magicians: Make a list of magician's names. Pass the list to a function called `show_magicians()`, which prints the name of each magician in the list.

8-10. Great Magicians: Start with a copy of your program from Exercise 8-9. Write a function called `make_great()` that modifies the list of magicians by adding the phrase *the Great* to each magician's name. Call `show_magicians()` to see that the list has actually been modified.

8-11. Unchanged Magicians: Start with your work from Exercise 8-10. Call the function `make_great()` with a copy of the list of magicians' names. Because the original list will be unchanged, return the new list and store it in a separate list. Call `show_magicians()` with each list to show that you have one list of the original names and one list with *the Great* added to each magician's name.

Passing an Arbitrary Number of Arguments

Sometimes you won't know ahead of time how many arguments a function needs to accept. Fortunately, Python allows a function to collect an arbitrary number of arguments from the calling statement.

For example, consider a function that builds a pizza. It needs to accept a number of toppings, but you can't know ahead of time how many toppings a person will want. The function in the following example has one parameter, *toppings, but this parameter collects as many arguments as the calling line provides:

pizza.py

```
def make_pizza(*toppings):
    """Print the list of toppings that have been requested."""
    print(toppings)

make_pizza('pepperoni')
make_pizza('mushrooms', 'green peppers', 'extra cheese')
```

The asterisk in the parameter name *toppings tells Python to make an empty tuple called toppings and pack whatever values it receives into this tuple. The print statement in the function body produces output showing that Python can handle a function call with one value and a call with three values. It treats the different calls similarly. Note that Python packs the arguments into a tuple, even if the function receives only one value:

```
('pepperoni',)
('mushrooms', 'green peppers', 'extra cheese')
```

Now we can replace the print statement with a loop that runs through the list of toppings and describes the pizza being ordered:

```
def make_pizza(*toppings):
    """Summarize the pizza we are about to make."""
    print("\nMaking a pizza with the following toppings:")
    for topping in toppings:
        print("- " + topping)

make_pizza('pepperoni')
make_pizza('mushrooms', 'green peppers', 'extra cheese')
```

The function responds appropriately, whether it receives one value or three values:

```
Making a pizza with the following toppings:
- pepperoni

Making a pizza with the following toppings:
- mushrooms
- green peppers
- extra cheese
```

This syntax works no matter how many arguments the function receives.

Mixing Positional and Arbitrary Arguments

If you want a function to accept several different kinds of arguments, the parameter that accepts an arbitrary number of arguments must be placed last in the function definition. Python matches positional and keyword arguments first and then collects any remaining arguments in the final parameter.

For example, if the function needs to take in a size for the pizza, that parameter must come before the parameter `*toppings`:

```
def make_pizza(size, *toppings):
    """Summarize the pizza we are about to make."""
    print("\nMaking a " + str(size) +
          "-inch pizza with the following toppings:")
    for topping in toppings:
        print("- " + topping)

make_pizza(16, 'pepperoni')
make_pizza(12, 'mushrooms', 'green peppers', 'extra cheese')
```

In the function definition, Python stores the first value it receives in the parameter `size`. All other values that come after are stored in the tuple `toppings`. The function calls include an argument for the size first, followed by as many toppings as needed.

Now each pizza has a size and a number of toppings, and each piece of information is printed in the proper place, showing size first and toppings after:

```
Making a 16-inch pizza with the following toppings:
- pepperoni

Making a 12-inch pizza with the following toppings:
- mushrooms
- green peppers
- extra cheese
```

Using Arbitrary Keyword Arguments

Sometimes you'll want to accept an arbitrary number of arguments, but you won't know ahead of time what kind of information will be passed to the function. In this case, you can write functions that accept as many key-value pairs as the calling statement provides. One example involves building user profiles: you know you'll get information about a user, but you're not sure what kind of information you'll receive. The function `build_profile()` in the following example always takes in a first and last name, but it accepts an arbitrary number of keyword arguments as well:

user_profile.py

```
def build_profile(first, last, **user_info):
    """Build a dictionary containing everything we know about a user."""
    profile = {}
❶   profile['first_name'] = first
    profile['last_name'] = last
❷   for key, value in user_info.items():
        profile[key] = value
    return profile

user_profile = build_profile('albert', 'einstein',
                             location='princeton',
                             field='physics')
print(user_profile)
```

The definition of `build_profile()` expects a first and last name, and then it allows the user to pass in as many name-value pairs as they want. The double asterisks before the parameter `**user_info` cause Python to create an empty dictionary called `user_info` and pack whatever name-value pairs it receives into this dictionary. Within the function, you can access the name-value pairs in `user_info` just as you would for any dictionary.

In the body of `build_profile()`, we make an empty dictionary called `profile` to hold the user's profile. At ❶ we add the first and last names to this dictionary because we'll always receive these two pieces of information from the user. At ❷ we loop through the additional key-value pairs in the dictionary `user_info` and add each pair to the `profile` dictionary. Finally, we return the `profile` dictionary to the function call line.

We call `build_profile()`, passing it the first name `'albert'`, the last name `'einstein'`, and the two key-value pairs `location='princeton'` and `field='physics'`. We store the returned `profile` in `user_profile` and print `user_profile`:

```
{'first_name': 'albert', 'last_name': 'einstein',
'location': 'princeton', 'field': 'physics'}
```

The returned dictionary contains the user's first and last names and, in this case, the location and field of study as well. The function would work no matter how many additional key-value pairs are provided in the function call.

You can mix positional, keyword, and arbitrary values in many different ways when writing your own functions. It's useful to know that all these argument types exist because you'll see them often when you start reading other people's code. It takes practice to learn to use the different types correctly and to know when to use each type. For now, remember to use the simplest approach that gets the job done. As you progress you'll learn to use the most efficient approach each time.

TRY IT YOURSELF

8-12. Sandwiches: Write a function that accepts a list of items a person wants on a sandwich. The function should have one parameter that collects as many items as the function call provides, and it should print a summary of the sandwich that is being ordered. Call the function three times, using a different number of arguments each time.

8-13. User Profile: Start with a copy of *user_profile.py* from page 153. Build a profile of yourself by calling `build_profile()`, using your first and last names and three other key-value pairs that describe you.

8-14. Cars: Write a function that stores information about a car in a dictionary. The function should always receive a manufacturer and a model name. It should then accept an arbitrary number of keyword arguments. Call the function with the required information and two other name-value pairs, such as a color or an optional feature. Your function should work for a call like this one:

```
car = make_car('subaru', 'outback', color='blue', tow_package=True)
```

Print the dictionary that's returned to make sure all the information was stored correctly.

Storing Your Functions in Modules

One advantage of functions is the way they separate blocks of code from your main program. By using descriptive names for your functions, your main program will be much easier to follow. You can go a step further by storing your functions in a separate file called a *module* and then *importing* that module into your main program. An `import` statement tells Python to make the code in a module available in the currently running program file.

Storing your functions in a separate file allows you to hide the details of your program's code and focus on its higher-level logic. It also allows you to reuse functions in many different programs. When you store your functions in separate files, you can share those files with other programmers without having to share your entire program. Knowing how to import functions also allows you to use libraries of functions that other programmers have written.

There are several ways to import a module, and I'll show you each of these briefly.

Importing an Entire Module

To start importing functions, we first need to create a module. A *module* is a file ending in *.py* that contains the code you want to import into your program. Let's make a module that contains the function `make_pizza()`. To make this module, we'll remove everything from the file *pizza.py* except the function `make_pizza()`:

pizza.py

```
def make_pizza(size, *toppings):
    """Summarize the pizza we are about to make."""
    print("\nMaking a " + str(size) +
          "-inch pizza with the following toppings:")
    for topping in toppings:
        print("- " + topping)
```

Now we'll make a separate file called *making_pizzas.py* in the same directory as *pizza.py*. This file imports the module we just created and then makes two calls to `make_pizza()`:

making_pizzas.py

```
import pizza

❶ pizza.make_pizza(16, 'pepperoni')
pizza.make_pizza(12, 'mushrooms', 'green peppers', 'extra cheese')
```

When Python reads this file, the line `import pizza` tells Python to open the file *pizza.py* and copy all the functions from it into this program. You don't actually see code being copied between files because Python copies the code behind the scenes as the program runs. All you need to know is that any function defined in *pizza.py* will now be available in *making_pizzas.py*.

To call a function from an imported module, enter the name of the module you imported, `pizza`, followed by the name of the function, `make_pizza()`, separated by a dot ❶. This code produces the same output as the original program that didn't import a module:

```
Making a 16-inch pizza with the following toppings:
- pepperoni

Making a 12-inch pizza with the following toppings:
- mushrooms
- green peppers
- extra cheese
```

This first approach to importing, in which you simply write `import` followed by the name of the module, makes every function from the module available in your program. If you use this kind of `import` statement to import an entire module named *module_name.py*, each function in the module is available through the following syntax:

```
module_name.function_name()
```

Importing Specific Functions

You can also import a specific function from a module. Here's the general syntax for this approach:

```
from module_name import function_name
```

You can import as many functions as you want from a module by separating each function's name with a comma:

```
from module_name import function_0, function_1, function_2
```

The *making_pizzas.py* example would look like this if we want to import just the function we're going to use:

```
from pizza import make_pizza

make_pizza(16, 'pepperoni')
make_pizza(12, 'mushrooms', 'green peppers', 'extra cheese')
```

With this syntax, you don't need to use the dot notation when you call a function. Because we've explicitly imported the function `make_pizza()` in the `import` statement, we can call it by name when we use the function.

Using as to Give a Function an Alias

If the name of a function you're importing might conflict with an existing name in your program or if the function name is long, you can use a short, unique *alias*—an alternate name similar to a nickname for the function. You'll give the function this special nickname when you import the function.

Here we give the function `make_pizza()` an alias, `mp()`, by importing `make_pizza as mp`. The `as` keyword renames a function using the alias you provide:

```
from pizza import make_pizza as mp

mp(16, 'pepperoni')
mp(12, 'mushrooms', 'green peppers', 'extra cheese')
```

The `import` statement shown here renames the function `make_pizza()` to `mp()` in this program. Any time we want to call `make_pizza()` we can simply write `mp()` instead, and Python will run the code in `make_pizza()` while avoiding any confusion with another `make_pizza()` function you might have written in this program file.

The general syntax for providing an alias is:

```
from module_name import function_name as fn
```

Using as to Give a Module an Alias

You can also provide an alias for a module name. Giving a module a short alias, like `p` for `pizza`, allows you to call the module's functions more quickly. Calling `p.make_pizza()` is more concise than calling `pizza.make_pizza()`:

```
import pizza as p

p.make_pizza(16, 'pepperoni')
p.make_pizza(12, 'mushrooms', 'green peppers', 'extra cheese')
```

The module `pizza` is given the alias `p` in the `import` statement, but all of the module's functions retain their original names. Calling the functions by writing `p.make_pizza()` is not only more concise than writing `pizza.make_pizza()`, but also redirects your attention from the module name and allows you to focus on the descriptive names of its functions. These function names, which clearly tell you what each function does, are more important to the readability of your code than using the full module name.

The general syntax for this approach is:

```
import module_name as mn
```

Importing All Functions in a Module

You can tell Python to import every function in a module by using the asterisk (*) operator:

```
from pizza import *

make_pizza(16, 'pepperoni')
make_pizza(12, 'mushrooms', 'green peppers', 'extra cheese')
```

The asterisk in the `import` statement tells Python to copy every function from the module `pizza` into this program file. Because every function is imported, you can call each function by name without using the dot notation. However, it's best not to use this approach when you're working with larger modules that you didn't write: if the module has a function name that matches an existing name in your project, you can get some unexpected results. Python may see several functions or variables with the same name, and instead of importing all the functions separately, it will overwrite the functions.

The best approach is to import the function or functions you want, or import the entire module and use the dot notation. This leads to clear code that's easy to read and understand. I include this section so you'll recognize `import` statements like the following when you see them in other people's code:

```
from module_name import *
```

Styling Functions

You need to keep a few details in mind when you're styling functions. Functions should have descriptive names, and these names should use lowercase letters and underscores. Descriptive names help you and others understand what your code is trying to do. Module names should use these conventions as well.

Every function should have a comment that explains concisely what the function does. This comment should appear immediately after the function definition and use the docstring format. In a well-documented function, other programmers can use the function by reading only the description in the docstring. They should be able to trust that the code works as described, and as long as they know the name of the function, the arguments it needs, and the kind of value it returns, they should be able to use it in their programs.

If you specify a default value for a parameter, no spaces should be used on either side of the equal sign:

```
def function_name(parameter_0, parameter_1='default value')
```

The same convention should be used for keyword arguments in function calls:

```
function_name(value_0, parameter_1='value')
```

PEP 8 (*https://www.python.org/dev/peps/pep-0008/*) recommends that you limit lines of code to 79 characters so every line is visible in a reasonably sized editor window. If a set of parameters causes a function's definition to be longer than 79 characters, press ENTER after the opening parenthesis on the definition line. On the next line, press TAB twice to separate the list of arguments from the body of the function, which will only be indented one level.

Most editors automatically line up any additional lines of parameters to match the indentation you have established on the first line:

```
def function_name(
        parameter_0, parameter_1, parameter_2,
        parameter_3, parameter_4, parameter_5):
    function body...
```

If your program or module has more than one function, you can separate each by two blank lines to make it easier to see where one function ends and the next one begins.

All `import` statements should be written at the beginning of a file. The only exception is if you use comments at the beginning of your file to describe the overall program.

TRY IT YOURSELF

8-15. Printing Models: Put the functions for the example *print_models.py* in a separate file called *printing_functions.py*. Write an `import` statement at the top of *print_models.py*, and modify the file to use the imported functions.

8-16. Imports: Using a program you wrote that has one function in it, store that function in a separate file. Import the function into your main program file, and call the function using each of these approaches:

```
import module_name
from module_name import function_name
from module_name import function_name as fn
import module_name as mn
from module_name import *
```

8-17. Styling Functions: Choose any three programs you wrote for this chapter, and make sure they follow the styling guidelines described in this section.

Summary

In this chapter you learned how to write functions and to pass arguments so that your functions have access to the information they need to do their work. You learned how to use positional and keyword arguments, and how to accept an arbitrary number of arguments. You saw functions that display output and functions that return values. You learned how to use functions with lists, dictionaries, `if` statements, and `while` loops. You also saw how to store your functions in separate files called *modules*, so your program files will be simpler and easier to understand. Finally, you learned to style your functions so your programs will continue to be well-structured and as easy as possible for you and others to read.

One of your goals as a programmer should be to write simple code that does what you want it to, and functions help you do this. They allow you to write blocks of code and leave them alone once you know they work. When you know a function does its job correctly, you can trust that it will continue to work and move on to your next coding task.

Functions allow you to write code once and then reuse that code as many times as you want. When you need to run the code in a function, all you need to do is write a one-line call and the function does its job. When you need to modify a function's behavior, you only have to modify one block of code, and your change takes effect everywhere you've made a call to that function.

Using functions makes your programs easier to read, and good function names summarize what each part of a program does. Reading a series of function calls gives you a much quicker sense of what a program does than reading a long series of code blocks.

Functions also make your code easier to test and debug. When the bulk of your program's work is done by a set of functions, each of which has a specific job, it's much easier to test and maintain the code you've written. You can write a separate program that calls each function and tests whether each function works in all the situations it may encounter. When you do this, you can be confident that your functions will work properly each time you call them.

In Chapter 9 you'll learn to write classes. *Classes* combine functions and data into one neat package that can be used in flexible and efficient ways.

9

CLASSES

Object-oriented programming is one of the most effective approaches to writing software. In object-oriented programming you write *classes* that represent real-world things and situations, and you create *objects* based on these classes. When you write a class, you define the general behavior that a whole category of objects can have. When you create individual objects from the class, each object is automatically equipped with the general behavior; you can then give each object whatever unique traits you desire. You'll be amazed how well real-world situations can be modeled with object-oriented programming.

Making an object from a class is called *instantiation*, and you work with *instances* of a class. In this chapter you'll write classes and create instances of those classes. You'll specify the kind of information that can be stored in instances, and you'll define actions that can be taken with these instances. You'll also write classes that extend the functionality of existing classes, so similar classes can share code efficiently. You'll store your classes in modules and import classes written by other programmers into your own program files.

Understanding object-oriented programming will help you see the world as a programmer does. It'll help you really know your code, not just what's happening line by line, but also the bigger concepts behind it. Knowing the logic behind classes will train you to think logically so you can write programs that effectively address almost any problem you encounter.

Classes also make life easier for you and the other programmers you'll need to work with as you take on increasingly complex challenges. When you and other programmers write code based on the same kind of logic, you'll be able to understand each other's work. Your programs will make sense to many collaborators, allowing everyone to accomplish more.

Creating and Using a Class

You can model almost anything using classes. Let's start by writing a simple class, `Dog`, that represents a dog—not one dog in particular, but any dog. What do we know about most pet dogs? Well, they all have a name and age. We also know that most dogs sit and roll over. Those two pieces of information (name and age) and those two behaviors (sit and roll over) will go in our `Dog` class because they're common to most dogs. This class will tell Python how to make an object representing a dog. After our class is written, we'll use it to make individual instances, each of which represents one specific dog.

Creating the Dog Class

Each instance created from the `Dog` class will store a `name` and an `age`, and we'll give each dog the ability to `sit()` and `roll_over()`:

dog.py

```
❶ class Dog():
❷     """A simple attempt to model a dog."""

❸     def __init__(self, name, age):
          """Initialize name and age attributes."""
❹         self.name = name
          self.age = age

❺     def sit(self):
          """Simulate a dog sitting in response to a command."""
          print(self.name.title() + " is now sitting.")

      def roll_over(self):
          """Simulate rolling over in response to a command."""
          print(self.name.title() + " rolled over!")
```

There's a lot to notice here, but don't worry. You'll see this structure throughout this chapter and have lots of time to get used to it. At ❶ we define a class called Dog. By convention, capitalized names refer to classes in Python. The parentheses in the class definition are empty because we're creating this class from scratch. At ❷ we write a docstring describing what this class does.

The __init__() Method

A function that's part of a class is a *method*. Everything you learned about functions applies to methods as well; the only practical difference for now is the way we'll call methods. The `__init__()` method at ❸ is a special method Python runs automatically whenever we create a new instance based on the `Dog` class. This method has two leading underscores and two trailing underscores, a convention that helps prevent Python's default method names from conflicting with your method names.

We define the `__init__()` method to have three parameters: `self`, `name`, and `age`. The `self` parameter is required in the method definition, and it must come first before the other parameters. It must be included in the definition because when Python calls this `__init__()` method later (to create an instance of `Dog`), the method call will automatically pass the `self` argument. Every method call associated with a class automatically passes `self`, which is a reference to the instance itself; it gives the individual instance access to the attributes and methods in the class. When we make an instance of `Dog`, Python will call the `__init__()` method from the `Dog` class. We'll pass `Dog()` a name and an age as arguments; `self` is passed automatically, so we don't need to pass it. Whenever we want to make an instance from the `Dog` class, we'll provide values for only the last two parameters, `name` and `age`.

The two variables defined at ❹ each have the prefix `self`. Any variable prefixed with `self` is available to every method in the class, and we'll also be able to access these variables through any instance created from the class. `self.name = name` takes the value stored in the parameter `name` and stores it in the variable `name`, which is then attached to the instance being created. The same process happens with `self.age = age`. Variables that are accessible through instances like this are called *attributes*.

The `Dog` class has two other methods defined: `sit()` and `roll_over()` ❺. Because these methods don't need additional information like a name or age, we just define them to have one parameter, `self`. The instances we create later will have access to these methods. In other words, they'll be able to sit and roll over. For now, `sit()` and `roll_over()` don't do much. They simply print a message saying the dog is sitting or rolling over. But the concept can be extended to realistic situations: if this class were part of an actual computer game, these methods would contain code to make an animated dog sit and roll over. If this class was written to control a robot, these methods would direct movements that cause a dog robot to sit and roll over.

Creating Classes in Python 2.7

When you create a class in Python 2.7, you need to make one minor change. You include the term object in parentheses when you create a class:

```
class ClassName(object):
    --snip--
```

This makes Python 2.7 classes behave more like Python 3 classes, which makes your work easier overall.

The Dog class would be defined like this in Python 2.7:

```
class Dog(object):
    --snip--
```

Making an Instance from a Class

Think of a class as a set of instructions for how to make an instance. The class Dog is a set of instructions that tells Python how to make individual instances representing specific dogs.

Let's make an instance representing a specific dog:

```
class Dog():
    --snip--

❶ my_dog = Dog('willie', 6)

❷ print("My dog's name is " + my_dog.name.title() + ".")
❸ print("My dog is " + str(my_dog.age) + " years old.")
```

The Dog class we're using here is the one we just wrote in the previous example. At ❶ we tell Python to create a dog whose name is 'willie' and whose age is 6. When Python reads this line, it calls the __init__() method in Dog with the arguments 'willie' and 6. The __init__() method creates an instance representing this particular dog and sets the name and age attributes using the values we provided. The __init__() method has no explicit return statement, but Python automatically returns an instance representing this dog. We store that instance in the variable my_dog. The naming convention is helpful here: we can usually assume that a capitalized name like Dog refers to a class, and a lowercase name like my_dog refers to a single instance created from a class.

Accessing Attributes

To access the attributes of an instance, you use dot notation. At ❷ we access the value of my_dog's attribute name by writing:

```
my_dog.name
```

Dot notation is used often in Python. This syntax demonstrates how Python finds an attribute's value. Here Python looks at the instance my_dog and then finds the attribute name associated with my_dog. This is the same attribute referred to as self.name in the class Dog. At ❸ we use the same approach to work with the attribute age. In our first print statement, my_dog.name.title() makes 'willie', the value of my_dog's name attribute, start with a capital letter. In the second print statement, str(my_dog.age) converts 6, the value of my_dog's age attribute, to a string.

The output is a summary of what we know about my_dog:

```
My dog's name is Willie.
My dog is 6 years old.
```

Calling Methods

After we create an instance from the class Dog, we can use dot notation to call any method defined in Dog. Let's make our dog sit and roll over:

```
class Dog():
    --snip--

my_dog = Dog('willie', 6)
my_dog.sit()
my_dog.roll_over()
```

To call a method, give the name of the instance (in this case, my_dog) and the method you want to call, separated by a dot. When Python reads my_dog.sit(), it looks for the method sit() in the class Dog and runs that code. Python interprets the line my_dog.roll_over() in the same way.

Now Willie does what we tell him to:

```
Willie is now sitting.
Willie rolled over!
```

This syntax is quite useful. When attributes and methods have been given appropriately descriptive names like name, age, sit(), and roll_over(), we can easily infer what a block of code, even one we've never seen before, is supposed to do.

Creating Multiple Instances

You can create as many instances from a class as you need. Let's create a second dog called your_dog:

```
class Dog():
    --snip--

my_dog = Dog('willie', 6)
your_dog = Dog('lucy', 3)

print("My dog's name is " + my_dog.name.title() + ".")
print("My dog is " + str(my_dog.age) + " years old.")
my_dog.sit()
```

```
print("\nYour dog's name is " + your_dog.name.title() + ".")
print("Your dog is " + str(your_dog.age) + " years old.")
your_dog.sit()
```

In this example we create a dog named Willie and a dog named Lucy. Each dog is a separate instance with its own set of attributes, capable of the same set of actions:

```
My dog's name is Willie.
My dog is 6 years old.
Willie is now sitting.

Your dog's name is Lucy.
Your dog is 3 years old.
Lucy is now sitting.
```

Even if we used the same name and age for the second dog, Python would still create a separate instance from the `Dog` class. You can make as many instances from one class as you need, as long as you give each instance a unique variable name or it occupies a unique spot in a list or dictionary.

TRY IT YOURSELF

9-1. Restaurant: Make a class called `Restaurant`. The `__init__()` method for `Restaurant` should store two attributes: a `restaurant_name` and a `cuisine_type`. Make a method called `describe_restaurant()` that prints these two pieces of information, and a method called `open_restaurant()` that prints a message indicating that the restaurant is open.

Make an instance called `restaurant` from your class. Print the two attributes individually, and then call both methods.

9-2. Three Restaurants: Start with your class from Exercise 9-1. Create three different instances from the class, and call `describe_restaurant()` for each instance.

9-3. Users: Make a class called `User`. Create two attributes called `first_name` and `last_name`, and then create several other attributes that are typically stored in a user profile. Make a method called `describe_user()` that prints a summary of the user's information. Make another method called `greet_user()` that prints a personalized greeting to the user.

Create several instances representing different users, and call both methods for each user.

Working with Classes and Instances

You can use classes to represent many real-world situations. Once you write a class, you'll spend most of your time working with instances created from that class. One of the first tasks you'll want to do is modify the attributes associated with a particular instance. You can modify the attributes of an instance directly or write methods that update attributes in specific ways.

The Car Class

Let's write a new class representing a car. Our class will store information about the kind of car we're working with, and it will have a method that summarizes this information:

car.py

```
class Car():
    """A simple attempt to represent a car."""

❶   def __init__(self, make, model, year):
        """Initialize attributes to describe a car."""
        self.make = make
        self.model = model
        self.year = year

❷   def get_descriptive_name(self):
        """Return a neatly formatted descriptive name."""
        long_name = str(self.year) + ' ' + self.make + ' ' + self.model
        return long_name.title()

❸ my_new_car = Car('audi', 'a4', 2016)
print(my_new_car.get_descriptive_name())
```

At ❶ in the `Car` class, we define the `__init__()` method with the `self` parameter first, just like we did before with our `Dog` class. We also give it three other parameters: `make`, `model`, and `year`. The `__init__()` method takes in these parameters and stores them in the attributes that will be associated with instances made from this class. When we make a new `Car` instance, we'll need to specify a make, model, and year for our instance.

At ❷ we define a method called `get_descriptive_name()` that puts a car's `year`, `make`, and `model` into one string neatly describing the car. This will spare us from having to print each attribute's value individually. To work with the attribute values in this method, we use `self.make`, `self.model`, and `self.year`. At ❸ we make an instance from the `Car` class and store it in the variable `my_new_car`. Then we call `get_descriptive_name()` to show what kind of car we have:

```
2016 Audi A4
```

To make the class more interesting, let's add an attribute that changes over time. We'll add an attribute that stores the car's overall mileage.

Setting a Default Value for an Attribute

Every attribute in a class needs an initial value, even if that value is 0 or an empty string. In some cases, such as when setting a default value, it makes sense to specify this initial value in the body of the `__init__()` method; if you do this for an attribute, you don't have to include a parameter for that attribute.

Let's add an attribute called `odometer_reading` that always starts with a value of 0. We'll also add a method `read_odometer()` that helps us read each car's odometer:

```
class Car():

    def __init__(self, make, model, year):
        """Initialize attributes to describe a car."""
        self.make = make
        self.model = model
        self.year = year
❶       self.odometer_reading = 0

    def get_descriptive_name(self):
        --snip--

❷   def read_odometer(self):
        """Print a statement showing the car's mileage."""
        print("This car has " + str(self.odometer_reading) + " miles on it.")

my_new_car = Car('audi', 'a4', 2016)
print(my_new_car.get_descriptive_name())
my_new_car.read_odometer()
```

This time when Python calls the `__init__()` method to create a new instance, it stores the make, model, and year values as attributes like it did in the previous example. Then Python creates a new attribute called `odometer_reading` and sets its initial value to 0 ❶. We also have a new method called `read_odometer()` at ❷ that makes it easy to read a car's mileage.

Our car starts with a mileage of 0:

```
2016 Audi A4
This car has 0 miles on it.
```

Not many cars are sold with exactly 0 miles on the odometer, so we need a way to change the value of this attribute.

Modifying Attribute Values

You can change an attribute's value in three ways: you can change the value directly through an instance, set the value through a method, or increment the value (add a certain amount to it) through a method. Let's look at each of these approaches.

Modifying an Attribute's Value Directly

The simplest way to modify the value of an attribute is to access the attribute directly through an instance. Here we set the odometer reading to 23 directly:

```
class Car():
    --snip--

my_new_car = Car('audi', 'a4', 2016)
print(my_new_car.get_descriptive_name())

❶ my_new_car.odometer_reading = 23
my_new_car.read_odometer()
```

At ❶ we use dot notation to access the car's `odometer_reading` attribute and set its value directly. This line tells Python to take the instance `my_new_car`, find the attribute `odometer_reading` associated with it, and set the value of that attribute to 23:

```
2016 Audi A4
This car has 23 miles on it.
```

Sometimes you'll want to access attributes directly like this, but other times you'll want to write a method that updates the value for you.

Modifying an Attribute's Value Through a Method

It can be helpful to have methods that update certain attributes for you. Instead of accessing the attribute directly, you pass the new value to a method that handles the updating internally.

Here's an example showing a method called `update_odometer()`:

```
class Car():
    --snip--

❶     def update_odometer(self, mileage):
        """Set the odometer reading to the given value."""
        self.odometer_reading = mileage

my_new_car = Car('audi', 'a4', 2016)
print(my_new_car.get_descriptive_name())

❷ my_new_car.update_odometer(23)
my_new_car.read_odometer()
```

The only modification to `Car` is the addition of `update_odometer()` at ❶. This method takes in a mileage value and stores it in `self.odometer_reading`. At ❷ we call `update_odometer()` and give it `23` as an argument (corresponding to the mileage parameter in the method definition). It sets the odometer reading to 23, and read_odometer() prints the reading:

```
2016 Audi A4
This car has 23 miles on it.
```

We can extend the method update_odometer() to do additional work every time the odometer reading is modified. Let's add a little logic to make sure no one tries to roll back the odometer reading:

```
class Car():
    --snip--

    def update_odometer(self, mileage):
        """
        Set the odometer reading to the given value.
        Reject the change if it attempts to roll the odometer back.
        """
❶       if mileage >= self.odometer_reading:
            self.odometer_reading = mileage
        else:
❷           print("You can't roll back an odometer!")
```

Now update_odometer() checks that the new reading makes sense before modifying the attribute. If the new mileage, mileage, is greater than or equal to the existing mileage, self.odometer_reading, you can update the odometer reading to the new mileage ❶. If the new mileage is less than the existing mileage, you'll get a warning that you can't roll back an odometer ❷.

Incrementing an Attribute's Value Through a Method

Sometimes you'll want to increment an attribute's value by a certain amount rather than set an entirely new value. Say we buy a used car and put 100 miles on it between the time we buy it and the time we register it. Here's a method that allows us to pass this incremental amount and add that value to the odometer reading:

```
class Car():
    --snip--

    def update_odometer(self, mileage):
        --snip--

❶   def increment_odometer(self, miles):
        """Add the given amount to the odometer reading."""
        self.odometer_reading += miles

❷ my_used_car = Car('subaru', 'outback', 2013)
print(my_used_car.get_descriptive_name())

❸ my_used_car.update_odometer(23500)
my_used_car.read_odometer()
```

```
❹ my_used_car.increment_odometer(100)
  my_used_car.read_odometer()
```

The new method `increment_odometer()` at ❶ takes in a number of miles, and adds this value to `self.odometer_reading`. At ❷ we create a used car, `my_used_car`. We set its odometer to 23,500 by calling `update_odometer()` and passing it `23500` at ❸. At ❹ we call `increment_odometer()` and pass it `100` to add the 100 miles that we drove between buying the car and registering it:

```
2013 Subaru Outback
This car has 23500 miles on it.
This car has 23600 miles on it.
```

You can easily modify this method to reject negative increments so no one uses this function to roll back an odometer.

NOTE *You can use methods like this to control how users of your program update values such as an odometer reading, but anyone with access to the program can set the odometer reading to any value by accessing the attribute directly. Effective security takes extreme attention to detail in addition to basic checks like those shown here.*

TRY IT YOURSELF

9-4. Number Served: Start with your program from Exercise 9-1 (page 166). Add an attribute called `number_served` with a default value of 0. Create an instance called `restaurant` from this class. Print the number of customers the restaurant has served, and then change this value and print it again.

Add a method called `set_number_served()` that lets you set the number of customers that have been served. Call this method with a new number and print the value again.

Add a method called `increment_number_served()` that lets you increment the number of customers who've been served. Call this method with any number you like that could represent how many customers were served in, say, a day of business.

9-5. Login Attempts: Add an attribute called `login_attempts` to your `User` class from Exercise 9-3 (page 166). Write a method called `increment_login_attempts()` that increments the value of `login_attempts` by 1. Write another method called `reset_login_attempts()` that resets the value of `login_attempts` to 0.

Make an instance of the `User` class and call `increment_login_attempts()` several times. Print the value of `login_attempts` to make sure it was incremented properly, and then call `reset_login_attempts()`. Print `login_attempts` again to make sure it was reset to 0.

Inheritance

You don't always have to start from scratch when writing a class. If the class you're writing is a specialized version of another class you wrote, you can use *inheritance*. When one class *inherits* from another, it automatically takes on all the attributes and methods of the first class. The original class is called the *parent class*, and the new class is the *child class*. The child class inherits every attribute and method from its parent class but is also free to define new attributes and methods of its own.

The __init__() Method for a Child Class

The first task Python has when creating an instance from a child class is to assign values to all attributes in the parent class. To do this, the `__init__()` method for a child class needs help from its parent class.

As an example, let's model an electric car. An electric car is just a specific kind of car, so we can base our new `ElectricCar` class on the `Car` class we wrote earlier. Then we'll only have to write code for the attributes and behavior specific to electric cars.

Let's start by making a simple version of the `ElectricCar` class, which does everything the `Car` class does:

electric_car.py

```
❶ class Car():
    """A simple attempt to represent a car."""

    def __init__(self, make, model, year):
        self.make = make
        self.model = model
        self.year = year
        self.odometer_reading = 0

    def get_descriptive_name(self):
        long_name = str(self.year) + ' ' + self.make + ' ' + self.model
        return long_name.title()

    def read_odometer(self):
        print("This car has " + str(self.odometer_reading) + " miles on it.")

    def update_odometer(self, mileage):
        if mileage >= self.odometer_reading:
            self.odometer_reading = mileage
        else:
            print("You can't roll back an odometer!")

    def increment_odometer(self, miles):
        self.odometer_reading += miles

❷ class ElectricCar(Car):
    """Represent aspects of a car, specific to electric vehicles."""
```

```
❸     def __init__(self, make, model, year):
          """Initialize attributes of the parent class."""
❹         super().__init__(make, model, year)


❺ my_tesla = ElectricCar('tesla', 'model s', 2016)
  print(my_tesla.get_descriptive_name())
```

At ❶ we start with `Car`. When you create a child class, the parent class must be part of the current file and must appear before the child class in the file. At ❷ we define the child class, `ElectricCar`. The name of the parent class must be included in parentheses in the definition of the child class. The `__init__()` method at ❸ takes in the information required to make a `Car` instance.

The `super()` function at ❹ is a special function that helps Python make connections between the parent and child class. This line tells Python to call the `__init__()` method from `ElectricCar`'s parent class, which gives an `ElectricCar` instance all the attributes of its parent class. The name *super* comes from a convention of calling the parent class a *superclass* and the child class a *subclass*.

We test whether inheritance is working properly by trying to create an electric car with the same kind of information we'd provide when making a regular car. At ❺ we make an instance of the `ElectricCar` class, and store it in `my_tesla`. This line calls the `__init__()` method defined in `ElectricCar`, which in turn tells Python to call the `__init__()` method defined in the parent class `Car`. We provide the arguments `'tesla'`, `'model s'`, and `2016`.

Aside from `__init__()`, there are no attributes or methods yet that are particular to an electric car. At this point we're just making sure the electric car has the appropriate `Car` behaviors:

```
2016 Tesla Model S
```

The `ElectricCar` instance works just like an instance of `Car`, so now we can begin defining attributes and methods specific to electric cars.

Inheritance in Python 2.7

In Python 2.7, inheritance is slightly different. The `ElectricCar` class would look like this:

```
class Car(object):
    def __init__(self, make, model, year):
        --snip--

class ElectricCar(Car):
    def __init__(self, make, model, year):
        super(ElectricCar, self).__init__(make, model, year)
        --snip--
```

The super() function needs two arguments: a reference to the child class and the self object. These arguments are necessary to help Python make proper connections between the parent and child classes. When you use inheritance in Python 2.7, make sure you define the parent class using the object syntax as well.

Defining Attributes and Methods for the Child Class

Once you have a child class that inherits from a parent class, you can add any new attributes and methods necessary to differentiate the child class from the parent class.

Let's add an attribute that's specific to electric cars (a battery, for example) and a method to report on this attribute. We'll store the battery size and write a method that prints a description of the battery:

```
class Car():
    --snip--

class ElectricCar(Car):
    """Represent aspects of a car, specific to electric vehicles."""

    def __init__(self, make, model, year):
        """
        Initialize attributes of the parent class.
        Then initialize attributes specific to an electric car.
        """
        super().__init__(make, model, year)
❶       self.battery_size = 70

❷   def describe_battery(self):
        """Print a statement describing the battery size."""
        print("This car has a " + str(self.battery_size) + "-kWh battery.")

my_tesla = ElectricCar('tesla', 'model s', 2016)
print(my_tesla.get_descriptive_name())
my_tesla.describe_battery()
```

At ❶ we add a new attribute self.battery_size and set its initial value to, say, 70. This attribute will be associated with all instances created from the ElectricCar class but won't be associated with any instances of Car. We also add a method called describe_battery() that prints information about the battery at ❷. When we call this method, we get a description that is clearly specific to an electric car:

```
2016 Tesla Model S
This car has a 70-kWh battery.
```

There's no limit to how much you can specialize the ElectricCar class. You can add as many attributes and methods as you need to model an electric car to whatever degree of accuracy you need. An attribute or method that could belong to any car, rather than one that's specific to an electric car, should be added to the Car class instead of the ElectricCar class. Then anyone who uses the Car class will have that functionality available as well, and the ElectricCar class will only contain code for the information and behavior specific to electric vehicles.

Overriding Methods from the Parent Class

You can override any method from the parent class that doesn't fit what you're trying to model with the child class. To do this, you define a method in the child class with the same name as the method you want to override in the parent class. Python will disregard the parent class method and only pay attention to the method you define in the child class.

Say the class Car had a method called fill_gas_tank(). This method is meaningless for an all-electric vehicle, so you might want to override this method. Here's one way to do that:

```
def ElectricCar(Car):
    --snip--

    def fill_gas_tank():
        """Electric cars don't have gas tanks."""
        print("This car doesn't need a gas tank!")
```

Now if someone tries to call fill_gas_tank() with an electric car, Python will ignore the method fill_gas_tank() in Car and run this code instead. When you use inheritance, you can make your child classes retain what you need and override anything you don't need from the parent class.

Instances as Attributes

When modeling something from the real world in code, you may find that you're adding more and more detail to a class. You'll find that you have a growing list of attributes and methods and that your files are becoming lengthy. In these situations, you might recognize that part of one class can be written as a separate class. You can break your large class into smaller classes that work together.

For example, if we continue adding detail to the ElectricCar class, we might notice that we're adding many attributes and methods specific to the car's battery. When we see this happening, we can stop and move those attributes and methods to a separate class called Battery. Then we can use a Battery instance as an attribute in the ElectricCar class:

```
class Car():
    --snip--

❶ class Battery():
    """A simple attempt to model a battery for an electric car."""

❷     def __init__(self, battery_size=70):
        """Initialize the battery's attributes."""
        self.battery_size = battery_size
```

```
❸     def describe_battery(self):
          """Print a statement describing the battery size."""
          print("This car has a " + str(self.battery_size) + "-kWh battery.")


  class ElectricCar(Car):
      """Represent aspects of a car, specific to electric vehicles."""

      def __init__(self, make, model, year):
          """
          Initialize attributes of the parent class.
          Then initialize attributes specific to an electric car.
          """
          super().__init__(make, model, year)
❹         self.battery = Battery()


  my_tesla = ElectricCar('tesla', 'model s', 2016)

  print(my_tesla.get_descriptive_name())
  my_tesla.battery.describe_battery()
```

At ❶ we define a new class called Battery that doesn't inherit from any other class. The __init__() method at ❷ has one parameter, battery_size, in addition to self. This is an optional parameter that sets the battery's size to 70 if no value is provided. The method describe_battery() has been moved to this class as well ❸.

In the ElectricCar class, we now add an attribute called self.battery ❹. This line tells Python to create a new instance of Battery (with a default size of 70, because we're not specifying a value) and store that instance in the attribute self.battery. This will happen every time the __init__() method is called; any ElectricCar instance will now have a Battery instance created automatically.

We create an electric car and store it in the variable my_tesla. When we want to describe the battery, we need to work through the car's battery attribute:

```
my_tesla.battery.describe_battery()
```

This line tells Python to look at the instance my_tesla, find its battery attribute, and call the method describe_battery() that's associated with the Battery instance stored in the attribute.

The output is identical to what we saw previously:

```
2016 Tesla Model S
This car has a 70-kWh battery.
```

This looks like a lot of extra work, but now we can describe the battery in as much detail as we want without cluttering the `ElectricCar` class. Let's add another method to `Battery` that reports the range of the car based on the battery size:

```
class Car():
    --snip--

class Battery():
    --snip--

❶     def get_range(self):
        """Print a statement about the range this battery provides."""
        if self.battery_size == 70:
            range = 240
        elif self.battery_size == 85:
            range = 270

        message = "This car can go approximately " + str(range)
        message += " miles on a full charge."
        print(message)

class ElectricCar(Car):
    --snip--

my_tesla = ElectricCar('tesla', 'model s', 2016)
print(my_tesla.get_descriptive_name())
my_tesla.battery.describe_battery()
❷ my_tesla.battery.get_range()
```

The new method `get_range()` at ❶ performs some simple analysis. If the battery's capacity is 70 kWh, `get_range()` sets the range to 240 miles, and if the capacity is 85 kWh, it sets the range to 270 miles. It then reports this value. When we want to use this method, we again have to call it through the car's `battery` attribute at ❷.

The output tells us the range of the car based on its battery size:

```
2016 Tesla Model S
This car has a 70-kWh battery.
This car can go approximately 240 miles on a full charge.
```

Modeling Real-World Objects

As you begin to model more complicated items like electric cars, you'll wrestle with interesting questions. Is the range of an electric car a property of the battery or of the car? If we're only describing one car, it's probably fine to maintain the association of the method `get_range()` with the `Battery` class. But if we're describing a manufacturer's entire line of cars, we probably want to move `get_range()` to the `ElectricCar` class. The `get_range()` method would still check the battery size before determining the range, but it would report a range specific to the kind of car it's associated with. Alternatively, we could maintain the association of the `get_range()` method with the battery but pass it a parameter such as `car_model`. The `get_range()` method would then report a range based on the battery size and car model.

This brings you to an interesting point in your growth as a programmer. When you wrestle with questions like these, you're thinking at a higher logical level rather than a syntax-focused level. You're thinking not about Python, but about how to represent the real world in code. When you reach this point, you'll realize there are often no right or wrong approaches to modeling real-world situations. Some approaches are more efficient than others, but it takes practice to find the most efficient representations. If your code is working as you want it to, you're doing well! Don't be discouraged if you find you're ripping apart your classes and rewriting them several times using different approaches. In the quest to write accurate, efficient code, everyone goes through this process.

TRY IT YOURSELF

9-6. Ice Cream Stand: An ice cream stand is a specific kind of restaurant. Write a class called `IceCreamStand` that inherits from the `Restaurant` class you wrote in Exercise 9-1 (page 166) or Exercise 9-4 (page 171). Either version of the class will work; just pick the one you like better. Add an attribute called `flavors` that stores a list of ice cream flavors. Write a method that displays these flavors. Create an instance of `IceCreamStand`, and call this method.

9-7. Admin: An administrator is a special kind of user. Write a class called `Admin` that inherits from the `User` class you wrote in Exercise 9-3 (page 166) or Exercise 9-5 (page 171). Add an attribute, `privileges`, that stores a list of strings like `"can add post"`, `"can delete post"`, `"can ban user"`, and so on. Write a method called `show_privileges()` that lists the administrator's set of privileges. Create an instance of `Admin`, and call your method.

9-8. Privileges: Write a separate `Privileges` class. The class should have one attribute, `privileges`, that stores a list of strings as described in Exercise 9-7. Move the `show_privileges()` method to this class. Make a `Privileges` instance as an attribute in the `Admin` class. Create a new instance of `Admin` and use your method to show its privileges.

9-9. Battery Upgrade: Use the final version of *electric_car.py* from this section. Add a method to the `Battery` class called `upgrade_battery()`. This method should check the battery size and set the capacity to 85 if it isn't already. Make an electric car with a default battery size, call `get_range()` once, and then call `get_range()` a second time after upgrading the battery. You should see an increase in the car's range.

Importing Classes

As you add more functionality to your classes, your files can get long, even when you use inheritance properly. In keeping with the overall philosophy of Python, you'll want to keep your files as uncluttered as possible. To help, Python lets you store classes in modules and then import the classes you need into your main program.

Importing a Single Class

Let's create a module containing just the `Car` class. This brings up a subtle naming issue: we already have a file named *car.py* in this chapter, but this module should be named *car.py* because it contains code representing a car. We'll resolve this naming issue by storing the `Car` class in a module named *car.py*, replacing the *car.py* file we were previously using. From now on, any program that uses this module will need a more specific filename, such as *my_car.py*. Here's *car.py* with just the code from the class `Car`:

car.py ❶

```
"""A class that can be used to represent a car."""

class Car():
    """A simple attempt to represent a car."""

    def __init__(self, make, model, year):
        """Initialize attributes to describe a car."""
        self.make = make
        self.model = model
        self.year = year
        self.odometer_reading = 0

    def get_descriptive_name(self):
        """Return a neatly formatted descriptive name."""
        long_name = str(self.year) + ' ' + self.make + ' ' + self.model
        return long_name.title()

    def read_odometer(self):
        """Print a statement showing the car's mileage."""
        print("This car has " + str(self.odometer_reading) + " miles on it.")

    def update_odometer(self, mileage):
        """
        Set the odometer reading to the given value.
        Reject the change if it attempts to roll the odometer back.
        """
        if mileage >= self.odometer_reading:
            self.odometer_reading = mileage
        else:
            print("You can't roll back an odometer!")

    def increment_odometer(self, miles):
        """Add the given amount to the odometer reading."""
        self.odometer_reading += miles
```

At ❶ we include a module-level docstring that briefly describes the contents of this module. You should write a docstring for each module you create.

Now we make a separate file called *my_car.py*. This file will import the Car class and then create an instance from that class:

my_car.py

```
❶ from car import Car

my_new_car = Car('audi', 'a4', 2016)
print(my_new_car.get_descriptive_name())

my_new_car.odometer_reading = 23
my_new_car.read_odometer()
```

The import statement at ❶ tells Python to open the car module and import the class Car. Now we can use the Car class as if it were defined in this file. The output is the same as we saw earlier:

```
2016 Audi A4
This car has 23 miles on it.
```

Importing classes is an effective way to program. Picture how long this program file would be if the entire Car class were included. When you instead move the class to a module and import the module, you still get all the same functionality, but you keep your main program file clean and easy to read. You also store most of the logic in separate files; once your classes work as you want them to, you can leave those files alone and focus on the higher-level logic of your main program.

Storing Multiple Classes in a Module

You can store as many classes as you need in a single module, although each class in a module should be related somehow. The classes Battery and ElectricCar both help represent cars, so let's add them to the module *car.py*:

car.py

```
"""A set of classes used to represent gas and electric cars."""

class Car():
    --snip--

class Battery():
    """A simple attempt to model a battery for an electric car."""

    def __init__(self, battery_size=60):
        """Initialize the batteery's attributes."""
        self.battery_size = battery_size

    def describe_battery(self):
        """Print a statement describing the battery size."""
        print("This car has a " + str(self.battery_size) + "-kWh battery.")

    def get_range(self):
```

```
        """Print a statement about the range this battery provides."""
        if self.battery_size == 70:
            range = 240
        elif self.battery_size == 85:
            range = 270

        message = "This car can go approximately " + str(range)
        message += " miles on a full charge."
        print(message)

class ElectricCar(Car):
    """Models aspects of a car, specific to electric vehicles."""

    def __init__(self, make, model, year):
        """
        Initialize attributes of the parent class.
        Then initialize attributes specific to an electric car.
        """
        super().__init__(make, model, year)
        self.battery = Battery()
```

Now we can make a new file called *my_electric_car.py*, import the ElectricCar class, and make an electric car:

my_electric_car.py

```
from car import ElectricCar

my_tesla = ElectricCar('tesla', 'model s', 2016)

print(my_tesla.get_descriptive_name())
my_tesla.battery.describe_battery()
my_tesla.battery.get_range()
```

This has the same output we saw earlier, even though most of the logic is hidden away in a module:

```
2016 Tesla Model S
This car has a 70-kWh battery.
This car can go approximately 240 miles on a full charge.
```

Importing Multiple Classes from a Module

You can import as many classes as you need into a program file. If we want to make a regular car and an electric car in the same file, we need to import both classes, Car and ElectricCar:

my_cars.py

```
❶ from car import Car, ElectricCar

❷ my_beetle = Car('volkswagen', 'beetle', 2016)
  print(my_beetle.get_descriptive_name())

❸ my_tesla = ElectricCar('tesla', 'roadster', 2016)
  print(my_tesla.get_descriptive_name())
```

You import multiple classes from a module by separating each class with a comma ❶. Once you've imported the necessary classes, you're free to make as many instances of each class as you need.

In this example we make a regular Volkswagen Beetle at ❷ and an electric Tesla Roadster at ❸:

```
2016 Volkswagen Beetle
2016 Tesla Roadster
```

Importing an Entire Module

You can also import an entire module and then access the classes you need using dot notation. This approach is simple and results in code that is easy to read. Because every call that creates an instance of a class includes the module name, you won't have naming conflicts with any names used in the current file.

Here's what it looks like to import the entire car module and then create a regular car and an electric car:

my_cars.py

```
❶ import car

❷ my_beetle = car.Car('volkswagen', 'beetle', 2016)
  print(my_beetle.get_descriptive_name())

❸ my_tesla = car.ElectricCar('tesla', 'roadster', 2016)
  print(my_tesla.get_descriptive_name())
```

At ❶ we import the entire car module. We then access the classes we need through the *module_name.class_name* syntax. At ❷ we again create a Volkswagen Beetle, and at ❸ we create a Tesla Roadster.

Importing All Classes from a Module

You can import every class from a module using the following syntax:

```
from module_name import *
```

This method is not recommended for two reasons. First, it's helpful to be able to read the import statements at the top of a file and get a clear sense of which classes a program uses. With this approach it's unclear which classes you're using from the module. This approach can also lead to confusion with names in the file. If you accidentally import a class with the same name as something else in your program file, you can create errors that are hard to diagnose. I show this here because even though it's not a recommended approach, you're likely to see it in other people's code.

If you need to import many classes from a module, you're better off importing the entire module and using the *module_name.class_name* syntax.

You won't see all the classes used at the top of the file, but you'll see clearly where the module is used in the program. You'll also avoid the potential naming conflicts that can arise when you import every class in a module.

Importing a Module into a Module

Sometimes you'll want to spread out your classes over several modules to keep any one file from growing too large and avoid storing unrelated classes in the same module. When you store your classes in several modules, you may find that a class in one module depends on a class in another module. When this happens, you can import the required class into the first module.

For example, let's store the `Car` class in one module and the `ElectricCar` and `Battery` classes in a separate module. We'll make a new module called *electric_car.py*—replacing the *electric_car.py* file we created earlier—and copy just the `Battery` and `ElectricCar` classes into this file:

electric_car.py

```
"""A set of classes that can be used to represent electric cars."""

❶ from car import Car

class Battery():
    --snip--

class ElectricCar(Car):
    --snip--
```

The class `ElectricCar` needs access to its parent class `Car`, so we import `Car` directly into the module at ❶. If we forget this line, Python will raise an error when we try to make an `ElectricCar` instance. We also need to update the `Car` module so it contains only the `Car` class:

car.py

```
"""A class that can be used to represent a car."""

class Car():
    --snip--
```

Now we can import from each module separately and create whatever kind of car we need:

my_cars.py

```
❶ from car import Car
from electric_car import ElectricCar

my_beetle = Car('volkswagen', 'beetle', 2016)
print(my_beetle.get_descriptive_name())

my_tesla = ElectricCar('tesla', 'roadster', 2016)
print(my_tesla.get_descriptive_name())
```

At ❶ we import `Car` from its module, and `ElectricCar` from its module. We then create one regular car and one electric car. Both kinds of cars are created correctly:

```
2016 Volkswagen Beetle
2016 Tesla Roadster
```

Finding Your Own Workflow

As you can see, Python gives you many options for how to structure code in a large project. It's important to know all these possibilities so you can determine the best ways to organize your projects as well as understand other people's projects.

When you're starting out, keep your code structure simple. Try doing everything in one file and moving your classes to separate modules once everything is working. If you like how modules and files interact, try storing your classes in modules when you start a project. Find an approach that lets you write code that works, and go from there.

TRY IT YOURSELF

9-10. Imported Restaurant: Using your latest `Restaurant` class, store it in a module. Make a separate file that imports `Restaurant`. Make a `Restaurant` instance, and call one of `Restaurant`'s methods to show that the `import` statement is working properly.

9-11. Imported Admin: Start with your work from Exercise 9-8 (page 178). Store the classes `User`, `Privileges`, and `Admin` in one module. Create a separate file, make an `Admin` instance, and call `show_privileges()` to show that everything is working correctly.

9-12. Multiple Modules: Store the `User` class in one module, and store the `Privileges` and `Admin` classes in a separate module. In a separate file, create an `Admin` instance and call `show_privileges()` to show that everything is still working correctly.

The Python Standard Library

The *Python standard library* is a set of modules included with every Python installation. Now that you have a basic understanding of how classes work, you can start to use modules like these that other programmers have written. You can use any function or class in the standard library by including a simple `import` statement at the top of your file. Let's look at one class, `OrderedDict`, from the module `collections`.

Dictionaries allow you to connect pieces of information, but they don't keep track of the order in which you add key-value pairs. If you're creating a dictionary and want to keep track of the order in which key-value pairs are added, you can use the `OrderedDict` class from the `collections` module. Instances of the `OrderedDict` class behave almost exactly like dictionaries except they keep track of the order in which key-value pairs are added.

Let's revisit the *favorite_languages.py* example from Chapter 6. This time we'll keep track of the order in which people respond to the poll:

favorite_languages.py

```
❶ from collections import OrderedDict

❷ favorite_languages = OrderedDict()

❸ favorite_languages['jen'] = 'python'
  favorite_languages['sarah'] = 'c'
  favorite_languages['edward'] = 'ruby'
  favorite_languages['phil'] = 'python'

❹ for name, language in favorite_languages.items():
      print(name.title() + "'s favorite language is " +
          language.title() + ".")
```

We begin by importing the `OrderedDict` class from the module `collections` at ❶. At ❷ we create an instance of the `OrderedDict` class and store this instance in `favorite_languages`. Notice there are no curly brackets; the call to `OrderedDict()` creates an empty ordered dictionary for us and stores it in `favorite_languages`. We then add each name and language to `favorite_languages` one at a time ❸. Now when we loop through `favorite_languages` at ❹, we know we'll always get responses back in the order they were added:

```
Jen's favorite language is Python.
Sarah's favorite language is C.
Edward's favorite language is Ruby.
Phil's favorite language is Python.
```

This is a great class to be aware of because it combines the main benefit of lists (retaining your original order) with the main feature of dictionaries (connecting pieces of information). As you begin to model real-world situations that you care about, you'll probably come across a situation where an ordered dictionary is exactly what you need. As you learn more about the standard library, you'll become familiar with a number of modules like this that help you handle common situations.

NOTE *You can also download modules from external sources. You'll see a number of these examples in Part II, where we'll need external modules to complete each project.*

TRY IT YOURSELF

9-13. OrderedDict Rewrite: Start with Exercise 6-4 (page 108), where you used a standard dictionary to represent a glossary. Rewrite the program using the `OrderedDict` class and make sure the order of the output matches the order in which key-value pairs were added to the dictionary.

9-14. Dice: The module `random` contains functions that generate random numbers in a variety of ways. The function `randint()` returns an integer in the range you provide. The following code returns a number between 1 and 6:

```
from random import randint
x = randint(1, 6)
```

Make a class `Die` with one attribute called `sides`, which has a default value of 6. Write a method called `roll_die()` that prints a random number between 1 and the number of sides the die has. Make a 6-sided die and roll it 10 times.

Make a 10-sided die and a 20-sided die. Roll each die 10 times.

9-15. Python Module of the Week: One excellent resource for exploring the Python standard library is a site called *Python Module of the Week*. Go to *http://pymotw.com/* and look at the table of contents. Find a module that looks interesting to you and read about it, or explore the documentation of the `collections` and `random` modules.

Styling Classes

A few styling issues related to classes are worth clarifying, especially as your programs become more complicated.

Class names should be written in *CamelCaps*. To do this, capitalize the first letter of each word in the name, and don't use underscores. Instance and module names should be written in lowercase with underscores between words.

Every class should have a docstring immediately following the class definition. The docstring should be a brief description of what the class does, and you should follow the same formatting conventions you used for writing docstrings in functions. Each module should also have a docstring describing what the classes in a module can be used for.

You can use blank lines to organize code, but don't use them excessively. Within a class you can use one blank line between methods, and within a module you can use two blank lines to separate classes.

If you need to import a module from the standard library and a module that you wrote, place the import statement for the standard library module first. Then add a blank line and the import statement for the module you wrote. In programs with multiple import statements, this convention makes it easier to see where the different modules used in the program come from.

Summary

In this chapter you learned how to write your own classes. You learned how to store information in a class using attributes and how to write methods that give your classes the behavior they need. You learned to write `__init__()` methods that create instances from your classes with exactly the attributes you want. You saw how to modify the attributes of an instance directly and through methods. You learned that inheritance can simplify the creation of classes that are related to each other, and you learned to use instances of one class as attributes in another class to keep each class simple.

You saw how storing classes in modules and importing classes you need into the files where they'll be used can keep your projects organized. You started learning about the Python standard library, and you saw an example based on the `OrderedDict` class from the `collections` module. Finally, you learned to style your classes using Python conventions.

In Chapter 10 you'll learn to work with files so you can save the work you've done in a program and the work you've allowed users to do. You'll also learn about *exceptions*, a special Python class designed to help you respond to errors when they arise.

10

FILES AND EXCEPTIONS

Now that you've mastered the basic skills you need to write organized programs that are easy to use, it's time to think about making your programs even more relevant and usable. In this chapter you'll learn to work with files so your programs can quickly analyze lots of data. You'll learn to handle errors so your programs don't crash when they encounter unexpected situations. You'll learn about *exceptions*, which are special objects Python creates to manage errors that arise while a program is running. You'll also learn about the `json` module, which allows you to save user data so it isn't lost when your program stops running.

Learning to work with files and save data will make your programs easier for people to use. Users will be able to choose what data to enter and when to enter it. People can run your program, do some work, and then close the program and pick up where they left off later. Learning to handle exceptions will help you deal with situations in which files don't exist and deal with other problems that can cause your programs to crash. This will make your programs more robust when they encounter bad data, whether it comes from innocent mistakes or from malicious attempts to break your programs. With the skills you'll learn in this chapter, you'll make your programs more applicable, usable, and stable.

Reading from a File

An incredible amount of data is available in text files. Text files can contain weather data, traffic data, socioeconomic data, literary works, and more. Reading from a file is particularly useful in data analysis applications, but it's also applicable to any situation in which you want to analyze or modify information stored in a file. For example, you can write a program that reads in the contents of a text file and rewrites the file with formatting that allows a browser to display it.

When you want to work with the information in a text file, the first step is to read the file into memory. You can read the entire contents of a file, or you can work through the file one line at a time.

Reading an Entire File

To begin, we need a file with a few lines of text in it. Let's start with a file that contains *pi* to 30 decimal places with 10 decimal places per line:

pi_digits.txt

```
3.1415926535
  8979323846
  2643383279
```

To try the following examples yourself, you can enter these lines in an editor and save the file as *pi_digits.txt*, or you can download the file from the book's resources through *https://www.nostarch.com/pythoncrashcourse/*. Save the file in the same directory where you'll store this chapter's programs.

Here's a program that opens this file, reads it, and prints the contents of the file to the screen:

file_reader.py

```
with open('pi_digits.txt') as file_object:
    contents = file_object.read()
    print(contents)
```

The first line of this program has a lot going on. Let's start by looking at the `open()` function. To do any work with a file, even just printing its contents, you first need to *open* the file to access it. The `open()` function needs one argument: the name of the file you want to open. Python looks for this file in the directory where the program that's currently being executed is stored. In this example, *file_reader.py* is currently running, so Python looks for *pi_digits.txt* in the directory where *file_reader.py* is stored. The `open()` function returns an object representing the file. Here, `open('pi_digits.txt')` returns an object representing *pi_digits.txt*. Python stores this object in `file_object`, which we'll work with later in the program.

The keyword `with` closes the file once access to it is no longer needed. Notice how we call `open()` in this program but not `close()`. You could open and close the file by calling `open()` and `close()`, but if a bug in your program prevents the `close()` statement from being executed, the file may never close. This may seem trivial, but improperly closed files can cause data to be lost or corrupted. And if you call `close()` too early in your program, you'll find yourself trying to work with a *closed* file (a file you can't access), which leads to more errors. It's not always easy to know exactly when you should close a file, but with the structure shown here, Python will figure that out for you. All you have to do is open the file and work with it as desired, trusting that Python will close it automatically when the time is right.

Once we have a file object representing *pi_digits.txt*, we use the `read()` method in the second line of our program to read the entire contents of the file and store it as one long string in `contents`. When we print the value of `contents`, we get the entire text file back:

```
3.1415926535
  8979323846
  2643383279

```

The only difference between this output and the original file is the extra blank line at the end of the output. The blank line appears because `read()` returns an empty string when it reaches the end of the file; this empty string shows up as a blank line. If you want to remove the extra blank line, you can use `rstrip()` in the `print` statement:

```
with open('pi_digits.txt') as file_object:
    contents = file_object.read()
    print(contents.rstrip())
```

Recall that Python's `rstrip()` method removes, or strips, any whitespace characters from the right side of a string. Now the output matches the contents of the original file exactly:

```
3.1415926535
  8979323846
  2643383279
```

File Paths

When you pass a simple filename like *pi_digits.txt* to the `open()` function, Python looks in the directory where the file that's currently being executed (that is, your *.py* program file) is stored.

Sometimes, depending on how you organize your work, the file you want to open won't be in the same directory as your program file. For example, you might store your program files in a folder called *python_work*; inside *python_work*, you might have another folder called *text_files* to distinguish your program files from the text files they're manipulating. Even though *text_files* is in *python_work*, just passing `open()` the name of a file in *text_files* won't work, because Python will only look in *python_work* and stop there; it won't go on and look in *text_files*. To get Python to open files from a directory other than the one where your program file is stored, you need to provide a *file path*, which tells Python to look in a specific location on your system.

Because *text_files* is inside *python_work*, you could use a relative file path to open a file from *text_files*. A *relative file path* tells Python to look for a given location relative to the directory where the currently running program file is stored. On Linux and OS X, you'd write:

```
with open('text_files/filename.txt') as file_object:
```

This line tells Python to look for the desired *.txt* file in the folder *text_files* and assumes that *text_files* is located inside *python_work* (which it is). On Windows systems, you use a backslash (\) instead of a forward slash (/) in the file path:

```
with open('text_files\filename.txt') as file_object:
```

You can also tell Python exactly where the file is on your computer regardless of where the program that's being executed is stored. This is called an *absolute file path*. You use an absolute path if a relative path doesn't work. For instance, if you've put *text_files* in some folder other than *python_work*—say, a folder called *other_files*—then just passing `open()` the path `'text_files/filename.txt'` won't work because Python will only look for that location inside *python_work*. You'll need to write out a full path to clarify where you want Python to look.

Absolute paths are usually longer than relative paths, so it's helpful to store them in a variable and then pass that variable to `open()`. On Linux and OS X, absolute paths look like this:

```
file_path = '/home/ehmatthes/other_files/text_files/filename.txt'
with open(file_path) as file_object:
```

and on Windows they look like this:

```
file_path = 'C:\Users\ehmatthes\other_files\text_files\filename.txt'
with open(file_path) as file_object:
```

Using absolute paths, you can read files from any location on your system. For now it's easiest to store files in the same directory as your program files or in a folder such as *text_files* within the directory that stores your program files.

NOTE *Windows systems will sometimes interpret forward slashes in file paths correctly. If you're using Windows and you're not getting the results you expect, make sure you try using backslashes.*

Reading Line by Line

When you're reading a file, you'll often want to examine each line of the file. You might be looking for certain information in the file, or you might want to modify the text in the file in some way. For example, you might want to read through a file of weather data and work with any line that includes the word *sunny* in the description of that day's weather. In a news report, you might look for any line with the tag `<headline>` and rewrite that line with a specific kind of formatting.

You can use a `for` loop on the file object to examine each line from a file one at a time:

file_reader.py

```
❶ filename = 'pi_digits.txt'

❷ with open(filename) as file_object:
❸     for line in file_object:
          print(line)
```

At ❶ we store the name of the file we're reading from in the variable `filename`. This is a common convention when working with files. Because the variable `filename` doesn't represent the actual file—it's just a string telling Python where to find the file—you can easily swap out `'pi_digits.txt'` for the name of another file you want to work with. After we call `open()`, an object representing the file and its contents is stored in the variable `file_object` ❷. We again use the `with` syntax to let Python open and close the file properly. To examine the file's contents, we work through each line in the file by looping over the file object ❸.

When we print each line, we find even more blank lines:

```
3.1415926535

  8979323846

  2643383279

```

These blank lines appear because an invisible newline character is at the end of each line in the text file. The `print` statement adds its own newline each time we call it, so we end up with two newline characters at the end of each line: one from the file and one from the `print` statement. Using `rstrip()` on each line in the `print` statement eliminates these extra blank lines:

```
filename = 'pi_digits.txt'

with open(filename) as file_object:
    for line in file_object:
        print(line.rstrip())
```

Now the output matches the contents of the file once again:

```
3.1415926535
  8979323846
  2643383279
```

Making a List of Lines from a File

When you use with, the file object returned by open() is only available inside the with block that contains it. If you want to retain access to a file's contents outside the with block, you can store the file's lines in a list inside the block and then work with that list. You can process parts of the file immediately and postpone some processing for later in the program.

The following example stores the lines of *pi_digits.txt* in a list inside the with block and then prints the lines outside the with block:

```
filename = 'pi_digits.txt'

with open(filename) as file_object:
❶     lines = file_object.readlines()

❷ for line in lines:
    print(line.rstrip())
```

At ❶ the readlines() method takes each line from the file and stores it in a list. This list is then stored in lines, which we can continue to work with after the with block ends. At ❷ we use a simple for loop to print each line from lines. Because each item in lines corresponds to each line in the file, the output matches the contents of the file exactly.

Working with a File's Contents

After you've read a file into memory, you can do whatever you want with that data, so let's briefly explore the digits of *pi*. First, we'll attempt to build a single string containing all the digits in the file with no whitespace in it:

pi_string.py

```
filename = 'pi_digits.txt'

with open(filename) as file_object:
    lines = file_object.readlines()

❶ pi_string = ''
❷ for line in lines:
    pi_string += line.rstrip()

❸ print(pi_string)
print(len(pi_string))
```

We start by opening the file and storing each line of digits in a list, just as we did in the previous example. At ❶ we create a variable, pi_string, to hold the digits of *pi*. We then create a loop that adds each line of digits to pi_string and removes the newline character from each line ❷. At ❸ we print this string and also show how long the string is:

```
3.1415926535  8979323846  2643383279
36
```

The variable pi_string contains the whitespace that was on the left side of the digits in each line, but we can get rid of that by using strip() instead of rstrip():

```
filename = 'pi_30_digits.txt'

with open(filename) as file_object:
    lines = file_object.readlines()

pi_string = ''
for line in lines:
    pi_string += line.strip()

print(pi_string)
print(len(pi_string))
```

Now we have a string containing *pi* to 30 decimal places. The string is 32 characters long because it also includes the leading 3 and a decimal point:

```
3.141592653589793238462643383279
32
```

NOTE *When Python reads from a text file, it interprets all text in the file as a string. If you read in a number and want to work with that value in a numerical context, you'll have to convert it to an integer using the* int() *function or convert it to a float using the* float() *function.*

Large Files: One Million Digits

So far we've focused on analyzing a text file that contains only three lines, but the code in these examples would work just as well on much larger files. If we start with a text file that contains *pi* to 1,000,000 decimal places instead of just 30, we can create a single string containing all these digits. We don't need to change our program at all except to pass it a different file. We'll also print just the first 50 decimal places, so we don't have to watch a million digits scroll by in the terminal:

pi_string.py

```
filename = 'pi_million_digits.txt'

with open(filename) as file_object:
    lines = file_object.readlines()
```

```
pi_string = ''
for line in lines:
    pi_string += line.strip()

print(pi_string[:52] + "...")
print(len(pi_string))
```

The output shows that we do indeed have a string containing *pi* to 1,000,000 decimal places:

```
3.14159265358979323846264338327950288419716939937510...
1000002
```

Python has no inherent limit to how much data you can work with; you can work with as much data as your system's memory can handle.

NOTE *To run this program (and many of the examples that follow), you'll need to download the resources available at* https://www.nostarch.com/pythoncrashcourse/.

Is Your Birthday Contained in Pi?

I've always been curious to know if my birthday appears anywhere in the digits of *pi*. Let's use the program we just wrote to find out if someone's birthday appears anywhere in the first million digits of *pi*. We can do this by expressing each birthday as a string of digits and seeing if that string appears anywhere in `pi_string`:

```
filename = 'pi_million_digits.txt'

with open(filename) as file_object:
    lines = file_object.readlines()

pi_string = ''
for line in lines:
    pi_string += line.rstrip()

❶ birthday = input("Enter your birthday, in the form mmddyy: ")
❷ if birthday in pi_string:
    print("Your birthday appears in the first million digits of pi!")
else:
    print("Your birthday does not appear in the first million digits of pi.")
```

At ❶ we prompt for the user's birthday, and then at ❷ we check if that string is in `pi_string`. Let's try it:

```
Enter your birthdate, in the form mmddyy: 120372
Your birthday appears in the first million digits of pi!
```

My birthday does appear in the digits of *pi*! Once you've read from a file, you can analyze its contents in just about any way you can imagine.

TRY IT YOURSELF

10-1. Learning Python: Open a blank file in your text editor and write a few lines summarizing what you've learned about Python so far. Start each line with the phrase *In Python you can....* Save the file as *learning_python.txt* in the same directory as your exercises from this chapter. Write a program that reads the file and prints what you wrote three times. Print the contents once by reading in the entire file, once by looping over the file object, and once by storing the lines in a list and then working with them outside the `with` block.

10-2. Learning C: You can use the `replace()` method to replace any word in a string with a different word. Here's a quick example showing how to replace `'dog'` with `'cat'` in a sentence:

```
>>> message = "I really like dogs."
>>> message.replace('dog', 'cat')
'I really like cats.'
```

Read in each line from the file you just created, *learning_python.txt*, and replace the word *Python* with the name of another language, such as *C*. Print each modified line to the screen.

Writing to a File

One of the simplest ways to save data is to write it to a file. When you write text to a file, the output will still be available after you close the terminal containing your program's output. You can examine output after a program finishes running, and you can share the output files with others as well. You can also write programs that read the text back into memory and work with it again later.

Writing to an Empty File

To write text to a file, you need to call `open()` with a second argument telling Python that you want to write to the file. To see how this works, let's write a simple message and store it in a file instead of printing it to the screen:

write_message.py

```
filename = 'programming.txt'

❶ with open(filename, 'w') as file_object:
❷     file_object.write("I love programming.")
```

The call to `open()` in this example has two arguments ❶. The first argument is still the name of the file we want to open. The second argument, `'w'`, tells Python that we want to open the file in *write mode*. You can open a file in *read mode* ('r'), *write mode* ('w'), *append mode* ('a'), or a mode that allows you to read and write to the file ('r+'). If you omit the mode argument, Python opens the file in read-only mode by default.

The open() function automatically creates the file you're writing to if it doesn't already exist. However, be careful opening a file in write mode ('w') because if the file does exist, Python will erase the file before returning the file object.

At ❷ we use the write() method on the file object to write a string to the file. This program has no terminal output, but if you open the file *programming.txt*, you'll see one line:

programming.txt

```
I love programming.
```

This file behaves like any other file on your computer. You can open it, write new text in it, copy from it, paste to it, and so forth.

NOTE *Python can only write strings to a text file. If you want to store numerical data in a text file, you'll have to convert the data to string format first using the* str() *function.*

Writing Multiple Lines

The write() function doesn't add any newlines to the text you write. So if you write more than one line without including newline characters, your file may not look the way you want it to:

```
filename = 'programming.txt'

with open(filename, 'w') as file_object:
    file_object.write("I love programming.")
    file_object.write("I love creating new games.")
```

If you open *programming.txt*, you'll see the two lines squished together:

```
I love programming.I love creating new games.
```

Including newlines in your write() statements makes each string appear on its own line:

```
filename = 'programming.txt'

with open(filename, 'w') as file_object:
    file_object.write("I love programming.\n")
    file_object.write("I love creating new games.\n")
```

The output now appears on separate lines:

```
I love programming.
I love creating new games.
```

You can also use spaces, tab characters, and blank lines to format your output, just as you've been doing with terminal-based output.

Appending to a File

If you want to add content to a file instead of writing over existing content, you can open the file in *append mode*. When you open a file in append mode, Python doesn't erase the file before returning the file object. Any lines you write to the file will be added at the end of the file. If the file doesn't exist yet, Python will create an empty file for you.

Let's modify *write_message.py* by adding some new reasons we love programming to the existing file *programming.txt*:

write_message.py

```
filename = 'programming.txt'

❶ with open(filename, 'a') as file_object:
❷     file_object.write("I also love finding meaning in large datasets.\n")
      file_object.write("I love creating apps that can run in a browser.\n")
```

At ❶ we use the 'a' argument to open the file for appending rather than writing over the existing file. At ❷ we write two new lines, which are added to *programming.txt*:

programming.txt

```
I love programming.
I love creating new games.
I also love finding meaning in large datasets.
I love creating apps that can run in a browser.
```

We end up with the original contents of the file, followed by the new content we just added.

> **TRY IT YOURSELF**
>
> **10-3. Guest:** Write a program that prompts the user for their name. When they respond, write their name to a file called *guest.txt*.
>
> **10-4. Guest Book:** Write a `while` loop that prompts users for their name. When they enter their name, print a greeting to the screen and add a line recording their visit in a file called *guest_book.txt*. Make sure each entry appears on a new line in the file.
>
> **10-5. Programming Poll:** Write a `while` loop that asks people why they like programming. Each time someone enters a reason, add their reason to a file that stores all the responses.

Exceptions

Python uses special objects called *exceptions* to manage errors that arise during a program's execution. Whenever an error occurs that makes Python unsure what to do next, it creates an exception object. If you write code that handles the exception, the program will continue running. If you don't handle the exception, the program will halt and show a *traceback*, which includes a report of the exception that was raised.

Exceptions are handled with try-except blocks. A try-except block asks Python to do something, but it also tells Python what to do if an exception is raised. When you use try-except blocks, your programs will continue running even if things start to go wrong. Instead of tracebacks, which can be confusing for users to read, users will see friendly error messages that you write.

Handling the ZeroDivisionError Exception

Let's look at a simple error that causes Python to raise an exception. You probably know that it's impossible to divide a number by zero, but let's ask Python to do it anyway:

division.py

```
print(5/0)
```

Of course Python can't do this, so we get a traceback:

```
Traceback (most recent call last):
  File "division.py", line 1, in <module>
    print(5/0)
❶ ZeroDivisionError: division by zero
```

The error reported at ❶ in the traceback, ZeroDivisionError, is an exception object. Python creates this kind of object in response to a situation where it can't do what we ask it to. When this happens, Python stops the program and tells us the kind of exception that was raised. We can use this information to modify our program. We'll tell Python what to do when this kind of exception occurs; that way, if it happens again, we're prepared.

Using try-except Blocks

When you think an error may occur, you can write a try-except block to handle the exception that might be raised. You tell Python to try running some code, and you tell it what to do if the code results in a particular kind of exception.

Here's what a try-except block for handling the ZeroDivisionError exception looks like:

```
try:
    print(5/0)
except ZeroDivisionError:
    print("You can't divide by zero!")
```

We put print(5/0), the line that caused the error, inside a try block. If the code in a try block works, Python skips over the except block. If the code in the try block causes an error, Python looks for an except block whose error matches the one that was raised and runs the code in that block.

In this example, the code in the try block produces a ZeroDivisionError, so Python looks for an except block telling it how to respond. Python then runs the code in that block, and the user sees a friendly error message instead of a traceback:

```
You can't divide by zero!
```

If more code followed the try-except block, the program would continue running because we told Python how to handle the error. Let's look at an example where catching an error can allow a program to continue running.

Using Exceptions to Prevent Crashes

Handling errors correctly is especially important when the program has more work to do after the error occurs. This happens often in programs that prompt users for input. If the program responds to invalid input appropriately, it can prompt for more valid input instead of crashing.

Let's create a simple calculator that does only division:

division.py

```
print("Give me two numbers, and I'll divide them.")
print("Enter 'q' to quit.")

while True:
❶     first_number = input("\nFirst number: ")
      if first_number == 'q':
          break
❷     second_number = input("Second number: ")
      if second_number == 'q':
          break
❸     answer = int(first_number) / int(second_number)
      print(answer)
```

This program prompts the user to input a first_number ❶ and, if the user does not enter *q* to quit, a second_number ❷. We then divide these two numbers to get an answer ❸. This program does nothing to handle errors, so asking it to divide by zero causes it to crash:

```
Give me two numbers, and I'll divide them.
Enter 'q' to quit.

First number: 5
Second number: 0
Traceback (most recent call last):
  File "division.py", line 9, in <module>
    answer = int(first_number) / int(second_number)
ZeroDivisionError: division by zero
```

It's bad that the program crashed, but it's also not a good idea to let users see tracebacks. Nontechnical users will be confused by them, and in a malicious setting, attackers will learn more than you want them to know from a traceback. For example, they'll know the name of your program file, and they'll see a part of your code that isn't working properly. A skilled attacker can sometimes use this information to determine which kind of attacks to use against your code.

The else Block

We can make this program more error resistant by wrapping the line that might produce errors in a `try-except` block. The error occurs on the line that performs the division, so that's where we'll put the `try-except` block. This example also includes an `else` block. Any code that depends on the `try` block executing successfully goes in the `else` block:

```
print("Give me two numbers, and I'll divide them.")
print("Enter 'q' to quit.")

while True:
    first_number = input("\nFirst number: ")
    if first_number == 'q':
        break
    second_number = input("Second number: ")
❶   try:
        answer = int(first_number) / int(second_number)
❷   except ZeroDivisionError:
        print("You can't divide by 0!")
❸   else:
        print(answer)
```

We ask Python to try to complete the division operation in a `try` block ❶, which includes only the code that might cause an error. Any code that depends on the `try` block succeeding is added to the `else` block. In this case if the division operation is successful, we use the `else` block to print the result ❸.

The `except` block tells Python how to respond when a `ZeroDivisionError` arises ❷. If the `try` statement doesn't succeed because of a division by zero error, we print a friendly message telling the user how to avoid this kind of error. The program continues to run, and the user never sees a traceback:

```
Give me two numbers, and I'll divide them.
Enter 'q' to quit.

First number: 5
Second number: 0
You can't divide by 0!
```

```
First number: 5
Second number: 2
2.5

First number: q
```

The try-except-else block works like this: Python attempts to run the code in the try statement. The only code that should go in a try statement is code that might cause an exception to be raised. Sometimes you'll have additional code that should run only if the try block was successful; this code goes in the else block. The except block tells Python what to do in case a certain exception arises when it tries to run the code in the try statement.

By anticipating likely sources of errors, you can write robust programs that continue to run even when they encounter invalid data and missing resources. Your code will be resistant to innocent user mistakes and malicious attacks.

Handling the FileNotFoundError Exception

One common issue when working with files is handling missing files. The file you're looking for might be in a different location, the filename may be misspelled, or the file may not exist at all. You can handle all of these situations in a straightforward way with a try-except block.

Let's try to read a file that doesn't exist. The following program tries to read in the contents of *Alice in Wonderland*, but I haven't saved the file *alice.txt* in the same directory as *alice.py*:

alice.py

```
filename = 'alice.txt'

with open(filename) as f_obj:
    contents = f_obj.read()
```

Python can't read from a missing file, so it raises an exception:

```
Traceback (most recent call last):
  File "alice.py", line 3, in <module>
    with open(filename) as f_obj:
FileNotFoundError: [Errno 2] No such file or directory: 'alice.txt'
```

The last line of the traceback reports a FileNotFoundError: this is the exception Python creates when it can't find the file it's trying to open. In this example, the open() function produces the error, so to handle it, the try block will begin just before the line that contains open():

```
filename = 'alice.txt'

try:
    with open(filename) as f_obj:
        contents = f_obj.read()
```

```
except FileNotFoundError:
    msg = "Sorry, the file " + filename + " does not exist."
    print(msg)
```

In this example, the code in the try block produces a FileNotFoundError, so Python looks for an except block that matches that error. Python then runs the code in that block, and the result is a friendly error message instead of a traceback:

```
Sorry, the file alice.txt does not exist.
```

The program has nothing more to do if the file doesn't exist, so the error-handling code doesn't add much to this program. Let's build on this example and see how exception handling can help when you're working with more than one file.

Analyzing Text

You can analyze text files containing entire books. Many classic works of literature are available as simple text files because they are in the public domain. The texts used in this section come from Project Gutenberg (*http://gutenberg.org/*). Project Gutenberg maintains a collection of literary works that are available in the public domain, and it's a great resource if you're interested in working with literary texts in your programming projects.

Let's pull in the text of *Alice in Wonderland* and try to count the number of words in the text. We'll use the string method split(), which can build a list of words from a string. Here's what split() does with a string containing just the title "Alice in Wonderland":

```
>>> title = "Alice in Wonderland"
>>> title.split()
['Alice', 'in', 'Wonderland']
```

The split() method separates a string into parts wherever it finds a space and stores all the parts of the string in a list. The result is a list of words from the string, although some punctuation may also appear with some of the words. To count the number of words in *Alice in Wonderland*, we'll use split() on the entire text. Then we'll count the items in the list to get a rough idea of the number of words in the text:

```
filename = 'alice.txt'

try:
    with open(filename) as f_obj:
        contents = f_obj.read()
except FileNotFoundError:
    msg = "Sorry, the file " + filename + " does not exist."
    print(msg)
```

```
    else:
        # Count the approximate number of words in the file.
❶       words = contents.split()
❷       num_words = len(words)
❸       print("The file " + filename + " has about " + str(num_words) + " words.")
```

I moved the file *alice.txt* to the correct directory, so the try block will work this time. At ❶ we take the string contents, which now contains the entire text of *Alice in Wonderland* as one long string, and use the split() method to produce a list of all the words in the book. When we use len() on this list to examine its length, we get a good approximation of the number of words in the original string ❷. At ❸ we print a statement that reports how many words were found in the file. This code is placed in the else block because it will work only if the code in the try block was executed successfully. The output tells us how many words are in *alice.txt*:

```
The file alice.txt has about 29461 words.
```

The count is a little high because extra information is provided by the publisher in the text file used here, but it's a good approximation of the length of *Alice in Wonderland.*

Working with Multiple Files

Let's add more books to analyze. But before we do, let's move the bulk of this program to a function called count_words(). By doing so, it will be easier to run the analysis for multiple books:

word_count.py

```
def count_words(filename):
❶   """Count the approximate number of words in a file."""
    try:
        with open(filename) as f_obj:
            contents = f_obj.read()
    except FileNotFoundError:
        msg = "Sorry, the file " + filename + " does not exist."
        print(msg)
    else:
        # Count approximate number of words in the file.
        words = contents.split()
        num_words = len(words)
        print("The file " + filename + " has about " + str(num_words) +
            " words.")

filename = 'alice.txt'
count_words(filename)
```

Most of this code is unchanged. We simply indented it and moved it into the body of count_words(). It's a good habit to keep comments up to date when you're modifying a program, so we changed the comment to a docstring and reworded it slightly ❶.

Now we can write a simple loop to count the words in any text we want to analyze. We do this by storing the names of the files we want to analyze in a list, and then we call `count_words()` for each file in the list. We'll try to count the words for *Alice in Wonderland, Siddhartha, Moby Dick,* and *Little Women,* which are all available in the public domain. I've intentionally left *siddhartha.txt* out of the directory containing *word_count.py*, so we can see how well our program handles a missing file:

```
def count_words(filename):
    --snip--

filenames = ['alice.txt', 'siddhartha.txt', 'moby_dick.txt', 'little_women.txt']
for filename in filenames:
    count_words(filename)
```

The missing *siddhartha.txt* file has no effect on the rest of the program's execution:

```
The file alice.txt has about 29461 words.
Sorry, the file siddhartha.txt does not exist.
The file moby_dick.txt has about 215136 words.
The file little_women.txt has about 189079 words.
```

Using the `try-except` block in this example provides two significant advantages. We prevent our users from seeing a traceback, and we let the program continue analyzing the texts it's able to find. If we don't catch the `FileNotFoundError` that *siddhartha.txt* raised, the user would see a full traceback, and the program would stop running after trying to analyze *Siddhartha*. It would never analyze *Moby Dick* or *Little Women*.

Failing Silently

In the previous example, we informed our users that one of the files was unavailable. But you don't need to report every exception you catch. Sometimes you'll want the program to fail silently when an exception occurs and continue on as if nothing happened. To make a program fail silently, you write a `try` block as usual, but you explicitly tell Python to do nothing in the `except` block. Python has a `pass` statement that tells it to do nothing in a block:

```
def count_words(filename):
    """Count the approximate number of words in a file."""
    try:
        --snip--
    except FileNotFoundError:
❶         pass
    else:
        --snip--

filenames = ['alice.txt', 'siddhartha.txt', 'moby_dick.txt', 'little_women.txt']
for filename in filenames:
    count_words(filename)
```

The only difference between this listing and the previous one is the `pass` statement at ❶. Now when a `FileNotFoundError` is raised, the code in the `except` block runs, but nothing happens. No traceback is produced, and there's no output in response to the error that was raised. Users see the word counts for each file that exists, but they don't see any indication that a file was not found:

```
The file alice.txt has about 29461 words.
The file moby_dick.txt has about 215136 words.
The file little_women.txt has about 189079 words.
```

The `pass` statement also acts as a placeholder. It's a reminder that you're choosing to do nothing at a specific point in your program's execution and that you might want to do something there later. For example, in this program we might decide to write any missing filenames to a file called *missing_files.txt*. Our users wouldn't see this file, but we'd be able to read the file and deal with any missing texts.

Deciding Which Errors to Report

How do you know when to report an error to your users and when to fail silently? If users know which texts are supposed to be analyzed, they might appreciate a message informing them why some texts were not analyzed. If users expect to see some results but don't know which books are supposed to be analyzed, they might not need to know that some texts were unavailable. Giving users information they aren't looking for can decrease the usability of your program. Python's error-handling structures give you fine-grained control over how much to share with users when things go wrong; it's up to you to decide how much information to share.

Well-written, properly tested code is not very prone to internal errors, such as syntax or logical errors. But every time your program depends on something external, such as user input, the existence of a file, or the availability of a network connection, there is a possibility of an exception being raised. A little experience will help you know where to include exception handling blocks in your program and how much to report to users about errors that arise.

TRY IT YOURSELF

10-6. Addition: One common problem when prompting for numerical input occurs when people provide text instead of numbers. When you try to convert the input to an `int`, you'll get a `TypeError`. Write a program that prompts for two numbers. Add them together and print the result. Catch the `TypeError` if either input value is not a number, and print a friendly error message. Test your program by entering two numbers and then by entering some text instead of a number.

(continued)

10-7. Addition Calculator: Wrap your code from Exercise 10-6 in a `while` loop so the user can continue entering numbers even if they make a mistake and enter text instead of a number.

10-8. Cats and Dogs: Make two files, *cats.txt* and *dogs.txt*. Store at least three names of cats in the first file and three names of dogs in the second file. Write a program that tries to read these files and print the contents of the file to the screen. Wrap your code in a `try-except` block to catch the `FileNotFound` error, and print a friendly message if a file is missing. Move one of the files to a different location on your system, and make sure the code in the `except` block executes properly.

10-9. Silent Cats and Dogs: Modify your `except` block in Exercise 10-8 to fail silently if either file is missing.

10-10. Common Words: Visit Project Gutenberg (*http://gutenberg.org/*) and find a few texts you'd like to analyze. Download the text files for these works, or copy the raw text from your browser into a text file on your computer.

You can use the `count()` method to find out how many times a word or phrase appears in a string. For example, the following code counts the number of times `'row'` appears in a string:

```
>>> line = "Row, row, row your boat"
>>> line.count('row')
2
>>> line.lower().count('row')
3
```

Notice that converting the string to lowercase using `lower()` catches all appearances of the word you're looking for, regardless of how it's formatted.

Write a program that reads the files you found at Project Gutenberg and determines how many times the word `'the'` appears in each text.

Storing Data

Many of your programs will ask users to input certain kinds of information. You might allow users to store preferences in a game or provide data for a visualization. Whatever the focus of your program is, you'll store the information users provide in data structures such as lists and dictionaries. When users close a program, you'll almost always want to save the information they entered. A simple way to do this involves storing your data using the `json` module.

The json module allows you to dump simple Python data structures into a file and load the data from that file the next time the program runs. You can also use json to share data between different Python programs. Even better, the JSON data format is not specific to Python, so you can share data you store in the JSON format with people who work in many other programming languages. It's a useful and portable format, and it's easy to learn.

NOTE *The JSON (JavaScript Object Notation) format was originally developed for JavaScript. However, it has since become a common format used by many languages, including Python.*

Using json.dump() and json.load()

Let's write a short program that stores a set of numbers and another program that reads these numbers back into memory. The first program will use json.dump() to store the set of numbers, and the second program will use json.load().

The json.dump() function takes two arguments: a piece of data to store and a file object it can use to store the data. Here's how you can use json.dump() to store a list of numbers:

number_writer.py

```
import json

numbers = [2, 3, 5, 7, 11, 13]

❶ filename = 'numbers.json'
❷ with open(filename, 'w') as f_obj:
❸     json.dump(numbers, f_obj)
```

We first import the json module and then create a list of numbers to work with. At ❶ we choose a filename in which to store the list of numbers. It's customary to use the file extension *.json* to indicate that the data in the file is stored in the JSON format. Then we open the file in write mode, which allows json to write the data to the file ❷. At ❸ we use the json.dump() function to store the list numbers in the file *numbers.json*.

This program has no output, but let's open the file *numbers.json* and look at it. The data is stored in a format that looks just like Python:

```
[2, 3, 5, 7, 11, 13]
```

Now we'll write a program that uses json.load() to read the list back into memory:

number_reader.py

```
import json

❶ filename = 'numbers.json'
❷ with open(filename) as f_obj:
❸     numbers = json.load(f_obj)

print(numbers)
```

At ❶ we make sure to read from the same file we wrote to. This time when we open the file, we open it in read mode because Python only needs to read from the file ❷. At ❸ we use the `json.load()` function to load the information stored in *numbers.json*, and we store it in the variable `numbers`. Finally we print the recovered list of numbers and see that it's the same list created in *number_writer.py*:

```
[2, 3, 5, 7, 11, 13]
```

This is a simple way to share data between two programs.

Saving and Reading User-Generated Data

Saving data with `json` is useful when you're working with user-generated data, because if you don't store your user's information somehow, you'll lose it when the program stops running. Let's look at an example where we prompt the user for their name the first time they run a program and then remember their name when they run the program again.

Let's start by storing the user's name:

remember_me.py

```
import json

❶ username = input("What is your name? ")

filename = 'username.json'
with open(filename, 'w') as f_obj:
❷     json.dump(username, f_obj)
❸     print("We'll remember you when you come back, " + username + "!")
```

At ❶ we prompt for a username to store. Next, we use `json.dump()`, passing it a username and a file object, to store the username in a file ❷. Then we print a message informing the user that we've stored their information ❸:

```
What is your name? Eric
We'll remember you when you come back, Eric!
```

Now let's write a new program that greets a user whose name has already been stored:

greet_user.py

```
import json

filename = 'username.json'

with open(filename) as f_obj:
❶     username = json.load(f_obj)
❷     print("Welcome back, " + username + "!")
```

At ❶ we use json.load() to read the information stored in *username.json* into the variable username. Now that we've recovered the username, we can welcome them back ❷:

```
Welcome back, Eric!
```

We need to combine these two programs into one file. When someone runs *remember_me.py*, we want to retrieve their username from memory if possible; therefore, we'll start with a try block that attempts to recover the username. If the file *username.json* doesn't exist, we'll have the except block prompt for a username and store it in *username.json* for next time:

remember_me.py

```
import json

# Load the username, if it has been stored previously.
#  Otherwise, prompt for the username and store it.
filename = 'username.json'
try:
❶    with open(filename) as f_obj:
❷        username = json.load(f_obj)
❸ except FileNotFoundError:
❹    username = input("What is your name? ")
❺    with open(filename, 'w') as f_obj:
        json.dump(username, f_obj)
        print("We'll remember you when you come back, " + username + "!")
else:
    print("Welcome back, " + username + "!")
```

There's no new code here; blocks of code from the last two examples are just combined into one file. At ❶ we try to open the file *username.json*. If this file exists, we read the username back into memory ❷ and print a message welcoming back the user in the else block. If this is the first time the user runs the program, *username.json* won't exist and a FileNotFoundError will occur ❸. Python will move on to the except block where we prompt the user to enter their username ❹. We then use json.dump() to store the username and print a greeting ❺.

Whichever block executes, the result is a username and an appropriate greeting. If this is the first time the program runs, this is the output:

```
What is your name? Eric
We'll remember you when you come back, Eric!
```

Otherwise:

```
Welcome back, Eric!
```

This is the output you see if the program was already run at least once.

Refactoring

Often, you'll come to a point where your code will work, but you'll recognize that you could improve the code by breaking it up into a series of functions that have specific jobs. This process is called *refactoring*. Refactoring makes your code cleaner, easier to understand, and easier to extend.

We can refactor *remember_me.py* by moving the bulk of its logic into one or more functions. The focus of *remember_me.py* is on greeting the user, so let's move all of our existing code into a function called greet_user():

remember_me.py

```
import json

def greet_user():
❶     """Greet the user by name."""
    filename = 'username.json'
    try:
        with open(filename) as f_obj:
            username = json.load(f_obj)
    except FileNotFoundError:
        username = input("What is your name? ")
        with open(filename, 'w') as f_obj:
            json.dump(username, f_obj)
            print("We'll remember you when you come back, " + username + "!")
    else:
        print("Welcome back, " + username + "!")

greet_user()
```

Because we're using a function now, we update the comments with a docstring that reflects how the program currently works ❶. This file is a little cleaner, but the function greet_user() is doing more than just greeting the user—it's also retrieving a stored username if one exists and prompting for a new username if one doesn't exist.

Let's refactor greet_user() so it's not doing so many different tasks. We'll start by moving the code for retrieving a stored username to a separate function:

```
import json

def get_stored_username():
❶     """Get stored username if available."""
    filename = 'username.json'
    try:
        with open(filename) as f_obj:
            username = json.load(f_obj)
    except FileNotFoundError:
❷         return None
    else:
        return username
```

```
def greet_user():
    """Greet the user by name."""
    username = get_stored_username()
❸   if username:
        print("Welcome back, " + username + "!")
    else:
        username = input("What is your name? ")
        filename = 'username.json'
        with open(filename, 'w') as f_obj:
            json.dump(username, f_obj)
            print("We'll remember you when you come back, " + username + "!")

greet_user()
```

The new function `get_stored_username()` has a clear purpose, as stated in the docstring at ❶. This function retrieves a stored username and returns the username if it finds one. If the file *username.json* doesn't exist, the function returns `None` ❷. This is good practice: a function should either return the value you're expecting, or it should return `None`. This allows us to perform a simple test with the return value of the function. At ❸ we print a welcome back message to the user if the attempt to retrieve a username was successful, and if it doesn't, we prompt for a new username.

We should factor one more block of code out of `greet_user()`. If the username doesn't exist, we should move the code that prompts for a new username to a function dedicated to that purpose:

```
import json

def get_stored_username():
    """Get stored username if available."""
    --snip--

def get_new_username():
    """Prompt for a new username."""
    username = input("What is your name? ")
    filename = 'username.json'
    with open(filename, 'w') as f_obj:
        json.dump(username, f_obj)
    return username

def greet_user():
    """Greet the user by name."""
    username = get_stored_username()
    if username:
        print("Welcome back, " + username + "!")
    else:
        username = get_new_username()
        print("We'll remember you when you come back, " + username + "!")

greet_user()
```

Each function in this final version of *remember_me.py* has a single, clear purpose. We call `greet_user()`, and that function prints an appropriate message: it either welcomes back an existing user or greets a new user. It does this by calling `get_stored_username()`, which is responsible only for retrieving a stored username if one exists. Finally, `greet_user()` calls `get_new_username()` if necessary, which is responsible only for getting a new username and storing it. This compartmentalization of work is an essential part of writing clear code that will be easy to maintain and extend.

TRY IT YOURSELF

10-11. Favorite Number: Write a program that prompts for the user's favorite number. Use `json.dump()` to store this number in a file. Write a separate program that reads in this value and prints the message, "I know your favorite number! It's _____."

10-12. Favorite Number Remembered: Combine the two programs from Exercise 10-11 into one file. If the number is already stored, report the favorite number to the user. If not, prompt for the user's favorite number and store it in a file. Run the program twice to see that it works.

10-13. Verify User: The final listing for *remember_me.py* assumes either that the user has already entered their username or that the program is running for the first time. We should modify it in case the current user is not the person who last used the program.

Before printing a welcome back message in `greet_user()`, ask the user if this is the correct username. If it's not, call `get_new_username()` to get the correct username.

Summary

In this chapter, you learned how to work with files. You learned to read an entire file at once and read through a file's contents one line at a time. You learned to write to a file and append text onto the end of a file. You read about exceptions and how to handle the exceptions you're likely to see in your programs. Finally, you learned how to store Python data structures so you can save information your users provide, preventing them from having to start over each time they run a program.

In Chapter 11 you'll learn efficient ways to test your code. This will help you trust that the code you develop is correct, and it will help you identify bugs that are introduced as you continue to build on the programs you've written.

11

TESTING YOUR CODE

When you write a function or a class, you can also write tests for that code. Testing proves that your code works as it's supposed to in response to all the input types it's designed to receive. When you write tests, you can be confident that your code will work correctly as more people begin to use your programs. You'll also be able to test new code as you add it to make sure your changes don't break your program's existing behavior. Every programmer makes mistakes, so every programmer must test their code often, catching problems before users encounter them.

In this chapter you'll learn to test your code using tools in Python's `unittest` module. You'll learn to build a test case and check that a set of inputs results in the output you want. You'll see what a passing test looks like and what a failing test looks like, and you'll learn how a failing test can help you improve your code. You'll learn to test functions and classes, and you'll start to understand how many tests to write for a project.

Testing a Function

To learn about testing, we need code to test. Here's a simple function that takes in a first and last name, and returns a neatly formatted full name:

name_function.py

```
def get_formatted_name(first, last):
    """Generate a neatly formatted full name."""
    full_name = first + ' ' + last
    return full_name.title()
```

The function `get_formatted_name()` combines the first and last name with a space in between to complete a full name, and then capitalizes and returns the full name. To check that `get_formatted_name()` works, let's make a program that uses this function. The program *names.py* lets users enter a first and last name, and see a neatly formatted full name:

names.py

```
from name_function import get_formatted_name

print("Enter 'q' at any time to quit.")
while True:
    first = input("\nPlease give me a first name: ")
    if first == 'q':
        break
    last = input("Please give me a last name: ")
    if last == 'q':
        break

    formatted_name = get_formatted_name(first, last)
    print("\tNeatly formatted name: " + formatted_name + '.')
```

This program imports `get_formatted_name()` from *name_function.py*. The user can enter a series of first and last names, and see the formatted full names that are generated:

```
Enter 'q' at any time to quit.

Please give me a first name: janis
Please give me a last name: joplin
        Neatly formatted name: Janis Joplin.

Please give me a first name: bob
Please give me a last name: dylan
        Neatly formatted name: Bob Dylan.

Please give me a first name: q
```

We can see that the names generated here are correct. But let's say we want to modify `get_formatted_name()` so it can also handle middle names. As we do so, we want to make sure we don't break the way the function handles names that have only a first and last name. We could test our code by running *names.py* and entering a name like `Janis Joplin` every time we modify `get_formatted_name()`, but that would become tedious. Fortunately, Python provides an efficient way to automate the testing of a function's output. If we automate the testing of `get_formatted_name()`, we can always be confident that the function will work when given the kinds of names we've written tests for.

Unit Tests and Test Cases

The module `unittest` from the Python standard library provides tools for testing your code. A *unit test* verifies that one specific aspect of a function's behavior is correct. A *test case* is a collection of unit tests that together prove that a function behaves as it's supposed to, within the full range of situations you expect it to handle. A good test case considers all the possible kinds of input a function could receive and includes tests to represent each of these situations. A test case with *full coverage* includes a full range of unit tests covering all the possible ways you can use a function. Achieving full coverage on a large project can be daunting. It's often good enough to write tests for your code's critical behaviors and then aim for full coverage only if the project starts to see widespread use.

A Passing Test

The syntax for setting up a test case takes some getting used to, but once you've set up the test case it's straightforward to add more unit tests for your functions. To write a test case for a function, import the `unittest` module and the function you want to test. Then create a class that inherits from `unittest.TestCase`, and write a series of methods to test different aspects of your function's behavior.

Here's a test case with one method that verifies that the function `get_formatted_name()` works correctly when given a first and last name:

test_name_function.py

```
import unittest
from name_function import get_formatted_name

❶ class NamesTestCase(unittest.TestCase):
    """Tests for 'name_function.py'."""

    def test_first_last_name(self):
        """Do names like 'Janis Joplin' work?"""
❷       formatted_name = get_formatted_name('janis', 'joplin')
❸       self.assertEqual(formatted_name, 'Janis Joplin')

unittest.main()
```

First, we import `unittest` and the function we want to test, `get_formatted_name()`. At ❶ we create a class called `NamesTestCase`, which will contain a series of unit tests for `get_formatted_name()`. You can name the class anything you want, but it's best to call it something related to the function you're about to test and to use the word *Test* in the class name. This class must inherit from the class unittest.TestCase so Python knows how to run the tests you write.

NamesTestCase contains a single method that tests one aspect of get_formatted_name(). We call this method test_first_last_name() because we're verifying that names with only a first and last name are formatted correctly. Any method that starts with test_ will be run automatically when we run *test_name_function.py*. Within this test method, we call the function we want to test and store a return value that we're interested in testing. In this example we call get_formatted_name() with the arguments 'janis' and 'joplin', and store the result in formatted_name ❷.

At ❸ we use one of unittest's most useful features: an *assert* method. Assert methods verify that a result you received matches the result you expected to receive. In this case, because we know get_formatted_name() is supposed to return a capitalized, properly spaced full name, we expect the value in formatted_name to be Janis Joplin. To check if this is true, we use unittest's assertEqual() method and pass it formatted_name and 'Janis Joplin'. The line

```
self.assertEqual(formatted_name, 'Janis Joplin')
```

says, "Compare the value in formatted_name to the string 'Janis Joplin'. If they are equal as expected, fine. But if they don't match, let me know!"

The line unittest.main() tells Python to run the tests in this file. When we run *test_name_function.py*, we get the following output:

```
.
----------------------------------------------------------------------
Ran 1 test in 0.000s

OK
```

The dot on the first line of output tells us that a single test passed. The next line tells us that Python ran one test, and it took less than 0.001 seconds to run. The final OK tells us that all unit tests in the test case passed.

This output indicates that the function get_formatted_name() will always work for names that have a first and last name unless we modify the function. When we modify get_formatted_name(), we can run this test again. If the test case passes, we know the function will still work for names like Janis Joplin.

A Failing Test

What does a failing test look like? Let's modify get_formatted_name() so it can handle middle names, but we'll do so in a way that breaks the function for names with just a first and last name, like Janis Joplin.

Here's a new version of get_formatted_name() that requires a middle name argument:

name_function.py

```
def get_formatted_name(first, middle, last):
    """Generate a neatly formatted full name."""
    full_name = first + ' ' + middle + ' ' + last
    return full_name.title()
```

This version should work for people with middle names, but when we test it, we see that we've broken the function for people with just a first and last name. This time, running the file *test_name_function.py* gives this output:

```
❶ E
  ======================================================================
❷ ERROR: test_first_last_name (__main__.NamesTestCase)
  ----------------------------------------------------------------------
❸ Traceback (most recent call last):
    File "test_name_function.py", line 8, in test_first_last_name
      formatted_name = get_formatted_name('janis', 'joplin')
  TypeError: get_formatted_name() missing 1 required positional argument: 'last'

  ----------------------------------------------------------------------
❹ Ran 1 test in 0.000s

❺ FAILED (errors=1)
```

There's a lot of information here because there's a lot you might need to know when a test fails. The first item in the output is a single E ❶, which tells us one unit test in the test case resulted in an error. Next, we see that test_first_last_name() in NamesTestCase caused an error ❷. Knowing which test failed is critical when your test case contains many unit tests. At ❸ we see a standard traceback, which reports that the function call get_formatted_name('janis', 'joplin') no longer works because it's missing a required positional argument.

We also see that one unit test was run ❹. Finally, we see an additional message that the overall test case failed and that one error occurred when running the test case ❺. This information appears at the end of the output so you see it right away; you don't want to scroll up through a long output listing to find out how many tests failed.

Responding to a Failed Test

What do you do when a test fails? Assuming you're checking the right conditions, a passing test means the function is behaving correctly and a failing test means there's an error in the new code you wrote. So when a test fails, don't change the test. Instead, fix the code that caused the test to fail. Examine the changes you just made to the function, and figure out how those changes broke the desired behavior.

In this case `get_formatted_name()` used to require only two parameters: a first name and a last name. Now it requires a first name, middle name, and last name. The addition of that mandatory middle name parameter broke the desired behavior of `get_formatted_name()`. The best option here is to make the middle name optional. Once we do, our test for names like `Janis Joplin` should pass again, and we should be able to accept middle names as well. Let's modify `get_formatted_name()` so middle names are optional and then run the test case again. If it passes, we'll move on to making sure the function handles middle names properly.

To make middle names optional, we move the parameter `middle` to the end of the parameter list in the function definition and give it an empty default value. We also add an `if` test that builds the full name properly, depending on whether or not a middle name is provided:

name_function.py

```
def get_formatted_name(first, last, middle=''):
    """Generate a neatly formatted full name."""
    if middle:
        full_name = first + ' ' + middle + ' ' + last
    else:
        full_name = first + ' ' + last
    return full_name.title()
```

In this new version of `get_formatted_name()`, the middle name is optional. If a middle name is passed to the function (`if middle:`), the full name will contain a first, middle, and last name. Otherwise, the full name will consist of just a first and last name. Now the function should work for both kinds of names. To find out if the function still works for names like `Janis Joplin`, let's run *test_name_function.py* again:

```
.
----------------------------------------------------------------------
Ran 1 test in 0.000s

OK
```

The test case passes now. This is ideal; it means the function works for names like `Janis Joplin` again without us having to test the function manually. Fixing our function was easy because the failed test helped us identify the new code that broke existing behavior.

Adding New Tests

Now that we know get_formatted_name() works for simple names again, let's write a second test for people who include a middle name. We do this by adding another method to the class NamesTestCase:

```
import unittest
from name_function import get_formatted_name

class NamesTestCase(unittest.TestCase):
    """Tests for 'name_function.py'."""

    def test_first_last_name(self):
        """Do names like 'Janis Joplin' work?"""
        formatted_name = get_formatted_name('janis', 'joplin')
        self.assertEqual(formatted_name, 'Janis Joplin')

    def test_first_last_middle_name(self):
        """Do names like 'Wolfgang Amadeus Mozart' work?"""
❶       formatted_name = get_formatted_name(
            'wolfgang', 'mozart', 'amadeus')
        self.assertEqual(formatted_name, 'Wolfgang Amadeus Mozart')

unittest.main()
```

We name this new method test_first_last_middle_name(). The method name must start with *test_* so the method runs automatically when we run *test_name_function.py*. We name the method to make it clear which behavior of get_formatted_name() we're testing. As a result, if the test fails, we know right away what kinds of names are affected. It's fine to have long method names in your TestCase classes. They need to be descriptive so you can make sense of the output when your tests fail, and because Python calls them automatically, you'll never have to write code that calls these methods.

To test the function, we call get_formatted_name() with a first, last, and middle name ❶, and then we use assertEqual() to check that the returned full name matches the full name (first, middle, and last) that we expect. When we run *test_name_function.py* again, both tests pass:

```
..
----------------------------------------------------------------------
Ran 2 tests in 0.000s

OK
```

Great! We now know that the function still works for names like Janis Joplin, and we can be confident that it will work for names like Wolfgang Amadeus Mozart as well.

TRY IT YOURSELF

11-1. City, Country: Write a function that accepts two parameters: a city name and a country name. The function should return a single string of the form *City, Country*, such as `Santiago, Chile`. Store the function in a module called *city_functions.py*.

Create a file called *test_cities.py* that tests the function you just wrote (remember that you need to import `unittest` and the function you want to test). Write a method called `test_city_country()` to verify that calling your function with values such as `'santiago'` and `'chile'` results in the correct string. Run *test_cities.py*, and make sure `test_city_country()` passes.

11-2. Population: Modify your function so it requires a third parameter, `population`. It should now return a single string of the form *City, Country – population xxx*, such as `Santiago, Chile - population 5000000`. Run *test_cities.py* again. Make sure `test_city_country()` fails this time.

Modify the function so the `population` parameter is optional. Run *test_cities.py* again, and make sure `test_city_country()` passes again.

Write a second test called `test_city_country_population()` that verifies you can call your function with the values `'santiago'`, `'chile'`, and `'population=5000000'`. Run *test_cities.py* again, and make sure this new test passes.

Testing a Class

In the first part of this chapter, you wrote tests for a single function. Now you'll write tests for a class. You'll use classes in many of your own programs, so it's helpful to be able to prove that your classes work correctly. If you have passing tests for a class you're working on, you can be confident that improvements you make to the class won't accidentally break its current behavior.

A Variety of Assert Methods

Python provides a number of assert methods in the `unittest.TestCase` class. As mentioned earlier, assert methods test whether a condition you believe is true at a specific point in your code is indeed true. If the condition is true as expected, your assumption about how that part of your program behaves is confirmed; you can be confident that no errors exist. If the condition you assume is true is actually not true, Python raises an exception.

Table 11-1 describes six commonly used assert methods. With these methods you can verify that returned values equal or don't equal expected values, that values are `True` or `False`, and that values are `in` or `not in` a given list. You can use these methods only in a class that inherits from unittest .TestCase, so let's look at how we can use one of these methods in the context of testing an actual class.

Table 11-1: Assert Methods Available from the unittest Module

Method	Use
assertEqual(a, b)	Verify that a == b
assertNotEqual(a, b)	Verify that a != b
assertTrue(x)	Verify that x is True
assertFalse(x)	Verify that x is False
assertIn(*item*, *list*)	Verify that *item* is in *list*
assertNotIn(*item*, *list*)	Verify that *item* is not in *list*

A Class to Test

Testing a class is similar to testing a function—much of your work involves testing the behavior of the methods in the class. But there are a few differences, so let's write a class to test. Consider a class that helps administer anonymous surveys:

survey.py

```
class AnonymousSurvey():
    """Collect anonymous answers to a survey question."""

❶   def __init__(self, question):
        """Store a question, and prepare to store responses."""
        self.question = question
        self.responses = []

❷   def show_question(self):
        """Show the survey question."""
        print(question)

❸   def store_response(self, new_response):
        """Store a single response to the survey."""
        self.responses.append(new_response)

❹   def show_results(self):
        """Show all the responses that have been given."""
        print("Survey results:")
        for response in responses:
            print('- ' + response)
```

This class starts with a survey question that you provide ❶ and includes an empty list to store responses. The class has methods to print the survey question ❷, add a new response to the response list ❸, and print all the responses stored in the list ❹. To create an instance from this class, all you have to provide is a question. Once you have an instance representing a particular survey, you display the survey question with `show_question()`, store a response using `store_response()`, and show results with `show_results()`.

To show that the `AnonymousSurvey` class works, let's write a program that uses the class:

language_survey.py

```
from survey import AnonymousSurvey

# Define a question, and make a survey.
question = "What language did you first learn to speak?"
my_survey = AnonymousSurvey(question)

# Show the question, and store responses to the question.
my_survey.show_question()
print("Enter 'q' at any time to quit.\n")
while True:
    response = input("Language: ")
    if response == 'q':
        break
    my_survey.store_response(response)

# Show the survey results.
print("\nThank you to everyone who participated in the survey!")
my_survey.show_results()
```

This program defines a question (`"What language did you first learn to speak?"`) and creates an `AnonymousSurvey` object with that question. The program calls `show_question()` to display the question and then prompts for responses. Each response is stored as it is received. When all responses have been entered (the user inputs `q` to quit), `show_results()` prints the survey results:

```
What language did you first learn to speak?
Enter 'q' at any time to quit.

Language: English
Language: Spanish
Language: English
Language: Mandarin
Language: q

Thank you to everyone who participated in the survey!
Survey results:
- English
- Spanish
- English
- Mandarin
```

This class works for a simple anonymous survey. But let's say we want to improve `AnonymousSurvey` and the module it's in, `survey`. We could allow each user to enter more than one response. We could write a method to list only unique responses and to report how many times each response was given. We could write another class to manage nonanonymous surveys.

Implementing such changes would risk affecting the current behavior of the class `AnonymousSurvey`. For example, it's possible that while trying to allow each user to enter multiple responses, we could accidentally change how single responses are handled. To ensure we don't break existing behavior as we develop this module, we can write tests for the class.

Testing the AnonymousSurvey Class

Let's write a test that verifies one aspect of the way `AnonymousSurvey` behaves. We'll write a test to verify that a single response to the survey question is stored properly. We'll use the `assertIn()` method to verify that the response is in the list of responses after it's been stored:

test_survey.py

```
import unittest
from survey import AnonymousSurvey

❶ class TestAnonmyousSurvey(unittest.TestCase):
    """Tests for the class AnonymousSurvey"""

❷     def test_store_single_response(self):
        """Test that a single response is stored properly."""
        question = "What language did you first learn to speak?"
❸         my_survey = AnonymousSurvey(question)
        my_survey.store_response('English')

❹         self.assertIn('English', my_survey.responses)

unittest.main()
```

We start by importing the `unittest` module and the class we want to test, `AnonymousSurvey`. We call our test case `TestAnonymousSurvey`, which again inherits from `unittest.TestCase` ❶. The first test method will verify that when we store a response to the survey question, the response ends up in the survey's list of responses. A good descriptive name for this method is `test_store_single_response()` ❷. If this test fails, we'll know from the method name shown in the output of the failing test that there was a problem storing a single response to the survey.

To test the behavior of a class, we need to make an instance of the class. At ❸ we create an instance called `my_survey` with the question `"What language did you first learn to speak?"` We store a single response, `English`, using the `store_response()` method. Then we verify that the response was stored correctly by asserting that `English` is in the list `my_survey.responses` ❹.

When we run *test_survey.py*, the test passes:

```
.
----------------------------------------------------------------------
Ran 1 test in 0.001s

OK
```

This is good, but a survey is useful only if it generates more than one response. Let's verify that three responses can be stored correctly. To do this, we add another method to `TestAnonymousSurvey`:

```
import unittest
from survey import AnonymousSurvey

class TestAnonymousSurvey(unittest.TestCase):
    """Tests for the class AnonymousSurvey"""

    def test_store_single_response(self):
        """Test that a single response is stored properly."""
        --snip--

    def test_store_three_responses(self):
        """Test that three individual responses are stored properly."""
        question = "What language did you first learn to speak?"
        my_survey = AnonymousSurvey(question)
❶       responses = ['English', 'Spanish', 'Mandarin']
        for response in responses:
            my_survey.store_response(response)

❷       for response in responses:
            self.assertIn(response, my_survey.responses)

unittest.main()
```

We call the new method `test_store_three_responses()`. We create a survey object just like we did in `test_store_single_response()`. We define a list containing three different responses ❶, and then we call `store_response()` for each of these responses. Once the responses have been stored, we write another loop and assert that each response is now in `my_survey.responses` ❷.

When we run *test_survey.py* again, both tests (for a single response and for three responses) pass:

```
..
----------------------------------------------------------------------
Ran 2 tests in 0.000s

OK
```

This works perfectly. However, these tests are a bit repetitive, so we'll use another feature of `unittest` to make them more efficient.

The setUp() Method

In *test_survey.py* we created a new instance of `AnonymousSurvey` in each test method, and we created new responses in each method. The `unittest.TestCase` class has a `setUp()` method that allows you to create these objects once and then use them in each of your test methods. When you include a `setUp()` method in a `TestCase` class, Python runs the `setUp()` method before running each method starting with *test_*. Any objects created in the `setUp()` method are then available in each test method you write.

Let's use `setUp()` to create a survey instance and a set of responses that can be used in `test_store_single_response()` and `test_store_three_responses()`:

```
import unittest
from survey import AnonymousSurvey

class TestAnonymousSurvey(unittest.TestCase):
    """Tests for the class AnonymousSurvey."""

    def setUp(self):
        """
        Create a survey and a set of responses for use in all test methods.
        """
        question = "What language did you first learn to speak?"
❶       self.my_survey = AnonymousSurvey(question)
❷       self.responses = ['English', 'Spanish', 'Mandarin']

    def test_store_single_response(self):
        """Test that a single response is stored properly."""
        self.my_survey.store_response(self.responses[0])
        self.assertIn(self.responses[0], self.my_survey.responses)

    def test_store_three_responses(self):
        """Test that three individual responses are stored properly."""
        for response in self.responses:
            self.my_survey.store_response(response)
        for response in self.responses:
            self.assertIn(response, self.my_survey.responses)

unittest.main()
```

The method `setUp()` does two things: it creates a survey instance ❶, and it creates a list of responses ❷. Each of these is prefixed by `self`, so they can be used anywhere in the class. This makes the two test methods simpler, because neither one has to make a survey instance or a response. The method `test_store_single_response()` verifies that the first response in `self.responses`—`self.responses[0]`—can be stored correctly, and `test_store_single_response()` verifies that all three responses in `self.responses` can be stored correctly.

When we run *test_survey.py* again, both tests still pass. These tests would be particularly useful when trying to expand `AnonymousSurvey` to handle multiple responses for each person. After modifying the code to accept multiple responses, you could run these tests and make sure you haven't affected the ability to store a single response or a series of individual responses.

When you're testing your own classes, the `setUp()` method can make your test methods easier to write. You make one set of instances and attributes in `setUp()` and then use these instances in all your test methods. This is much easier than making a new set of instances and attributes in each test method.

NOTE *When a test case is running, Python prints one character for each unit test as it is completed. A passing test prints a dot, a test that results in an error prints an* `E`*, and a test that results in a failed assertion prints an* `F`*. This is why you'll see a different number of dots and characters on the first line of output when you run your test cases. If a test case takes a long time to run because it contains many unit tests, you can watch these results to get a sense of how many tests are passing.*

TRY IT YOURSELF

11-3. Employee: Write a class called `Employee`. The `__init__()` method should take in a first name, a last name, and an annual salary, and store each of these as attributes. Write a method called `give_raise()` that adds $5000 to the annual salary by default but also accepts a different raise amount.

Write a test case for `Employee`. Write two test methods, `test_give_default_raise()` and `test_give_custom_raise()`. Use the `setUp()` method so you don't have to create a new employee instance in each test method. Run your test case, and make sure both tests pass.

Summary

In this chapter you learned to write tests for functions and classes using tools in the `unittest` module. You learned to write a class that inherits from `unittest.TestCase`, and you learned to write test methods that verify specific behaviors your functions and classes should exhibit. You learned to use the `setUp()` method to efficiently create instances and attributes from your classes that can be used in all the test methods for a class.

Testing is an important topic that many beginners don't learn. You don't have to write tests for all the simple projects you try as a beginner. But as soon as you start to work on projects that involve significant development effort, you should test the critical behaviors of your functions and classes. You'll be more confident that new work on your project won't break the parts that work, and this will give you the freedom to make improvements to your code. If you accidentally break existing functionality, you'll know right away, so you can still fix the problem easily. Responding to a failed test that you ran is much easier than responding to a bug report from an unhappy user.

Other programmers respect your projects more if you include some initial tests. They'll feel more comfortable experimenting with your code and be more willing to work with you on projects. If you want to contribute to a project that other programmers are working on, you'll be expected to show that your code passes existing tests and you'll usually be expected to write tests for new behavior you introduce to the project.

Play around with tests to become familiar with the process of testing your code. Write tests for the most critical behaviors of your functions and classes, but don't aim for full coverage in early projects unless you have a specific reason to do so.

PART II

PROJECTS

Congratulations! You now know enough about Python to start building interactive and meaningful projects. Creating your own projects will teach you new skills and solidify your understanding of the concepts introduced in Part I.

Part II contains three types of projects, and you can choose to do any or all of these projects in whichever order you like. Here's a brief description of each project to help you decide which to dig into first.

Alien Invasion: Making a Game with Python

In the Alien Invasion project (Chapters 12, 13, and 14), you'll use the Pygame package to develop a 2D game in which the aim is to shoot down a fleet of aliens as they drop down the screen in levels that increase in speed and difficulty. At the end of the project, you'll have learned skills that will enable you to develop your own 2D games in Pygame.

Data Visualization

The Data Visualization project starts in Chapter 15, in which you'll learn to generate data and create a series of functional and beautiful visualizations of that data using matplotlib and Pygal. Chapter 16 teaches you to access data from online sources and feed it into a visualization package to create plots of weather data and a world population map. Finally, Chapter 17 shows you how to write a program to automatically download and visualize data. Learning to make visualizations allows you to explore the field of data mining, which is a highly sought-after skill in the world today.

Web Applications

In the Web Applications project (Chapters 18, 19, and 20), you'll use the Django package to create a simple web application that allows users to keep a journal about any number of topics they've been learning about. Users will create an account with a username and password, enter a topic, and then make entries about what they're learning. You'll also learn how to deploy your app so anyone in the world can access it.

After completing this project, you'll be able to start building your own simple web applications, and you'll be ready to delve into more thorough resources on building applications with Django.

PROJECT 1

ALIEN INVASION

12

A SHIP THAT FIRES BULLETS

Let's build a game! We'll use Pygame, a collection of fun, powerful Python modules that manage graphics, animation, and even sound, making it easier for you to build sophisticated games. With Pygame handling tasks like drawing images to the screen, you can skip much of the tedious, difficult coding and focus on the higher-level logic of game dynamics.

In this chapter, you'll set up Pygame and then create a ship that moves right and left, and fires bullets in response to player input. In the next two chapters, you'll create a fleet of aliens to destroy, and then continue to make refinements, such as setting limits on the number of ships you can use and adding a scoreboard.

From this chapter you'll also learn to manage large projects that span multiple files. We'll refactor a lot of code and manage file contents to keep our project organized and the code efficient.

Making games is an ideal way to have fun while learning a language. It's deeply satisfying to watch others play a game you wrote, and writing a simple game will help you understand how professional games are written. As you work through this chapter, enter and run the code to understand how each block of code contributes to overall gameplay. Experiment with different values and settings to gain a better understanding of how to refine interactions in your own games.

NOTE *Alien Invasion will span a number of different files, so make a new folder on your system called* alien_invasion. *Be sure to save all files for the project to this folder so your* `import` *statements will work correctly.*

Planning Your Project

When building a large project, it's important to prepare a plan before you begin to write your code. Your plan will keep you focused and make it more likely that you'll complete the project.

Let's write a description of the overall gameplay. Although this description doesn't cover every detail of Alien Invasion, it provides a clear idea of how to start building the game:

> In Alien Invasion, the player controls a ship that appears at the bottom center of the screen. The player can move the ship right and left using the arrow keys and shoot bullets using the spacebar. When the game begins, a fleet of aliens fills the sky and moves across and down the screen. The player shoots and destroys the aliens. If the player shoots all the aliens, a new fleet appears that moves faster than the previous fleet. If any alien hits the player's ship or reaches the bottom of the screen, the player loses a ship. If the player loses three ships, the game ends.

For the first phase of development, we'll make a ship that can move right and left. The ship should be able to fire bullets when the player presses the spacebar. After setting up this behavior, we can turn our attention to the aliens and refine the gameplay.

Installing Pygame

Before you begin coding, install Pygame. Here's how to do so on Linux, OS X, and Microsoft Windows.

If you're using Python 3 on Linux or if you're using OS X, you'll need to use pip to install Pygame. pip is a program that handles the downloading and installing of Python packages for you. The following sections will show you how to install packages with pip.

If you're using Python 2.7 on Linux or if you're using Windows, you won't need pip to install Pygame. Instead, move on to "Installing Pygame on Linux" on page 238 or "Installing Pygame on Windows" on page 240.

NOTE *Instructions for installing pip on all systems are included in the sections that follow because you'll need pip for the data visualization and web application projects. These instructions are also included in the online resources at* https://www.nostarch.com/pythoncrashcourse/. *If you have trouble with the instructions here, see if the online instructions work for you.*

Installing Python Packages with pip

The most recent versions of Python come with pip installed, so first check whether pip is already on your system. With Python 3, pip is sometimes called *pip3*.

Checking for pip on Linux and OS X

Open a terminal window and enter the following command:

```
$ pip --version
❶ pip 7.0.3 from /usr/local/lib/python3.5/dist-packages (python 3.5)
$
```

If you have only one version of Python installed on your system and you see output similar to this, move on to either "Installing Pygame on Linux" on page 238 or "Installing Pygame on OS X" on page 239. If you get an error message, try using `pip3` instead of `pip`. If neither version is installed on your system, go to "Installing pip" on page 238.

If you have more than one version of Python on your system, verify that pip is associated with the version of Python you're using—for example, `python 3.5` at ❶. If pip is associated with the correct version of Python, move on to "Installing Pygame on Linux" on page 238 or "Installing Pygame on OS X" on page 239. If pip is associated with the wrong version of Python, try using `pip3` instead of `pip`. If neither command works for the version of Python you're using, go to "Installing pip" on page 238.

Checking for pip on Windows

Open a terminal window and enter the following command:

```
$ python -m pip --version
❶ pip 7.0.3 from C:\Python35\lib\site-packages (python 3.5)
$
```

If your system has only one version of Python installed and you see output similar to this, move on to "Installing Pygame on Windows" on page 240. If you get an error message, try using `pip3` instead of `pip`. If neither version is installed on your system, move on to "Installing pip" on page 238.

If your system has more than one version of Python installed, verify that pip is associated with the version of Python you're using—for example, `python 3.5` at ❶. If pip is associated with the correct version of Python, move on to "Installing Pygame on Windows" on page 240. If pip is associated with the wrong version of Python, try using pip3 instead of pip. If neither command works for the version of Python you're using, move on to "Installing pip" next.

Installing pip

To install pip, go to *https://bootstrap.pypa.io/get-pip.py*. Save the file if prompted to do so. If the code for *get-pip.py* appears in your browser, copy and paste the program into your text editor and save the file as *get-pip.py*. Once *get-pip.py* is saved on your computer, you'll need to run it with administrative privileges because pip will be installing new packages to your system.

NOTE *If you can't find* get-pip.py, *go to* https://pip.pypa.io/, *click* ***Installation*** *in the left panel, and then under "Install pip," follow the link to* get-pip.py.

Installing pip on Linux and OS X

Use the following command to run *get-pip.py* with administrative privileges:

```
$ sudo python get-pip.py
```

NOTE *If you use the command* python3 *to start a terminal session, you should use* **sudo python3 get-pip.py** *here.*

After the program runs, use the command **pip --version** (or **pip3 --version**) to make sure pip was installed correctly.

Installing pip on Windows

Use the following command to run *get-pip.py*:

```
$ python get-pip.py
```

If you use a different command to run Python in a terminal, make sure you use that command to run *get-pip.py*. For example, your command might be python3 get-pip.py or C:\Python35\python get-pip.py.

After the program runs, run the command **python -m pip --version** to make sure pip was installed successfully.

Installing Pygame on Linux

If you're using Python 2.7, install Pygame using the package manager. Open a terminal window and run the following command, which will download and install Pygame onto your system:

```
$ sudo apt-get install python-pygame
```

Test your installation in a terminal session by entering the following:

```
$ python
>>> import pygame
>>>
```

If no output appears, Python has imported Pygame and you're ready to move on to "Starting the Game Project" on page 240.

If you're running Python 3, two steps are required: installing the libraries Pygame depends on, and downloading and installing Pygame.

Enter the following to install the libraries Pygame needs. (If you use a command such as `python3.5` on your system, replace `python3-dev` with `python3.5-dev`.)

```
$ sudo apt-get install python3-dev mercurial
$ sudo apt-get install libsdl-image1.2-dev libsdl2-dev libsdl-ttf2.0-dev
```

This will install the libraries needed to run Alien Invasion successfully. If you want to enable some more advanced functionality in Pygame, such as the ability to add sounds, you can also add the following libraries:

```
$ sudo apt-get install libsdl-mixer1.2-dev libportmidi-dev
$ sudo apt-get install libswscale-dev libsmpeg-dev libavformat-dev libavcode-dev
$ sudo apt-get install python-numpy
```

Now install Pygame by entering the following (use `pip3` if that's appropriate for your system):

```
$ pip install --user hg+http://bitbucket.org/pygame/pygame
```

The output will pause for a moment after informing you which libraries Pygame found. Press ENTER, even though some libraries are missing. You should see a message stating that Pygame installed successfully.

To confirm the installation, run a Python terminal session and try to import Pygame by entering the following:

```
$ python3
>>> import pygame
>>>
```

If this works, move on to "Starting the Game Project" on page 240.

Installing Pygame on OS X

You'll need Homebrew to install some packages that Pygame depends on. If you haven't already installed Homebrew, see Appendix A for instructions.

To install the libraries that Pygame depends on, enter the following:

```
$ brew install hg sdl sdl_image sdl_ttf
```

This will install the libraries needed to run Alien Invasion. You should see output scroll by as each library is installed.

If you also want to enable more advanced functionality, such as including sound in games, you can install two additional libraries:

```
$ brew install sdl_mixer portmidi
```

Use the following command to install Pygame (use `pip` rather than `pip3` if you're running Python 2.7):

```
$ pip3 install --user hg+http://bitbucket.org/pygame/pygame
```

Start a Python terminal session and import Pygame to check whether the installation was successful (enter `python` rather than `python3` if you're running Python 2.7):

```
$ python3
>>> import pygame
>>>
```

If the `import` statement works, move on to "Starting the Game Project" below.

Installing Pygame on Windows

The Pygame project is hosted on a code-sharing site called Bitbucket. To install Pygame on your version of Windows, find a Windows installer at *https://bitbucket.org/pygame/pygame/downloads/* that matches the version of Python you're running. If you don't see an appropriate installer listed at Bitbucket, check *http://www.lfd.uci.edu/~gohlke/pythonlibs/#pygame.*

After you've downloaded the appropriate file, run the installer if it's a *.exe* file.

If you have a file ending in *.whl,* copy the file to your project directory. Open a command window, navigate to the folder that you copied the installer to, and use pip to run the installer:

```
> python -m pip install --user pygame-1.9.2a0-cp35-none-win32.whl
```

Starting the Game Project

Now we'll start building our game by first creating an empty Pygame window to which we can later draw our game elements, such as the ship and the aliens. We'll also have our game respond to user input, set the background color, and load a ship image.

Creating a Pygame Window and Responding to User Input

First, we'll create an empty Pygame window. Here's the basic structure of a game written in Pygame:

alien_invasion.py

```
import sys

import pygame

def run_game():
    # Initialize game and create a screen object.
❶   pygame.init()
❷   screen = pygame.display.set_mode((1200, 800))
    pygame.display.set_caption("Alien Invasion")

    # Start the main loop for the game.
❸   while True:

        # Watch for keyboard and mouse events.
❹       for event in pygame.event.get():
❺           if event.type == pygame.QUIT:
                sys.exit()

        # Make the most recently drawn screen visible.
❻       pygame.display.flip()

run_game()
```

First, we import the sys and pygame modules. The pygame module contains the functionality needed to make a game. We'll use the sys module to exit the game when the player quits.

Alien Invasion starts as the function `run_game()`. The line `pygame.init()` at ❶ initializes background settings that Pygame needs to work properly. At ❷, we call `pygame.display.set_mode()` to create a display window called `screen`, on which we'll draw all of the game's graphical elements. The argument `(1200, 800)` is a tuple that defines the dimensions of the game window. By passing these dimensions to `pygame.display.set_mode()`, we create a game window 1200 pixels wide by 800 pixels high. (You can adjust these values depending on the size of your display.)

The `screen` object is called a surface. A *surface* in Pygame is a part of the screen where you display a game element. Each element in the game, like the aliens or the ship, is a surface. The surface returned by `display.set_mode()` represents the entire game window. When we activate the game's animation loop, this surface is automatically redrawn on every pass through the loop.

The game is controlled by a `while` loop ❸ that contains an event loop and code that manages screen updates. An *event* is an action that the user performs while playing the game, such as pressing a key or moving the mouse. To make our program respond to events, we'll write an *event loop* to *listen* for an event and perform an appropriate task depending on the kind of event that occurred. The `for` loop at ❹ is an event loop.

To access the events detected by Pygame, we'll use the `pygame.event.get()` method. Any keyboard or mouse event will cause the `for` loop to run. Inside the loop, we'll write a series of `if` statements to detect and respond to specific events. For example, when the player clicks the game window's close button, a `pygame.QUIT` event is detected and we call `sys.exit()` to exit the game ❺.

The call to `pygame.display.flip()` at ❻ tells Pygame to make the most recently drawn screen visible. In this case it draws an empty screen each time through the `while` loop to erase the old screen so that only the new screen is visible. When we move the game elements around, `pygame.display.flip()` will continually update the display to show the new positions of elements and hide the old ones, creating the illusion of smooth movement.

The last line in this basic game structure calls `run_game()`, which initializes the game and starts the main loop.

Run this code now, and you should see an empty Pygame window.

Setting the Background Color

Pygame creates a black screen by default, but that's boring. Let's set a different background color:

alien_invasion.py

```
--snip--
def run_game():
    --snip--
    pygame.display.set_caption("Alien Invasion")

    # Set the background color.
❶   bg_color = (230, 230, 230)

    # Start the main loop for the game.
    while True:

        # Watch for keyboard and mouse events.
        --snip--

        # Redraw the screen during each pass through the loop.
❷       screen.fill(bg_color)

        # Make the most recently drawn screen visible.
        pygame.display.flip()

run_game()
```

First, we create a background color and store it in `bg_color` ❶. This color needs to be specified only once, so we define its value before entering the main `while` loop.

Colors in Pygame are specified as RGB colors: a mix of red, green, and blue. Each color value can range from 0 to 255. The color value (255, 0, 0) is red, (0, 255, 0) is green, and (0, 0, 255) is blue. You can mix RGB values to create 16 million colors. The color value (230, 230, 230) mixes equal amounts of red, blue, and green, which produces a light gray background color.

At ❷, we fill the screen with the background color using the `screen.fill()` method, which takes only one argument: a color.

Creating a Settings Class

Each time we introduce new functionality into our game, we'll typically introduce some new settings as well. Instead of adding settings throughout the code, let's write a module called `settings` that contains a class called `Settings` to store all the settings in one place. This approach allows us to pass around one settings object instead of many individual settings. In addition, it makes our function calls simpler and makes it easier to modify the game's appearance as our project grows. To modify the game, we'll simply change some values in *settings.py* instead of searching for different settings throughout our files.

Here's the initial `Settings` class:

settings.py

```
class Settings():
    """A class to store all settings for Alien Invasion."""

    def __init__(self):
        """Initialize the game's settings."""
        # Screen settings
        self.screen_width = 1200
        self.screen_height = 800
        self.bg_color = (230, 230, 230)
```

To make an instance of `Settings` and use it to access our settings, modify *alien_invasion.py* as follows:

alien_invasion.py

```
--snip--
import pygame

from settings import Settings

def run_game():
    # Initialize pygame, settings, and screen object.
    pygame.init()
❶   ai_settings = Settings()
❷   screen = pygame.display.set_mode(
        (ai_settings.screen_width, ai_settings.screen_height))
    pygame.display.set_caption("Alien Invasion")

    # Start the main loop for the game.
    while True:
        --snip--
        # Redraw the screen during each pass through the loop.
❸       screen.fill(ai_settings.bg_color)

        # Make the most recently drawn screen visible.
        pygame.display.flip()

run_game()
```

We import `Settings` into the main program file, and then create an instance of `Settings` and store it in `ai_settings` after making the call to `pygame.init()` ❶. When we create a screen ❷, we use the `screen_width` and `screen_height` attributes of `ai_settings`, and then we use `ai_settings` to access the background color when filling the screen at ❸ as well.

Adding the Ship Image

Now let's add the ship to our game. To draw the player's ship on screen, we'll load an image and then use the Pygame method `blit()` to draw the image.

When choosing artwork for your games, be sure to pay attention to licensing. The safest and cheapest way to start is to use freely licensed graphics that you can modify from a website like *http://pixabay.com/*.

You can use almost any type of image file in your game, but it's easiest if you use a bitmap (*.bmp*) file because Pygame loads bitmaps by default. Although you can configure Pygame to use other file types, some file types depend on certain image libraries that must be installed on your computer. (Most images you'll find are in *.jpg*, *.png*, or *.gif* formats, but you can convert them to bitmaps using tools like Photoshop, GIMP, and Paint.)

Pay particular attention to the background color in your chosen image. Try to find a file with a transparent background that you can replace with any background color using an image editor. Your games will look best if the image's background color matches your game's background color. Alternatively, you can match your game's background to the image's background.

For Alien Invasion, you can use the file *ship.bmp* (Figure 12-1), which is available in the book's resources through *https://www.nostarch.com/pythoncrashcourse/*. The file's background color matches the settings we're using in this project. Make a folder called *images* inside your main project folder (*alien_invasion*). Save the file *ship.bmp* in the *images* folder.

Figure 12-1: The ship for Alien Invasion

Creating the Ship Class

After choosing an image for the ship, we need to display it onscreen. To use our ship, we'll write a module called `ship`, which contains the class `Ship`. This class will manage most of the behavior of the player's ship.

ship.py

```
import pygame

class Ship():

    def __init__(self, screen):
        """Initialize the ship and set its starting position."""
        self.screen = screen

        # Load the ship image and get its rect.
❶       self.image = pygame.image.load('images/ship.bmp')
❷       self.rect = self.image.get_rect()
❸       self.screen_rect = screen.get_rect()

        # Start each new ship at the bottom center of the screen.
❹       self.rect.centerx = self.screen_rect.centerx
        self.rect.bottom = self.screen_rect.bottom

❺   def blitme(self):
        """Draw the ship at its current location."""
        self.screen.blit(self.image, self.rect)
```

First, we import the `pygame` module. The `__init__()` method of `Ship` takes two parameters: the `self` reference and the `screen` where we'll draw the ship. To load the image, we call `pygame.image.load()` ❶. This function returns a surface representing the ship, which we store in `self.image`.

Once the image is loaded, we use `get_rect()` to access the surface's `rect` attribute ❷. One reason Pygame is so efficient is that it lets you treat game elements like rectangles (*rects*), even if they're not exactly shaped like rectangles. Treating an element as a rectangle is efficient because rectangles are simple geometric shapes. This approach usually works well enough that no one playing the game will notice that we're not working with the exact shape of each game element.

When working with a `rect` object, you can use the x- and y-coordinates of the top, bottom, left, and right edges of the rectangle, as well as the center. You can set any of these values to determine the current position of the rect.

When you're centering a game element, work with the `center`, `centerx`, or `centery` attributes of a rect. When you're working at an edge of the screen, work with the `top`, `bottom`, `left`, or `right` attributes. When you're adjusting the horizontal or vertical placement of the rect, you can just use the `x` and `y` attributes, which are the x- and y-coordinates of its top-left corner. These attributes spare you from having to do calculations that game developers formerly had to do manually, and you'll find you'll use them often.

NOTE *In Pygame, the origin (0, 0) is at the top-left corner of the screen, and coordinates increase as you go down and to the right. On a 1200 by 800 screen, the origin is at the top-left corner, and the bottom-right corner has the coordinates (1200, 800).*

We'll position the ship at the bottom center of the screen. To do so, first store the screen's rect in `self.screen_rect` ❸, and then make the value of `self.rect.centerx` (the x-coordinate of the ship's center) match the `centerx` attribute of the screen's rect ❹. Make the value of `self.rect.bottom` (the y-coordinate of the ship's bottom) equal to the value of the screen rect's `bottom` attribute. Pygame will use these `rect` attributes to position the ship image so it's centered horizontally and aligned with the bottom of the screen.

At ❺ we define the `blitme()` method, which will draw the image to the screen at the position specified by `self.rect`.

Drawing the Ship to the Screen

Now let's update *alien_invasion.py* so it creates a ship and calls the ship's `blitme()` method:

alien_invasion.py

```
--snip--
from settings import Settings
from ship import Ship

def run_game():
    --snip--
    pygame.display.set_caption("Alien Invasion")

    # Make a ship.
❶   ship = Ship(screen)

    # Start the main loop for the game.
    while True:
        --snip--
        # Redraw the screen during each pass through the loop.
        screen.fill(ai_settings.bg_color)
❷       ship.blitme()

        # Make the most recently drawn screen visible.
        pygame.display.flip()

run_game()
```

We import `Ship` and then make an instance of `Ship` (named `ship`) after the screen has been created. It must come before the main `while` loop ❶ so we don't make a new instance of the ship on each pass through the loop. We draw the ship onscreen by calling `ship.blitme()` after filling the background, so the ship appears on top of the background ❷.

When you run *alien_invasion.py* now, you should see an empty game screen with our rocket ship sitting at the bottom center, as shown in Figure 12-2.

Figure 12-2: Alien Invasion with the ship at the bottom center of the screen

Refactoring: the game_functions Module

In larger projects, you'll often refactor code you've written before adding more code. *Refactoring* simplifies the structure of the code you've already written, making it easier to build on. In this section we'll create a new module called `game_functions`, which will store a number of functions that make Alien Invasion work. The `game_functions` module will prevent *alien_invasion.py* from becoming too lengthy and will make the logic in *alien_invasion.py* easier to follow.

The check_events() Function

We'll start by moving the code that manages events to a separate function called `check_events()`. This will simplify `run_game()` and isolate the event management loop. Isolating the event loop allows you to manage events separately from other aspects of the game, like updating the screen.

Place `check_events()` in a separate module called `game_functions`:

game_functions.py

```
import sys

import pygame

def check_events():
    """Respond to keypresses and mouse events."""
    for event in pygame.event.get():
        if event.type == pygame.QUIT:
            sys.exit()
```

This module imports sys and pygame, which are used in the event checking loop. The function needs no parameters at this point, and the body is copied from the event loop in *alien_invasion.py*.

Now let's modify *alien_invasion.py* so it imports the game_functions module, and we'll replace the event loop with a call to check_events():

alien_invasion.py

```
import pygame

from settings import Settings
from ship import Ship
import game_functions as gf

def run_game():
    --snip--
    # Start the main loop for the game.
    while True:
        gf.check_events()

        # Redraw the screen during each pass through the loop.
        --snip--
```

We no longer need to import sys directly into the main program file, because it's only being used in the game_functions module now. We give the imported game_functions module the alias gf for simplification.

The update_screen() Function

Let's move the code for updating the screen to a separate function called update_screen() in *game_functions.py* to further simplify run_game():

game_functions.py

```
--snip--

def check_events():
    --snip--

def update_screen(ai_settings, screen, ship):
    """Update images on the screen and flip to the new screen."""
    # Redraw the screen during each pass through the loop.
    screen.fill(ai_settings.bg_color)
    ship.blitme()

    # Make the most recently drawn screen visible.
    pygame.display.flip()
```

The new update_screen() function takes three parameters: ai_settings, screen, and ship. Now we need to update the while loop from *alien_invasion.py* with a call to update_screen():

alien_invasion.py

```
--snip--
    # Start the main loop for the game.
```

```
    while True:
        gf.check_events()
        gf.update_screen(ai_settings, screen, ship)

run_game()
```

These two functions make the `while` loop simpler and will make further development easier. Instead of working inside `run_game()`, we can do most of our work in the module `game_functions`.

Because we wanted to start out working with code in a single file, we didn't introduce the `game_functions` module right away. This approach gives you an idea of a realistic development process: you start out writing your code as simply as possible, and refactor it as your project becomes more complex.

Now that our code is restructured to make it easier to add to, we can work on the dynamic aspects of the game!

TRY IT YOURSELF

12-1. Blue Sky: Make a Pygame window with a blue background.

12-2. Game Character: Find a bitmap image of a game character you like or convert an image to a bitmap. Make a class that draws the character at the center of the screen and match the background color of the image to the background color of the screen, or vice versa.

Piloting the Ship

Let's give the player the ability to move the ship right and left. To do this, we'll write code that responds when the player presses the right or left arrow key. We'll focus on movement to the right first, and then we'll apply the same principles to control movement to the left. As you do this, you'll learn how to control the movement of images on the screen.

Responding to a Keypress

Whenever the player presses a key, that keypress is registered in Pygame as an event. Each event is picked up by the `pygame.event.get()` method, so we need to specify in our `check_events()` function what kind of events to check for. Each keypress is registered as a `KEYDOWN` event.

When a `KEYDOWN` event is detected, we need to check whether the key that was pressed is one that triggers a certain event. For example, if the right arrow key is pressed, we increase the ship's rect.centerx value to move the ship to the right:

game_functions.py

```
def check_events(ship):
    """Respond to keypresses and mouse events."""
    for event in pygame.event.get():
        if event.type == pygame.QUIT:
            sys.exit()

❶       elif event.type == pygame.KEYDOWN:
❷           if event.key == pygame.K_RIGHT:
                # Move the ship to the right.
❸               ship.rect.centerx += 1
```

We give the check_events() function a ship parameter, because the ship needs to move to the right when the right arrow key is pressed. Inside check_events() we add an elif block to the event loop to respond when Pygame detects a KEYDOWN event ❶. We check if the key pressed is the right arrow key (pygame.K_RIGHT) by reading the event.key attribute ❷. If the right arrow key was pressed, we move the ship to the right by increasing the value of ship.rect.centerx by 1 ❸.

We need to update the call to check_events() in *alien_invasion.py* so it passes ship as an argument:

alien_invasion.py

```
    # Start the main loop for the game.
    while True:
        gf.check_events(ship)
        gf.update_screen(ai_settings, screen, ship)
```

If you run *alien_invasion.py* now, you should see the ship move to the right one pixel every time you press the right arrow key. That's a start, but it's not an efficient way to control the ship. Let's improve this control by allowing continuous movement.

Allowing Continuous Movement

When the player holds down the right arrow key, we want the ship to continue moving right until the player releases the key. We'll have our game detect a pygame.KEYUP event so we'll know when the right arrow key is released; then we'll use the KEYDOWN and KEYUP events together with a flag called moving_right to implement continuous motion.

When the ship is motionless, the moving_right flag will be False. When the right arrow key is pressed, we'll set the flag to True, and when it's released, we'll set the flag to False again.

The Ship class controls all attributes of the ship, so we'll give it an attribute called moving_right and an update() method to check the status of the moving_right flag. The update() method will change the position of the ship if the flag is set to True. We'll call this method any time we want to update the position of the ship.

Here are the changes to the Ship class:

ship.py

```
class Ship():

    def __init__(self, screen):
        --snip--
        # Start each new ship at the bottom center of the screen.
        self.rect.centerx = self.screen_rect.centerx
        self.rect.bottom = self.screen_rect.bottom

        # Movement flag
❶       self.moving_right = False

❷   def update(self):
        """Update the ship's position based on the movement flag."""
        if self.moving_right:
            self.rect.centerx += 1

    def blitme(self):
        --snip--
```

We add a self.moving_right attribute in the __init__() method and set it to False initially ❶. Then we add update(), which moves the ship right if the flag is True ❷.

Now modify check_events() so that moving_right is set to True when the right arrow key is pressed and False when the key is released:

game_functions.py

```
def check_events(ship):
    """Respond to keypresses and mouse events."""
    for event in pygame.event.get():
        --snip--
        elif event.type == pygame.KEYDOWN:
            if event.key == pygame.K_RIGHT:
❶               ship.moving_right = True

❷       elif event.type == pygame.KEYUP:
            if event.key == pygame.K_RIGHT:
                ship.moving_right = False
```

At ❶, we modify how the game responds when the player presses the right arrow key: instead of changing the ship's position directly, we merely set moving_right to True. At ❷, we add a new elif block, which responds to KEYUP events. When the player releases the right arrow key (K_RIGHT), we set moving_right to False.

Finally, we modify the while loop in *alien_invasion.py* so it calls the ship's update() method on each pass through the loop:

alien_invasion.py

```
    # Start the main loop for the game.
    while True:
        gf.check_events(ship)
        ship.update()
        gf.update_screen(ai_settings, screen, ship)
```

The ship's position will update after we've checked for keyboard events and before we update the screen. This allows the ship's position to be updated in response to player input and ensures the updated position is used when drawing the ship to the screen.

When you run *alien_invasion.py* and hold down the right arrow key, the ship should move continuously to the right until you release the key.

Moving Both Left and Right

Now that the ship can move continuously to the right, adding movement to the left is easy. We'll again modify the `Ship` class and the `check_events()` function. Here are the relevant changes to `__init__()` and `update()` in `Ship`:

ship.py

```
    def __init__(self, screen):
        --snip--
        # Movement flags
        self.moving_right = False
        self.moving_left = False

    def update(self):
        """Update the ship's position based on movement flags."""
        if self.moving_right:
            self.rect.centerx += 1
        if self.moving_left:
            self.rect.centerx -= 1
```

In `__init__()`, we add a `self.moving_left` flag. In `update()`, we use two separate `if` blocks rather than an `elif` in `update()` to allow the ship's `rect.centerx` value to be increased and then decreased if both arrow keys are held down. This results in the ship standing still. If we used `elif` for motion to the left, the right arrow key would always have priority. Doing it this way makes the movements more accurate when switching from left to right, when the player might momentarily hold down both keys.

We have to make two adjustments to `check_events()`:

game_functions.py

```
def check_events(ship):
    """Respond to keypresses and mouse events."""
    for event in pygame.event.get():
        --snip--
        elif event.type == pygame.KEYDOWN:
            if event.key == pygame.K_RIGHT:
                ship.moving_right = True
            elif event.key == pygame.K_LEFT:
                ship.moving_left = True

        elif event.type == pygame.KEYUP:
            if event.key == pygame.K_RIGHT:
                ship.moving_right = False
            elif event.key == pygame.K_LEFT:
                ship.moving_left = False
```

If a KEYDOWN event occurs for the K_LEFT key, we set moving_left to True. If a KEYUP event occurs for the K_LEFT key, we set moving_left to False. We can use elif blocks here because each event is connected to only one key. If the player presses both keys at once, two separate events will be detected.

If you run *alien_invasion.py* now, you should be able to move the ship continuously to the right and left. If you hold down both keys, the ship should stop moving.

Next, we'll further refine the movement of the ship. Let's adjust the ship's speed and limit how far the ship can move so it doesn't disappear off the sides of the screen.

Adjusting the Ship's Speed

Currently, the ship moves one pixel per cycle through the while loop, but we can take finer control of the ship's speed by adding a ship_speed_factor attribute to the Settings class. We'll use this attribute to determine how far to move the ship on each pass through the loop. Here's the new attribute in *settings.py*:

settings.py

```
class Settings():
    """A class to store all settings for Alien Invasion."""

    def __init__(self):
        --snip--

        # Ship settings
        self.ship_speed_factor = 1.5
```

We set the initial value of ship_speed_factor to 1.5. When we want to move the ship, we'll adjust its position by 1.5 pixels rather than 1 pixel.

We're using decimal values for the speed setting to give us finer control of the ship's speed when we increase the tempo of the game later on. However, rect attributes such as centerx store only integer values, so we need to make some modifications to Ship:

ship.py

```
class Ship():

❶     def __init__(self, ai_settings, screen):
        """Initialize the ship and set its starting position."""
        self.screen = screen
❷         self.ai_settings = ai_settings
        --snip--

        # Start each new ship at the bottom center of the screen.
        --snip--

        # Store a decimal value for the ship's center.
❸         self.center = float(self.rect.centerx)

        # Movement flags
        self.moving_right = False
        self.moving_left = False
```

```
    def update(self):
        """Update the ship's position based on movement flags."""
        # Update the ship's center value, not the rect.
        if self.moving_right:
❹           self.center += self.ai_settings.ship_speed_factor
        if self.moving_left:
            self.center -= self.ai_settings.ship_speed_factor

        # Update rect object from self.center.
❺       self.rect.centerx = self.center

    def blitme(self):
        --snip--
```

At ❶, we add `ai_settings` to the list of parameters for `__init__()`, so the ship will have access to its speed setting. We then turn the `ai_settings` parameter into an attribute, so we can use it in `update()` ❷. Now that we're adjusting the position of the ship by fractions of a pixel, we need to store the position in a variable that can store a decimal value. You can use a decimal value to set a rect's attribute, but the rect will store only the integer portion of that value. To store the ship's position accurately, we define a new attribute `self.center`, which can hold decimal values ❸. We use the `float()` function to convert the value of `self.rect.centerx` to a decimal and store this value in `self.center`.

Now when we change the ship's position in `update()`, the value of `self.center` is adjusted by the amount stored in `ai_settings.ship_speed_factor` ❹. After `self.center` has been updated, we use the new value to update `self.rect.centerx`, which controls the position of the ship ❺. Only the integer portion of `self.center` will be stored in `self.rect.centerx`, but that's fine for displaying the ship.

We need to pass `ai_settings` as an argument when we create an instance of `Ship` in *alien_invasion.py*:

alien_invasion.py

```
--snip--
def run_game():
    --snip--
    # Make a ship.
    ship = Ship(ai_settings, screen)
    --snip--
```

Now any value of `ship_speed_factor` greater than one will make the ship move faster. This will be helpful in making the ship respond quickly enough to shoot down aliens, and it will let us change the tempo of the game as the player progresses in gameplay.

Limiting the Ship's Range

At this point the ship will disappear off either edge of the screen if you hold down an arrow key long enough. Let's correct this so the ship stops moving when it reaches the edge of the screen. We do this by modifying the `update()` method in `Ship`:

ship.py

```
    def update(self):
        """Update the ship's position based on movement flags."""
        # Update the ship's center value, not the rect.
❶       if self.moving_right and self.rect.right < self.screen_rect.right:
            self.center += self.ai_settings.ship_speed_factor
❷       if self.moving_left and self.rect.left > 0:
            self.center -= self.ai_settings.ship_speed_factor

        # Update rect object from self.center.
        self.rect.centerx = self.center
```

This code checks the position of the ship before changing the value of `self.center`. The code `self.rect.right` returns the x-coordinate value of the right edge of the ship's `rect`. If this value is less than the value returned by `self.screen_rect.right`, the ship hasn't reached the right edge of the screen ❶. The same goes for the left edge: if the value of the left side of the `rect` is greater than zero, the ship hasn't reached the left edge of the screen ❷. This ensures the ship is within these bounds before adjusting the value of `self.center`.

If you run *alien_invasion.py* now, the ship should stop moving at either edge of the screen.

Refactoring check_events()

The `check_events()` function will increase in length as we continue to develop the game, so let's break `check_events()` into two more functions: one that handles `KEYDOWN` events and another that handles `KEYUP` events:

game_functions.py

```
def check_keydown_events(event, ship):
    """Respond to keypresses."""
    if event.key == pygame.K_RIGHT:
        ship.moving_right = True
    elif event.key == pygame.K_LEFT:
        ship.moving_left = True

def check_keyup_events(event, ship):
    """Respond to key releases."""
    if event.key == pygame.K_RIGHT:
        ship.moving_right = False
    elif event.key == pygame.K_LEFT:
        ship.moving_left = False
```

```
def check_events(ship):
    """Respond to keypresses and mouse events."""
    for event in pygame.event.get():
        if event.type == pygame.QUIT:
            sys.exit()
        elif event.type == pygame.KEYDOWN:
            check_keydown_events(event, ship)
        elif event.type == pygame.KEYUP:
            check_keyup_events(event, ship)
```

We make two new functions: `check_keydown_events()` and `check_keyup_events()`. Each needs an `event` parameter and a `ship` parameter. The bodies of these two functions are copied from `check_events()`, and we've replaced the old code with calls to the new functions. The `check_events()` function is simpler now with this cleaner code structure, which will make it easier to develop further responses to player input.

A Quick Recap

In the next section, we'll add the ability to shoot bullets, which involves a new file called *bullet.py* and some modifications to some of the files we already have. Right now, we have four files containing a number of classes, functions, and methods. To be clear about how the project is organized, let's review each of these files before adding more functionality.

alien_invasion.py

The main file, *alien_invasion.py*, creates a number of important objects used throughout the game: the settings are stored in `ai_settings`, the main display surface is stored in `screen`, and a `ship` instance is created in this file as well. Also stored in *alien_invasion.py* is the main loop of the game, which is a `while` loop that calls `check_events()`, `ship.update()`, and `update_screen()`.

alien_invasion.py is the only file you need to run when you want to play Alien Invasion. The other files—*settings.py*, *game_functions.py*, *ship.py*—contain code that is imported, directly or indirectly, into this file.

settings.py

The *settings.py* file contains the `Settings` class. This class only has an `__init__()` method, which initializes attributes controlling the game's appearance and the ship's speed.

game_functions.py

The *game_functions.py* file contains a number of functions that carry out the bulk of the work in the game. The `check_events()` function detects relevant events, such as keypresses and releases, and processes each of these types of events through the helper functions `check_keydown_events()` and check_keyup_events(). For now, these functions manage the movement of the ship. The game_functions module also contains update_screen(), which redraws the screen on each pass through the main loop.

ship.py

The *ship.py* file contains the Ship class. Ship has an __init__() method, an update() method to manage the ship's position, and a blitme() method to draw the ship to the screen. The actual image of the ship is stored in *ship.bmp*, which is in the *images* folder.

TRY IT YOURSELF

12-3. Rocket: Make a game that begins with a rocket in the center of the screen. Allow the player to move the rocket up, down, left, or right using the four arrow keys. Make sure the rocket never moves beyond any edge of the screen.

12-4. Keys: Make a Pygame file that creates an empty screen. In the event loop, print the event.key attribute whenever a pygame.KEYDOWN event is detected. Run the program and press various keys to see how Pygame responds.

Shooting Bullets

Now let's add the ability to shoot bullets. We'll write code that fires a bullet (a small rectangle) when the player presses the spacebar. Bullets will then travel straight up the screen until they disappear off the top of the screen.

Adding the Bullet Settings

First, update *settings.py* to include the values we'll need for a new Bullet class, at the end of the __init__() method:

settings.py

```
    def __init__(self):
        --snip--
        # Bullet settings
        self.bullet_speed_factor = 1
        self.bullet_width = 3
        self.bullet_height = 15
        self.bullet_color = 60, 60, 60
```

These settings create dark gray bullets with a width of 3 pixels and a height of 15 pixels. The bullets will travel slightly slower than the ship.

Creating the Bullet Class

Now create a *bullet.py* file to store our Bullet class. Here's the first part of *bullet.py*:

bullet.py

```
import pygame
from pygame.sprite import Sprite

class Bullet(Sprite):
    """A class to manage bullets fired from the ship"""

    def __init__(self, ai_settings, screen, ship):
        """Create a bullet object at the ship's current position."""
        super(Bullet, self).__init__()
        self.screen = screen

        # Create a bullet rect at (0, 0) and then set correct position.
❶       self.rect = pygame.Rect(0, 0, ai_settings.bullet_width,
            ai_settings.bullet_height)
❷       self.rect.centerx = ship.rect.centerx
❸       self.rect.top = ship.rect.top

        # Store the bullet's position as a decimal value.
❹       self.y = float(self.rect.y)

❺       self.color = ai_settings.bullet_color
        self.speed_factor = ai_settings.bullet_speed_factor
```

The Bullet class inherits from Sprite, which we import from the pygame.sprite module. When you use sprites, you can group related elements in your game and act on all the grouped elements at once. To create a bullet instance, __init__() needs the ai_settings, screen, and ship instances, and we call super() to inherit properly from Sprite.

NOTE *The call* super(Bullet, self).__init__() *uses Python 2.7 syntax. This works in Python 3 too, or you can also write this call more simply as* super().__init__().

At ❶, we create the bullet's rect attribute. The bullet is not based on an image so we have to build a rect from scratch using the pygame.Rect() class. This class requires the x- and y-coordinates of the top-left corner of the rect, and the width and height of the rect. We initialize the rect at (0, 0), but we'll move it to the correct location in the next two lines, because the bullet's position is dependent on the ship's position. We get the width and height of the bullet from the values stored in ai_settings.

At ❷, we set the bullet's centerx to be the same as the ship's rect.centerx. The bullet should emerge from the top of the ship, so we set the top of the bullet's rect to match the top of the ship's rect, making it look like the bullet is fired from the ship ❸.

We store a decimal value for the bullet's y-coordinate so we can make fine adjustments to the bullet's speed ❹. At ❺, we store the bullet's color and speed settings in self.color and self.speed_factor.

Here's the second part of *bullet.py*, `update()` and `draw_bullet()`:

bullet.py

```
    def update(self):
        """Move the bullet up the screen."""
        # Update the decimal position of the bullet.
❶       self.y -= self.speed_factor
        # Update the rect position.
❷       self.rect.y = self.y

    def draw_bullet(self):
        """Draw the bullet to the screen."""
❸       pygame.draw.rect(self.screen, self.color, self.rect)
```

The `update()` method manages the bullet's position. When a bullet is fired, it moves up the screen, which corresponds to a decreasing y-coordinate value; so to update the position, we subtract the amount stored in `self.speed_factor` from `self.y` ❶. We then use the value of `self.y` to set the value of `self.rect.y` ❷. The `speed_factor` attribute allows us to increase the speed of the bullets as the game progresses or as needed to refine the game's behavior. Once fired, a bullet's x-coordinate value never changes, so it will only travel vertically in a straight line.

When we want to draw a bullet, we'll call `draw_bullet()`. The `draw.rect()` function fills the part of the screen defined by the bullet's `rect` with the color stored in `self.color` ❸.

Storing Bullets in a Group

Now that we have a `Bullet` class and the necessary settings defined, we can write code to fire a bullet each time the player presses the spacebar. First, we'll create a group in *alien_invasion.py* to store all the live bullets so we can manage the bullets that have already been fired. This group will be an instance of the class `pygame.sprite.Group`, which behaves like a list with some extra functionality that's helpful when building games. We'll use this group to draw bullets to the screen on each pass through the main loop and to update each bullet's position:

alien_invasion.py

```
import pygame
from pygame.sprite import Group
--snip--

def run_game():
    --snip--
    # Make a ship.
    ship = Ship(ai_settings, screen)
    # Make a group to store bullets in.
❶   bullets = Group()

    # Start the main loop for the game.
    while True:
        gf.check_events(ai_settings, screen, ship, bullets)
        ship.update()
```

```
❷         bullets.update()
          gf.update_screen(ai_settings, screen, ship, bullets)

run_game()
```

We import Group from pygame.sprite. At ❶, we make an instance of Group and call it bullets. This group is created outside of the while loop so we don't create a new group of bullets each time the loop cycles.

NOTE *If you make a group like this inside the loop, you'll be creating thousands of groups of bullets and your game will probably slow to a crawl. If your game freezes up, look carefully at what's happening in your main* while *loop.*

We pass bullets to check_events() and update_screen(). We'll need to work with bullets in check_events() when the spacebar is pressed, and we'll need to update the bullets that are being drawn to the screen in update_screen().

When you call update() on a group ❷, the group automatically calls update() for each sprite in the group. The line bullets.update() calls bullet.update() for each bullet we place in the group bullets.

Firing Bullets

In *game_functions.py*, we need to modify check_keydown_events() to fire a bullet when the spacebar is pressed. We don't need to change check_keyup_events() because nothing happens when the key is released. We also need to modify update_screen() to make sure each bullet is redrawn to the screen before we call flip(). Here are the relevant changes to *game_functions.py*:

game_functions.py

```
--snip--
from bullet import Bullet

❶ def check_keydown_events(event, ai_settings, screen, ship, bullets):
      --snip--
❷     elif event.key == pygame.K_SPACE:
          # Create a new bullet and add it to the bullets group.
          new_bullet = Bullet(ai_settings, screen, ship)
          bullets.add(new_bullet)
         --snip--

❸ def check_events(ai_settings, screen, ship, bullets):
      """Respond to keypresses and mouse events."""
      for event in pygame.event.get():
          --snip--
          elif event.type == pygame.KEYDOWN:
              check_keydown_events(event, ai_settings, screen, ship, bullets)
          --snip--

❹ def update_screen(ai_settings, screen, ship, bullets):
      --snip--
      # Redraw all bullets behind ship and aliens.
❺     for bullet in bullets.sprites():
          bullet.draw_bullet()
```

```
        ship.blitme()
        --snip--
```

The group bullets is passed to check_keydown_events() ❶. When the player presses the spacebar, we create a new bullet (a Bullet instance that we name new_bullet) and add it to the group bullets ❷ using the add() method; the code bullets.add(new_bullet) stores the new bullet in the group bullets.

We need to add bullets as a parameter in the definition of check_events() ❸, and we need to pass bullets as an argument in the call to check_keydown_events() as well.

We give the bullets parameter to update_screen() at ❹, which draws the bullets to the screen. The bullets.sprites() method returns a list of all sprites in the group bullets. To draw all fired bullets to the screen, we loop through the sprites in bullets and call draw_bullet() on each one ❺.

If you run *alien_invasion.py* now, you should be able to move the ship right and left, and fire as many bullets as you want. The bullets travel up the screen and disappear when they reach the top, as shown in Figure 12-3. You can alter the size, color, and speed of the bullets in *settings.py*.

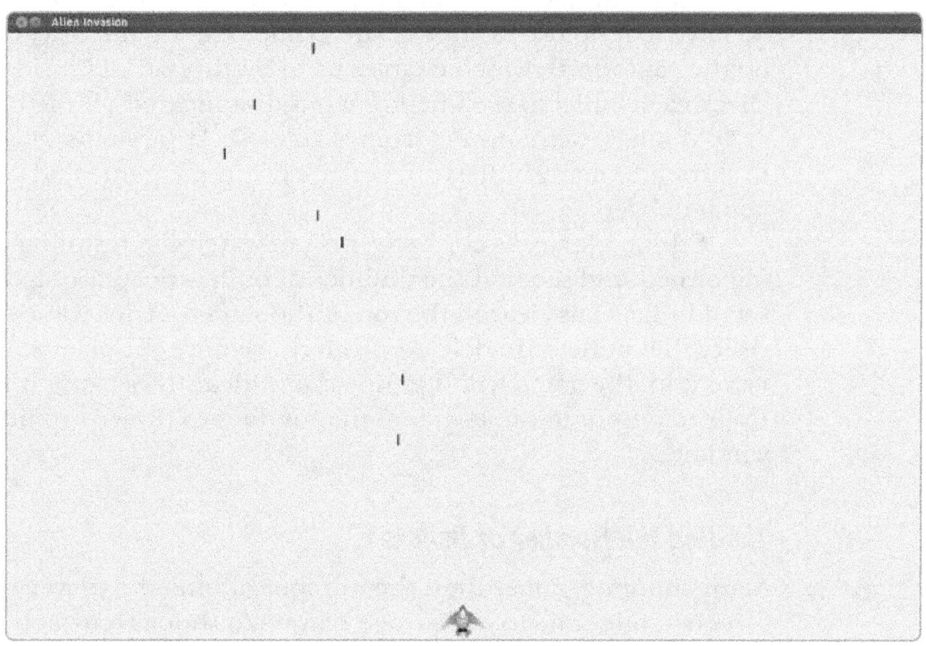

Figure 12-3: The ship after firing a series of bullets

Deleting Old Bullets

At the moment, the bullets disappear when they reach the top, but only because Pygame can't draw them above the top of the screen. The bullets actually continue to exist; their y-coordinate values just grow increasingly negative. This is a problem, because they continue to consume memory and processing power.

We need to get rid of these old bullets, or the game will slow down from doing so much unnecessary work. To do this, we need to detect when the `bottom` value of a bullet's `rect` has a value of 0, which indicates the bullet has passed off the top of the screen:

alien_invasion.py

```
# Start the main loop for the game.
while True:
    gf.check_events(ai_settings, screen, ship, bullets)
    ship.update()
    bullets.update()

    # Get rid of bullets that have disappeared.
❶   for bullet in bullets.copy():
❷       if bullet.rect.bottom <= 0:
❸           bullets.remove(bullet)
❹   print(len(bullets))

    gf.update_screen(ai_settings, screen, ship, bullets)
```

You shouldn't remove items from a list or group within a `for` loop, so we have to loop over a copy of the group. We use the `copy()` method to set up the `for` loop ❶, which enables us to modify `bullets` inside the loop. We check each bullet to see whether it has disappeared off the top of the screen at ❷. If it has, we remove it from `bullets` ❸. At ❹ we insert a `print` statement to show how many bullets currently exist in the game and verify that they're being deleted.

If this code works correctly, we can watch the terminal output while firing bullets and see that the number of bullets decreases to zero after each set of bullets has cleared the top of the screen. After you run the game and verify that bullets are deleted properly, remove the `print` statement. If you leave it in, the game will slow down significantly because it takes more time to write output to the terminal than it does to draw graphics to the game window.

Limiting the Number of Bullets

Many shooting games limit the number of bullets a player can have on the screen at one time to encourage players to shoot accurately. We'll do the same in Alien Invasion.

First, store the number of bullets allowed in *settings.py*:

settings.py

```
        # Bullet settings
        self.bullet_width = 3
        self.bullet_height = 15
        self.bullet_color = 60, 60, 60
        self.bullets_allowed = 3
```

This limits the player to three bullets at a time. We'll use this setting in *game_functions.py* to check how many bullets exist before creating a new bullet in `check_keydown_events()`:

game_functions.py

```
def check_keydown_events(event, ai_settings, screen, ship, bullets):
    --snip--
    elif event.key == pygame.K_SPACE:
        # Create a new bullet and add it to the bullets group.
        if len(bullets) < ai_settings.bullets_allowed:
            new_bullet = Bullet(ai_settings, screen, ship)
            bullets.add(new_bullet)
```

When the spacebar is pressed, we check the length of `bullets`. If `len(bullets)` is less than three, we create a new bullet. But if three bullets are already active, nothing happens when the spacebar is pressed. If you run the game now, you should be able to fire bullets only in groups of three.

Creating the update_bullets() Function

We want to keep our main *alien_invasion.py* program file as simple as possible, so now that we've written and checked the bullet management code we can move it to the `game_functions` module. We'll create a new function called `update_bullets()` and add it to the end of *game_functions.py*:

game_functions.py

```
def update_bullets(bullets):
    """Update position of bullets and get rid of old bullets."""
    # Update bullet positions.
    bullets.update()

    # Get rid of bullets that have disappeared.
    for bullet in bullets.copy():
        if bullet.rect.bottom <= 0:
            bullets.remove(bullet)
```

The code for `update_bullets()` is cut and pasted from *alien_invasion.py*; the only parameter it needs is the group `bullets`.

The `while` loop in *alien_invasion.py* looks simple again:

alien_invasion.py

```
    # Start the main loop for the game.
    while True:
❶       gf.check_events(ai_settings, screen, ship, bullets)
❷       ship.update()
❸       gf.update_bullets(bullets)
❹       gf.update_screen(ai_settings, screen, ship, bullets)
```

We've made it so that our main loop contains only minimal code so we can quickly read the function names and understand what's happening in the game. The main loop checks for player input at ❶, and then it updates the position of the ship at ❷ and any bullets that have been fired at ❸. We then use the updated positions to draw a new screen at ❹.

Creating the fire_bullet() Function

Let's move the code for firing a bullet to a separate function so we can use a single line of code to fire a bullet and keep the `elif` block in `check_keydown_events()` simple:

game_functions.py

```
def check_keydown_events(event, ai_settings, screen, ship, bullets):
    """Respond to keypresses."""
    --snip--
    elif event.key == pygame.K_SPACE:
        fire_bullet(ai_settings, screen, ship, bullets)

def fire_bullet(ai_settings, screen, ship, bullets):
    """Fire a bullet if limit not reached yet."""
    # Create a new bullet and add it to the bullets group.
    if len(bullets) < ai_settings.bullets_allowed:
        new_bullet = Bullet(ai_settings, screen, ship)
        bullets.add(new_bullet)
```

The function `fire_bullet()` simply contains the code that was used to fire a bullet when the spacebar is pressed, and we add a call to `fire_bullet()` in `check_keydown_events()` when the spacebar is pressed.

Run *alien_invasion.py* one more time, and make sure you can still fire bullets without errors.

TRY IT YOURSELF

12-5. Sideways Shooter: Write a game that places a ship on the left side of the screen and allows the player to move the ship up and down. Make the ship fire a bullet that travels right across the screen when the player presses the spacebar. Make sure bullets are deleted once they disappear off the screen.

Summary

In this chapter, you learned to make a plan for a game. You learned the basic structure of a game written in Pygame. You learned to set a background color and store settings in a separate class where they can be made available to all parts of the game. You saw how to draw an image to the screen and give the player control over the movement of game elements. You learned to create elements that move on their own, like bullets flying up a screen, and how to delete objects that are no longer needed. You learned to refactor code in a project on a regular basis to facilitate ongoing development.

In Chapter 13, we'll add aliens to Alien Invasion. By the end of Chapter 13, you'll be able to shoot down aliens, hopefully before they reach your ship!

13

ALIENS!

In this chapter we'll add aliens to Alien Invasion. First, we'll add one alien near the top of the screen, and then we'll generate a whole fleet of aliens. We'll make the fleet advance sideways and down, and we'll get rid of any aliens hit by a bullet. Finally, we'll limit the number of ships a player has and end the game when the player runs out of ships.

As you work through this chapter, you'll learn more about Pygame and about managing a larger project. You'll also learn to detect collisions between game objects, like bullets and aliens. Detecting collisions helps you define interactions between elements in your games: you can confine a character inside the walls of a maze or pass a ball between two characters. We'll also continue to work from a plan that we revisit occasionally to maintain the focus of our code-writing sessions.

Before we start writing new code to add a fleet of aliens to the screen, let's look at the project and update our plan.

Reviewing Your Project

When you're beginning a new phase of development on a larger project, it's always a good idea to revisit your plan and clarify what you want to accomplish with the code you're about to write. In this chapter we will:

- Examine our code and determine if we need to refactor before implementing new features.
- Add a single alien to the top-left corner of the screen with appropriate spacing around it.
- Use the spacing around the first alien and the overall screen size to determine how many aliens can fit on the screen. We'll write a loop to create aliens to fill the upper portion of the screen.
- Make the fleet move sideways and down until the entire fleet is shot down, an alien hits the ship, or an alien reaches the ground. If the whole fleet is shot down, we'll create a new fleet. If an alien hits the ship or the ground, we'll destroy the ship and create a new fleet.
- Limit the number of ships the player can use, and end the game when the player has used up the allotment of ships.

We'll refine this plan as we implement features, but this is sufficient to start with.

You should also review code when you're about to begin working on a new series of features in a project. Because each new phase typically makes a project more complex, it's best to clean up cluttered or inefficient code.

Although we don't have much cleanup to do right now because we've been refactoring as we go, it's annoying to use the mouse to close the game each time we run it to test a new feature. Let's quickly add a keyboard shortcut to end the game when the user presses Q:

game_functions.py

```
def check_keydown_events(event, ai_settings, screen, ship, bullets):
    --snip--
    elif event.key == pygame.K_q:
        sys.exit()
```

In `check_keydown_events()` we add a new block that ends the game when Q is pressed. This is a fairly safe change because the Q key is far from the arrow keys and the spacebar, so it's unlikely a player will accidentally press Q and quit the game. Now, when testing, you can press Q to close the game rather than using your mouse to close the window.

Creating the First Alien

Placing one alien on the screen is like placing a ship on the screen. The behavior of each alien is controlled by a class called `Alien`, which we'll structure like the `Ship` class. We'll continue using bitmap images for simplicity. You can find your own image for an alien or use the one shown in Figure 13-1, which is available in the book's resources through *https://www.nostarch.com/pythoncrashcourse/*. This image has a gray background, which matches the screen's background color. Make sure to save the image file you choose in the *images* folder.

Figure 13-1: The alien we'll use to build the fleet

Creating the Alien Class

Now we'll write the Alien class:

alien.py

```
import pygame
from pygame.sprite import Sprite

class Alien(Sprite):
    """A class to represent a single alien in the fleet."""

    def __init__(self, ai_settings, screen):
        """Initialize the alien and set its starting position."""
        super(Alien, self).__init__()
        self.screen = screen
        self.ai_settings = ai_settings

        # Load the alien image and set its rect attribute.
        self.image = pygame.image.load('images/alien.bmp')
        self.rect = self.image.get_rect()

        # Start each new alien near the top left of the screen.
❶       self.rect.x = self.rect.width
        self.rect.y = self.rect.height

        # Store the alien's exact position.
        self.x = float(self.rect.x)

    def blitme(self):
        """Draw the alien at its current location."""
        self.screen.blit(self.image, self.rect)
```

Most of this class is like the Ship class except for the placement of the alien. We initially place each alien near the top-left corner of the screen, adding a space to the left of it that's equal to the alien's width and a space above it equal to its height ❶.

Creating an Instance of the Alien

Now we create an instance of Alien in *alien_invasion.py*:

alien_invasion.py

```
--snip--
from ship import Ship
from alien import Alien
import game_functions as gf

def run_game():
    --snip--
    # Make an alien.
    alien = Alien(ai_settings, screen)

    # Start the main loop for the game.
    while True:
        gf.check_events(ai_settings, screen, ship, bullets)
        ship.update()
        gf.update_bullets(bullets)
        gf.update_screen(ai_settings, screen, ship, alien, bullets)

run_game()
```

Here we're importing the new Alien class and creating an instance of Alien just before entering the main while loop. Because we're not changing the alien's position yet, we aren't adding anything new inside the loop; however, we do modify the call to update_screen() to pass it the alien instance.

Making the Alien Appear Onscreen

To make the alien appear onscreen, we call its blitme() method in update_screen():

game_functions.py

```
def update_screen(ai_settings, screen, ship, alien, bullets):
    --snip--

    # Redraw all bullets behind ship and aliens.
    for bullet in bullets:
        bullet.draw_bullet()
    ship.blitme()
    alien.blitme()

    # Make the most recently drawn screen visible.
    pygame.display.flip()
```

We draw the alien onscreen after the ship and the bullets have been drawn, so the aliens will be the top layer of the screen. Figure 13-2 shows the first alien on the screen.

Figure 13-2: The first alien appears.

Now that the first alien appears correctly, we'll write the code to draw an entire fleet.

Building the Alien Fleet

To draw a fleet, we need to figure out how many aliens can fit across the screen and how many rows of aliens can fit down the screen. We'll first figure out the horizontal spacing between aliens and create a row; then we'll determine the vertical spacing and create an entire fleet.

Determining How Many Aliens Fit in a Row

To figure out how many aliens fit in a row, let's look at how much horizontal space we have. The screen width is stored in `ai_settings.screen_width`, but we need an empty margin on either side of the screen. We'll make this margin the width of one alien. Because we have two margins, the available space for aliens is the screen width minus two alien widths:

```
available_space_x = ai_settings.screen_width - (2 * alien_width)
```

We also need to set the spacing between aliens; we'll make it one alien width. The space needed to display one alien is twice its width: one width for the alien and one width for the empty space to its right. To find the number of aliens that fit across the screen, we divide the available space by two times the width of an alien:

```
number_aliens_x = available_space_x / (2 * alien_width)
```

We'll include these calculations when we create the fleet.

NOTE *One great aspect about calculations in programming is that you don't have to be sure your formula is correct when you first write it. You can try it out and see if it works. At worst, you'll have a screen that's overcrowded with aliens or has too few aliens. You can revise your calculation based on what you see on the screen.*

Creating Rows of Aliens

To create a row, first create an empty group called aliens in *alien_invasion.py* to hold all of our aliens, and then call a function in *game_functions.py* to create a fleet:

alien_invasion.py

```
import pygame
from pygame.sprite import Group
from settings import Settings
from ship import Ship
import game_functions as gf

def run_game():
    --snip--
    # Make a ship, a group of bullets, and a group of aliens.
    ship = Ship(ai_settings, screen)
    bullets = Group()
❶   aliens = Group()

    # Create the fleet of aliens.
❷   gf.create_fleet(ai_settings, screen, aliens)

    # Start the main loop for the game.
    while True:
        --snip—
❸       gf.update_screen(ai_settings, screen, ship, aliens, bullets)

run_game()
```

Because we're no longer creating aliens directly in *alien_invasion.py*, we don't need to import the Alien class into this file.

Create an empty group to hold all of the aliens in the game ❶. Then, call the new function create_fleet() ❷, which we'll write shortly, and pass it the ai_settings, the screen object, and the empty group aliens. Next, modify the call to update_screen() to give it access to the group of aliens ❸.

We also need to modify update_screen():

game_functions.py

```
def update_screen(ai_settings, screen, ship, aliens, bullets):
    --snip--
    ship.blitme()
    aliens.draw(screen)

    # Make the most recently drawn screen visible.
    pygame.display.flip()
```

When you call draw() on a group, Pygame automatically draws each element in the group at the position defined by its rect attribute. In this case, aliens.draw(screen) draws each alien in the group to the screen.

Creating the Fleet

Now we can create the fleet. Here's the new function create_fleet(), which we place at the end of *game_functions.py*. We also need to import the Alien class, so make sure you add an import statement at the top of the file:

game_functions.py

```
--snip--
from bullet import Bullet
from alien import Alien
--snip--

def create_fleet(ai_settings, screen, aliens):
    """Create a full fleet of aliens."""
    # Create an alien and find the number of aliens in a row.
    # Spacing between each alien is equal to one alien width.
❶   alien = Alien(ai_settings, screen)
❷   alien_width = alien.rect.width
❸   available_space_x = ai_settings.screen_width - 2 * alien_width
❹   number_aliens_x = int(available_space_x / (2 * alien_width))

    # Create the first row of aliens.
❺   for alien_number in range(number_aliens_x):
        # Create an alien and place it in the row.
❻       alien = Alien(ai_settings, screen)
        alien.x = alien_width + 2 * alien_width * alien_number
        alien.rect.x = alien.x
        aliens.add(alien)
```

We've already thought through most of this code. We need to know the alien's width and height in order to place aliens, so we create an alien at ❶ before we perform calculations. This alien won't be part of the fleet, so don't add it to the group aliens. At ❷ we get the alien's width from its rect attribute and store this value in alien_width so we don't have to keep working through the rect attribute. At ❸ we calculate the horizontal space available for aliens and the number of aliens that can fit into that space.

The only change here from our original formulas is that we're using int() to ensure we end up with an integer number of aliens ❹ because we don't want to create partial aliens, and the range() function needs an integer. The `int()` function drops the decimal part of a number, effectively rounding down. (This is helpful because we'd rather have a little extra space in each row than an overly crowded row.)

Next, set up a loop that counts from 0 to the number of aliens we need to make ❺. In the main body of the loop, create a new alien and then set its x-coordinate value to place it in the row ❻. Each alien is pushed to the right one alien width from the left margin. Next, we multiply the alien width by 2 to account for the space each alien takes up, including the empty space to its right, and we multiply this amount by the alien's position in the row. Then we add each new alien to the group `aliens`.

When you run Alien Invasion, you should see the first row of aliens appear, as in Figure 13-3.

Figure 13-3: The first row of aliens

The first row is offset to the left, which is actually good for gameplay because we want the fleet to move right until it hits the edge of the screen, then drop down a bit, then move left, and so forth. Like the classic game *Space Invaders*, this movement is more interesting than having the fleet drop straight down. We'll continue this motion until all aliens are shot down or until an alien hits the ship or the bottom of the screen.

NOTE *Depending on the screen width you've chosen, the alignment of the first row of aliens may look slightly different on your system.*

Refactoring create_fleet()

If we were finished creating a fleet, we'd probably leave create_fleet() as is, but we have more work to do, so let's clean up the function a bit. Here's create_fleet() with two new functions: get_number_aliens_x() and create_alien():

game_functions.py

```
❶ def get_number_aliens_x(ai_settings, alien_width):
      """Determine the number of aliens that fit in a row."""
      available_space_x = ai_settings.screen_width - 2 * alien_width
      number_aliens_x = int(available_space_x / (2 * alien_width))
      return number_aliens_x

  def create_alien(ai_settings, screen, aliens, alien_number):
      """Create an alien and place it in the row."""
      alien = Alien(ai_settings, screen)
❷     alien_width = alien.rect.width
      alien.x = alien_width + 2 * alien_width * alien_number
      alien.rect.x = alien.x
      aliens.add(alien)

  def create_fleet(ai_settings, screen, aliens):
      """Create a full fleet of aliens."""
      # Create an alien and find the number of aliens in a row.
      alien = Alien(ai_settings, screen)
❸     number_aliens_x = get_number_aliens_x(ai_settings, alien.rect.width)

      # Create the first row of aliens.
      for alien_number in range(number_aliens_x):
❹         create_alien(ai_settings, screen, aliens, alien_number)
```

The body of get_number_aliens_x() is exactly as it was in create_fleet() ❶. The body of create_alien() is also unchanged from create_fleet() except that we use the alien that was just created to get the alien width ❷. At ❸ we replace the code for determining the horizontal spacing with a call to get_number_aliens_x(), and we remove the line referring to alien_width, because that's now handled inside create_alien(). At ❹ we call create_alien(). This refactoring will make it easier to add new rows and create an entire fleet.

Adding Rows

To finish the fleet, determine the number of rows that fit on the screen and then repeat the loop (for creating the aliens in one row) that number of times. To determine the number of rows, we find the available vertical space by subtracting the alien height from the top, the ship height from the bottom, and two alien heights from the bottom of the screen:

```
available_space_y = ai_settings.screen_height - 3 * alien_height - ship_height
```

The result will create some empty space above the ship, so the player has some time to start shooting aliens at the beginning of each level.

Each row needs some empty space below it, which we'll make equal to the height of one alien. To find the number of rows, we divide the available space by two times the height of an alien. (Again, if these calculations are off, we'll see it right away and adjust until we have reasonable spacing.)

```
number_rows = available_height_y / (2 * alien_height)
```

Now that we know how many rows fit in a fleet, we can repeat the code for creating a row:

game_functions.py

```
❶ def get_number_rows(ai_settings, ship_height, alien_height):
      """Determine the number of rows of aliens that fit on the screen."""
❷     available_space_y = (ai_settings.screen_height -
                              (3 * alien_height) - ship_height)
      number_rows = int(available_space_y / (2 * alien_height))
      return number_rows

  def create_alien(ai_settings, screen, aliens, alien_number, row_number):
      --snip--
      alien.x = alien_width + 2 * alien_width * alien_number
      alien.rect.x = alien.x
❸     alien.rect.y = alien.rect.height + 2 * alien.rect.height * row_number
      aliens.add(alien)

  def create_fleet(ai_settings, screen, ship, aliens):
      --snip--
      number_aliens_x = get_number_aliens_x(ai_settings, alien.rect.width)
      number_rows = get_number_rows(ai_settings, ship.rect.height,
          alien.rect.height)

      # Create the fleet of aliens.
❹     for row_number in range(number_rows):
          for alien_number in range(number_aliens_x):
              create_alien(ai_settings, screen, aliens, alien_number,
                  row_number)
```

To calculate the number of rows we can fit on the screen, we write our `available_space_y` and `number_rows` calculations into the function `get_number_rows()` ❶, which is similar to `get_number_aliens_x()`. The calculation is wrapped in parentheses so the outcome can be split over two lines, which results in lines of 79 characters or less as is recommended ❷. We use `int()` because we don't want to create a partial row of aliens.

To create multiple rows, we use two nested loops: one outer and one inner loop ❹. The inner loop creates the aliens in one row. The outer loop counts from 0 to the number of rows we want; Python will use the code for making a single row and repeat it `number_rows` times.

To nest the loops, write the new `for` loop and indent the code you want to repeat. (Most text editors make it easy to indent and unindent blocks of code, but for help see Appendix B.) Now when we call `create_alien()`, we include an argument for the row number so each row can be placed farther down the screen.

The definition of `create_alien()` needs a parameter to hold the row number. Within `create_alien()`, we change an alien's y-coordinate value when it's not in the first row ❸ by starting with one alien's height to create empty space at the top of the screen. Each row starts two alien heights below the last row, so we multiply the alien height by two and then by the row number. The first row number is 0, so the vertical placement of the first row is unchanged. All subsequent rows are placed farther down the screen.

The definition of `create_fleet()` also has a new parameter for the `ship` object, which means we need to include the `ship` argument in the call to `create_fleet()` in *alien_invasion.py*:

alien_invasion.py

```
# Create the fleet of aliens.
gf.create_fleet(ai_settings, screen, ship, aliens)
```

When you run the game now, you should see a fleet of aliens, as in Figure 13-4.

Figure 13-4: The full fleet appears.

In the next section, we'll make the fleet move!

TRY IT YOURSELF

13-1. Stars: Find an image of a star. Make a grid of stars appear on the screen.

13-2. Better Stars: You can make a more realistic star pattern by introducing randomness when you place each star. Recall that you can get a random number like this:

```
from random import randint
random_number = randint(-10,10)
```

This code returns a random integer between −10 and 10. Using your code in Exercise 13-1, adjust each star's position by a random amount.

Making the Fleet Move

Now let's make our fleet of aliens move to the right across the screen until it hits the edge, and then make it drop a set amount and move in the other direction. We'll continue this movement until all aliens have been shot down, one collides with the ship, or one reaches the bottom of the screen. Let's begin by making the fleet move to the right.

Moving the Aliens Right

To move the aliens, we'll use an `update()` method in *alien.py*, which we'll call for each alien in the group of aliens. First, add a setting to control the speed of each alien:

settings.py

```
def __init__(self):
    --snip--
    # Alien settings
    self.alien_speed_factor = 1
```

Then, use this setting to implement `update()`:

alien.py

```
def update(self):
    """Move the alien right."""
❶   self.x += self.ai_settings.alien_speed_factor
❷   self.rect.x = self.x
```

Each time we update an alien's position, we move it to the right by the amount stored in `alien_speed_factor`. We track the alien's exact position with the `self.x` attribute, which can hold decimal values ❶. We then use the value of `self.x` to update the position of the alien's rect ❷.

In the main while loop, we have calls to update the ship and bullets. Now we need to update the position of each alien as well:

alien_invasion.py

```
# Start the main loop for the game.
while True:
    gf.check_events(ai_settings, screen, ship, bullets)
    ship.update()
    gf.update_bullets(bullets)
    gf.update_aliens(aliens)
    gf.update_screen(ai_settings, screen, ship, aliens, bullets)
```

We update the aliens' positions after the bullets have been updated, because we'll soon be checking to see whether any bullets hit any aliens.

Finally, add the new function update_aliens() at the end of the file *game_functions.py*:

game_functions.py

```
def update_aliens(aliens):
    """Update the postions of all aliens in the fleet."""
    aliens.update()
```

We use the update() method on the aliens group, which automatically calls each alien's update() method. When you run Alien Invasion now, you should see the fleet move right and disappear off the side of the screen.

Creating Settings for Fleet Direction

Now we'll create the settings that will make the fleet move down the screen and to the left when it hits the right edge of the screen. Here's how to implement this behavior:

settings.py

```
        # Alien settings
        self.alien_speed_factor = 1
        self.fleet_drop_speed = 10
        # fleet_direction of 1 represents right; -1 represents left.
        self.fleet_direction = 1
```

The setting fleet_drop_speed controls how quickly the fleet drops down the screen each time an alien reaches either edge. It's helpful to separate this speed from the aliens' horizontal speed so you can adjust the two speeds independently.

To implement the setting fleet_direction, we could use a text value, such as 'left' or 'right', but we'd end up with if-elif statements testing for the fleet direction. Instead, because we have only two directions to deal with, let's use the values 1 and –1 and switch between them each time the fleet changes direction. (Using numbers also makes sense because moving right involves adding to each alien's x-coordinate value, and moving left involves subtracting from each alien's x-coordinate value.)

Checking to See Whether an Alien Has Hit the Edge

Now we need a method to check whether an alien is at either edge, and we need to modify `update()` to allow each alien to move in the appropriate direction:

alien.py

```
    def check_edges(self):
        """Return True if alien is at edge of screen."""
        screen_rect = self.screen.get_rect()
❶       if self.rect.right >= screen_rect.right:
            return True
❷       elif self.rect.left <= 0:
            return True

    def update(self):
        """Move the alien right or left."""
❸       self.x += (self.ai_settings.alien_speed_factor *
                        self.ai_settings.fleet_direction)
        self.rect.x = self.x
```

We can call the new method `check_edges()` on any alien to see if it's at the left or right edge. The alien is at the right edge if the `right` attribute of its `rect` is greater than or equal to the `right` attribute of the screen's `rect` ❶. It's at the left edge if its `left` value is less than or equal to 0 ❷.

We modify the method `update()` to allow motion to the left or right ❸ by multiplying the alien's speed factor by the value of `fleet_direction`. If `fleet_direction` is 1, the value of `alien_speed_factor` will be added to the alien's current position, moving the alien to the right; if `fleet_direction` is –1, the value will be subtracted from the alien's position, moving the alien to the left.

Dropping the Fleet and Changing Direction

When an alien reaches the edge, the entire fleet needs to drop down and change direction. We therefore need to make some substantial changes in *game_functions.py* because that's where we check to see if any aliens are at the left or right edge. We'll make this happen by writing the functions `check_fleet_edges()` and `change_fleet_direction()`, and then modifying `update_aliens()`:

game_functions.py

```
def check_fleet_edges(ai_settings, aliens):
    """Respond appropriately if any aliens have reached an edge."""
❶   for alien in aliens.sprites():
        if alien.check_edges():
            change_fleet_direction(ai_settings, aliens)
            break
```

```
def change_fleet_direction(ai_settings, aliens):
    """Drop the entire fleet and change the fleet's direction."""
    for alien in aliens.sprites():
❷       alien.rect.y += ai_settings.fleet_drop_speed
    ai_settings.fleet_direction *= -1

def update_aliens(ai_settings, aliens):
    """
    Check if the fleet is at an edge,
      and then update the postions of all aliens in the fleet.
    """
❸   check_fleet_edges(ai_settings, aliens)
    aliens.update()
```

In `check_fleet_edges()`, we loop through the fleet and call `check_edges()` on each alien ❶. If `check_edges()` returns `True`, we know an alien is at an edge and the whole fleet needs to change direction, so we call `change_fleet_direction()` and break out of the loop. In `change_fleet_direction()`, we loop through all the aliens and drop each one using the setting `fleet_drop_speed` ❷; then we change the value of `fleet_direction` by multiplying its current value by –1.

We've modified the function `update_aliens()` to determine whether any aliens are at an edge by calling `check_fleet_edges()` ❸. This function needs an `ai_settings` parameter, so we include an argument for `ai_settings` in the call to `update_aliens()`:

alien_invasion.py

```
    # Start the main loop for the game.
    while True:
        gf.check_events(ai_settings, screen, ship, bullets)
        ship.update()
        gf.update_bullets(bullets)
        gf.update_aliens(ai_settings, aliens)
        gf.update_screen(ai_settings, screen, ship, aliens, bullets)
```

If you run the game now, the fleet should move back and forth between the edges of the screen and drop down every time it hits an edge. Now we can begin shooting down aliens and watch for any aliens that hit the ship or reach the bottom of the screen.

TRY IT YOURSELF

13-3. Raindrops: Find an image of a raindrop and create a grid of raindrops. Make the raindrops fall toward the bottom of the screen until they disappear.

13-4. Steady Rain: Modify your code in Exercise 13-3 so that when a row of raindrops disappears off the bottom of the screen, a new row appears at the top of the screen and begins to fall.

Shooting Aliens

We've built our ship and a fleet of aliens, but when the bullets reach the aliens, they simply pass through because we aren't checking for collisions. In game programming, *collisions* happen when game elements overlap. To make the bullets shoot down aliens, we'll use the method sprite.groupcollide() to look for collisions between members of two groups.

Detecting Bullet Collisions

We want to know right away when a bullet hits an alien so we can make an alien disappear as soon as it's hit. To do this, we'll look for collisions immediately after updating a bullet's position.

The sprite.groupcollide() method compares each bullet's rect with each alien's rect and returns a dictionary containing the bullets and aliens that have collided. Each key in the dictionary is a bullet, and the corresponding value is the alien that was hit. (We'll use this dictionary when we implement a scoring system in Chapter 14.)

Use this code to check for collisions in the update_bullets() function:

game_functions.py

```
def update_bullets(aliens, bullets):
    """Update position of bullets and get rid of old bullets."""
    --snip--
    # Check for any bullets that have hit aliens.
    # If so, get rid of the bullet and the alien.
    collisions = pygame.sprite.groupcollide(bullets, aliens, True, True)
```

The new line we added loops through each bullet in the group bullets and then loops through each alien in the group aliens. Whenever the rects of a bullet and alien overlap, groupcollide() adds a key-value pair to the dictionary it returns. The two True arguments tell Pygame whether to delete the bullets and aliens that have collided. (To make a high-powered bullet that's able to travel to the top of the screen, destroying every alien in its path, you could set the first Boolean argument to False and keep the second Boolean argument set to True. The aliens hit would disappear, but all bullets would stay active until they disappeared off the top of the screen.)

We pass the argument aliens in the call to update_bullets():

alien_invasion.py

```
    # Start the main loop for the game.
    while True:
        gf.check_events(ai_settings, screen, ship, bullets)
        ship.update()
        gf.update_bullets(aliens, bullets)
        gf.update_aliens(ai_settings, aliens)
        gf.update_screen(ai_settings, screen, ship, aliens, bullets)
```

When you run Alien Invasion now, aliens you hit should disappear. Figure 13-5 shows a fleet that has been partially shot down.

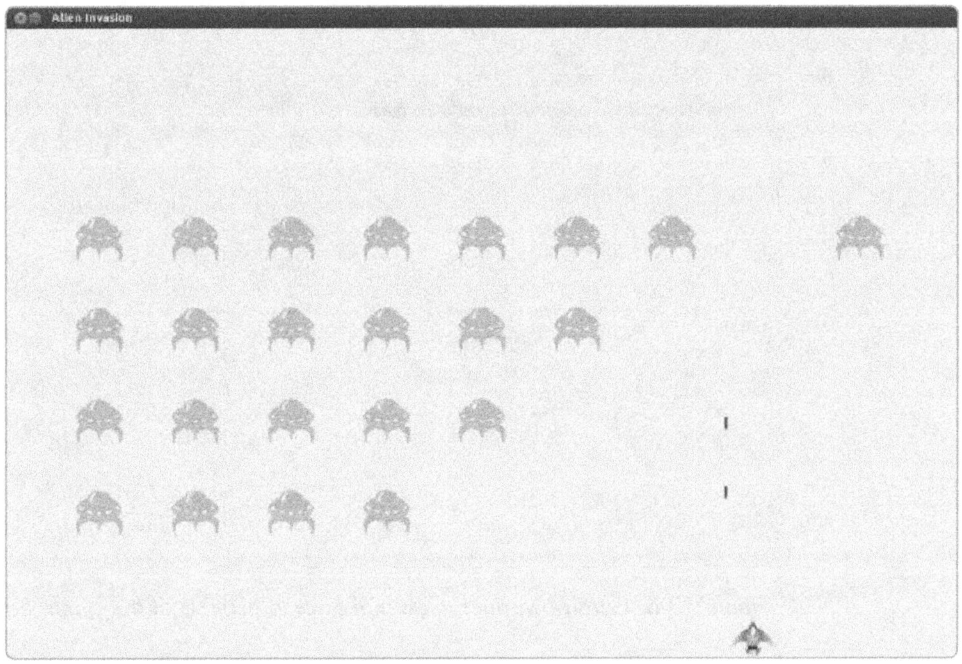

Figure 13-5: We can shoot aliens!

Making Larger Bullets for Testing

You can test many features of the game simply by running the game, but some features are tedious to test in the normal version of a game. For example, it's a lot of work to shoot down every alien on the screen multiple times to test if your code responds to an empty fleet correctly.

To test particular features, you can change certain game settings to focus on a particular area. For example, you might shrink the screen so there are fewer aliens to shoot down or increase the bullet speed and give yourself lots of bullets at once.

My favorite change for testing Alien Invasion is to use superwide bullets that remain active even after they've hit an alien (see Figure 13-6). Try setting `bullet_width` to 300 to see how quickly you can shoot down the fleet!

Changes like these will help you test the game more efficiently and possibly spark ideas for giving players bonus powers. (Just remember to restore the settings to normal once you're finished testing a feature.)

Figure 13-6: Extra-powerful bullets make some aspects of the game easier to test.

Repopulating the Fleet

One key feature of Alien Invasion is that the aliens are relentless: every time the fleet is destroyed, a new fleet should appear.

To make a new fleet of aliens appear after a fleet has been destroyed, first check to see whether the group `aliens` is empty. If it is, we call `create_fleet()`. We'll perform this check in `update_bullets()` because that's where individual aliens are destroyed:

game_functions.py

```
def update_bullets(ai_settings, screen, ship, aliens, bullets):
    --snip--
    # Check for any bullets that have hit aliens.
    # If so, get rid of the bullet and the alien.
    collisions = pygame.sprite.groupcollide(bullets, aliens, True, True)

❶   if len(aliens) == 0:
        # Destroy existing bullets and create new fleet.
❷       bullets.empty()
        create_fleet(ai_settings, screen, ship, aliens)
```

At ❶ we check whether the group `aliens` is empty. If it is, we get rid of any existing bullets by using the `empty()` method, which removes all the remaining sprites from a group ❷. We also call `create_fleet()`, which fills the screen with aliens again.

The definition of update_bullets() now has the additional parameters ai_settings, screen, and ship, so we need to update the call to update_bullets() in *alien_invasion.py*:

alien_invasion.py

```
    # Start the main loop for the game.
    while True:
        gf.check_events(ai_settings, screen, ship, bullets)
        ship.update()
        gf.update_bullets(ai_settings, screen, ship, aliens, bullets)
        gf.update_aliens(ai_settings, aliens)
        gf.update_screen(ai_settings, screen, ship, aliens, bullets)
```

Now a new fleet appears as soon as you destroy the current fleet.

Speeding Up the Bullets

If you've tried firing at the aliens in the game's current state, you may have noticed that the bullets have slowed down a bit. This is because Pygame is now doing more work on each pass through the loop. We can increase the speed of the bullets by adjusting the value of bullet_speed_factor in *settings.py*. If we increase this value (to 3, for example), the bullets should travel up the screen at a reasonable speed again:

settings.py

```
        # Bullet settings
        self.bullet_speed_factor = 3
        self.bullet_width = 3
        --snip--
```

The best value for this setting depends on the speed of your system, so find a value that works for you.

Refactoring update_bullets()

Let's refactor update_bullets() so it's not doing so many different tasks. We'll move the code for dealing with bullet-alien collisions to a separate function:

game_functions.py

```
def update_bullets(ai_settings, screen, ship, aliens, bullets):
    --snip--
    # Get rid of bullets that have disappeared.
    for bullet in bullets.copy():
        if bullet.rect.bottom <= 0:
            bullets.remove(bullet)

    check_bullet_alien_collisions(ai_settings, screen, ship, aliens, bullets)

def check_bullet_alien_collisions(ai_settings, screen, ship, aliens, bullets):
    """Respond to bullet-alien collisions."""
    # Remove any bullets and aliens that have collided.
    collisions = pygame.sprite.groupcollide(bullets, aliens, True, True)
```

```
    if len(aliens) == 0:
        # Destroy existing bullets and create new fleet.
        bullets.empty()
        create_fleet(ai_settings, screen, ship, aliens)
```

We've created a new function, `check_bullet_alien_collisions()`, to look for collisions between bullets and aliens, and to respond appropriately if the entire fleet has been destroyed. This keeps `update_bullets()` from growing too long and simplifies further development.

> **TRY IT YOURSELF**
>
> **13-5. Catch:** Create a game that places a character that you can move left and right at the bottom of the screen. Make a ball appear at a random position at the top of the screen and fall down the screen at a steady rate. If your character "catches" the ball by colliding with it, make the ball disappear. Make a new ball each time your character catches the ball or whenever the ball disappears off the bottom of the screen.

Ending the Game

What's the fun and challenge in a game if you can't lose? If the player doesn't shoot down the fleet quickly enough, we'll have the aliens destroy the ship if they hit it. At the same time, we'll limit the number of ships a player can use and we'll destroy the ship when an alien reaches the bottom of the screen. We'll end the game when the player has used up all their ships.

Detecting Alien-Ship Collisions

We'll start by checking for collisions between aliens and the ship so we can respond appropriately when an alien hits it. We'll check for alien-ship collisions immediately after updating the position of each alien:

game_functions.py

```
def update_aliens(ai_settings, ship, aliens):
    """
    Check if the fleet is at an edge,
      and then update the postions of all aliens in the fleet.
    """
    check_fleet_edges(ai_settings, aliens)
    aliens.update()

    # Look for alien-ship collisions.
❶   if pygame.sprite.spritecollideany(ship, aliens):
❷       print("Ship hit!!!")
```

The method spritecollideany() takes two arguments: a sprite and a group. The method looks for any member of the group that's collided with the sprite and stops looping through the group as soon as it finds one member that has collided with the sprite. Here, it loops through the group aliens and returns the first alien it finds that has collided with ship.

If no collisions occur, spritecollideany() returns None and the if block at ❶ won't execute. If it finds an alien that's collided with the ship, it returns that alien and the if block executes: it prints *Ship hit!!!* ❷. (When an alien hits the ship, we'll need to do a number of tasks: we'll need to delete all remaining aliens and bullets, recenter the ship, and create a new fleet. Before we write code to do all this, we need to know that our approach for detecting alien-ship collisions works correctly. Writing a print statement is a simple way to ensure we're detecting collisions properly.)

Now we need to pass ship to update_aliens():

alien_invasion.py

```
    # Start the main loop for the game.
    while True:
        gf.check_events(ai_settings, screen, ship, bullets)
        ship.update()
        gf.update_bullets(ai_settings, screen, ship, aliens, bullets)
        gf.update_aliens(ai_settings, ship, aliens)
        gf.update_screen(ai_settings, screen, ship, aliens, bullets)
```

Now when you run Alien Invasion, *Ship hit!!!* should appear in the terminal whenever an alien runs into the ship. When testing this feature, set alien_drop_speed to a higher value such as 50 or 100 so that the aliens will reach your ship faster.

Responding to Alien-Ship Collisions

Now we need to figure out what happens when an alien collides with the ship. Instead of destroying the ship instance and creating a new one, we'll count how many times the ship has been hit by tracking statistics for the game. (Tracking statistics will also be useful for scoring.)

Let's write a new class, GameStats, to track game statistics, and save it as *game_stats.py*:

game_stats.py

```
class GameStats():
    """Track statistics for Alien Invasion."""

    def __init__(self, ai_settings):
        """Initialize statistics."""
        self.ai_settings = ai_settings
❶       self.reset_stats()

    def reset_stats(self):
        """Initialize statistics that can change during the game."""
        self.ships_left = self.ai_settings.ship_limit
```

We'll make one GameStats instance for the entire time Alien Invasion is running, but we'll need to reset some statistics each time the player starts a new game. To do this, we'll initialize most of the statistics in the method reset_stats() instead of directly in __init__(). We'll call this method from __init__() so the statistics are set properly when the GameStats instance is first created ❶, but we'll also be able to call reset_stats() any time the player starts a new game.

Right now we have only one statistic, ships_left, the value of which will change throughout the game. The number of ships the player starts with is stored in *settings.py* as ship_limit:

settings.py

```
    # Ship settings
    self.ship_speed_factor = 1.5
    self.ship_limit = 3
```

We also need to make a few changes in *alien_invasion.py*, to create an instance of GameStats:

alien_invasion.py

```
  --snip--
  from settings import Settings
❶ from game_stats import GameStats
  --snip--

  def run_game():
      --snip--
      pygame.display.set_caption("Alien Invasion")

      # Create an instance to store game statistics.
❷     stats = GameStats(ai_settings)
      --snip--
      # Start the main loop for the game.
      while True:
          --snip--
          gf.update_bullets(ai_settings, screen, ship, aliens, bullets)
❸         gf.update_aliens(ai_settings, stats, screen, ship, aliens, bullets)
          --snip--
```

We import the new GameStats class ❶, make a stats instance ❷, and then add the stats, screen, and ship arguments in the call to update_aliens() ❸. We'll use these arguments to track the number of ships the player has left and to build a new fleet when an alien hits the ship.

When an alien hits the ship, we subtract one from the number of ships left, destroy all existing aliens and bullets, create a new fleet, and reposition the ship in the middle of the screen. (We'll also pause the game for a moment so the player can notice the collision and regroup before a new fleet appears.)

Let's put most of this code in the function ship_hit():

game_functions.py

```
  import sys
❶ from time import sleep

  import pygame
  --snip--
```

```
def ship_hit(ai_settings, stats, screen, ship, aliens, bullets):
    """Respond to ship being hit by alien."""
    # Decrement ships_left.
❷   stats.ships_left -= 1

    # Empty the list of aliens and bullets.
❸   aliens.empty()
    bullets.empty()

    # Create a new fleet and center the ship.
❹   create_fleet(ai_settings, screen, ship, aliens)
    ship.center_ship()

    # Pause.
❺   sleep(0.5)

❻ def update_aliens(ai_settings, stats, screen, ship, aliens, bullets):
    --snip--
    # Look for alien-ship collisions.
    if pygame.sprite.spritecollideany(ship, aliens):
        ship_hit(ai_settings, stats, screen, ship, aliens, bullets)
```

We first import the sleep() function from the time module to pause the game ❶. The new function ship_hit() coordinates the response when the ship is hit by an alien. Inside ship_hit(), the number of ships left is reduced by 1 ❷, after which we empty the groups aliens and bullets ❸.

Next, we create a new fleet and center the ship ❹. (We'll add the method center_ship() to Ship in a moment.) Finally, we pause after the updates have been made to all the game elements but before any changes have been drawn to the screen so the player can see that their ship has been hit ❺. The screen will freeze momentarily, and the player will see that the alien has hit the ship. When the sleep() function ends, the code will move on to the update_screen() function, which will draw the new fleet to the screen.

We also update the definition of update_aliens() to include the parameters stats, screen, and bullets ❻ so it can pass these values in the call to ship_hit().

Here's the new method center_ship(); add it to the end of *ship.py*:

ship.py

```
    def center_ship(self):
        """Center the ship on the screen."""
        self.center = self.screen_rect.centerx
```

To center the ship, we set the value of the ship's center attribute to match the center of the screen, which we get through the screen_rect attribute.

NOTE *Notice that we never make more than one ship; we make only one ship instance for the whole game and recenter it whenever the ship has been hit. The statistic* ships_left *will tell us when the player has run out of ships.*

Run the game, shoot a few aliens, and let an alien hit the ship. The game should pause, and a new fleet should appear with the ship centered at the bottom of the screen again.

Aliens that Reach the Bottom of the Screen

If an alien reaches the bottom of the screen, we'll respond the same way we do when an alien hits the ship. Add a new function to perform this check, and call it from `update_aliens()`:

game_functions.py

```
def check_aliens_bottom(ai_settings, stats, screen, ship, aliens, bullets):
    """Check if any aliens have reached the bottom of the screen."""
    screen_rect = screen.get_rect()
    for alien in aliens.sprites():
❶       if alien.rect.bottom >= screen_rect.bottom:
            # Treat this the same as if the ship got hit.
            ship_hit(ai_settings, stats, screen, ship, aliens, bullets)
            break

def update_aliens(ai_settings, stats, screen, ship, aliens, bullets):
    --snip--
    # Look for aliens hitting the bottom of the screen.
❷   check_aliens_bottom(ai_settings, stats, screen, ship, aliens, bullets)
```

The function `check_aliens_bottom()` checks to see whether any aliens have reached the bottom of the screen. An alien reaches the bottom when its `rect.bottom` value is greater than or equal to the screen's `rect.bottom` attribute ❶. If an alien reaches the bottom, we call `ship_hit()`. If one alien hits the bottom, there's no need to check the rest, so we break out of the loop after calling `ship_hit()`.

We call `check_aliens_bottom()` after updating the positions of all the aliens and after looking for alien-ship collisions ❷. Now a new fleet will appear every time the ship is hit by an alien or an alien reaches the bottom of the screen.

Game Over!

Alien Invasion feels more complete now, but the game never ends. The value of `ships_left` just grows increasingly negative. Let's add a `game_active` flag as an attribute to `GameStats` to end the game when the player runs out of ships:

game_stats.py

```
    def __init__(self, settings):
        --snip--
        # Start Alien Invasion in an active state.
        self.game_active = True
```

Now we add code to ship_hit() that sets game_active to False if the player has used up all their ships:

game_functions.py

```
def ship_hit(ai_settings, stats, screen, ship, aliens, bullets):
    """Respond to ship being hit by alien."""
    if stats.ships_left > 0:
        # Decrement ships_left.
        stats.ships_left -= 1
        --snip--
        # Pause.
        sleep(0.5)

    else:
        stats.game_active = False
```

Most of ship_hit() is unchanged. We've moved all of the existing code into an if block, which tests to make sure the player has at least one ship remaining. If so, we create a new fleet, pause, and move on. If the player has no ships left, we set game_active to False.

Identifying When Parts of the Game Should Run

In *alien_invasion.py* we need to identify the parts of the game that should always run and the parts that should run only when the game is active:

alien_invasion.py

```
    # Start the main loop for the game.
    while True:
        gf.check_events(ai_settings, screen, ship, bullets)

        if stats.game_active:
            ship.update()
            gf.update_bullets(ai_settings, screen, ship, aliens, bullets)
            gf.update_aliens(ai_settings, stats, screen, ship, aliens, bullets)

        gf.update_screen(ai_settings, screen, ship, aliens, bullets)
```

In the main loop, we always need to call check_events(), even if the game is inactive. For example, we still need to know if the user presses Q to quit the game or clicks the button to close the window. We also continue updating the screen so we can make changes to the screen while waiting to see whether the player chooses to start a new game. The rest of the function calls only need to happen when the game is active, because when the game is inactive, we don't need to update the positions of game elements.

Now when you play Alien Invasion, the game should freeze when you've used up all of your ships.

TRY IT YOURSELF

13-6. Game Over: Using your code from Exercise 13-5 (page 284), keep track of the number of times the player misses the ball. When they've missed the ball three times, end the game.

Summary

In this chapter you learned how to add a large number of identical elements to a game by creating a fleet of aliens. You learned how to use nested loops to create a grid of elements, and you made a large set of game elements move by calling each element's `update()` method. You learned to control the direction of objects on the screen and how to respond to events, such as when the fleet reaches the edge of the screen. You also learned how to detect and respond to collisions when bullets hit aliens and aliens hit the ship. Finally, you learned how to track the statistics in a game and use a `game_active` flag to determine when the game was over.

In the final chapter of this project, we'll add a Play button so the player can choose when to start their first game and whether to play again when the game ends. We'll speed up the game each time the player shoots down the entire fleet, and we'll add a scoring system. The final result will be a fully playable game!

14

SCORING

In this chapter we'll finish the Alien Invasion game. We'll add a Play button to start a game on demand or to restart a game once it ends. We'll also change the game so it speeds up when the player moves up a level, and we'll implement a scoring system. By the end of the chapter, you'll know enough to start writing games that increase in difficulty as a player progresses and that show scores.

Adding the Play Button

In this section we'll add a Play button that appears before a game begins and reappears when the game ends so the player can play again.

Right now the game begins as soon as you run *alien_invasion.py*. Let's start the game in an inactive state and then prompt the player to click a Play button to begin. To do this, enter the following in *game_stats.py*:

game_stats.py

```
    def __init__(self, ai_settings):
        """Initialize statistics."""
        self.ai_settings = ai_settings
        self.reset_stats()

        # Start game in an inactive state.
        self.game_active = False

    def reset_stats(self):
        --snip--
```

Now the game should start in an inactive state with no way for the player to start it until we make a Play button.

Creating a Button Class

Because Pygame doesn't have a built-in method for making buttons, we'll write a `Button` class to create a filled rectangle with a label. You can use this code to make any button in a game. Here's the first part of the `Button` class; save it as *button.py*:

button.py

```
import pygame.font

class Button():

❶   def __init__(self, ai_settings, screen, msg):
        """Initialize button attributes."""
        self.screen = screen
        self.screen_rect = screen.get_rect()

        # Set the dimensions and properties of the button.
❷       self.width, self.height = 200, 50
        self.button_color = (0, 255, 0)
        self.text_color = (255, 255, 255)
❸       self.font = pygame.font.SysFont(None, 48)

        # Build the button's rect object and center it.
❹       self.rect = pygame.Rect(0, 0, self.width, self.height)
        self.rect.center = self.screen_rect.center

        # The button message needs to be prepped only once.
❺       self.prep_msg(msg)
```

First we import the pygame.font module, which lets Pygame render text to the screen. The __init__() method takes the parameters self, the ai_settings and screen objects, and msg, which contains the text for the button ❶. We set the button dimensions at ❷, and then we set button_color to color the button's rect object bright green and set text_color to render the text in white.

At ❸ we prepare a font attribute for rendering text. The None argument tells Pygame to use the default font, and 48 determines the size of the text. To center the button on the screen, we create a rect for the button ❹ and set its center attribute to match that of the screen.

Pygame works with text by rendering the string you want to display as an image. At ❺ we call prep_msg() to handle this rendering.

Here's the code for prep_msg():

button.py

```
    def prep_msg(self, msg):
        """Turn msg into a rendered image and center text on the button."""
❶       self.msg_image = self.font.render(msg, True, self.text_color,
            self.button_color)
❷       self.msg_image_rect = self.msg_image.get_rect()
        self.msg_image_rect.center = self.rect.center
```

The prep_msg() method needs a self parameter and the text to be rendered as an image (msg). The call to font.render() turns the text stored in msg into an image, which we then store in msg_image ❶. The font.render() method also takes a Boolean value to turn antialiasing on or off (antialiasing makes the edges of the text smoother). The remaining arguments are the specified font color and background color. We set antialiasing to True and set the text background to the same color as the button. (If you don't include a background color, Pygame will try to render the font with a transparent background.)

At ❷ we center the text image on the button by creating a rect from the image and setting its center attribute to match that of the button.

Finally, we create a draw_button() method that we can call to display the button onscreen:

button.py

```
    def draw_button(self):
        # Draw blank button and then draw message.
        self.screen.fill(self.button_color, self.rect)
        self.screen.blit(self.msg_image, self.msg_image_rect)
```

We call screen.fill() to draw the rectangular portion of the button. Then we call screen.blit() to draw the text image to the screen, passing it an image and the rect object associated with the image. This completes the Button class.

Drawing the Button to the Screen

We'll use the Button class to create a Play button. Because we need only one Play button, we'll create the button directly in *alien_invasion.py* as shown here:

alien_invasion.py

```
--snip--
from game_stats import GameStats
from button import Button
--snip--

def run_game():
    --snip--
    pygame.display.set_caption("Alien Invasion")

    # Make the Play button.
❶   play_button = Button(ai_settings, screen, "Play")
    --snip--

    # Start the main loop for the game.
    while True:
        --snip--
❷       gf.update_screen(ai_settings, screen, stats, ship, aliens, bullets,
            play_button)

run_game()
```

We import Button and create an instance called play_button ❶, and then we pass play_button to update_screen() so the button appears when the screen updates ❷.

Next, modify update_screen() so the Play button appears only when the game is inactive:

game_functions.py

```
def update_screen(ai_settings, screen, stats, ship, aliens, bullets,
        play_button):
    """Update images on the screen and flip to the new screen."""
    --snip--

    # Draw the play button if the game is inactive.
    if not stats.game_active:
        play_button.draw_button()

    # Make the most recently drawn screen visible.
    pygame.display.flip()
```

To make the Play button visible above all other elements on the screen, we draw it after all other game elements have been drawn and before flipping to a new screen. Now when you run Alien Invasion you should see a Play button in the center of the screen, as shown in Figure 14-1.

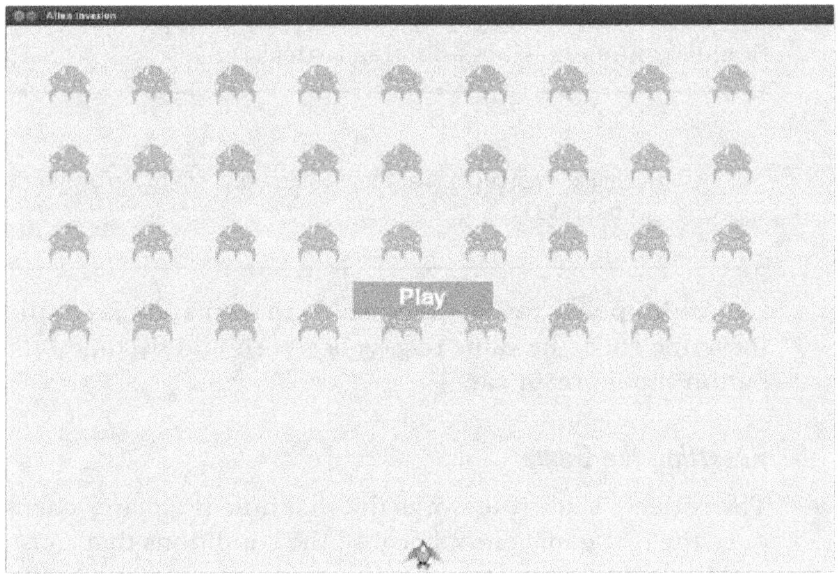

Figure 14-1: A Play button appears when the game is inactive.

Starting the Game

To start a new game when the player clicks Play, add the following code to *game_functions.py* to monitor mouse events over the button:

game_functions.py

```
def check_events(ai_settings, screen, stats, play_button, ship, bullets):
    """Respond to keypresses and mouse events."""
    for event in pygame.event.get():
        if event.type == pygame.QUIT:
            --snip--
❶       elif event.type == pygame.MOUSEBUTTONDOWN:
❷           mouse_x, mouse_y = pygame.mouse.get_pos()
❸           check_play_button(stats, play_button, mouse_x, mouse_y)

def check_play_button(stats, play_button, mouse_x, mouse_y):
    """Start a new game when the player clicks Play."""
❹   if play_button.rect.collidepoint(mouse_x, mouse_y):
        stats.game_active = True
```

We've updated the definition of `check_events()` to accept the `stats` and `play_button` parameters. We'll use `stats` to access the `game_active` flag and `play_button` to check whether the Play button has been clicked.

Pygame detects a `MOUSEBUTTONDOWN` event when the player clicks anywhere on the screen ❶, but we want to restrict our game to respond to mouse clicks only on the Play button. To accomplish this, we use `pygame.mouse.get_pos()`, which returns a tuple containing the x- and y-coordinates of the mouse cursor when the mouse button is clicked ❷. We send these values to the function `check_play_button()` ❸, which uses `collidepoint()` to see if the point of the mouse click overlaps the region defined by the Play button's `rect` ❹. If so, we set `game_active` to `True`, and the game begins!

The call to check_events() in *alien_invasion.py* needs to pass two additional arguments, stats and play_button:

alien_invasion.py

```
    # Start the main loop for the game.
    while True:
        gf.check_events(ai_settings, screen, stats, play_button, ship,
            bullets)
        --snip--
```

At this point, you should be able to start and play a full game. When the game ends, the value of game_active should become False and the Play button should reappear.

Resetting the Game

The code we just wrote works the first time the player clicks Play but not once the first game ends, because the conditions that caused the game to end haven't been reset.

To reset the game each time the player clicks Play, we need to reset the game statistics, clear out the old aliens and bullets, build a new fleet, and center the ship, as shown here:

game_functions.py

```
def check_play_button(ai_settings, screen, stats, play_button, ship, aliens,
        bullets, mouse_x, mouse_y):
    """Start a new game when the player clicks Play."""
    if play_button.rect.collidepoint(mouse_x, mouse_y):
        # Reset the game statistics.
❶       stats.reset_stats()
        stats.game_active = True

        # Empty the list of aliens and bullets.
❷       aliens.empty()
        bullets.empty()

        # Create a new fleet and center the ship.
❸       create_fleet(ai_settings, screen, ship, aliens)
        ship.center_ship()
```

We update the definition of check_play_button() so it has access to ai_settings, stats, ship, aliens, and bullets. It needs these objects to reset the settings that have changed during the game and to refresh the visual elements of the game.

At ❶ we reset the game statistics, which gives the player three new ships. Then we set game_active to True (so the game will begin as soon as the code in this function finishes running), empty the aliens and bullets groups ❷, and create a new fleet and center the ship ❸.

The definition of check_events() needs to be modified, as does the call to check_play_button():

game_functions.py

```
def check_events(ai_settings, screen, stats, play_button, ship, aliens,
        bullets):
    """Respond to keypresses and mouse events."""
    for event in pygame.event.get():
        if event.type == pygame.QUIT:
            --snip--
        elif event.type == pygame.MOUSEBUTTONDOWN:
            mouse_x, mouse_y = pygame.mouse.get_pos()
❶           check_play_button(ai_settings, screen, stats, play_button, ship,
                aliens, bullets, mouse_x, mouse_y)
```

The definition of check_events() needs the aliens parameter, which it will pass to check_play_button(). We then update the call to check_play_button() so it passes the appropriate arguments ❶.

Now update the call to check_events() in *alien_invasion.py* so it passes the aliens argument:

alien_invasion.py

```
    # Start the main loop for the game.
    while True:
        gf.check_events(ai_settings, screen, stats, play_button, ship,
            aliens, bullets)
        --snip--
```

The game will now reset properly each time you click Play, allowing you to play it as many times as you want!

Deactivating the Play Button

One issue with our Play button is that the button region on the screen will continue to respond to clicks even when the Play button isn't visible. Click the Play button area by accident once a game has begun and the game will restart!

To fix this, set the game to start only when game_active is False:

game_functions.py

```
def check_play_button(ai_settings, screen, stats, play_button, ship, aliens,
        bullets, mouse_x, mouse_y):
    """Start a new game when the player clicks Play."""
❶   button_clicked = play_button.rect.collidepoint(mouse_x, mouse_y)
❷   if button_clicked and not stats.game_active:
        # Reset the game statistics.
        --snip--
```

The flag button_clicked stores a True or False value ❶, and the game will restart only if Play is clicked *and* the game is not currently active ❷. To test this behavior, start a new game and repeatedly click where the Play button should be. If everything works as expected, clicking the Play button area should have no effect on the gameplay.

Hiding the Mouse Cursor

We want the mouse cursor visible in order to begin play, but once play begins it only gets in the way. To fix this, we'll make it invisible once the game becomes active:

game_functions.py

```
def check_play_button(ai_settings, screen, stats, play_button, ship, aliens,
        bullets, mouse_x, mouse_y):
    """Start new game when the player clicks Play."""
    button_clicked = play_button.rect.collidepoint(mouse_x, mouse_y)
    if button_clicked and not stats.game_active:
        # Hide the mouse cursor.
        pygame.mouse.set_visible(False)
        --snip--
```

Passing `False` to `set_visible()` tells Pygame to hide the cursor when the mouse is over the game window.

We'll make the cursor reappear once the game ends so the player can click Play to begin a new game. Here's the code to do that:

game_functions.py

```
def ship_hit(ai_settings, screen, stats, ship, aliens, bullets):
    """Respond to ship being hit by alien."""
    if stats.ships_left > 0:
        --snip--
    else:
        stats.game_active = False
        pygame.mouse.set_visible(True)
```

We make the cursor visible again as soon as the game becomes inactive, which happens in `ship_hit()`. Attention to details like this makes your game seem more professional and allows the player to focus on playing rather than figuring out the user interface.

TRY IT YOURSELF

14-1. Press P to Play: Because Alien Invasion uses keyboard input to control the ship, it's best to start the game with a keypress. Add code that lets the player press P to start. It may help to move some code from `check_play_button()` to a `start_game()` function that can be called from both `check_play_button()` and `check_keydown_events()`.

14-2. Target Practice: Create a rectangle at the right edge of the screen that moves up and down at a steady rate. Then have a ship appear on the left side of the screen that the player can move up and down while firing bullets at the moving, rectangular target. Add a Play button that starts the game, and when the player misses the target three times, end the game and make the Play button reappear. Let the player restart the game with this Play button.

Leveling Up

In our current game, once a player shoots down the entire alien fleet, the player reaches a new level, but the game difficulty doesn't change. Let's liven things up a bit and make the game more challenging by increasing the speed of the game each time a player clears the screen.

Modifying the Speed Settings

We'll first reorganize the `Settings` class to group the game settings into static and changing ones. We'll also make sure that settings that change over the course of a game reset when we start a new game. Here's the `__init__()` method for *settings.py*:

settings.py

```
    def __init__(self):
        """Initialize the game's static settings."""
        # Screen settings
        self.screen_width = 1200
        self.screen_height = 800
        self.bg_color = (230, 230, 230)

        # Ship settings
        self.ship_limit = 3

        # Bullet settings
        self.bullet_width = 3
        self.bullet_height = 15
        self.bullet_color = 60, 60, 60
        self.bullets_allowed = 3

        # Alien settings
        self.fleet_drop_speed = 10

        # How quickly the game speeds up
❶       self.speedup_scale = 1.1

❷       self.initialize_dynamic_settings()
```

We continue to initialize the settings that stay constant in the `__init__()` method. At ❶ we add a `speedup_scale` setting to control how quickly the game speeds up: a value of 2 will double the game speed every time the player reaches a new level; a value of 1 will keep the speed constant. A speed value like 1.1 should increase the speed enough to make the game challenging but not impossible. Finally, we call `initialize_dynamic_settings()` to initialize the values for attributes that need to change throughout the course of a game ❷.

Here's the code for `initialize_dynamic_settings()`:

settings.py

```
    def initialize_dynamic_settings(self):
        """Initialize settings that change throughout the game."""
        self.ship_speed_factor = 1.5
        self.bullet_speed_factor = 3
```

```
        self.alien_speed_factor = 1

        # fleet_direction of 1 represents right; -1 represents left.
        self.fleet_direction = 1
```

This method sets the initial values for the ship, bullet, and alien speeds. We'll increase these speeds as the player progresses in the game and reset them each time the player starts a new game. We include `fleet_direction` in this method so the aliens always move right at the beginning of a new game. To increase the speeds of the ship, bullets, and aliens each time the player reaches a new level, use `increase_speed()`:

settings.py

```
    def increase_speed(self):
        """Increase speed settings."""
        self.ship_speed_factor *= self.speedup_scale
        self.bullet_speed_factor *= self.speedup_scale
        self.alien_speed_factor *= self.speedup_scale
```

To increase the speed of these game elements, we multiply each speed setting by the value of `speedup_scale`.

We increase the game's tempo by calling `increase_speed()` in `check_bullet_alien_collisions()` when the last alien in a fleet has been shot down but before creating a new fleet:

game_functions.py

```
def check_bullet_alien_collisions(ai_settings, screen, ship, aliens, bullets):
    --snip--
    if len(aliens) == 0:
        # Destroy existing bullets, speed up game, and create new fleet.
        bullets.empty()
        ai_settings.increase_speed()
        create_fleet(ai_settings, screen, ship, aliens)
```

Changing the values of the speed settings `ship_speed_factor`, `alien_speed_factor`, and `bullet_speed_factor` is enough to speed up the entire game!

Resetting the Speed

We need to return any changed settings to their initial values each time the player starts a new game, or each new game would start with the increased speed settings of the previous game:

game_functions.py

```
def check_play_button(ai_settings, screen, stats, play_button, ship, aliens,
        bullets, mouse_x, mouse_y):
    """Start a new game when the player clicks Play."""
    button_clicked = play_button.rect.collidepoint(mouse_x, mouse_y)
    if button_clicked and not stats.game_active:
        # Reset the game settings.
        ai_settings.initialize_dynamic_settings()

        # Hide the mouse cursor.
        pygame.mouse.set_visible(False)
        --snip--
```

Playing Alien Invasion should be more fun and challenging now. Each time you clear the screen, the game should speed up and become slightly more difficult. If the game becomes too difficult too quickly, decrease the value of `settings.speedup_scale`, or if the game isn't challenging enough, increase the value slightly. Find a sweet spot by ramping up the difficulty in a reasonable amount of time. The first couple of screens should be easy, the next few challenging but doable, and subsequent screens almost impossibly difficult.

TRY IT YOURSELF

14-3. Challenging Target Practice: Start with your work from Exercise 14-2 (page 298). Make the target move faster as the game progresses, and restart at the original speed when the player clicks Play.

Scoring

Let's implement a scoring system to track the game's score in real time, as well as to display the high score, level, and the number of ships remaining.

The score is a game statistic, so we'll add a `score` attribute to `GameStats`:

game_stats.py

```
class GameStats():
    --snip--
    def reset_stats(self):
        """Initialize statistics that can change during the game."""
        self.ships_left = self.ai_settings.ship_limit
        self.score = 0
```

To reset the score each time a new game starts, we initialize `score` in `reset_stats()` rather than `__init__()`.

Displaying the Score

To display the score on the screen, we first create a new class, `Scoreboard`. For now this class will just display the current score, but we'll use it to report the high score, level, and number of ships remaining as well. Here's the first part of the class; save it as *scoreboard.py*:

scoreboard.py

```
import pygame.font

class Scoreboard():
    """A class to report scoring information."""

❶   def __init__(self, ai_settings, screen, stats):
        """Initialize scorekeeping attributes."""
        self.screen = screen
```

```
        self.screen_rect = screen.get_rect()
        self.ai_settings = ai_settings
        self.stats = stats

        # Font settings for scoring information.
❷       self.text_color = (30, 30, 30)
❸       self.font = pygame.font.SysFont(None, 48)

        # Prepare the initial score image.
❹       self.prep_score()
```

Because Scoreboard writes text to the screen, we begin by importing the pygame.font module. Next, we give __init__() the parameters ai_settings, screen, and stats so it can report the values we're tracking ❶. Then, we set a text color ❷ and instantiate a font object ❸.

To turn the text to be displayed into an image, we call prep_score() ❹, which we define here:

scoreboard.py

```
    def prep_score(self):
        """Turn the score into a rendered image."""
❶       score_str = str(self.stats.score)
❷       self.score_image = self.font.render(score_str, True, self.text_color,
            self.ai_settings.bg_color)

        # Display the score at the top right of the screen.
❸       self.score_rect = self.score_image.get_rect()
❹       self.score_rect.right = self.screen_rect.right - 20
❺       self.score_rect.top = 20
```

In prep_score(), we first turn the numerical value stats.score into a string ❶, and then pass this string to render(), which creates the image ❷. To display the score clearly onscreen, we pass the screen's background color to render() as well as a text color.

We'll position the score in the upper-right corner of the screen and have it expand to the left as the score increases and the width of the number grows. To make sure the score always lines up with the right side of the screen, we create a rect called score_rect ❸ and set its right edge 20 pixels from the right screen edge ❹. We then place the top edge 20 pixels down from the top of the screen ❺.

Finally, we create a show_score() method to display the rendered score image:

scoreboard.py

```
    def show_score(self):
        """Draw score to the screen."""
        self.screen.blit(self.score_image, self.score_rect)
```

This method draws the score image to the screen at the location specified by score_rect.

Making a Scoreboard

To display the score, we'll create a `Scoreboard` instance in *alien_invasion.py*:

alien_invasion.py

```
--snip--
from game_stats import GameStats
from scoreboard import Scoreboard
--snip--
def run_game():
    --snip--
    # Create an instance to store game statistics and create a scoreboard.
    stats = GameStats(ai_settings)
❶   sb = Scoreboard(ai_settings, screen, stats)
    --snip--
    # Start the main loop for the game.
    while True:
        --snip--
❷       gf.update_screen(ai_settings, screen, stats, sb, ship, aliens,
            bullets, play_button)

run_game()
```

We import the new `Scoreboard` class and make an instance called `sb` after creating the stats instance ❶. We then pass `sb` to `update_screen()` so the score can be drawn to the screen ❷.

To display the score, modify `update_screen()` like this:

game_functions.py

```
def update_screen(ai_settings, screen, stats, sb, ship, aliens, bullets,
        play_button):
    --snip--
    # Draw the score information.
    sb.show_score()

    # Draw the play button if the game is inactive.
    if not stats.game_active:
        play_button.draw_button()

    # Make the most recently drawn screen visible.
    pygame.display.flip()
```

We add `sb` to the list of parameters that define `update_screen()` and call `show_score()` just before the Play button is drawn.

When you run Alien Invasion now, you should see 0 at the top right of the screen. (For now we just want to make sure that the score appears in the right place before developing the scoring system further.) Figure 14-2 shows the score as it appears before the game starts.

Figure 14-2: The score appears at the top-right corner of the screen.

Now to assign point values to each alien!

Updating the Score as Aliens Are Shot Down

To write a live score to the screen, we update the value of `stats.score` whenever an alien is hit, and then call `prep_score()` to update the score image. But first, let's determine how many points a player gets each time they shoot down an alien:

settings.py

```
    def initialize_dynamic_settings(self):
        --snip--

        # Scoring
        self.alien_points = 50
```

We'll increase the point value of each alien as the game progresses. To make sure this point value is reset each time a new game starts, we set the value in `initialize_dynamic_settings()`.

Update the score each time an alien is shot down in `check_bullet_alien_collisions()`:

game_functions.py

```
def check_bullet_alien_collisions(ai_settings, screen, stats, sb, ship,
        aliens, bullets):
    """Respond to bullet-alien collisions."""
    # Remove any bullets and aliens that have collided.
    collisions = pygame.sprite.groupcollide(bullets, aliens, True, True)
```

```
    if collisions:
❶       stats.score += ai_settings.alien_points
        sb.prep_score()
    --snip--
```

We update the definition of check_bullet_alien_collisions() to include the stats and sb parameters so it can update the score and the scoreboard. When a bullet hits an alien, Pygame returns a collisions dictionary. We check whether the dictionary exists, and if it does, the alien's value is added to the score ❶. We then call prep_score() to create a new image for the updated score.

We need to modify update_bullets() to make sure the appropriate arguments are passed between functions:

game_functions.py

```
def update_bullets(ai_settings, screen, stats, sb, ship, aliens, bullets):
    """Update position of bullets and get rid of old bullets."""
    --snip--

    check_bullet_alien_collisions(ai_settings, screen, stats, sb, ship,
        aliens, bullets)
```

The definition of update_bullets() needs the additional parameters stats and sb. The call to check_bullet_alien_collisions() needs to include the stats and sb arguments as well.

We also need to modify the call to update_bullets() in the main while loop:

alien_invasion.py

```
    # Start the main loop for the game.
    while True:
        gf.check_events(ai_settings, screen, stats, play_button, ship,
            aliens, bullets)
        if stats.game_active:
            ship.update()
            gf.update_bullets(ai_settings, screen, stats, sb, ship, aliens,
                bullets)
            --snip--
```

The call to update_bullets() needs the stats and sb arguments.

Now when you play Alien Invasion, you should be able to rack up points!

Making Sure to Score All Hits

As currently written, our code could miss some aliens. For example, if two bullets collide with aliens during the same pass through the loop or if we make an extra wide bullet to hit multiple aliens, the player will receive points only for one of the aliens killed. To fix this, let's refine the way that alien bullet collisions are detected.

In check_bullet_alien_collisions(), any bullet that collides with an alien becomes a key in the collisions dictionary. The value associated with each bullet is a list of aliens it has collided with. We loop through the collisions dictionary to make sure we award points for each alien hit:

game_functions.py

```
def check_bullet_alien_collisions(ai_settings, screen, stats, sb, ship,
        aliens, bullets):
    --snip--
    if collisions:
❶       for aliens in collisions.values():
            stats.score += ai_settings.alien_points * len(aliens)
            sb.prep_score()
    --snip--
```

If the collisions dictionary has been defined, we loop through all values in the collisions dictionary. Remember that each value is a list of aliens hit by a single bullet. We multiply the value of each alien by the number of aliens in each list and add this amount to the current score. To test this, change the width of a bullet to 300 pixels and verify that you receive points for each alien you hit with your extra wide bullets; then return the bullet width to normal.

Increasing Point Values

Because the game gets more difficult each time a player reaches a new level, aliens in later levels should be worth more points. To implement this functionality, we'll add code to increase the point value when the game's speed increases:

settings.py

```
class Settings():
    """A class to store all settings for Alien Invasion."""

    def __init__(self):
        --snip--
        # How quickly the game speeds up
        self.speedup_scale = 1.1
        # How quickly the alien point values increase
❶       self.score_scale = 1.5

        self.initialize_dynamic_settings()

    def increase_speed(self):
        """Increase speed settings and alien point values."""
        self.ship_speed_factor *= self.speedup_scale
        self.bullet_speed_factor *= self.speedup_scale
        self.alien_speed_factor *= self.speedup_scale

❷       self.alien_points = int(self.alien_points * self.score_scale)
```

We define a rate at which points increase, which we call score_scale ❶. A small increase in speed (1.1) makes the game grow challenging quickly, but in order to see a notable difference in scoring you need to change the alien point value by a larger amount (1.5). Now when we increase the speed of the game, we also increase the point value of each hit ❷. We use the `int()` function to increase the point value by whole integers.

To see the value of each alien, add a `print` statement to the method `increase_speed()` in `Settings`:

settings.py

```
    def increase_speed(self):
        --snip--
        self.alien_points = int(self.alien_points * self.score_scale)
        print(self.alien_points)
```

You should see the new point value in the terminal every time you reach a new level.

NOTE *Be sure to remove the `print` statement after verifying that the point value is increasing, or it may affect the performance of your game and distract the player.*

Rounding the Score

Most arcade-style shooting games report scores as multiples of 10, so let's follow that lead with our scoring. Let's also format the score to include comma separators in large numbers. We'll make this change in `Scoreboard`:

scoreboard.py

```
    def prep_score(self):
        """Turn the score into a rendered image."""
❶       rounded_score = int(round(self.stats.score, -1))
❷       score_str = "{:,}".format(rounded_score)
        self.score_image = self.font.render(score_str, True, self.text_color,
            self.ai_settings.bg_color)
        --snip--
```

The `round()` function normally rounds a decimal number to a set number of decimal places given as the second argument. However, if you pass a negative number as the second argument, `round()` will round the value to the nearest 10, 100, 1000, and so on. The code at ❶ tells Python to round the value of `stats.score` to the nearest 10 and store it in `rounded_score`.

NOTE *In Python 2.7, `round()` always returns a decimal value, so we use `int()` to make sure the score is reported as an integer. If you're using Python 3, you can leave out the call to `int()`.*

At ❷, a string formatting directive tells Python to insert commas into numbers when converting a numerical value to a string—for example, to output `1,000,000` instead of `1000000`. Now when you run the game, you should see a neatly formatted, rounded score even when you rack up lots of points, as shown in Figure 14-3.

Figure 14-3: Rounded score with comma separators

High Scores

Every player wants to beat a game's high score, so let's track and report high scores to give players something to work toward. We'll store high scores in GameStats:

game_stats.py

```
    def __init__(self, ai_settings):
        --snip--
        # High score should never be reset.
        self.high_score = 0
```

Because the high score should never be reset, we initialize high_score in __init__() rather than in reset_stats().

Now we'll modify Scoreboard to display the high score. Let's start with the __init__() method:

scoreboard.py

```
    def __init__(self, ai_settings, screen, stats):
        --snip--
        # Prepare the initial score images.
        self.prep_score()
❶       self.prep_high_score()
```

The high score will be displayed separately from the score, so we need a new method, prep_high_score(), to prepare the high score image ❶.

Here's the prep_high_score() method:

scoreboard.py

```
    def prep_high_score(self):
        """Turn the high score into a rendered image."""
❶       high_score = int(round(self.stats.high_score, -1))
```

```
❷           high_score_str = "{:,}".format(high_score)
❸           self.high_score_image = self.font.render(high_score_str, True,
                self.text_color, self.ai_settings.bg_color)

            # Center the high score at the top of the screen.
            self.high_score_rect = self.high_score_image.get_rect()
❹           self.high_score_rect.centerx = self.screen_rect.centerx
❺           self.high_score_rect.top = self.score_rect.top
```

We round the high score to the nearest 10 ❶ and format it with commas ❷. We then generate an image from the high score ❸, center the high score rect horizontally ❹, and set its `top` attribute to match the top of the score image ❺.

The `show_score()` method now draws the current score at the top right and the high score at the top center of the screen:

scoreboard.py

```
    def show_score(self):
        """Draw the score to the screen."""
        self.screen.blit(self.score_image, self.score_rect)
        self.screen.blit(self.high_score_image, self.high_score_rect)
```

To check for high scores, we'll write a new function, `check_high_score()`, in *game_functions.py*:

game_functions.py

```
  def check_high_score(stats, sb):
      """Check to see if there's a new high score."""
❶     if stats.score > stats.high_score:
          stats.high_score = stats.score
          sb.prep_high_score()
```

The function `check_high_score()` takes two parameters, `stats` and `sb`. It uses `stats` to check the current score and the high score, and it needs `sb` to modify the high score image when necessary. At ❶ we check the current score against the high score. If the current score is greater, we update the value of `high_score` and call `prep_high_score()` to update the image of the high score.

We need to call `check_high_score()` each time an alien is hit after updating the score in `check_bullet_alien_collisions()`:

game_functions.py

```
def check_bullet_alien_collisions(ai_settings, screen, stats, sb, ship,
        aliens, bullets):
    --snip--
    if collisions:
        for aliens in collisions.values():
            stats.score += ai_settings.alien_points * len(aliens)
            sb.prep_score()
        check_high_score(stats, sb)
    --snip--
```

We call `check_high_score()` when the `collisions` dictionary is present, and we do so after updating the score for all the aliens that have been hit.

The first time you play Alien Invasion your score will be the high score, so it will be displayed as both the current and high score. But when you start a second game, your high score should appear in the middle and your current score at the right, as shown in Figure 14-4.

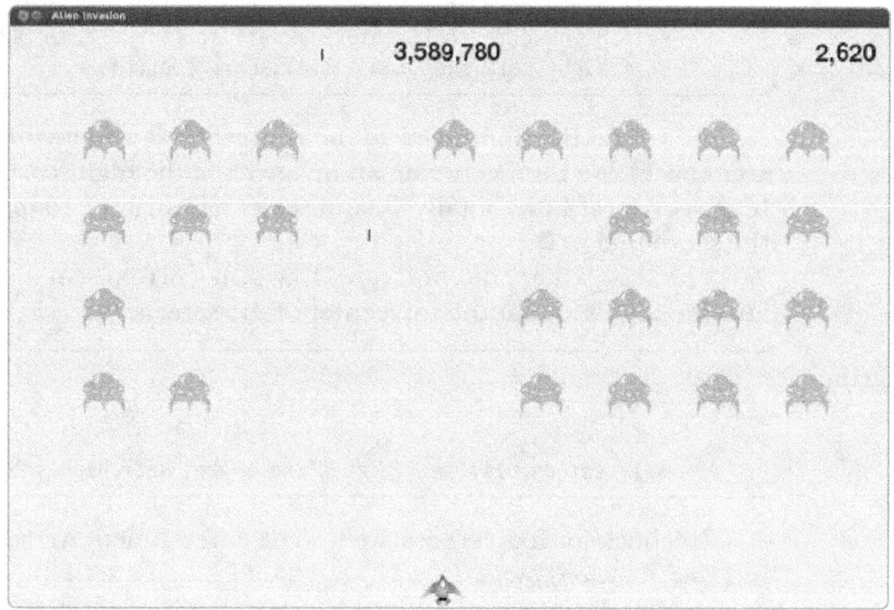

Figure 14-4: The high score is shown at the top center of the screen.

Displaying the Level

To display the player's level in the game, we first need an attribute in `GameStats` representing the current level. To reset the level at the start of each new game, initialize it in `reset_stats()`:

game_stats.py

```
def reset_stats(self):
    """Initialize statistics that can change during the game."""
    self.ships_left = self.ai_settings.ship_limit
    self.score = 0
    self.level = 1
```

To have `Scoreboard` display the current level (just below the current score), we call a new method, `prep_level()`, from `__init__()`:

scoreboard.py

```
def __init__(self, ai_settings, screen, stats):
    --snip--

    # Prepare the initial score images.
    self.prep_score()
    self.prep_high_score()
    self.prep_level()
```

Here's prep_level():

scoreboard.py

```
    def prep_level(self):
        """Turn the level into a rendered image."""
❶       self.level_image = self.font.render(str(self.stats.level), True,
                self.text_color, self.ai_settings.bg_color)

        # Position the level below the score.
        self.level_rect = self.level_image.get_rect()
❷       self.level_rect.right = self.score_rect.right
❸       self.level_rect.top = self.score_rect.bottom + 10
```

The method prep_level() creates an image from the value stored in stats.level ❶ and sets the image's right attribute to match the score's right attribute ❷. It then sets the top attribute 10 pixels beneath the bottom of the score image to leave space between the score and the level ❸.

We also need to update show_score():

scoreboard.py

```
    def show_score(self):
        """Draw scores and ships to the screen."""
        self.screen.blit(self.score_image, self.score_rect)
        self.screen.blit(self.high_score_image, self.high_score_rect)
        self.screen.blit(self.level_image, self.level_rect)
```

This adds a line to draw the level image to the screen.

We'll increment stats.level and update the level image in check_bullet_alien_collisions():

game_functions.py

```
def check_bullet_alien_collisions(ai_settings, screen, stats, sb, ship,
        aliens, bullets):
    --snip--
    if len(aliens) == 0:
        # If the entire fleet is destroyed, start a new level.
        bullets.empty()
        ai_settings.increase_speed()

        # Increase level.
❶       stats.level += 1
❷       sb.prep_level()

        create_fleet(ai_settings, screen, ship, aliens)
```

If a fleet is destroyed, we increment the value of stats.level ❶ and call prep_level() to make sure the new level is displayed correctly ❷.

To make sure the scoring and level images are updated properly at the start of a new game, trigger a reset when the Play button is clicked:

game_functions.py

```
def check_play_button(ai_settings, screen, stats, sb, play_button, ship,
        aliens, bullets, mouse_x, mouse_y):
    """Start a new game when the player clicks Play."""
    button_clicked = play_button.rect.collidepoint(mouse_x, mouse_y)
    if button_clicked and not stats.game_active:
```

```
        --snip--

        # Reset the game statistics.
        stats.reset_stats()
        stats.game_active = True

        # Reset the scoreboard images.
❶       sb.prep_score()
        sb.prep_high_score()
        sb.prep_level()

        # Empty the list of aliens and bullets.
        aliens.empty()
        bullets.empty()

        --snip--
```

The definition of check_play_button() needs the sb object. To reset the scoreboard images, we call prep_score(), prep_high_score(), and prep_level() after resetting the relevant game settings ❶.

Now pass sb from check_events() so check_play_button() has access to the scoreboard object:

game_functions.py

```
def check_events(ai_settings, screen, stats, sb, play_button, ship, aliens,
        bullets):
    """Respond to keypresses and mouse events."""
    for event in pygame.event.get():
        if event.type == pygame.QUIT:
            --snip--
        elif event.type == pygame.MOUSEBUTTONDOWN:
            mouse_x, mouse_y = pygame.mouse.get_pos()
❶           check_play_button(ai_settings, screen, stats, sb, play_button,
                ship, aliens, bullets, mouse_x, mouse_y)
```

The definition of check_events() needs sb as a parameter, so the call to check_play_button() can include sb as an argument ❶.

Finally, update the call to check_events() in *alien_invasion.py* so it passes sb as well:

alien_invasion.py

```
    # Start the main loop for the game.
    while True:
        gf.check_events(ai_settings, screen, stats, sb, play_button, ship,
            aliens, bullets)
        --snip--
```

Now you can see how many levels you've completed, as shown in Figure 14-5.

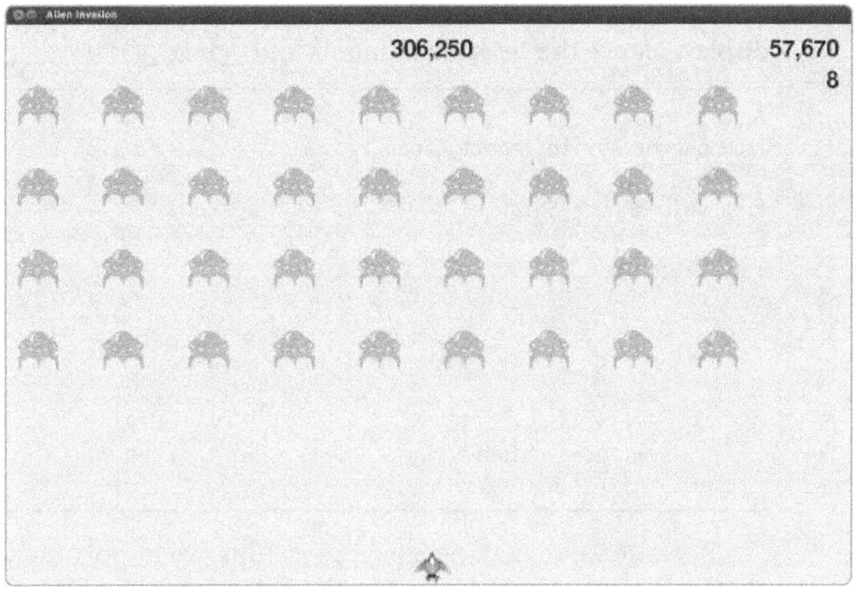

Figure 14-5: The current level is reported just below the current score.

NOTE *In some classic games, the scores have labels, such as Score, High Score, and Level. We've omitted these labels because the meaning of each number becomes clear once you've played the game. To include these labels, add them to the score strings just before the calls to* `font.render()` *in* `Scoreboard`*.*

Displaying the Number of Ships

Finally, let's display the number of ships the player has left, but this time, let's use a graphic. To do so, we'll draw ships in the upper-left corner of the screen to represent how many ships are left, like many classic arcade games do.

First, we need to make `Ship` inherit from `Sprite` so we can create a group of ships:

ship.py

```
import pygame
from pygame.sprite import Sprite

❶ class Ship(Sprite):

      def __init__(self, ai_settings, screen):
          """Initialize the ship and set its starting position."""
❷         super(Ship, self).__init__()
          --snip--
```

Here we import `Sprite`, make sure `Ship` inherits from `Sprite` ❶, and call `super()` at the beginning of `__init__()` ❷.

Next, we need to modify Scoreboard to create a group of ships we can display. Here's the import statements and __init__():

scoreboard.py

```
import pygame.font
from pygame.sprite import Group

from ship import Ship

class Scoreboard():
    """A class to report scoring information."""

    def __init__(self, ai_settings, screen, stats):
        --snip--
        self.prep_level()
        self.prep_ships()
       --snip--
```

Because we're making a group of ships, we import the Group and Ship classes. We call prep_ships() after the call to prep_level().

Here's prep_ships():

scoreboard.py

```
    def prep_ships(self):
        """Show how many ships are left."""
❶       self.ships = Group()
❷       for ship_number in range(self.stats.ships_left):
            ship = Ship(self.ai_settings, self.screen)
❸           ship.rect.x = 10 + ship_number * ship.rect.width
❹           ship.rect.y = 10
❺           self.ships.add(ship)
```

The prep_ships() method creates an empty group, self.ships, to hold the ship instances ❶. To fill this group, a loop runs once for every ship the player has left ❷. Inside the loop we create a new ship and set each ship's x-coordinate value so the ships appear next to each other with a 10-pixel margin on the left side of the group of ships ❸. We set the y-coordinate value 10 pixels down from the top of the screen so the ships line up with the score image ❹. Finally, we add each new ship to the group ships ❺.

Now we need to draw the ships to the screen:

scoreboard.py

```
    def show_score(self):
        --snip--
        self.screen.blit(self.level_image, self.level_rect)
        # Draw ships.
        self.ships.draw(self.screen)
```

To display the ships on the screen, we call draw() on the group, and Pygame draws each ship.

To show the player how many ships they have to start with, we call prep_ships() when a new game starts. We do this in check_play_button() in *game_functions.py*:

game_functions.py

```
def check_play_button(ai_settings, screen, stats, sb, play_button, ship,
        aliens, bullets, mouse_x, mouse_y):
    """Start a new game when the player clicks Play."""
    button_clicked = play_button.rect.collidepoint(mouse_x, mouse_y)
    if button_clicked and not stats.game_active:
        --snip--
        # Reset the scoreboard images.
        sb.prep_score()
        sb.prep_high_score()
        sb.prep_level()
        sb.prep_ships()
        --snip--
```

We also call prep_ships() when a ship is hit to update the display of ship images when the player loses a ship:

game_functions.py

```
❶ def update_aliens(ai_settings, screen, stats, sb, ship, aliens, bullets):
      --snip--
      # Look for alien-ship collisions.
      if pygame.sprite.spritecollideany(ship, aliens):
❷         ship_hit(ai_settings, screen, stats, sb, ship, aliens, bullets)

      # Look for aliens hitting the bottom of the screen.
❸     check_aliens_bottom(ai_settings, screen, stats, sb, ship, aliens, bullets)

❹ def ship_hit(ai_settings, screen, stats, sb, ship, aliens, bullets):
      """Respond to ship being hit by alien."""
      if stats.ships_left > 0:
          # Decrement ships_left.
          stats.ships_left -= 1

          # Update scoreboard.
❺         sb.prep_ships()

          # Empty the list of aliens and bullets.
          --snip--
```

We first add the parameter sb to the definition of update_aliens() ❶. We then pass sb to ship_hit() ❷ and check_aliens_bottom() so each has access to the scoreboard object ❸.

Then we update the definition of ship_hit() to include sb ❹. We call prep_ships() after decreasing the value of ships_left ❺, so the correct number of ships is displayed each time a ship is destroyed.

There's a call to ship_hit() in check_aliens_bottom(), so update that function as well:

game_functions.py

```
def check_aliens_bottom(ai_settings, screen, stats, sb, ship, aliens,
        bullets):
    """Check if any aliens have reached the bottom of the screen."""
    screen_rect = screen.get_rect()
    for alien in aliens.sprites():
        if alien.rect.bottom >= screen_rect.bottom:
            # Treat this the same as if a ship got hit.
            ship_hit(ai_settings, screen, stats, sb, ship, aliens, bullets)
            break
```

Now check_aliens_bottom() accepts sb as a parameter, and we add an sb argument in the call to ship_hit().

Finally, pass sb in the call to update_aliens() in *alien_invasion.py*:

alien_invasion.py

```
    # Start the main loop for the game.
    while True:
        --snip--
        if stats.game_active:
            ship.update()
            gf.update_bullets(ai_settings, screen, stats, sb, ship, aliens,
                bullets)
            gf.update_aliens(ai_settings, screen, stats, sb, ship, aliens,
                bullets)
        --snip--
```

Figure 14-6 shows the complete scoring system with the remaining ships displayed at the top left of the screen.

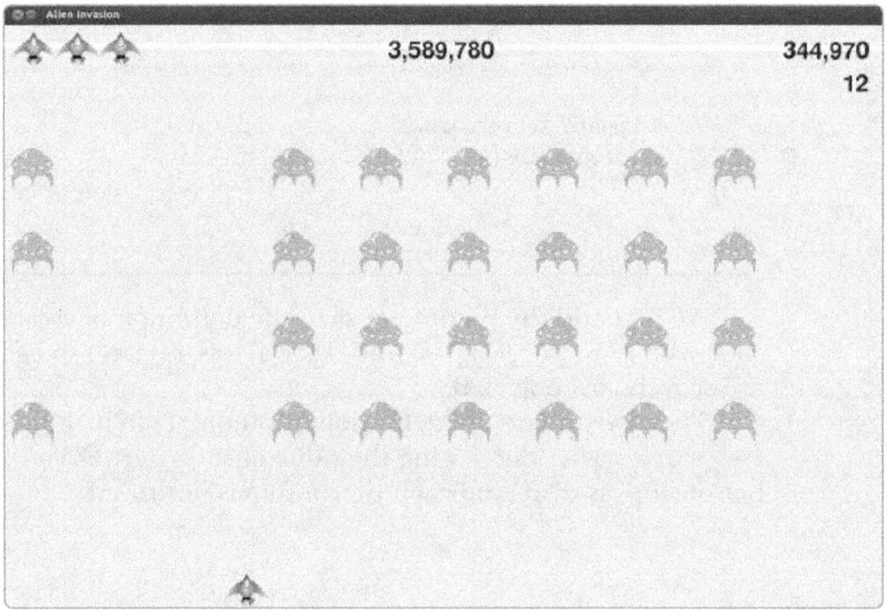

Figure 14-6: The complete scoring system for Alien Invasion

> **TRY IT YOURSELF**
>
> **14-4. All-Time High Score:** The high score is reset every time a player closes and restarts Alien Invasion. Fix this by writing the high score to a file before calling `sys.exit()` and reading the high score in when initializing its value in `GameStats`.
>
> **14-5. Refactoring:** Look for functions and methods that are doing more than one task, and refactor them to keep your code organized and efficient. For example, move some of the code in `check_bullet_alien_collisions()`, which starts a new level when the fleet of aliens has been destroyed, to a function called `start_new_level()`. Also, move the four separate method calls in the `__init__()` method in `Scoreboard` to a method called `prep_images()` to shorten `__init__()`. The `prep_images()` method could also help `check_play_button()` or `start_game()` if you've already refactored `check_play_button()`.
>
> **NOTE** *Before attempting to refactor the project, see Appendix D to learn how to restore the project to a working state if you introduce bugs while refactoring.*
>
> **14-6. Expanding Alien Invasion:** Think of a way to expand Alien Invasion. For example, you could program the aliens to shoot bullets down at the ship or add shields for your ship to hide behind, which can be destroyed by bullets from either side. Or use something like the `pygame.mixer` module to add sound effects like explosions and shooting sounds.

Summary

In this chapter you learned to build a Play button to start a new game and how to detect mouse events and hide the cursor in active games. You can use what you've learned to create other buttons in your games, like a Help button to display instructions on how to play. You also learned how to modify the speed of a game as it progresses, how to implement a progressive scoring system, and how to display information in textual and nontextual ways.

PROJECT 2

DATA VISUALIZATION

15

GENERATING DATA

Data visualization involves exploring data through visual representations. It's closely associated with *data mining*, which uses code to explore the patterns and connections in a data set. A data set can be just a small list of numbers that fits in one line of code or many gigabytes of data.

Making beautiful representations of data is about more than pretty pictures. When you have a simple, visually appealing representation of a data set, its meaning becomes clear to viewers. People will see patterns and significance in your data sets that they never knew existed.

Fortunately, you don't need a supercomputer to visualize complex data. With Python's efficiency, you can quickly explore data sets made of millions of individual data points on just a laptop. The data points don't have to be numbers, either. With the basics you learned in the first part of this book, you can analyze nonnumerical data as well.

People use Python for data-intensive work in genetics, climate research, political and economic analysis, and much more. Data scientists have written an impressive array of visualization and analysis tools in Python, many of which are available to you as well. One of the most popular tools is matplotlib, a mathematical plotting library. We'll use matplotlib to make simple plots, such as line graphs and scatter plots. After which, we'll create a more interesting data set based on the concept of a random walk—a visualization generated from a series of random decisions.

We'll also use a package called Pygal, which focuses on creating visualizations that work well on digital devices. You can use Pygal to emphasize and resize elements as the user interacts with your visualization, and you can easily resize the entire representation to fit on a tiny smartwatch or giant monitor. We'll use Pygal to explore what happens when you roll dice in various ways.

Installing matplotlib

First, you'll need to install matplotlib, which we'll use for our initial set of visualizations. If you haven't used pip yet, see "Installing Python Packages with pip" on page 237.

On Linux

If you're using the version of Python that came with your system, you can use your system's package manager to install matplotlib using just one line:

```
$ sudo apt-get install python3-matplotlib
```

If you're running Python 2.7, use this line:

```
$ sudo apt-get install python-matplotlib
```

If you installed a newer version of Python, you'll have to install a few libraries that matplotlib depends on:

```
$ sudo apt-get install python3.5-dev python3.5-tk tk-dev
$ sudo apt-get install libfreetype6-dev g++
```

Then use pip to install matplotlib:

```
$ pip install --user matplotlib
```

On OS X

Apple includes matplotlib with its standard Python installation. To check whether it's installed on your system, open a terminal session and try `import matplotlib`. If matplotlib isn't already on your system and you used Homebrew to install Python, install it like this:

```
$ pip install --user matplotlib
```

NOTE *You might need to use* `pip3` *instead of* `pip` *when installing packages. Also, if this command doesn't work, you might need to leave off the* `--user` *flag.*

On Windows

On Windows, you'll first need to install Visual Studio. Go to *https://dev.windows.com/*, click **Downloads**, and look for Visual Studio Community, which is a free set of developer tools for Windows. Download and run the installer.

Next you'll need an installer for matplotlib. Go to *https://pypi.python.org/pypi/matplotlib/* and look for a wheel file (a file ending in *.whl*) that matches the version of Python you're using. For example, if you're using a 32-bit version of Python 3.5, you'll need to download *matplotlib-1.4.3-cp35-none-win32.whl.*

NOTE *If you don't see a file matching your installed version of Python, look at what's available at* http://www.lfd.uci.edu/~gohlke/pythonlibs/#matplotlib. *This site tends to release installers a little earlier than the official matplotlib site.*

Copy the *.whl* file to your project folder, open a command window, and navigate to the project folder. Then use pip to install matplotlib:

```
> cd python_work
python_work> python -m pip install --user matplotlib-1.4.3-cp35-none-win32.whl
```

Testing matplotlib

After you've installed the necessary packages, test your installation by starting a terminal session with the `python` or `python3` command and importing matplotlib:

```
$ python3
>>> import matplotlib
>>>
```

If you don't see any error messages, then matplotlib is installed on your system, and you can move on to the next section.

NOTE *If you have trouble with your installation, see Appendix C. If all else fails, ask for help. Your issue will most likely be one that an experienced Python programmer can troubleshoot quickly with a little information from you.*

The matplotlib Gallery

To see the kinds of visualizations you can make with matplotlib, visit the sample gallery at *http://matplotlib.org/*. When you click a visualization in the gallery, you can see the code used to generate the plot.

Plotting a Simple Line Graph

Let's plot a simple line graph using matplotlib, and then customize it to create a more informative visualization of our data. We'll use the square number sequence 1, 4, 9, 16, 25 as the data for the graph.

Just provide matplotlib with the numbers as shown here, and matplotlib should do the rest:

mpl_squares.py

```
import matplotlib.pyplot as plt

squares = [1, 4, 9, 16, 25]
plt.plot(squares)
plt.show()
```

We first import the pyplot module using the alias plt so we don't have to type pyplot repeatedly. (You'll see this convention often in online examples, so we'll do the same here.) pyplot contains a number of functions that help generate charts and plots.

We create a list to hold the squares and then pass it to the plot() function, which will try to plot the numbers in a meaningful way. plt.show() opens matplotlib's viewer and displays the plot, as shown in Figure 15-1. The viewer allows you to zoom and navigate the plot, and if you click the disk icon, you can save any plot images you like.

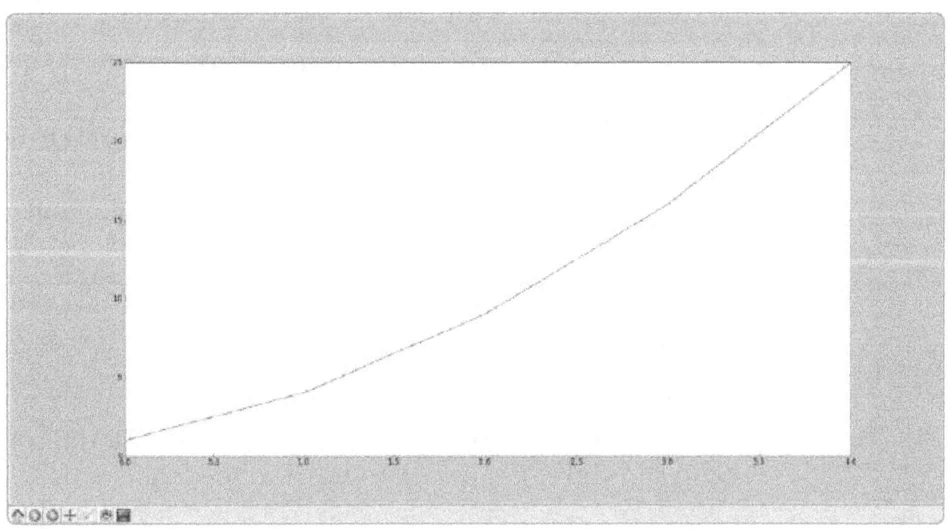

Figure 15-1: One of the simplest plots you can make in matplotlib

Changing the Label Type and Graph Thickness

Although the plot shown in Figure 15-1 shows that the numbers are increasing, the label type is too small and the line is too thin. Fortunately, matplotlib allows you to adjust every feature of a visualization.

We'll use a few of the available customizations to improve the readability of this plot, as shown here:

mpl_squares.py

```
import matplotlib.pyplot as plt

squares = [1, 4, 9, 16, 25]
❶ plt.plot(squares, linewidth=5)

# Set chart title and label axes.
❷ plt.title("Square Numbers", fontsize=24)
❸ plt.xlabel("Value", fontsize=14)
plt.ylabel("Square of Value", fontsize=14)

# Set size of tick labels.
❹ plt.tick_params(axis='both', labelsize=14)

plt.show()
```

The `linewidth` parameter at ❶ controls the thickness of the line that `plot()` generates. The `title()` function at ❷ sets a title for the chart. The `fontsize` parameters, which appear repeatedly throughout the code, control the size of the text on the chart.

The `xlabel()` and `ylabel()` functions allow you to set a title for each of the axes ❸, and the function `tick_params()` styles the tick marks ❹. The arguments shown here affect the tick marks on both the x- and y-axes (`axes='both'`) and set the font size of the tick mark labels to 14 (`labelsize=14`).

As you can see in Figure 15-2, the resulting chart is much easier to read. The label type is bigger, and the line graph is thicker.

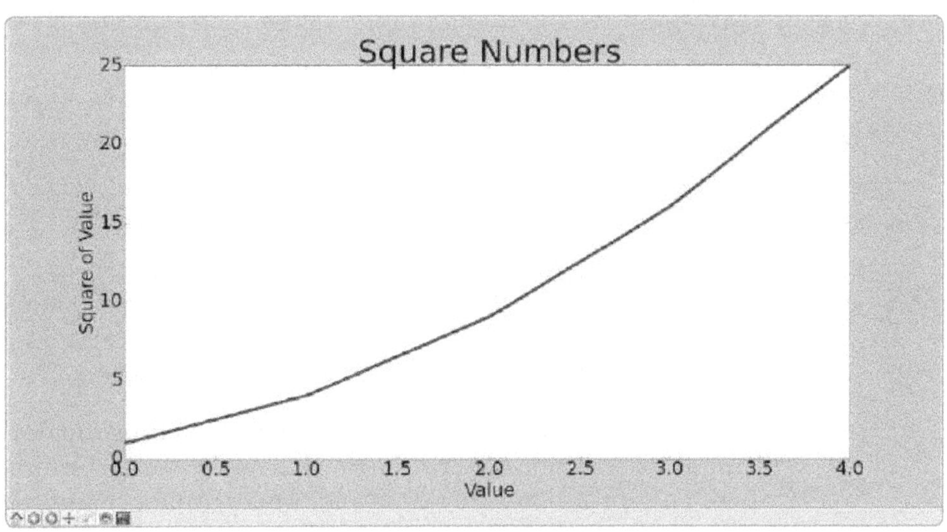

Figure 15-2: The chart is much easier to read now.

Correcting the Plot

But now that we can read the chart better, we see that the data is not plotted correctly. Notice at the end of the graph that the square of 4.0 is shown as 25! Let's fix that.

When you give `plot()` a sequence of numbers, it assumes the first data point corresponds to an x-coordinate value of 0, but our first point corresponds to an x-value of 1. We can override the default behavior by giving `plot()` both the input and output values used to calculate the squares:

mpl_squares.py

```
import matplotlib.pyplot as plt

input_values = [1, 2, 3, 4, 5]
squares = [1, 4, 9, 16, 25]
plt.plot(input_values, squares, linewidth=5)

# Set chart title and label axes.
--snip--
```

Now `plot()` will graph the data correctly because we've provided both the input and output values, so it doesn't have to assume how the output numbers were generated. The resulting plot, shown in Figure 15-3, is correct.

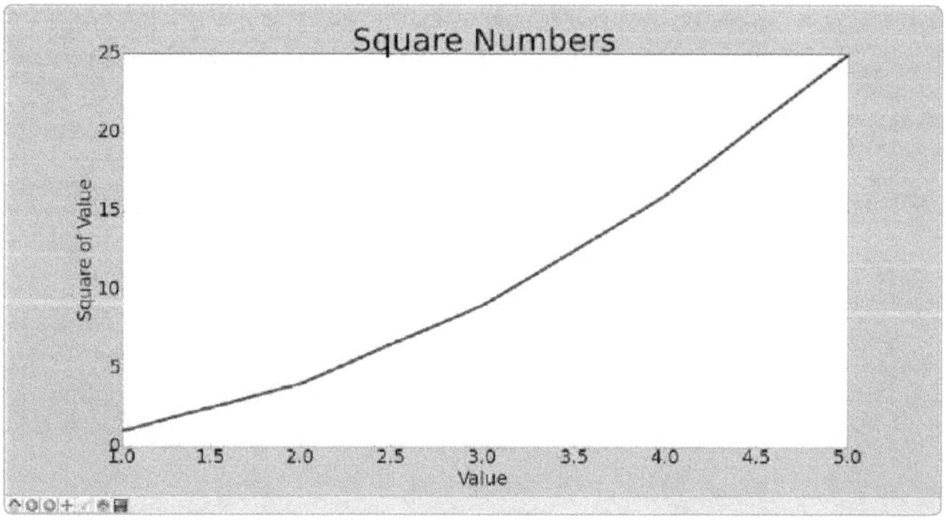

Figure 15-3: The data is now plotted correctly.

You can specify numerous arguments when using `plot()` and use a number of functions to customize your plots. We'll continue to explore these customization functions as we work with more interesting data sets throughout this chapter.

Plotting and Styling Individual Points with scatter()

Sometimes it's useful to be able to plot and style individual points based on certain characteristics. For example, you might plot small values in one color and larger values in a different color. You could also plot a large data set with one set of styling options and then emphasize individual points by replotting them with different options.

To plot a single point, use the scatter() function. Pass the single (*x*, *y*) values of the point of interest to scatter(), and it should plot those values:

scatter_squares.py

```
import matplotlib.pyplot as plt

plt.scatter(2, 4)
plt.show()
```

Let's style the output to make it more interesting. We'll add a title, label the axes, and make sure all the text is large enough to read:

```
import matplotlib.pyplot as plt

❶ plt.scatter(2, 4, s=200)

# Set chart title and label axes.
plt.title("Square Numbers", fontsize=24)
plt.xlabel("Value", fontsize=14)
plt.ylabel("Square of Value", fontsize=14)

# Set size of tick labels.
plt.tick_params(axis='both', which='major', labelsize=14)

plt.show()
```

At ❶ we call scatter() and use the s argument to set the size of the dots used to draw the graph. When you run *scatter_squares.py* now, you should see a single point in the middle of the chart, as shown in Figure 15-4.

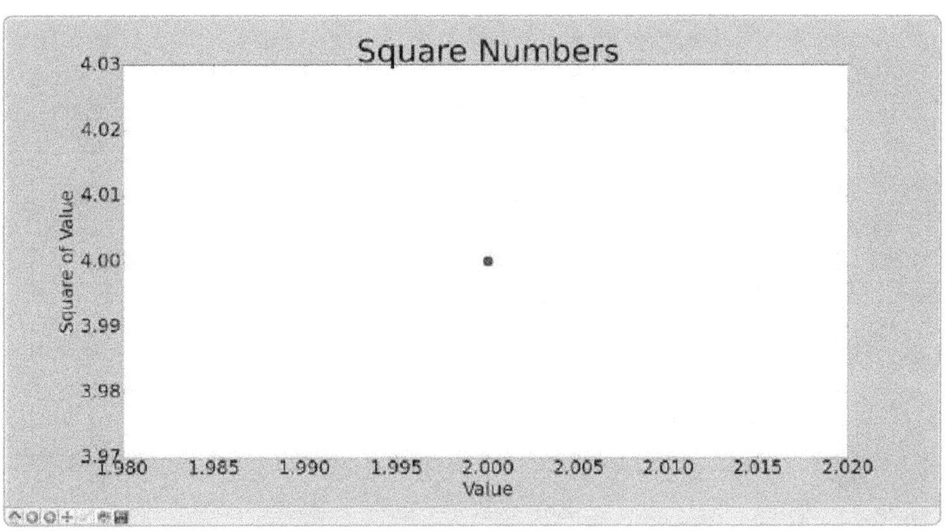

Figure 15-4: Plotting a single point

Plotting a Series of Points with scatter()

To plot a series of points, we can pass scatter() separate lists of x- and y-values, like this:

scatter_squares.py

```
import matplotlib.pyplot as plt

x_values = [1, 2, 3, 4, 5]
y_values = [1, 4, 9, 16, 25]

plt.scatter(x_values, y_values, s=100)

# Set chart title and label axes.
--snip--
```

The x_values list contains the numbers to be squared, and y_values contains the square of each number. When these lists are passed to scatter(), matplotlib reads one value from each list as it plots each point. The points to be plotted are (1, 1), (2, 4), (3, 9), (4, 16), and (5, 25); the result is shown in Figure 15-5.

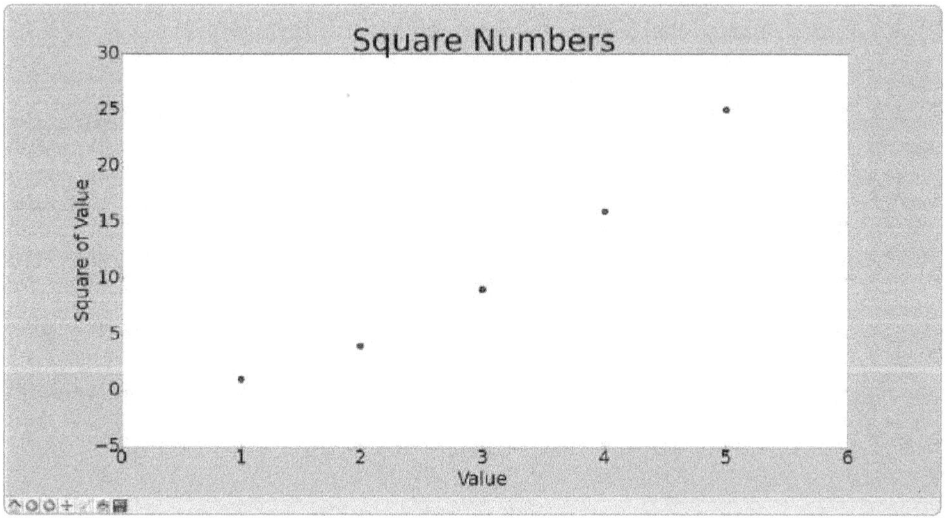

Figure 15-5: A scatter plot with multiple points

Calculating Data Automatically

Writing out lists by hand can be inefficient, especially when we have many points. Rather than passing our points in a list, let's use a loop in Python to do the calculations for us. Here's how this would look with 1000 points:

scatter_squares.py

```
import matplotlib.pyplot as plt

❶ x_values = list(range(1, 1001))
  y_values = [x**2 for x in x_values]

❷ plt.scatter(x_values, y_values, s=40)
```

```
    # Set chart title and label axes.
    --snip--

    # Set the range for each axis.
❸ plt.axis([0, 1100, 0, 1100000])

    plt.show()
```

We start with a list of x-values containing the numbers 1 through 1000 ❶. Next, a list comprehension generates the y-values by looping through the x-values (`for x in x_values`), squaring each number (`x**2`), and storing the results in `y_values`. We then pass the input and output lists to `scatter()` ❷.

Because this is a large data set, we use a smaller point size and we use the `axis()` function to specify the range of each axis ❸. The `axis()` function requires four values: the minimum and maximum values for the x-axis and the y-axis. Here, we run the x-axis from 0 to 1100 and the y-axis from 0 to 1,100,000. Figure 15-6 shows the result.

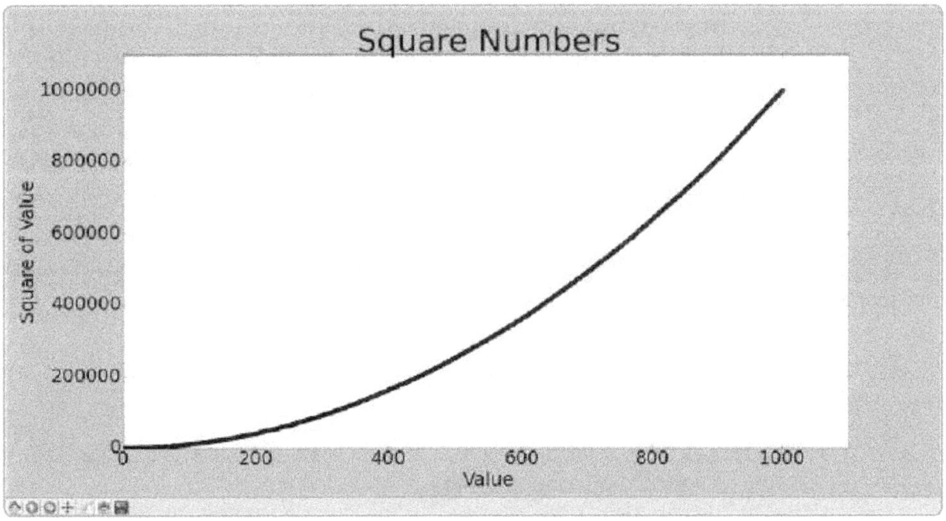

Figure 15-6: Python can plot 1000 points as easily as it plots 5 points.

Removing Outlines from Data Points

matplotlib lets you color points individually in a scatter plot. The default—blue dots with a black outline—works well for plots with a few points. But when plotting many points, the black outlines can blend together. To remove the outlines around points, pass the argument `edgecolor='none'` when you call `scatter()`:

```
plt.scatter(x_values, y_values, edgecolor='none', s=40)
```

Run *scatter_squares.py* using this call, and you should see only solid blue points in your plot.

Defining Custom Colors

To change the color of the points, pass c to scatter() with the name of a color to use, as shown here:

```
plt.scatter(x_values, y_values, c='red', edgecolor='none', s=40)
```

You can also define custom colors using the RGB color model. To define a color, pass the c argument a tuple with three decimal values (one each for red, green, and blue), using values between 0 and 1. For example, the following line would create a plot with light blue dots:

```
plt.scatter(x_values, y_values, c=(0, 0, 0.8), edgecolor='none', s=40)
```

Values closer to 0 produce dark colors, and values closer to 1 produce lighter colors.

Using a Colormap

A *colormap* is a series of colors in a gradient that moves from a starting to ending color. Colormaps are used in visualizations to emphasize a pattern in the data. For example, you might make low values a light color and high values a darker color.

The pyplot module includes a set of built-in colormaps. To use one of these colormaps, you need to specify how pyplot should assign a color to each point in the data set. Here's how to assign each point a color based on its y-value:

scatter_squares.py

```
import matplotlib.pyplot as plt

x_values = list(range(1001))
y_values = [x**2 for x in x_values]

plt.scatter(x_values, y_values, c=y_values, cmap=plt.cm.Blues,
    edgecolor='none', s=40)

# Set chart title and label axes.
--snip--
```

We pass the list of y-values to c and then tell pyplot which colormap to use through the cmap argument. This code colors the points with lower y-values light blue and the points with larger y-values dark blue. The resulting plot is shown in Figure 15-7.

NOTE *You can see all the colormaps available in* pyplot *at* http://matplotlib.org/; *go to* ***Examples****, scroll down to Color Examples, and click* ***colormaps_reference****.*

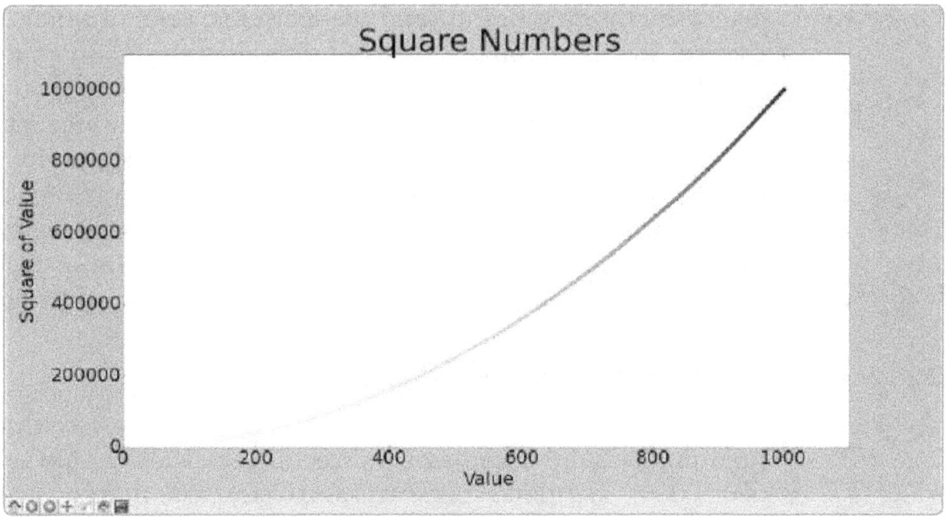

Figure 15-7: A plot using the `Blues` *colormap*

Saving Your Plots Automatically

If you want your program to automatically save the plot to a file, you can replace the call to `plt.show()` with a call to `plt.savefig()`:

```
plt.savefig('squares_plot.png', bbox_inches='tight')
```

The first argument is a filename for the plot image, which will be saved in the same directory as *scatter_squares.py*. The second argument trims extra whitespace from the plot. If you want the extra whitespace around the plot, you can omit this argument.

TRY IT YOURSELF

15-1. Cubes: A number raised to the third power is a *cube*. Plot the first five cubic numbers, and then plot the first 5000 cubic numbers.

15-2. Colored Cubes: Apply a colormap to your cubes plot.

Random Walks

In this section we'll use Python to generate data for a random walk and then use matplotlib to create a visually appealing representation of the generated data. A *random walk* is a path that has no clear direction but is determined by a series of random decisions, each of which is left entirely to chance. You might imagine a random walk as the path an ant would take if it had lost its mind and took every step in a random direction.

Random walks have practical applications in nature, physics, biology, chemistry, and economics. For example, a pollen grain floating on a drop of water moves across the surface of the water because it is constantly being pushed around by water molecules. Molecular motion in a water drop is random, so the path a pollen grain traces out on the surface is a random walk. The code we're about to write models many real-world situations.

Creating the RandomWalk() Class

To create a random walk, we'll create a `RandomWalk` class, which will make random decisions about which direction the walk should take. The class needs three attributes: one variable to store the number of points in the walk and two lists to store the x- and y-coordinate values of each point in the walk.

We'll use only two methods for the `RandomWalk` class: the `__init__()` method and `fill_walk()`, which will calculate the points in the walk. Let's start with `__init__()` as shown here:

random_walk.py

```
❶ from random import choice

  class RandomWalk():
      """A class to generate random walks."""

❷     def __init__(self, num_points=5000):
          """Initialize attributes of a walk."""
          self.num_points = num_points

          # All walks start at (0, 0).
❸         self.x_values = [0]
          self.y_values = [0]
```

To make random decisions, we'll store possible choices in a list and use `choice()` to decide which choice to use each time a decision is made ❶. We then set the default number of points in a walk to 5000—large enough to generate some interesting patterns but small enough to generate walks quickly ❷. Then at ❸ we make two lists to hold the x- and y-values, and we start each walk at point (0, 0).

Choosing Directions

We'll use `fill_walk()`, as shown here, to fill our walk with points and determine the direction of each step. Add this method to *random_walk.py*:

random_walk.py

```
      def fill_walk(self):
          """Calculate all the points in the walk."""

          # Keep taking steps until the walk reaches the desired length.
❶         while len(self.x_values) < self.num_points:
```

```
            # Decide which direction to go and how far to go in that direction.
❷           x_direction = choice([1, -1])
            x_distance = choice([0, 1, 2, 3, 4])
❸           x_step = x_direction * x_distance

            y_direction = choice([1, -1])
            y_distance = choice([0, 1, 2, 3, 4])
❹           y_step = y_direction * y_distance

            # Reject moves that go nowhere.
❺           if x_step == 0 and y_step == 0:
                continue

            # Calculate the next x and y values.
❻           next_x = self.x_values[-1] + x_step
            next_y = self.y_values[-1] + y_step

            self.x_values.append(next_x)
            self.y_values.append(next_y)
```

At ❶ we set up a loop that runs until the walk is filled with the correct number of points. The main part of this method tells Python how to simulate four random decisions: Will the walk go right or left? How far will it go in that direction? Will it go up or down? How far will it go in that direction?

We use `choice([1, -1])` to choose a value for `x_direction`, which returns either 1 for right movement or –1 for left ❷. Next, `choice([0, 1, 2, 3, 4])` tells Python how far to move in that direction (`x_distance`) by randomly selecting an integer between 0 and 4. (The inclusion of a 0 allows us to take steps along the y-axis as well as steps that have movement along both axes.)

At ❸ and ❹ we determine the length of each step in the *x* and *y* directions by multiplying the direction of movement by the distance chosen. A positive result for `x_step` moves us right, a negative result moves us left, and 0 moves us vertically. A positive result for `y_step` means move up, negative means move down, and 0 means move horizontally. If the value of both `x_step` and `y_step` are 0, the walk stops, but we continue the loop to prevent this ❺.

To get the next x-value for our walk, we add the value in `x_step` to the last value stored in `x_values` ❻ and do the same for the y-values. Once we have these values, we append them to `x_values` and `y_values`.

Plotting the Random Walk

Here's the code to plot all the points in the walk:

rw_visual.py

```
  import matplotlib.pyplot as plt

  from random_walk import RandomWalk

  # Make a random walk, and plot the points.
❶ rw = RandomWalk()
  rw.fill_walk()
```

```
❷ plt.scatter(rw.x_values, rw.y_values, s=15)
  plt.show()
```

We begin by importing `pyplot` and `RandomWalk`. We then create a random walk and store it in `rw` ❶, making sure to call `fill_walk()`. At ❷ we feed the walk's x- and y-values to `scatter()` and choose an appropriate dot size. Figure 15-8 shows the resulting plot with 5000 points. (The images in this section omit matplotlib's viewer, but you'll continue to see it when you run *rw_visual.py*.)

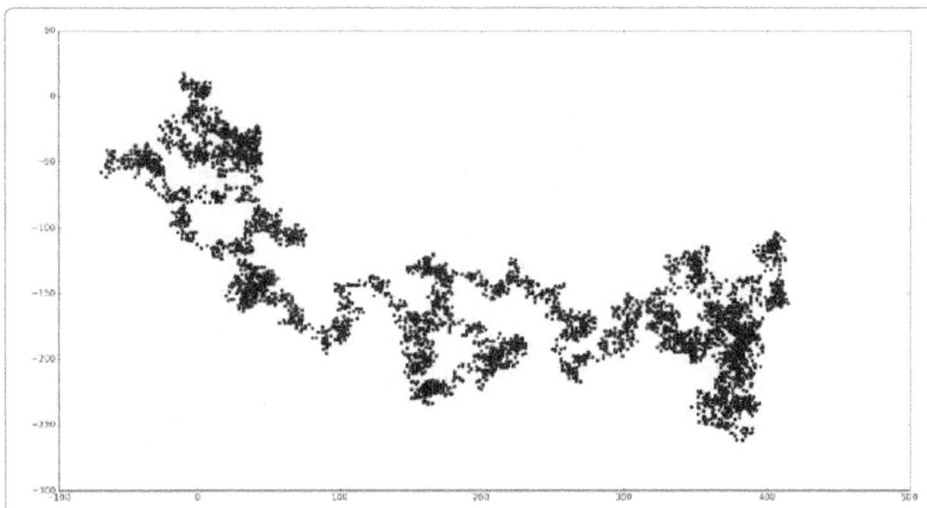

Figure 15-8: A random walk with 5000 points

Generating Multiple Random Walks

Every random walk is different, and it's fun to explore the various patterns that can be generated. One way to use the preceding code to make multiple walks without having to run the program several times is to wrap it in a `while` loop, like this:

rw_visual.py

```
import matplotlib.pyplot as plt

from random_walk import RandomWalk

# Keep making new walks, as long as the program is active.
while True:
    # Make a random walk, and plot the points.
    rw = RandomWalk()
    rw.fill_walk()
    plt.scatter(rw.x_values, rw.y_values, s=15)
    plt.show()

❶   keep_running = input("Make another walk? (y/n): ")
    if keep_running == 'n':
        break
```

This code will generate a random walk, display it in matplotlib's viewer, and pause with the viewer open. When you close the viewer, you'll be asked whether you want to generate another walk. Answer **y**, and you should be able to generate walks that stay near the starting point, that wander off mostly in one direction, that have thin sections connecting larger groups of points, and so on. When you want to end the program, enter **n**.

NOTE *If you're using Python 2.7, remember to use* `raw_input()` *instead of* `input()` *at* ❶.

Styling the Walk

In this section we'll customize our plots to emphasize the important characteristics of each walk and deemphasize distracting elements. To do so, we identify the characteristics we want to emphasize, such as where the walk began, where it ended, and the path taken. Next, we identify the characteristics to deemphasize, like tick marks and labels. The result should be a simple visual representation that clearly communicates the path taken in each random walk.

Coloring the Points

We'll use a colormap to show the order of the points in the walk and then remove the black outline from each dot so the color of the dots will be clearer. To color the points according to their position in the walk, we pass the `c` argument a list containing the position of each point. Because the points are plotted in order, the list just contains the numbers from 1 to 5000, as shown here:

rw_visual.py

```
--snip--
while True:
    # Make a random walk, and plot the points.
    rw = RandomWalk()
    rw.fill_walk()

❶   point_numbers = list(range(rw.num_points))
    plt.scatter(rw.x_values, rw.y_values, c=point_numbers, cmap=plt.cm.Blues,
        edgecolor='none', s=15)
    plt.show()

    keep_running = input("Make another walk? (y/n): ")
    --snip--
```

At ❶ we use `range()` to generate a list of numbers equal to the number of points in the walk. Then we store them in the list `point_numbers`, which we'll use to set the color of each point in the walk. We pass `point_numbers` to the `c` argument, use the `Blues` colormap, and then pass `edgecolor=none` to get rid of the black outline around each point. The result is a plot of the walk that varies from light to dark blue along a gradient, as shown in Figure 15-9.

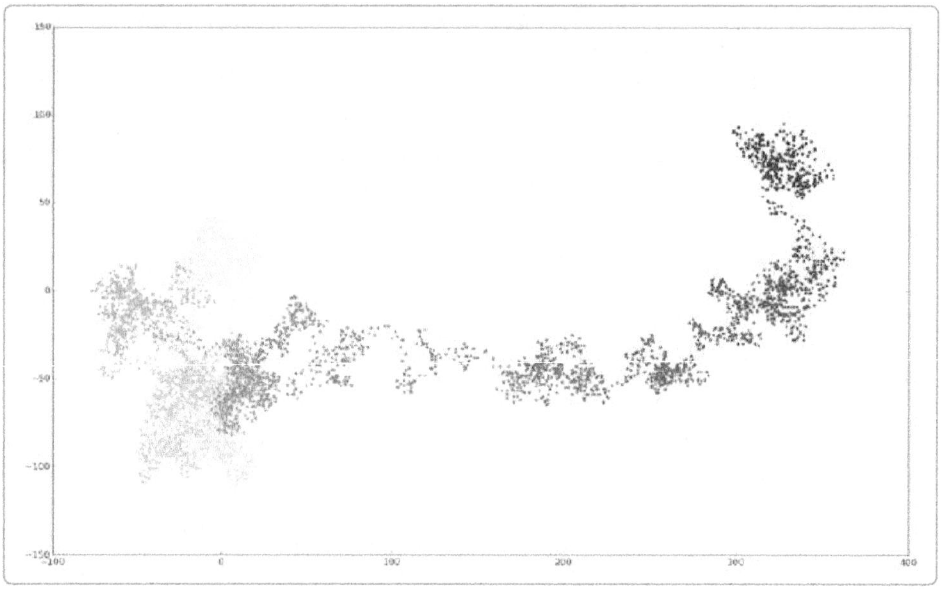

Figure 15-9: A random walk colored with the `Blues` colormap

Plotting the Starting and Ending Points

In addition to coloring points to show their position along the walk, it would be nice to see where each walk begins and ends. To do so, we can plot the first and last points individually once the main series has been plotted. We'll make the end points larger and color them differently to make them stand out, as shown here:

rw_visual.py

```
--snip--
while True:
    --snip--
    plt.scatter(rw.x_values, rw.y_values, c=point_numbers, cmap=plt.cm.Blues,
        edgecolor='none', s=15)

    # Emphasize the first and last points.
    plt.scatter(0, 0, c='green', edgecolors='none', s=100)
    plt.scatter(rw.x_values[-1], rw.y_values[-1], c='red', edgecolors='none',
        s=100)

    plt.show()
    --snip--
```

To show the starting point, we plot point (0, 0) in green in a larger size (`s=100`) than the rest of the points. To mark the end point, we plot the last x- and y-value in the walk in red with a size of 100. Make sure you insert this code just before the call to `plt.show()` so the starting and ending points are drawn on top of all the other points.

When you run this code, you should be able to spot exactly where each walk begins and ends. (If these end points don't stand out clearly, adjust their color and size until they do.)

Cleaning Up the Axes

Let's remove the axes in this plot so they don't distract us from the path of each walk. To turn the axes off, use this code:

rw_visual.py

```
--snip--
while True:
    --snip--
    plt.scatter(rw.x_values[-1], rw.y_values[-1], c='red', edgecolors='none',
        s=100)

    # Remove the axes.
❶   plt.axes().get_xaxis().set_visible(False)
    plt.axes().get_yaxis().set_visible(False)

    plt.show()
    --snip--
```

To modify the axes, use the `plt.axes()` function ❶ to set the visibility of each axis to `False`. As you continue to work with visualizations, you'll frequently see this chaining of methods.

Run *rw_visual.py* now; you should see a series of plots with no axes.

Adding Plot Points

Let's increase the number of points to give us more data to work with. To do so, we increase the value of `num_points` when we make a `RandomWalk` instance and adjust the size of each dot when drawing the plot, as shown here:

rw_visual.py

```
--snip--
while True:
    # Make a random walk, and plot the points.
    rw = RandomWalk(50000)
    rw.fill_walk()

    # Plot the points, and show the plot.
    point_numbers = list(range(rw.num_points))
    plt.scatter(rw.x_values, rw.y_values, c=point_numbers, cmap=plt.cm.Blues,
        edgecolor='none', s=1)
    --snip--
```

This example creates a random walk with 50,000 points (to mirror real-world data) and plots each point at size `s=1`. The resulting walk is wispy and cloud-like, as shown in Figure 15-10. As you can see, we've created a piece of art from a simple scatter plot!

Experiment with this code to see how much you can increase the number of points in a walk before your system starts to slow down significantly or the plot loses its visual appeal.

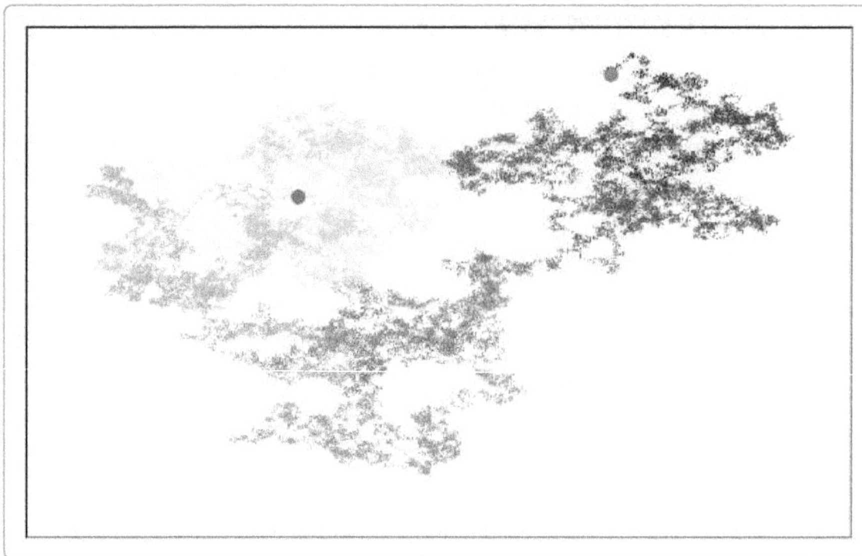

Figure 15-10: A walk with 50,000 points

Altering the Size to Fill the Screen

A visualization is much more effective at communicating patterns in data if it fits nicely on the screen. To make the plotting window better fit your screen, adjust the size of matplotlib's output, like this:

rw_visual.py

```
--snip--
while True:
    # Make a random walk, and plot the points.
    rw = RandomWalk()
    rw.fill_walk()

    # Set the size of the plotting window.
    plt.figure(figsize=(10, 6))
    --snip--
```

The `figure()` function controls the width, height, resolution, and background color of the plot. The `figsize` parameter takes a tuple, which tells matplotlib the dimensions of the plotting window in inches.

Python assumes that your screen resolution is 80 pixels per inch; if this code doesn't give you an accurate plot size, adjust the numbers as necessary. Or, if you know your system's resolution, pass `figure()` the resolution using the `dpi` parameter to set a plot size that makes effective use of the space available on your screen, as shown here:

```
plt.figure(dpi=128, figsize=(10, 6))
```

TRY IT YOURSELF

15-3. Molecular Motion: Modify *rw_visual.py* by replacing `plt.scatter()` with `plt.plot()`. To simulate the path of a pollen grain on the surface of a drop of water, pass in the `rw.x_values` and `rw.y_values`, and include a `linewidth` argument. Use 5000 instead of 50,000 points.

15-4. Modified Random Walks: In the class `RandomWalk`, `x_step` and `y_step` are generated from the same set of conditions. The direction is chosen randomly from the list `[1, -1]` and the distance from the list `[0, 1, 2, 3, 4]`. Modify the values in these lists to see what happens to the overall shape of your walks. Try a longer list of choices for the distance, such as 0 through 8, or remove the −1 from the *x* or *y* direction list.

15-5. Refactoring: The method `fill_walk()` is lengthy. Create a new method called `get_step()` to determine the direction and distance for each step, and then calculate the step. You should end up with two calls to `get_step()` in `fill_walk()`:

```
x_step = get_step()
y_step = get_step()
```

This refactoring should reduce the size of `fill_walk()` and make the method easier to read and understand.

Rolling Dice with Pygal

In this section we'll use the Python visualization package Pygal to produce scalable vector graphics files. These are useful in visualizations that are presented on differently sized screens because they scale automatically to fit the viewer's screen. If you plan to use your visualizations online, consider using Pygal so your work will look good on any device people use to view your visualizations.

In this project we'll analyze the results of rolling dice. If you roll one regular six-sided die, you have an equal chance of rolling any of the numbers from 1 through 6. However, when using two dice, you're more likely to roll certain numbers rather than others. We'll try to determine which numbers are most likely to occur by generating a data set that represents rolling dice. Then we'll plot the results of a large number of rolls to determine which results are more likely than others.

The study of rolling dice is often used in mathematics to explain various types of data analysis. But it also has real-world applications in casinos and other gambling scenarios, as well as in the way games like Monopoly and many role-playing games are played.

Installing Pygal

Install Pygal with pip. (If you haven't used pip yet, see "Installing Python Packages with pip" on page 237.)

On Linux and OS X, this should be something like:

```
pip install --user pygal
```

On Windows, this should be:

```
python -m pip install --user pygal
```

NOTE *You may need to use the command* pip3 *instead of* pip*, and if the command still doesn't work you may need to leave off the* --user *flag.*

The Pygal Gallery

To see what kind of visualizations are possible with Pygal, visit the gallery of chart types: go to *http://www.pygal.org/*, click **Documentation**, and then click **Chart types**. Each example includes source code, so you can see how the visualizations are generated.

Creating the Die Class

Here's a class to simulate the roll of one die:

die.py

```
from random import randint

class Die():
    """A class representing a single die."""

❶   def __init__(self, num_sides=6):
        """Assume a six-sided die."""
        self.num_sides = num_sides

    def roll(self):
        """"Return a random value between 1 and number of sides."""
❷       return randint(1, self.num_sides)
```

The __init__() method takes one optional argument. With this class, when an instance of our die is created, the number of sides will always be six if no argument is included. If an argument *is* included, that value is used to set the number of sides on the die ❶. (Dice are named for their number of sides: a six-sided die is a D6, an eight-sided die is a D8, and so on.)

The roll() method uses the randint() function to return a random number between 1 and the number of sides ❷. This function can return the starting value (1), the ending value (num_sides), or any integer between the two.

Rolling the Die

Before creating a visualization based on this class, let's roll a D6, print the results, and check that the results look reasonable:

die_visual.py

```
from die import Die

# Create a D6.
❶ die = Die()

# Make some rolls, and store results in a list.
results = []
❷ for roll_num in range(100):
    result = die.roll()
    results.append(result)

print(results)
```

At ❶ we create an instance of `Die` with the default six sides. At ❷ we roll the die 100 times and store the results of each roll in the list `results`. Here's a sample set of results:

```
[4, 6, 5, 6, 1, 5, 6, 3, 5, 3, 5, 3, 2, 2, 1, 3, 1, 5, 3, 6, 3, 6, 5, 4,
 1, 1, 4, 2, 3, 6, 4, 2, 6, 4, 1, 3, 2, 5, 6, 3, 6, 2, 1, 1, 3, 4, 1, 4,
 3, 5, 1, 4, 5, 5, 2, 3, 3, 1, 2, 3, 5, 6, 2, 5, 6, 1, 3, 2, 1, 1, 1, 6,
 5, 5, 2, 2, 6, 4, 1, 4, 5, 1, 1, 1, 4, 5, 3, 3, 1, 3, 5, 4, 5, 6, 5, 4,
 1, 5, 1, 2]
```

A quick scan of these results shows that the `Die` class seems to be working. We see the values 1 and 6, so we know the smallest and largest possible values are being returned, and because we don't see 0 or 7, we know all the results are in the appropriate range. We also see each number from 1 through 6, which indicates that all possible outcomes are represented.

Analyzing the Results

We analyze the results of rolling one D6 by counting how many times we roll each number:

die_visual.py

```
--snip--
# Make some rolls, and store results in a list.
results = []
❶ for roll_num in range(1000):
    result = die.roll()
    results.append(result)

# Analyze the results.
frequencies = []
❷ for value in range(1, die.num_sides+1):
❸     frequency = results.count(value)
❹     frequencies.append(frequency)

print(frequencies)
```

Because we're using Pygal to analyze instead of print the results, we can increase the number of simulated rolls to 1000 ❶. To analyze the rolls, we create the empty list `frequencies` to store the number of times each value is rolled. We loop through the possible values (1 through 6 in this case) at ❷, count how many times each number appears in `results` ❸, and then append this value to the `frequencies` list ❹. We then print this list before making a visualization:

```
[155, 167, 168, 170, 159, 181]
```

These results look reasonable: we see six frequencies, one for each possible number when you roll a D6, and we see that no frequency is significantly higher than any other. Now let's visualize these results.

Making a Histogram

With a list of frequencies, we can make a histogram of the results. A *histogram* is a bar chart showing how often certain results occur. Here's the code to create the histogram:

die_visual.py

```
import pygal
--snip--

# Analyze the results.
frequencies = []
for value in range(1, die.num_sides+1):
    frequency = results.count(value)
    frequencies.append(frequency)

# Visualize the results.
❶ hist = pygal.Bar()

hist.title = "Results of rolling one D6 1000 times."
❷ hist.x_labels = ['1', '2', '3', '4', '5', '6']
hist.x_title = "Result"
hist.y_title = "Frequency of Result"

❸ hist.add('D6', frequencies)
hist.render_to_file('die_visual.svg')
```

We make a bar chart by creating an instance of `pygal.Bar()`, which we store in `hist` ❶. We then set the `title` attribute of `hist` (just a string we use to label the histogram), use the possible results of rolling a D6 as the labels for the x-axis ❷, and add a title for each of the axes. We use `add()` to add a series of values to the chart at ❸ (passing it a label for the set of values to be added and a list of the values to appear on the chart). Finally, we render the chart to an SVG file, which expects a filename with the *.svg* extension.

The simplest way to look at the resulting histogram is in a web browser. Open a new tab in any web browser and then open the file *die_visual.svg* (in the folder where you saved *die_visual.py*). You should see a chart like the one in Figure 15-11. (I've modified this chart slightly for printing; by default Pygal generates charts with a darker background than what you see here.)

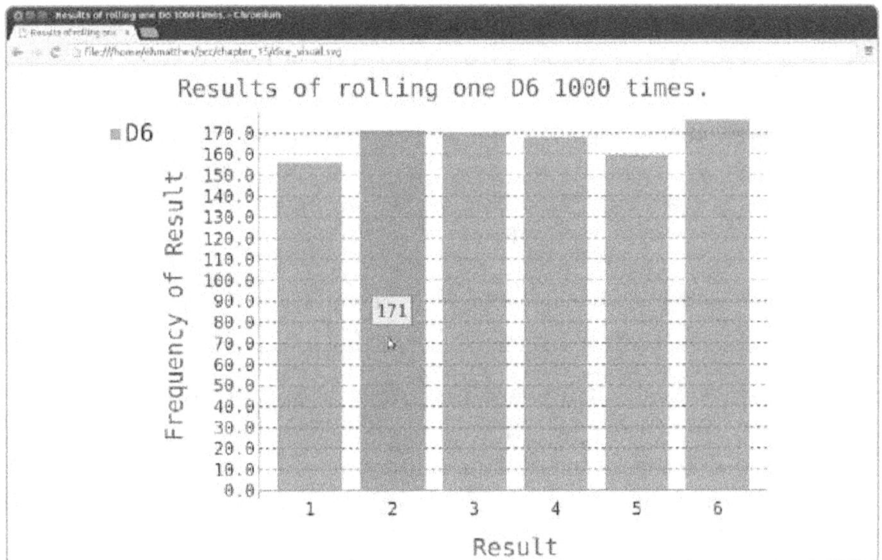

Figure 15-11: A simple bar chart created with Pygal

Notice that Pygal has made the chart interactive: hover your cursor over any bar in the chart and you'll see the data associated with it. This feature is particularly useful when plotting multiple data sets on the same chart.

Rolling Two Dice

Rolling two dice results in larger numbers and a different distribution of results. Let's modify our code to create two D6 dice to simulate the way we roll a pair of dice. Each time we roll the pair, we'll add the two numbers (one from each die) and store the sum in `results`. Save a copy of *die_visual.py* as *dice_visual.py*, and make the following changes:

dice_visual.py

```
import pygal

from die import Die

# Create two D6 dice.
die_1 = Die()
die_2 = Die()

# Make some rolls, and store results in a list.
results = []
for roll_num in range(1000):
❶    result = die_1.roll() + die_2.roll()
    results.append(result)

# Analyze the results.
frequencies = []
❷ max_result = die_1.num_sides + die_2.num_sides
```

```
❸ for value in range(2, max_result+1):
      frequency = results.count(value)
      frequencies.append(frequency)

  # Visualize the results.
  hist = pygal.Bar()

❹ hist.title = "Results of rolling two D6 dice 1000 times."
  hist.x_labels = ['2', '3', '4', '5', '6', '7', '8', '9', '10', '11', '12']
  hist.x_title = "Result"
  hist.y_title = "Frequency of Result"

  hist.add('D6 + D6', frequencies)
  hist.render_to_file('dice_visual.svg')
```

After creating two instances of `Die`, we roll the dice and calculate the sum of the two dice for each roll ❶. The largest possible result (12) is the sum of the largest number on both dice, which we store in `max_result` ❷. The smallest possible result (2) is the sum of the smallest number on both dice. When we analyze the results, we count the number of results for each value between 2 and `max_result` ❸. (We could have used `range(2, 13)`, but this would work only for two D6 dice. When modeling real-world situations, it's best to write code that can easily model a variety of situations. This code allows us to simulate rolling a pair of dice with any number of sides.)

When creating the chart, we update the title and the labels for the x-axis and data series ❹. (If the list `x_labels` were much longer, it would make sense to write a loop to generate this list automatically.)

After running this code, refresh the tab in your browser showing the chart; you should see a chart like the one in Figure 15-12.

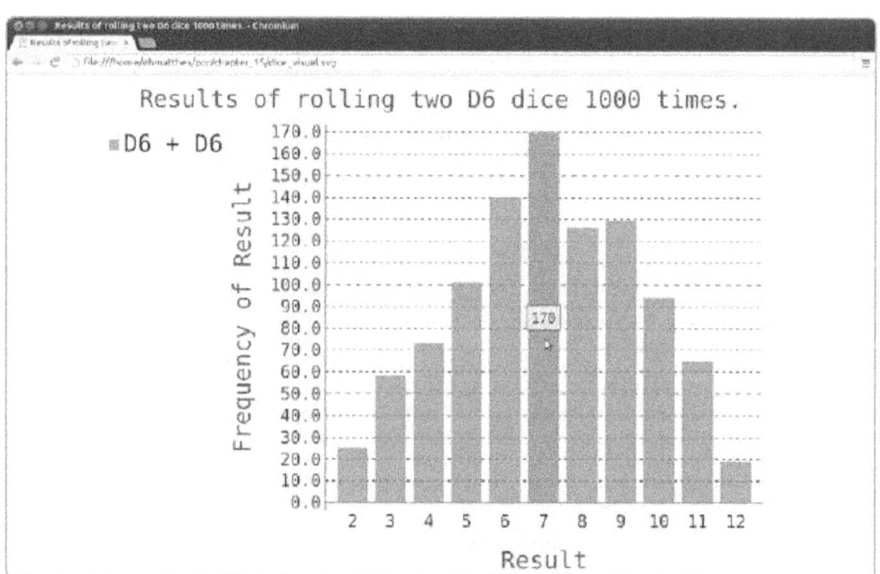

Figure 15-12: Simulated results of rolling two six-sided dice 1000 times

This graph shows the approximate results you're likely to get when you roll a pair of D6 dice. As you can see, you're least likely to roll a 2 or a 12 and most likely to roll a 7 because there are six ways to roll a 7, namely: 1 and 6, 2 and 5, 3 and 4, 4 and 3, 5 and 2, or 6 and 1.

Rolling Dice of Different Sizes

Let's create a six-sided die and a ten-sided die, and see what happens when we roll them 50,000 times:

different_dice.py

```
from die import Die

import pygal

# Create a D6 and a D10.
die_1 = Die()
❶ die_2 = Die(10)

# Make some rolls, and store results in a list.
results = []
for roll_num in range(50000):
    result = die_1.roll() + die_2.roll()
    results.append(result)

# Analyze the results.
--snip--

# Visualize the results.
hist = pygal.Bar()

❷ hist.title = "Results of rolling a D6 and a D10 50,000 times."
hist.x_labels = ['2', '3', '4', '5', '6', '7', '8', '9', '10', '11', '12',
    '13', '14', '15', '16']
hist.x_title = "Result"
hist.y_title = "Frequency of Result"

hist.add('D6 + D10', frequencies)
hist.render_to_file('dice_visual.svg')
```

To make a D10, we pass the argument `10` when creating the second `Die` instance ❶ and change the first loop to simulate 50,000 rolls instead of 1000. The lowest possible result is still 2, but the largest result is now 16; so we adjust the title, x-axis labels, and data series labels to reflect that ❷.

Figure 15-13 shows the resulting chart. Instead of one most likely result, there are five. This happens because there's still only one way to roll the smallest value (1 and 1) and the largest value (6 and 10), but the smaller die limits the number of ways you can generate the middle numbers: there are six ways to roll a 7, 8, 9, 10, and 11. Therefore, these are the most common results, and you're equally likely to roll any one of these numbers.

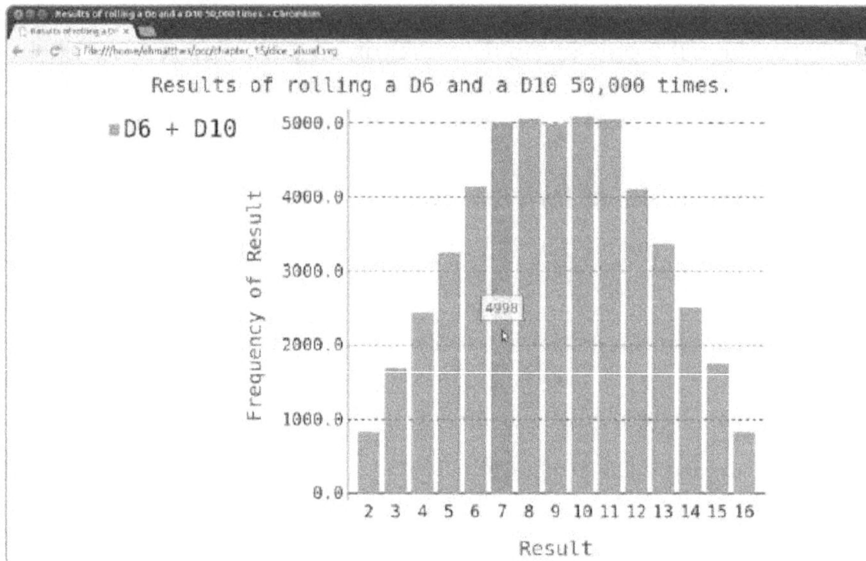

Figure 15-13: The results of rolling a six-sided die and a ten-sided die 50,000 times

Our ability to use Pygal to model the rolling of dice gives us considerable freedom in exploring this phenomenon. In just minutes you can simulate a tremendous number of rolls using a large variety of dice.

TRY IT YOURSELF

15-6. Automatic Labels: Modify *die.py* and *dice_visual.py* by replacing the list we used to set the value of `hist.x_labels` with a loop to generate this list automatically. If you're comfortable with list comprehensions, try replacing the other `for` loops in *die_visual.py* and *dice_visual.py* with comprehensions as well.

15-7. Two D8s: Create a simulation showing what happens if you roll two eight-sided dice 1000 times. Increase the number of rolls gradually until you start to see the limits of your system's capabilities.

15-8. Three Dice: If you roll three D6 dice, the smallest number you can roll is 3 and the largest number is 18. Create a visualization that shows what happens when you roll three D6 dice.

15-9. Multiplication: When you roll two dice, you usually add the two numbers together to get the result. Create a visualization that shows what happens if you multiply these numbers instead.

15-10. Practicing with Both Libraries: Try using matplotlib to make a die-rolling visualization, and use Pygal to make the visualization for a random walk.

Summary

In this chapter you learned to generate data sets and create visualizations of that data. You learned to create simple plots with matplotlib, and you saw how to use a scatter plot to explore random walks. You learned to create a histogram with Pygal and how to use a histogram to explore the results of rolling dice of different sizes.

Generating your own data sets with code is an interesting and powerful way to model and explore a wide variety of real-world situations. As you continue to work through the data visualization projects that follow, keep an eye out for situations you might be able to model with code. Look at the visualizations you see in news media, and see if you can identify those that were generated using methods similar to the ones you're learning in these projects.

In Chapter 16 we'll download data from online sources and continue to use matplotlib and Pygal to explore that data.

16

DOWNLOADING DATA

In this chapter you'll download data sets from online sources and create working visualizations of that data. An incredible variety of data can be found online, much of which hasn't been examined thoroughly. The ability to analyze this data allows you to discover patterns and connections that no one else has found.

We'll access and visualize data stored in two common data formats, CSV and JSON. We'll use Python's `csv` module to process weather data stored in the CSV (comma-separated values) format and analyze high and low temperatures over time in two different locations. We'll then use matplotlib to generate a chart based on our downloaded data to display variations in temperature in two very different environments: Sitka, Alaska, and Death Valley, California. Later in the chapter, we'll use the `json` module to access population data stored in the JSON format and use Pygal to draw a population map by country.

By the end of this chapter, you'll be prepared to work with different types and formats of data sets, and you'll have a deeper understanding of how to build complex visualizations. The ability to access and visualize online data of different types and formats is essential to working with a wide variety of real-world data sets.

The CSV File Format

One simple way to store data in a text file is to write the data as a series of values separated by commas, called *comma-separated values*. The resulting files are called *CSV* files. For example, here's one line of weather data in CSV format:

```
2014-1-5,61,44,26,18,7,-1,56,30,9,30.34,30.27,30.15,,,,10,4,,0.00,0,,195
```

This is weather data for January 5, 2014 in Sitka, Alaska. It includes the day's high and low temperatures, as well as a number of other measurements from that day. CSV files can be tricky for humans to read, but they're easy for programs to process and extract values from, which speeds up the data analysis process.

We'll begin with a small set of CSV-formatted weather data recorded in Sitka, which is available in the book's resources through *https://www.nostarch.com/pythoncrashcourse/*. Copy the file *sitka_weather_07-2014.csv* to the folder where you're writing this chapter's programs. (Once you download the book's resources, you'll have all the files you need for this project.)

NOTE *The weather data in this project was originally downloaded from* http://www.wunderground.com/history/.

Parsing the CSV File Headers

Python's `csv` module in the standard library parses the lines in a CSV file and allows us to quickly extract the values we're interested in. Let's start by examining the first line of the file, which contains a series of headers for the data:

highs_lows.py

```
import csv

filename = 'sitka_weather_07-2014.csv'
❶ with open(filename) as f:
❷     reader = csv.reader(f)
❸     header_row = next(reader)
      print(header_row)
```

After importing the csv module, we store the name of the file we're working with in `filename`. We then open the file and store the resulting file object in `f` ❶. Next, we call `csv.reader()` and pass it the file object as an argument to create a reader object associated with that file ❷. We store the reader object in `reader`.

The csv module contains a `next()` function, which returns the next line in the file when passed the reader object. In the preceding listing we call `next()` only once so we get the first line of the file, which contains the file headers ❸. We store the data that's returned in `header_row`. As you can see, `header_row` contains meaningful weather-related headers that tell us what information each line of data holds:

```
['AKDT', 'Max TemperatureF', 'Mean TemperatureF', 'Min TemperatureF',
'Max Dew PointF', 'MeanDew PointF', 'Min DewpointF', 'Max Humidity',
' Mean Humidity', ' Min Humidity', ' Max Sea Level PressureIn',
' Mean Sea Level PressureIn', ' Min Sea Level PressureIn',
' Max VisibilityMiles', ' Mean VisibilityMiles', ' Min VisibilityMiles',
' Max Wind SpeedMPH', ' Mean Wind SpeedMPH', ' Max Gust SpeedMPH',
'PrecipitationIn', ' CloudCover', ' Events', ' WindDirDegrees']
```

`reader` processes the first line of comma-separated values in the file and stores each as an item in a list. The header `AKDT` represents Alaska Daylight Time. The position of this header tells us that the first value in each line will be the date or time. The `Max TemperatureF` header tells us that the second value in each line is the maximum temperature for that date, in degrees Fahrenheit. You can read through the rest of the headers to determine the kind of information included in the file.

NOTE *The headers are not always formatted consistently: spaces and units are in odd places. This is common in raw data files but won't cause a problem.*

Printing the Headers and Their Positions

To make it easier to understand the file header data, print each header and its position in the list:

highs_lows.py

```
--snip--
with open(filename) as f:
    reader = csv.reader(f)
    header_row = next(reader)

❶   for index, column_header in enumerate(header_row):
        print(index, column_header)
```

We use `enumerate()` ❶ on the list to get the index of each item, as well as the value. (Note that we've removed the line `print(header_row)` in favor of this more detailed version.)

Here's the output showing the index of each header:

```
0 AKDT
1 Max TemperatureF
2 Mean TemperatureF
3 Min TemperatureF
--snip--
20 CloudCover
21 Events
22 WindDirDegrees
```

Here we see that the dates and their high temperatures are stored in columns 0 and 1. To explore this data, we'll process each row of data in *sitka_weather_07-2014.csv* and extract the values with the indices 0 and 1.

Extracting and Reading Data

Now that we know which columns of data we need, let's read in some of that data. First, we'll read in the high temperature for each day:

highs_lows.py

```
import csv

# Get high temperatures from file.
filename = 'sitka_weather_07-2014.csv'
with open(filename) as f:
    reader = csv.reader(f)
    header_row = next(reader)

❶   highs = []
❷   for row in reader:
❸       highs.append(row[1])

    print(highs)
```

We make an empty list called `highs` ❶ and then loop through the remaining rows in the file ❷. The reader object continues from where it left off in the CSV file and automatically returns each line following its current position. Because we've already read the header row, the loop will begin at the second line where the actual data begins. On each pass through the loop, we append the data from index 1, the second column, to `highs` ❸.

The following listing shows the data now stored in `highs`:

```
['64', '71', '64', '59', '69', '62', '61', '55', '57', '61', '57', '59', '57',
 '61', '64', '61', '59', '63', '60', '57', '69', '63', '62', '59', '57', '57',
 '61', '59', '61', '61', '66']
```

We've extracted the high temperature for each date and stored them neatly in a list as strings.

Next, convert these strings to numbers with `int()` so they can be read by matplotlib:

highs_lows.py

```
--snip--
    highs = []
    for row in reader:
❶        high = int(row[1])
        highs.append(high)

    print(highs)
```

We convert the strings to integers at ❶ before appending the temperatures to the list. The result is a list of daily highs in numerical format:

```
[64, 71, 64, 59, 69, 62, 61, 55, 57, 61, 57, 59, 57, 61, 64, 61, 59, 63, 60, 57,
 69, 63, 62, 59, 57, 57, 61, 59, 61, 61, 66]
```

Now let's create a visualization of this data.

Plotting Data in a Temperature Chart

To visualize the temperature data we have, we'll first create a simple plot of the daily highs using matplotlib, as shown here:

highs_lows.py

```
import csv

from matplotlib import pyplot as plt

# Get high temperatures from file.
--snip--

# Plot data.
fig = plt.figure(dpi=128, figsize=(10, 6))
❶ plt.plot(highs, c='red')

# Format plot.
❷ plt.title("Daily high temperatures, July 2014", fontsize=24)
❸ plt.xlabel('', fontsize=16)
plt.ylabel("Temperature (F)", fontsize=16)
plt.tick_params(axis='both', which='major', labelsize=16)

plt.show()
```

We pass the list of highs to `plot()` ❶ and pass `c='red'` to plot the points in red. (We'll plot the highs in red and the lows in blue.) We then specify a few other formatting details, such as font size and labels ❷, which you should recognize from Chapter 15. Because we have yet to add the dates, we won't label the x-axis, but `plt.xlabel()` does modify the font size to make the default labels more readable ❸. Figure 16-1 shows the resulting plot: a simple line graph of the high temperatures for July 2014, in Sitka, Alaska.

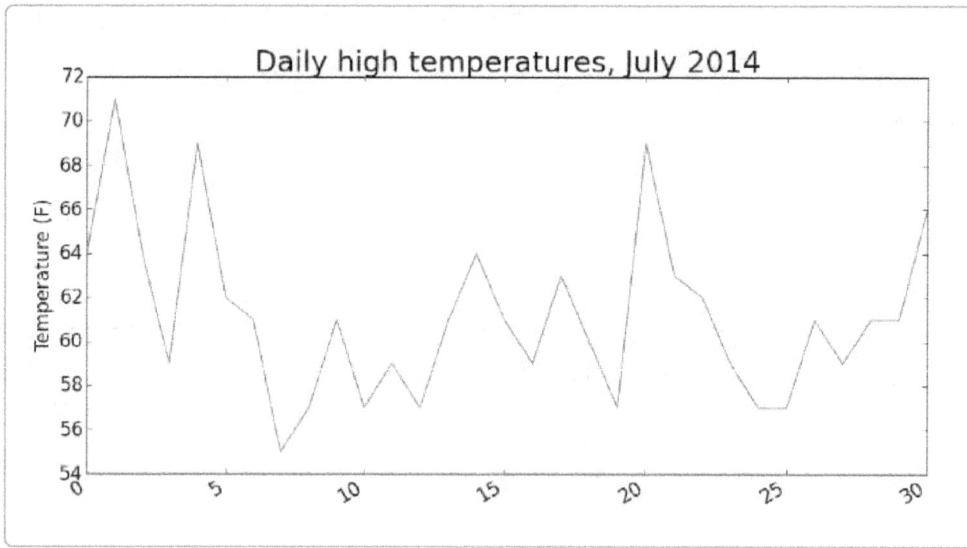

Figure 16-1: A line graph showing daily high temperatures for July 2014 in Sitka, Alaska

The datetime Module

Let's add dates to our graph to make it more useful. The first date from the weather data file is in the second row of the file:

```
2014-7-1,64,56,50,53,51,48,96,83,58,30.19,--snip--
```

The data will be read in as a string, so we need a way to convert the string `'2014-7-1'` to an object representing this date. We can construct an object representing July 1, 2014, using the `strptime()` method from the `datetime` module. Let's see how `strptime()` works in a terminal session:

```
>>> from datetime import datetime
>>> first_date = datetime.strptime('2014-7-1', '%Y-%m-%d')
>>> print(first_date)
2014-07-01 00:00:00
```

We first import the `datetime` class from the `datetime` module. Then we call the method `strptime()` with the string containing the date we want to work with as the first argument. The second argument tells Python how the date is formatted. In this example, `'%Y-'` tells Python to interpret the part of the string before the first dash as a four-digit year; `'%m-'` tells Python to interpret the part of the string before the second dash as a number representing the month; and `'%d'` tells Python to interpret the last part of the string as the day of the month, from 1 to 31.

The `strptime()` method can take a variety of arguments to determine how to interpret the date. Table 16-1 shows some of these arguments.

Table 16-1: Date and Time Formatting Arguments from the `datetime` Module

Argument	Meaning
`%A`	Weekday name, such as *Monday*
`%B`	Month name, such as *January*
`%m`	Month, as a number (01 to 12)
`%d`	Day of the month, as a number (01 to 31)
`%Y`	Four-digit year, such as 2015
`%y`	Two-digit year, such as 15
`%H`	Hour, in 24-hour format (00 to 23)
`%I`	Hour, in 12-hour format (01 to 12)
`%p`	AM or PM
`%M`	Minutes (00 to 59)
`%S`	Seconds (00 to 61)

Plotting Dates

Knowing how to process the dates in our CSV file, we can now improve our plot of the temperature data by extracting dates for the daily highs and passing the dates and the highs to `plot()`, as shown here:

highs_lows.py

```
import csv
from datetime import datetime

from matplotlib import pyplot as plt

# Get dates and high temperatures from file.
filename = 'sitka_weather_07-2014.csv'
with open(filename) as f:
    reader = csv.reader(f)
    header_row = next(reader)

❶   dates, highs = [], []
    for row in reader:
❷       current_date = datetime.strptime(row[0], "%Y-%m-%d")
        dates.append(current_date)

        high = int(row[1])
        highs.append(high)

# Plot data.
fig = plt.figure(dpi=128, figsize=(10, 6))
❸ plt.plot(dates, highs, c='red')

# Format plot.
plt.title("Daily high temperatures, July 2014", fontsize=24)
plt.xlabel('', fontsize=16)
```

```
❹ fig.autofmt_xdate()
  plt.ylabel("Temperature (F)", fontsize=16)
  plt.tick_params(axis='both', which='major', labelsize=16)

  plt.show()
```

We create two empty lists to store the dates and high temperatures from the file ❶. We then convert the data containing the date information (`row[0]`) to a `datetime` object ❷ and append it to `dates`. We pass the dates and the high temperature values to `plot()` at ❸. The call to `fig.autofmt_xdate()` at ❹ draws the date labels diagonally to prevent them from overlapping. Figure 16-2 shows the improved graph.

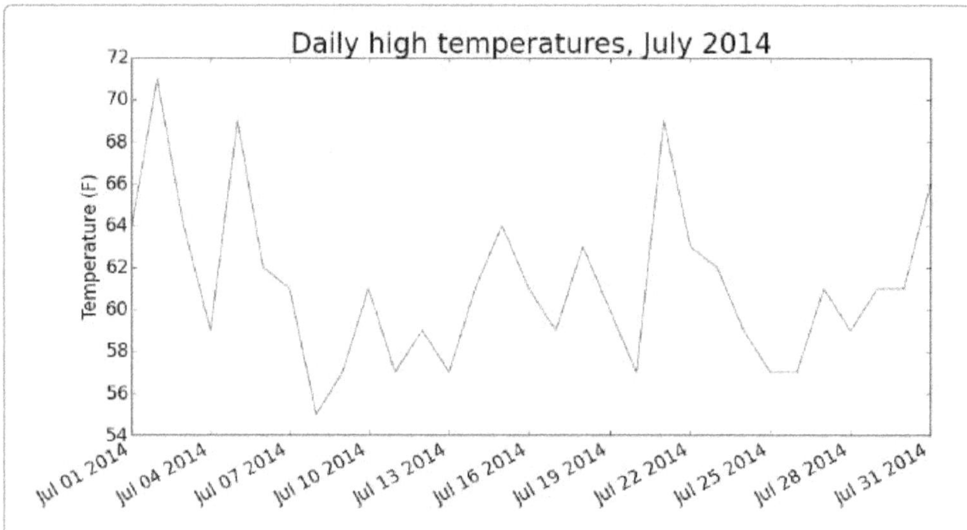

Figure 16-2: The graph is more meaningful now that it has dates on the x-axis.

Plotting a Longer Timeframe

With our graph set up, let's add more data to get a more complete picture of the weather in Sitka. Copy the file *sitka_weather_2014.csv*, which contains a full year's worth of Weather Underground data for Sitka, to the folder where you're storing this chapter's programs.

Now we can generate a graph for the entire year's weather:

highs_lows.py

```
  --snip--
  # Get dates and high temperatures from file.
❶ filename = 'sitka_weather_2014.csv'
  with open(filename) as f:
  --snip--
  # Format plot.
❷ plt.title("Daily high temperatures - 2014", fontsize=24)
  plt.xlabel('', fontsize=16)
  --snip--
```

We modify the filename to use the new data file *sitka_weather_2014.csv* ❶, and we update the title of our plot to reflect the change in its content ❷. Figure 16-3 shows the resulting plot.

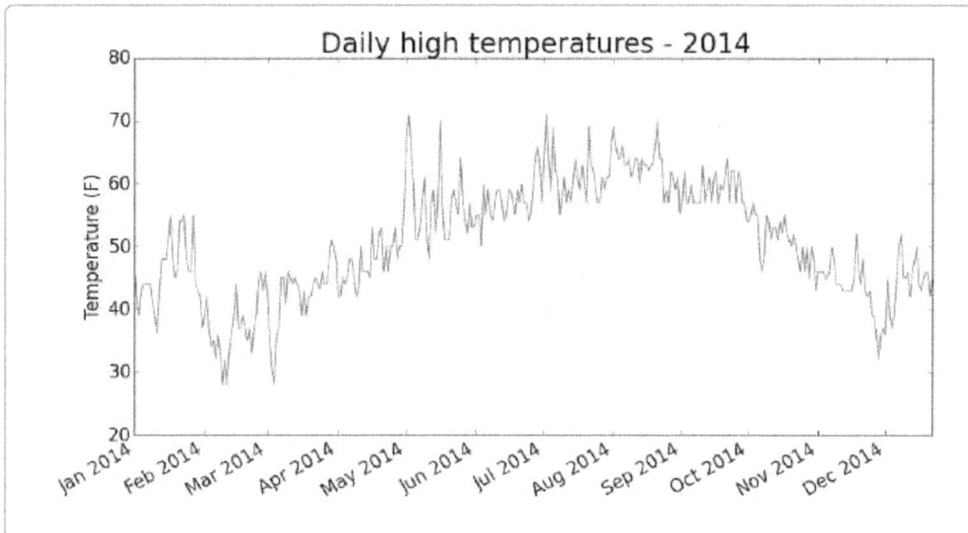

Figure 16-3: A year's worth of data

Plotting a Second Data Series

The reworked graph in Figure 16-3 displays a substantial amount of meaningful data, but we can make it even more useful by including the low temperatures. We need to extract the low temperatures from the data file and then add them to our graph, as shown here:

highs_lows.py

```
--snip--
# Get dates, high, and low temperatures from file.
filename = 'sitka_weather_2014.csv'
with open(filename) as f:
    reader = csv.reader(f)
    header_row = next(reader)

❶   dates, highs, lows = [], [], []
    for row in reader:
        current_date = datetime.strptime(row[0], "%Y-%m-%d")
        dates.append(current_date)

        high = int(row[1])
        highs.append(high)

❷       low = int(row[3])
        lows.append(low)
```

```
    # Plot data.
    fig = plt.figure(dpi=128, figsize=(10, 6))
    plt.plot(dates, highs, c='red')
❸ plt.plot(dates, lows, c='blue')

    # Format plot.
❹ plt.title("Daily high and low temperatures - 2014", fontsize=24)
    --snip--
```

At ❶ we add the empty list lows to hold low temperatures, and then we extract and store the low temperature for each date, from the fourth position in each row (row[3]) ❷. At ❸ we add a call to plot() for the low temperatures and color these values blue. Finally, we update the title ❹. Figure 16-4 shows the resulting chart.

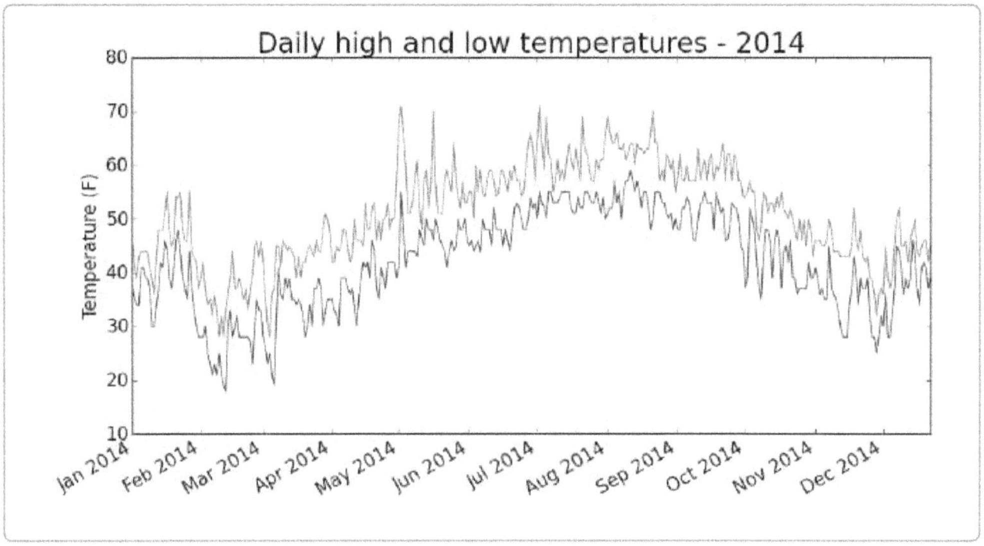

Figure 16-4: Two data series on the same plot

Shading an Area in the Chart

Having added two data series, we can now examine the range of temperatures for each day. Let's add a finishing touch to the graph by using shading to show the range between each day's high and low temperatures. To do so, we'll use the fill_between() method, which takes a series of x-values and two series of y-values, and fills the space between the two y-value series:

highs_lows.py

```
    --snip--
    # Plot data.
    fig = plt.figure(dpi=128, figsize=(10, 6))
❶ plt.plot(dates, highs, c='red', alpha=0.5)
    plt.plot(dates, lows, c='blue', alpha=0.5)
❷ plt.fill_between(dates, highs, lows, facecolor='blue', alpha=0.1)
    --snip--
```

The alpha argument at ❶ controls a color's transparency. An alpha value of 0 is completely transparent, and 1 (the default) is completely opaque. By setting alpha to 0.5 we make the red and blue plot lines appear lighter.

At ❷ we pass fill_between() the list dates for the x-values and then the two y-value series highs and lows. The facecolor argument determines the color of the shaded region, and we give it a low alpha value of 0.1 so the filled region connects the two data series without distracting from the information they represent. Figure 16-5 shows the plot with the shaded region between the highs and lows.

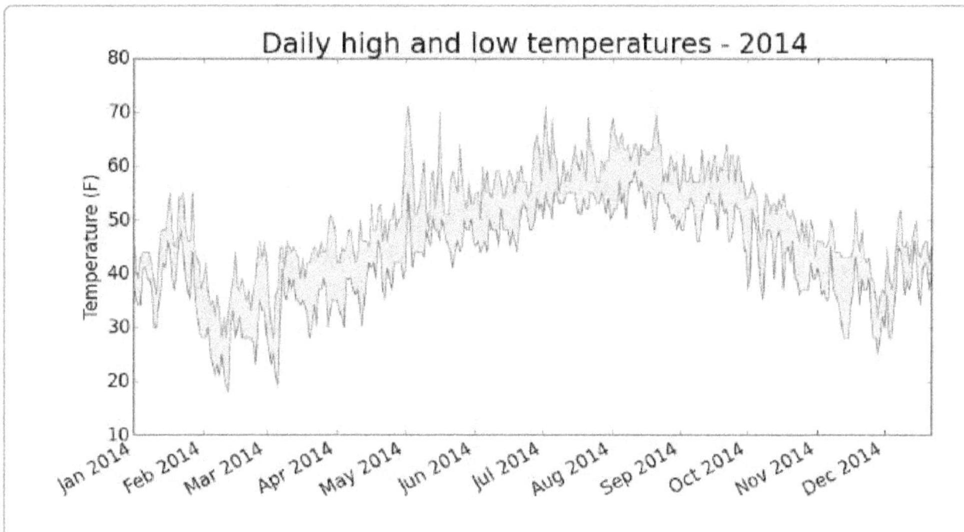

Figure 16-5: The region between the two data sets is shaded.

The shading helps make the range between the two data sets immediately apparent.

Error-Checking

We should be able to run the code from *highs_lows.py* using data for any location. But some weather stations occasionally malfunction and fail to collect some or all of the data they're supposed to. Missing data can result in exceptions that crash our programs if we don't handle them properly.

For example, let's see what happens when we attempt to generate a temperature plot for Death Valley, California. Copy the file *death_valley_2014.csv* to the folder where you're storing this chapter's programs, and then change *highs_lows.py* to generate a graph for Death Valley:

highs_lows.py

```
--snip--
# Get dates, high, and low temperatures from file.
filename = 'death_valley_2014.csv'
with open(filename) as f:
--snip--
```

When we run the program we get an error, as shown in the last line in the following output:

```
Traceback (most recent call last):
  File "highs_lows.py", line 17, in <module>
    high = int(row[1])
ValueError: invalid literal for int() with base 10: ''
```

The traceback tells us that Python can't process the high temperature for one of the dates because it can't turn an empty string ('') into an integer. A look through *death_valley_2014.csv* shows the problem:

```
2014-2-16,,,,,,,,,,,,,,,,,,,0.00,,,-1
```

It seems that on February 16, 2014, no data was recorded; the string for the high temperature is empty. To address this issue, we'll run error-checking code when the values are being read from the CSV file to handle exceptions that might arise when we parse our data sets. Here's how that works:

highs_lows.py

```
--snip--
# Get dates, high and low temperatures from file.
filename = 'death_valley_2014.csv'
with open(filename) as f:
    reader = csv.reader(f)
    header_row = next(reader)

    dates, highs, lows = [], [], []
    for row in reader:
❶       try:
            current_date = datetime.strptime(row[0], "%Y-%m-%d")
            high = int(row[1])
            low = int(row[3])
        except ValueError:
❷           print(current_date, 'missing data')
        else:
❸           dates.append(current_date)
            highs.append(high)
            lows.append(low)

# Plot data.
--snip--

# Format plot.
❹ title = "Daily high and low temperatures - 2014\nDeath Valley, CA"
plt.title(title, fontsize=20)
--snip--
```

Each time we examine a row, we try to extract the date and the high and low temperature ❶. If any data is missing, Python will raise a `ValueError` and we handle it by printing an error message that includes the date of the missing data ❷. After printing the error, the loop will continue processing the next row. If all data for a date is retrieved without error, the `else` block will run and the data will be appended to the appropriate lists ❸. Because we're plotting information for a new location, we update the title to include the location on the plot ❹.

When you run *highs_lows.py* now, you'll see that only one date had missing data:

```
2014-02-16 missing data
```

Figure 16-6 shows the resulting plot.

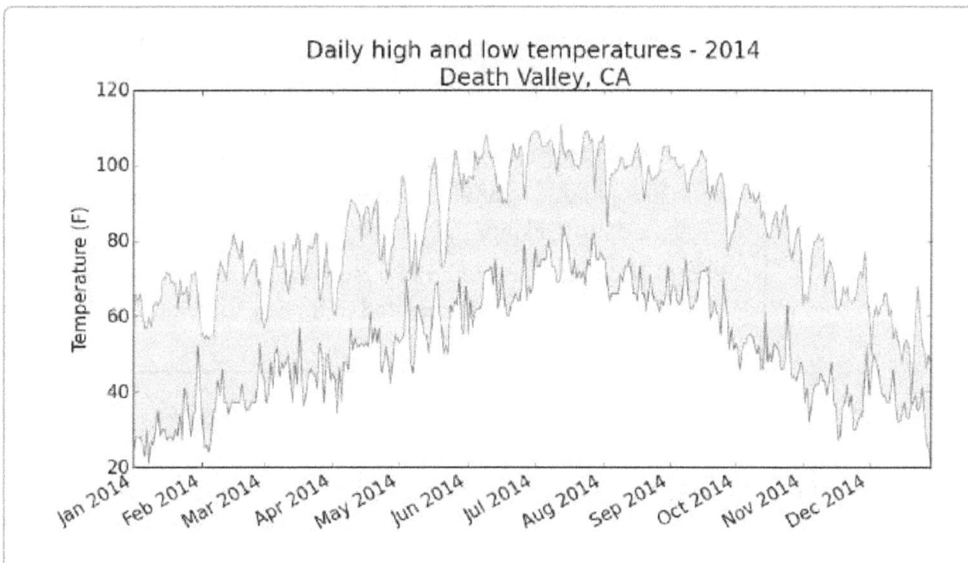

Figure 16-6: Daily high and low temperatures for Death Valley

Comparing this graph to the Sitka graph, we can see that Death Valley is warmer overall than southeast Alaska, as might be expected, but also that the range of temperatures each day is actually greater in the desert. The height of the shaded region makes this clear.

Many data sets you work with will have missing data, improperly formatted data, or incorrect data. Use the tools you learned in the first half of this book to deal with these situations. Here we used a `try-except-else` block to handle missing data. Sometimes you'll use `continue` to skip over some data or use `remove()` or `del` to eliminate some data after it's been extracted. You can use any approach that works, as long as the result is a meaningful, accurate visualization.

TRY IT YOURSELF

16-1. San Francisco: Are temperatures in San Francisco more like temperatures in Sitka or temperatures in Death Valley? Generate a high-low temperature plot for San Francisco and make a comparison. (You can download weather data for almost any location from *http://www.wunderground.com/history/*. Enter a location and date range, scroll to the bottom of the page, and find a link labeled *Comma-Delimited File*. Right-click this link, and save the data as a CSV file.)

16-2. Sitka-Death Valley Comparison: The temperature scales on the Sitka and Death Valley graphs reflect the different ranges of the data. To accurately compare the temperature range in Sitka to that of Death Valley, you need identical scales on the y-axis. Change the settings for the y-axis on one or both of the charts in Figures 16-5 and 16-6, and make a direct comparison between temperature ranges in Sitka and Death Valley (or any two places you want to compare). You can also try plotting the two data sets on the same chart.

16-3. Rainfall: Choose any location you're interested in, and make a visualization that plots its rainfall. Start by focusing on one month's data, and then once your code is working, run it for a full year's data.

16-4. Explore: Generate a few more visualizations that examine any other weather aspect you're interested in for any locations you're curious about.

Mapping Global Data Sets: JSON Format

In this section, you'll download location-based country data in the JSON format and work with it using the `json` module. Using Pygal's beginner-friendly mapping tool for country-based data, you'll create visualizations of this data that explore global patterns concerning the world's population distribution over different countries.

Downloading World Population Data

Copy the file *population_data.json*, which contains population data from 1960 through 2010 for most of the world's countries, to the folder where you're storing this chapter's programs. This data comes from one of the many data sets that the Open Knowledge Foundation (*http://data.okfn.org/*) makes freely available.

Extracting Relevant Data

Let's look at *population_data.json* to see how we might begin to process the data in the file:

population_data.json

```
[
  {
    "Country Name": "Arab World",
    "Country Code": "ARB",
    "Year": "1960",
    "Value": "96388069"
  },
  {
    "Country Name": "Arab World",
    "Country Code": "ARB",
    "Year": "1961",
    "Value": "98882541.4"
  },
  --snip--
]
```

The file is basically one long Python list. Each item is a dictionary with four keys: a country name, a country code, a year, and a value representing the population. We want to examine each country's name and population only in 2010, so start by writing a program to print just that information:

world_population.py

```
import json

# Load the data into a list.
filename = 'population_data.json'
with open(filename) as f:
❶    pop_data = json.load(f)

# Print the 2010 population for each country.
❷ for pop_dict in pop_data:
❸    if pop_dict['Year'] == '2010':
❹        country_name = pop_dict['Country Name']
        population = pop_dict['Value']
        print(country_name + ": " + population)
```

We first import the `json` module to be able to load the data properly from the file, and then we store the data in `pop_data` at ❶. The `json.load()` function converts the data into a format Python can work with: in this case, a list. At ❷ we loop through each item in `pop_data`. Each item is a dictionary with four key-value pairs, and we store each dictionary in `pop_dict`.

At ❸ we look for 2010 in the `'Year'` key of each dictionary. (Because the values in *population_data.json* are all in quotes, we do a string comparison.) If the year is 2010, we store the value associated with `'Country Name'` in `country_name` and the value associated with `'Value'` in `population` at ❹. We then print the name of each country and its population.

The output is a series of country names and population values:

```
Arab World: 357868000
Caribbean small states: 6880000
East Asia & Pacific (all income levels): 2201536674
--snip--
Zimbabwe: 12571000
```

Not all of the data we captured includes exact country names, but this is a good start. Now we need to convert the data into a format Pygal can work with.

Converting Strings into Numerical Values

Every key and value in *population_data.json* is stored as a string. To work with the population data, we need to convert the population strings to numerical values. We do this using the int() function:

world_population.py

```
--snip--
for pop_dict in pop_data:
    if pop_dict['Year'] == '2010':
        country_name = pop_dict['Country Name']
❶       population = int(pop_dict['Value'])
❷       print(country_name + ": " + str(population))
```

Now we've stored each population value in numerical format at ❶. When we print the population value, we need to convert it to a string at ❷.

However, this change results in an error for some values, as shown here:

```
Arab World: 357868000
Caribbean small states: 6880000
East Asia & Pacific (all income levels): 2201536674
--snip--
Traceback (most recent call last):
  File "print_populations.py", line 12, in <module>
    population = int(pop_dict['Value'])
❶ ValueError: invalid literal for int() with base 10: '1127437398.85751'
```

It's often the case that raw data isn't formatted consistently, so we come across errors a lot. Here the error occurs because Python can't directly turn a string that contains a decimal, '1127437398.85751', into an integer ❶. (This decimal value is probably the result of interpolation for years when a specific population count was not made.) We address this error by converting the string to a float and then converting that float to an integer:

world_population.py

```
--snip--
for pop_dict in pop_data:
    if pop_dict['Year'] == '2010':
        country = pop_dict['Country Name']
        population = int(float(pop_dict['Value']))
        print(country + ": " + str(population))
```

The float() function turns the string into a decimal, and the int() function drops the decimal part of the number and returns an integer. Now we can print a full set of population values for the year 2010 with no errors:

```
Arab World: 357868000
Caribbean small states: 6880000
East Asia & Pacific (all income levels): 2201536674
--snip--
Zimbabwe: 12571000
```

Each string was successfully converted to a float and then to an integer. Now that these population values are stored in a numerical format, we can use them to make a world population map.

Obtaining Two-Digit Country Codes

Before we can focus on mapping, we need to address one last aspect of the data. The mapping tool in Pygal expects data in a particular format: countries need to be provided as country codes and populations as values. Several standardized sets of country codes are frequently used when working with geopolitical data; the codes included in *population_data.json* are three-letter codes, but Pygal uses two-letter codes. We need a way to find the two-digit code from the country name.

Pygal's country codes are stored in a module called i18n, short for *internationalization*. The dictionary COUNTRIES contains the two-letter country codes as keys and the country names as values. To see these codes, import the dictionary from the i18n module and print its keys and values:

countries.py

```
from pygal.i18n import COUNTRIES

❶ for country_code in sorted(COUNTRIES.keys()):
    print(country_code, COUNTRIES[country_code])
```

In the for loop we tell Python to sort the keys in alphabetical order ❶. Then we print each country code and the country it's associated with:

```
ad Andorra
ae United Arab Emirates
af Afghanistan
--snip--
zw Zimbabwe
```

To extract the country code data, we write a function that searches through COUNTRIES and returns the country code. We'll write this in a separate module called country_codes so we can later import it into a visualization program:

country_codes.py

```
from pygal.i18n import COUNTRIES

❶ def get_country_code(country_name):
    """Return the Pygal 2-digit country code for the given country."""
```

```
❷     for code, name in COUNTRIES.items():
❸         if name == country_name:
              return code
      # If the country wasn't found, return None.
❹     return None

print(get_country_code('Andorra'))
print(get_country_code('United Arab Emirates'))
print(get_country_code('Afghanistan'))
```

We pass `get_country_code()` the name of the country and store it in the parameter `country_name` ❶. We then loop through the code-name pairs in `COUNTRIES` ❷. If the name of the country is found, the country code is returned ❸. We add a line after the loop to return `None` if the country name was not found ❹. Finally, we pass three country names to check that the function works. As expected, the program outputs three two-letter country codes:

```
ad
ae
af
```

Before using this function, remove the `print` statements from *country_codes.py*.

Next we import `get_country_code()` into *world_population.py*:

world_population.py

```
import json

from country_codes import get_country_code
--snip--

# Print the 2010 population for each country.
for pop_dict in pop_data:
    if pop_dict['Year'] == '2010':
        country_name = pop_dict['Country Name']
        population = int(float(pop_dict['Value']))
❶       code = get_country_code(country_name)
        if code:
❷           print(code + ": "+ str(population))
❸       else:
            print('ERROR - ' + country_name)
```

After extracting the country name and population, we store the country code in `code` or `None` if no code is available ❶. If a code is returned, the code and country's population are printed ❷. If the code is not available, we display an error message with the name of the country we can't find a code for ❸. Run this program, and you'll see some country codes with their populations and some error lines:

```
ERROR - Arab World
ERROR - Caribbean small states
ERROR - East Asia & Pacific (all income levels)
```

```
--snip--
af: 34385000
al: 3205000
dz: 35468000
--snip--
ERROR - Yemen, Rep.
zm: 12927000
zw: 12571000
```

The errors come from two sources. First, not all the classifications in the data set are by country; some population statistics are for regions (*Arab World*) and economic groups (*all income levels*). Second, some of the statistics use a different system for full names of countries (*Yemen, Rep.* instead of *Yemen*). For now, we'll omit country data that cause errors and see what our map looks like for the data that we recovered successfully.

Building a World Map

With the country codes we have, it's quick and simple to make a world map. Pygal includes a `Worldmap` chart type to help map global data sets. As an example of how to use `Worldmap`, we'll create a simple map that highlights North America, Central America, and South America:

americas.py

```
import pygal

❶ wm = pygal.Worldmap()
wm.title = 'North, Central, and South America'

❷ wm.add('North America', ['ca', 'mx', 'us'])
wm.add('Central America', ['bz', 'cr', 'gt', 'hn', 'ni', 'pa', 'sv'])
wm.add('South America', ['ar', 'bo', 'br', 'cl', 'co', 'ec', 'gf',
    'gy', 'pe', 'py', 'sr', 'uy', 've'])

❸ wm.render_to_file('americas.svg')
```

At ❶ we make an instance of the `Worldmap` class and set the map's `title` attribute. At ❷ we use the `add()` method, which takes in a label and a list of country codes for the countries we want to focus on. Each call to `add()` sets up a new color for the set of countries and adds that color to a key on the left of the graph with the label specified here. We want the entire region of North America represented in one color, so we place `'ca'`, `'mx'`, and `'us'` in the list we pass to the first `add()` call to highlight Canada, Mexico, and the United States together. We then do the same for the countries in Central America and South America.

The method `render_to_file()` at ❸ creates an *.svg* file containing the chart, which you can open in your browser. The output is a map highlighting North, Central, and South America in different colors, as shown in Figure 16-7.

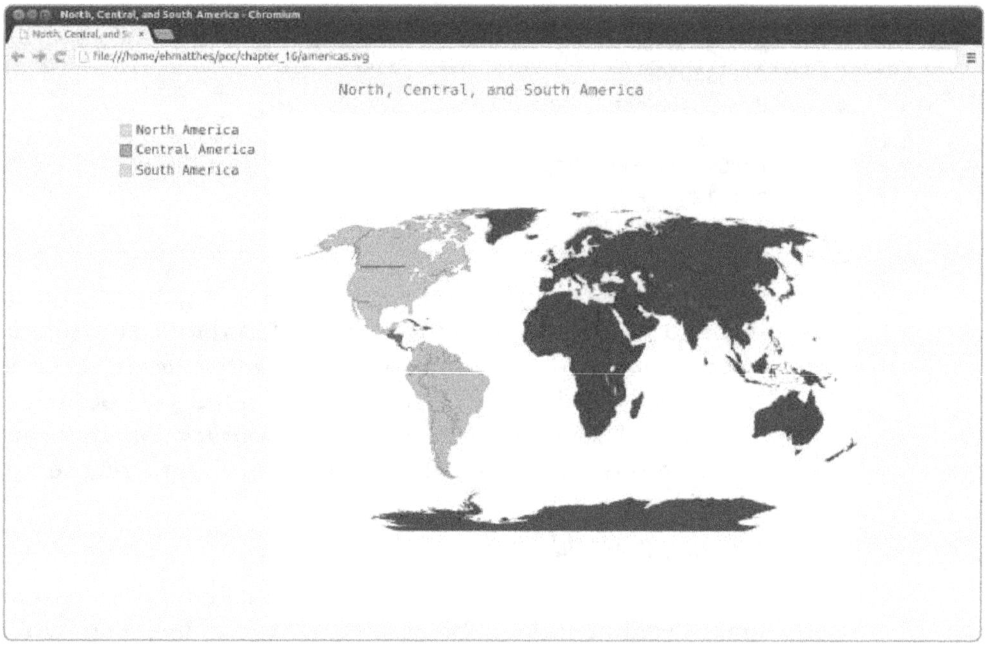

Figure 16-7: A simple instance of the `Worldmap` chart type

We now know how to make a map with colored areas, a key, and neat labels. Let's add data to our map to show information about a country.

Plotting Numerical Data on a World Map

To practice plotting numerical data on a map, create a map showing the populations of the three countries in North America:

na_populations.py

```
import pygal

wm = pygal.Worldmap()
wm.title = 'Populations of Countries in North America'
❶ wm.add('North America', {'ca': 34126000, 'us': 309349000, 'mx': 113423000})

wm.render_to_file('na_populations.svg')
```

First create a `Worldmap` instance and set a title. Then use the `add()` method, but this time pass a dictionary as the second argument instead of a list ❶. The dictionary has Pygal two-letter country codes as its keys and population numbers as its values. Pygal automatically uses these numbers to shade the countries from light (least populated) to dark (most populated). Figure 16-8 shows the resulting map.

Figure 16-8: Population sizes of countries in North America

This map is interactive: if you hover over each country, you'll see its population. Let's add more data to our map.

Plotting a Complete Population Map

To plot population numbers for the rest of the countries, we have to convert the country data we processed earlier into the dictionary format Pygal expects, which is two-letter country codes as keys and population numbers as values. Add the following code to *world_population.py*:

world_population.py

```
import json

import pygal

from country_codes import get_country_code

# Load the data into a list.
--snip--

# Build a dictionary of population data.
❶ cc_populations = {}
for pop_dict in pop_data:
    if pop_dict['Year'] == '2010':
        country = pop_dict['Country Name']
        population = int(float(pop_dict['Value']))
        code = get_country_code(country)
```

```
        if code:
❷           cc_populations[code] = population

❸ wm = pygal.Worldmap()
  wm.title = 'World Population in 2010, by Country'
❹ wm.add('2010', cc_populations)

  wm.render_to_file('world_population.svg')
```

We first import pygal. At ❶ we create an empty dictionary to store country codes and populations in the format Pygal expects. At ❷ we build the cc_populations dictionary using the country code as a key and the population as the value whenever a code is returned. We also remove all the print statements.

We make a Worldmap instance and set its title attribute ❸. When we call add(), we pass it the dictionary of country codes and population values ❹. Figure 16-9 shows the map that's generated.

Figure 16-9: The world's population in 2010

We don't have data for a few countries, which are colored in black, but most countries are colored according to their population size. You'll deal with the missing data later in this chapter, but first we'll alter the shading to more accurately reflect the population of the countries. Currently, our map shows many lightly shaded countries and two darkly shaded countries. The contrast between most of the countries isn't enough to indicate how populated they are relative to each other. We'll fix this by grouping countries into population levels and shading each group.

Grouping Countries by Population

Because China and India are more heavily populated than other countries, the map shows little contrast. China and India are each home to over a billion people, whereas the next most populous country is the United States with approximately 300 million people. Instead of plotting all countries as one group, let's separate the countries into three population levels: less than 10 million, between 10 million and 1 billion, and more than 1 billion:

world_population.py

```
--snip--
# Build a dictionary of population data.
cc_populations = {}
for pop_dict in pop_data:
    if pop_dict['Year'] == '2010':
        --snip--
        if code:
            cc_populations[code] = population

# Group the countries into 3 population levels.
❶ cc_pops_1, cc_pops_2, cc_pops_3 = {}, {}, {}
❷ for cc, pop in cc_populations.items():
    if pop < 10000000:
        cc_pops_1[cc] = pop
    elif pop < 1000000000:
        cc_pops_2[cc] = pop
    else:
        cc_pops_3[cc] = pop

# See how many countries are in each level.
❸ print(len(cc_pops_1), len(cc_pops_2), len(cc_pops_3))

wm = pygal.Worldmap()
wm.title = 'World Population in 2010, by Country'
❹ wm.add('0-10m', cc_pops_1)
wm.add('10m-1bn', cc_pops_2)
wm.add('>1bn', cc_pops_3)

wm.render_to_file('world_population.svg')
```

To group the countries, we create an empty dictionary for each category ❶. We then loop through `cc_populations` to check the population of each country ❷. The `if-elif-else` block adds an entry to the appropriate dictionary (`cc_pops_1`, `cc_pops_2`, or `cc_pops_3`) for each country code–population pair.

At ❸ we print the length of each of these dictionaries to find out the sizes of the groups. When we plot the data ❹, we make sure to add all three groups to the `Worldmap`. When you run this program, you'll first see the size of each group:

```
85 69 2
```

This output indicates that there are 85 countries with fewer than 10 million people, 69 countries with between 10 million and 1 billion people, and two outlier countries with over 1 billion. This seems like an even enough split for an informative map. Figure 16-10 shows the resulting map.

Figure 16-10: The world's population shown in three different groups

Now three different colors help us see the distinctions between population levels. Within each of the three levels, countries are shaded from light to dark for smallest to largest population.

Styling World Maps in Pygal

Although the population groups in our map are effective, the default color settings are pretty ugly: for example, here Pygal has chosen a garish pink and green motif. We'll use Pygal's styling directives to rectify the colors.

Let's direct Pygal to use one base color again, but this time we'll choose the color and apply more distinct shading for the three population groups:

world_population.py

```
import json

import pygal
❶ from pygal.style import RotateStyle
--snip--
# Group the countries into 3 population levels.
cc_pops_1, cc_pops_2, cc_pops_3 = {}, {}, {}
```

```
for cc, pop in cc_populations.items():
    if pop < 10000000:
        --snip--

❷ wm_style = RotateStyle('#336699')
❸ wm = pygal.Worldmap(style=wm_style)
wm.title = 'World Population in 2010, by Country'
--snip--
```

Pygal styles are stored in the style module from which we import the style RotateStyle ❶. This class takes one argument, an RGB color in hex format ❷. Pygal then chooses colors for each of the groups based on the color provided. The *hex format* is a string with a hash mark (#) followed by six characters: the first two represent the red component of the color, the next two represent the green component, and the last two represent the blue component. The component values can range from 00 (none of that color) to FF (maximum amount of that color). If you search online for *hex color chooser*, you should find a tool that will let you experiment with colors and give you the RGB values. The color used here (#336699) mixes a bit of red (33), a little more green (66), and even more blue (99) to give RotateStyle a light blue base color to work from.

RotateStyle returns a style object, which we store in wm_style. To use this style object, pass it as a keyword argument when you make an instance of Worldmap ❸. Figure 16-11 shows the updated chart.

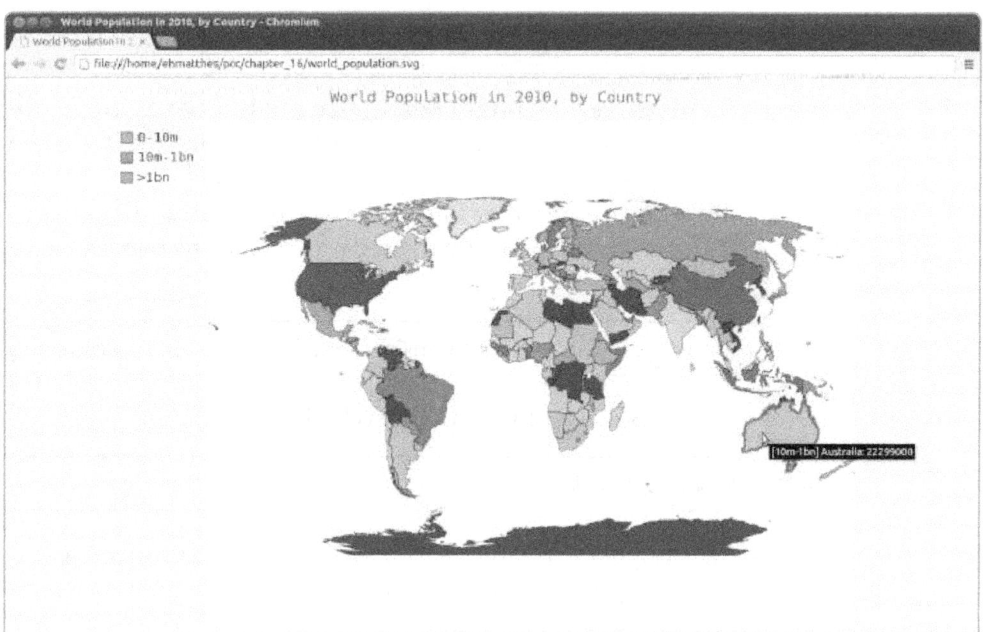

Figure 16-11: The three population groups in a unified color theme

This styling gives the map a unified look, and it results in groups that are easy to distinguish.

Lightening the Color Theme

Pygal tends to use dark themes by default. For the purposes of printing, I've lightened the style of my charts using `LightColorizedStyle`. This class changes the overall theme of the chart, including the background and labels as well as the individual country colors. To use it, first import the style:

```
from pygal.style import LightColorizedStyle
```

You can then use `LightColorizedStyle` on its own, as such:

```
wm_style = LightColorizedStyle
```

But this class gives you no direct control over the color used, so Pygal will choose a default base color. To set a color, use `LightColorizedStyle` as a base for `RotateStyle`. Import both `LightColorizedStyle` and `RotateStyle`:

```
from pygal.style import LightColorizedStyle, RotateStyle
```

Then create a style using `RotateStyle`, but pass it an additional `base_style` argument:

```
wm_style = RotateStyle('#336699', base_style=LightColorizedStyle)
```

This gives you a light overall theme but bases the country colors on the color you pass as an argument. With this style you'll see that your charts match the screenshots here a bit more closely.

While you're experimenting to find styling directives that work well for different visualizations, it can help to use aliases in your `import` statements:

```
from pygal.style import LightColorizedStyle as LCS, RotateStyle as RS
```

This will result in shorter style definitions:

```
wm_style = RS('#336699', base_style=LCS)
```

Using just this small set of styling directives gives you significant control over the appearance of charts and maps in Pygal.

TRY IT YOURSELF

16-5. All Countries: On the population maps we made in this section, our program couldn't automatically find two-letter codes for about 12 countries. Work out which countries are missing codes, and look through the `COUNTRIES` dictionary for the codes. Add an `if-elif` block to `get_country_code()` so it returns the correct country code values for these specific countries:

```
if country_name == 'Yemen, Rep.'
    return 'ye'
elif --snip--
```

Place this code after the `COUNTRIES` loop but before the `return None` statement. When you're finished, you should see a more complete map.

16-6. Gross Domestic Product: The Open Knowledge Foundation maintains a data set containing the gross domestic product (GDP) for each country in the world, which you can find at *http://data.okfn.org/data/core/gdp/*. Download the JSON version of this data set, and plot the GDP of each country in the world for the most recent year in the data set.

16-7. Choose Your Own Data: The World Bank maintains many data sets that are broken down for information on each country worldwide. Go to *http://data.worldbank.org/indicator/* and find a data set that looks interesting. Click the data set, click the **Download Data** link, and choose **CSV**. You'll receive three CSV files, two of which are labeled *Metadata*; use the third CSV file. Write a program that generates a dictionary with Pygal's two-letter country codes as its keys and your chosen data from the file as its values. Plot the data on a `Worldmap` and style the map as you like.

16-8. Testing the `country_codes` Module: When we wrote the `country_codes` module, we used `print` statements to check whether the `get_country_code()` function worked. Write a proper test for this function using what you learned in Chapter 11.

Summary

In this chapter you learned to work with online data sets. You learned how to process CSV and JSON files, and extract the data you want to focus on. Using historical weather data, you learned more about working with matplotlib, including how to use the `datetime` module and how to plot multiple data series on one chart. You learned to plot country data on a world map in Pygal and to style Pygal maps and charts.

As you gain experience with CSV and JSON files, you'll be able to process almost any data you want to analyze. Most online data sets can be downloaded in either or both of these formats. From working with these formats, you'll be able to learn other data formats as well.

In the next chapter, you'll write programs that automatically gather their own data from online sources, and then you'll create visualizations of that data. These are fun skills to have if you want to program as a hobby and critical skills if you're interested in programming professionally.

17

WORKING WITH APIs

In this chapter you'll learn how to write a self-contained program to generate a visualization based on data that it retrieves. Your program will use a web *application programming interface (API)* to automatically request specific information from a website rather than entire pages. It will then use that information to generate a visualization. Because programs written like this will always use current data to generate a visualization, even when that data might be rapidly changing, it will always be up to date.

Using a Web API

A web API is a part of a website designed to interact with programs that use very specific URLs to request certain information. This kind of request is called an *API call.* The requested data will be returned in an easily processed format, such as JSON or CSV. Most apps that rely on external data sources, such as apps that integrate with social media sites, rely on API calls.

Git and GitHub

We'll base our visualization on information from GitHub, a site that allows programmers to collaborate on projects. We'll use GitHub's API to request information about Python projects on the site and then generate an interactive visualization of the relative popularity of these projects in Pygal.

GitHub (*https://github.com/*) takes its name from Git, a distributed version control system that allows teams of programmers to collaborate on projects. Git helps people manage their individual work on a project, so changes made by one person won't interfere with changes other people are making. When you're implementing a new feature in a project, Git tracks the changes you make to each file. When your new code works, you *commit* the changes you've made, and Git records the new state of your project. If you make a mistake and want to revert your changes, you can easily return to any previously working state. (To learn more about version control using Git, see Appendix D.) Projects on GitHub are stored in *repositories*, which contain everything associated with the project: its code, information on its collaborators, any issues or bug reports, and so on.

When users on GitHub like a project, they can "star" it to show their support and keep track of projects they might want to use. In this chapter we'll write a program to automatically download information about the most-starred Python projects on GitHub, and then we'll create an informative visualization of these projects.

Requesting Data Using an API Call

GitHub's API lets you request a wide range of information through API calls. To see what an API call looks like, enter the following into your browser's address bar and press ENTER:

```
https://api.github.com/search/repositories?q=language:python&sort=stars
```

This call returns the number of Python projects currently hosted on GitHub, as well as information about the most popular Python repositories. Let's examine the call. The first part, `https://api.github.com/`, directs the request to the part of GitHub's website that responds to API calls. The next part, `search/repositories`, tells the API to conduct a search through all repositories on GitHub.

The question mark after `repositories` signals that we're about to pass an argument. The `q` stands for query, and the equal sign lets us begin specifying a query (q=). By using language:python, we indicate that we want information only on repositories that have Python as the primary language. The final part, &sort=stars, sorts the projects by the number of stars they've been given.

The following snippet shows the first few lines of the response. You can see from the response that this URL is not intended to be entered by humans.


```
{
  "total_count": 713062,
  "incomplete_results": false,
  "items": [
    {
      "id": 3544424,
      "name": "httpie",
      "full_name": "jkbrzt/httpie",
      --snip--
```


As you can see in the second line of output, GitHub found a total of 713,062 Python projects as of this writing. Because the value for "incomplete_results" is false, we know that the request was successful (it's not incomplete). If GitHub had been unable to fully process the API request, it would have returned true here. The "items" returned are displayed in the list that follows, which contains details about the most popular Python projects on GitHub.

Installing Requests

The requests package allows a Python program to easily request information from a website and examine the response that's returned. To install requests, issue a command like the following:

```
$ pip install --user requests
```

If you haven't used pip yet, see "Installing Python Packages with pip" on page 237. (You may need to use a slightly different version of this command, depending on your system's setup.)

Processing an API Response

Now we'll begin to write a program to issue an API call and process the results by identifying the most starred Python projects on GitHub:

python_repos.py

```
❶ import requests

  # Make an API call and store the response.
❷ url = 'https://api.github.com/search/repositories?q=language:python&sort=stars'
❸ r = requests.get(url)
❹ print("Status code:", r.status_code)
```

```
    # Store API response in a variable.
❺ response_dict = r.json()

    # Process results.
    print(response_dict.keys())
```

At ❶ we import the requests module. At ❷ we store the URL of the API call, and then we use requests to make the call ❸. We call get() and pass it the URL, and we store the response object in the variable r. The response object has an attribute called status_code, which tells us whether the request was successful. (A status code of 200 indicates a successful response.) At ❹ we print the value of status_code to make sure the call went through successfully.

The API returns the information in JSON format, so we use the json() method ❺ to convert the information to a Python dictionary. We store the resulting dictionary in response_dict.

Finally, we print the keys from response_dict and see this:

```
Status code: 200
dict_keys(['items', 'total_count', 'incomplete_results'])
```

Because the status code is 200, we know that the request was successful. The response dictionary contains only three keys: 'items', 'total_count', and 'incomplete_results'.

NOTE *Simple calls like this should return a complete set of results, so it's pretty safe to ignore the value associated with 'incomplete_results'. But when you're making more complex API calls, your program should check this value.*

Working with the Response Dictionary

Now that we have the information from the API call stored as a dictionary, we can work with the data stored there. Let's generate some output that summarizes the information. This is a good way to make sure we received the information we expected and to start examining the information we're interested in:

python_repos.py

```
    import requests

    # Make an API call and store the response.
    url = 'https://api.github.com/search/repositories?q=language:python&sort=stars'
    r = requests.get(url)
    print("Status code:", r.status_code)

    # Store API response in a variable.
    response_dict = r.json()
❶ print("Total repositories:", response_dict['total_count'])

    # Explore information about the repositories.
❷ repo_dicts = response_dict['items']
    print("Repositories returned:", len(repo_dicts))
```

```
# Examine the first repository.
❸ repo_dict = repo_dicts[0]
❹ print("\nKeys:", len(repo_dict))
❺ for key in sorted(repo_dict.keys()):
      print(key)
```

At ❶ we print the value associated with `'total_count'`, which represents the total number of Python repositories on GitHub.

The value associated with `'items'` is a list containing a number of dictionaries, each of which contains data about an individual Python repository. At ❷ we store this list of dictionaries in `repo_dicts`. We then print the length of `repo_dicts` to see how many repositories we have information for.

To take a closer look at the information returned about each repository, we pull out the first item from `repo_dicts` and store it in `repo_dict` ❸. We then print the number of keys in the dictionary to see how much information we have ❹. At ❺ we print all of the dictionary's keys to see what kind of information is included.

The results start to give us a clearer picture of the actual data:

```
Status code: 200
Total repositories: 713062
Repositories returned: 30

❶ Keys: 68
archive_url
assignees_url
blobs_url
--snip--
url
watchers
watchers_count
```

GitHub's API returns a lot of information about each repository: there are 68 keys in `repo_dict` ❶. When you look through these keys, you'll get a sense of the kind of information you can extract about a project. (The only way to know what information is available through an API is to read the documentation or to examine the information through code, as we're doing here.)

Let's pull out the values for some of the keys in `repo_dict`:

python_repos.py

```
--snip--
# Explore information about the repositories.
repo_dicts = response_dict['items']
print("Repositories returned:", len(repo_dicts))

# Examine the first repository.
repo_dict = repo_dicts[0]

print("\nSelected information about first repository:")
❶ print('Name:', repo_dict['name'])
❷ print('Owner:', repo_dict['owner']['login'])
```

```
❸ print('Stars:', repo_dict['stargazers_count'])
   print('Repository:', repo_dict['html_url'])
❹ print('Created:', repo_dict['created_at'])
❺ print('Updated:', repo_dict['updated_at'])
   print('Description:', repo_dict['description'])
```

Here we print out the values for a number of keys from the first repository's dictionary. At ❶ we print the name of the project. An entire dictionary represents the project's owner, so at ❷ we use the key `owner` to access the dictionary representing the owner and then use the key `login` to get the owner's login name. At ❸ we print how many stars the project has earned and the URL for the project's GitHub repository. We then show when it was created ❹ and when it was last updated ❺. Finally, we print the repository's description, and the output should look something like this:

```
Status code: 200
Total repositories: 713065
Repositories returned: 30

Selected information about first repository:
Name: httpie
Owner: jkbrzt
Stars: 16101
Repository: https://github.com/jkbrzt/httpie
Created: 2012-02-25T12:39:13Z
Updated: 2015-07-13T14:56:41Z
Description: CLI HTTP client; user-friendly cURL replacement featuring
intuitive UI, JSON support, syntax highlighting, wget-like downloads,
extensions, etc.
```

We can see that the most-starred Python project on GitHub as of this writing is HTTPie, its owner is user *jkbrzt*, and it has been starred by more than 16,000 GitHub users. We can see the URL for the project's repository, its creation date of February 2012, and that it was updated recently. Finally, the description tells us that HTTPie helps make HTTP calls from a terminal (*CLI* is short for *command line interface*).

Summarizing the Top Repositories

When we make a visualization for this data, we'll want to include more than one repository. Let's write a loop to print selected information about each of the repositories returned by the API call so we can include them all in the visualization:

python_repos.py

```
--snip--
# Explore information about the repositories.
repo_dicts = response_dict['items']
print("Repositories returned:", len(repo_dicts))
```

```
❶ print("\nSelected information about each repository:")
❷ for repo_dict in repo_dicts:
      print('\nName:', repo_dict['name'])
      print('Owner:', repo_dict['owner']['login'])
      print('Stars:', repo_dict['stargazers_count'])
      print('Repository:', repo_dict['html_url'])
      print('Description:', repo_dict['description'])
```

We print an introductory message at ❶. At ❷ we loop through all the dictionaries in repo_dicts. Inside the loop we print the name of each project, its owner, how many stars it has, its URL on GitHub, and the project's description:

```
Status code: 200
Total repositories: 713067
Repositories returned: 30

Selected information about each repository:

Name: httpie
Owner: jkbrzt
Stars: 16101
Repository: https://github.com/jkbrzt/httpie
Description: CLI HTTP client; user-friendly cURL replacement featuring
intuitive UI, JSON support, syntax highlighting, wget-like downloads,
extensions, etc.

Name: django
Owner: django
Stars: 15028
Repository: https://github.com/django/django
Description: The Web framework for perfectionists with deadlines.
--snip--

Name: powerline
Owner: powerline
Stars: 4315
Repository: https://github.com/powerline/powerline
Description: Powerline is a statusline plugin for vim, and provides
statuslines and prompts for several other applications, including zsh, bash,
tmux, IPython, Awesome and Qtile.
```

Some interesting projects appear in these results, and it might be worth taking a look at a few. But don't spend too long on it, because we're about to create a visualization that will make it much easier to read through the results.

Monitoring API Rate Limits

Most APIs are rate-limited, which means there's a limit to how many requests you can make in a certain amount of time. To see if you're approaching GitHub's limits, enter *https://api.github.com/rate_limit* into a web browser. You should see a response like this:

```
  {
    "resources": {
      "core": {
        "limit": 60,
        "remaining": 58,
        "reset": 1426082320
      },
❶     "search": {
❷       "limit": 10,
❸       "remaining": 8,
❹       "reset": 1426078803
      }
    },
    "rate": {
      "limit": 60,
      "remaining": 58,
      "reset": 1426082320
    }
  }
```

The information we're interested in is the rate limit for the search API ❶. We see at ❷ that the limit is 10 requests per minute and that we have 8 requests remaining for the current minute ❸. The reset value represents the time in *Unix* or *epoch time* (the number of seconds since midnight on January 1, 1970) when our quota will reset ❹. If you reach your quota, you'll get a short response that lets you know you've reached the API limit. If you reach the limit, just wait until your quota resets.

NOTE *Many APIs require you to register and obtain an API key in order to make API calls. As of this writing GitHub has no such requirement, but if you obtain an API key, your limits will be much higher.*

Visualizing Repositories Using Pygal

Now that we have some interesting data, let's make a visualization showing the relative popularity of Python projects on GitHub. We'll make an interactive bar chart: the height of each bar will represent the number of stars the project has acquired. Clicking a bar will take you to that project's home on GitHub. Here's an initial attempt:

python_repos.py

```
import requests
import pygal
from pygal.style import LightColorizedStyle as LCS, LightenStyle as LS
```

```
    # Make an API call and store the response.
    URL = 'https://api.github.com/search/repositories?q=language:python&sort=star'
    r = requests.get(URL)
    print("Status code:", r.status_code)

    # Store API response in a variable.
    response_dict = r.json()
    print("Total repositories:", response_dict['total_count'])

    # Explore information about the repositories.
    repo_dicts = response_dict['items']

❶ names, stars = [], []
    for repo_dict in repo_dicts:
❷        names.append(repo_dict['name'])
        stars.append(repo_dict['stargazers_count'])

    # Make visualization.
❸ my_style = LS('#333366', base_style=LCS)
❹ chart = pygal.Bar(style=my_style, x_label_rotation=45, show_legend=False)
    chart.title = 'Most-Starred Python Projects on GitHub'
    chart.x_labels = names

❺ chart.add('', stars)
    chart.render_to_file('python_repos.svg')
```

We start by importing pygal and the Pygal styles we'll need for the chart. We continue to print the status of the API call response and the total number of repositories found, so we'll know if there was a problem with the API call. We no longer print information about the specific projects that are returned, because that information will be included in the visualization.

At ❶ we create two empty lists to store the data we'll include in the chart. We'll need the name of each project in order to label the bars, and we'll need the number of stars to determine the height of the bars. In the loop, we append the name of each project and number of stars it has to these lists ❷.

Next we define a style using the LightenStyle class (alias LS) and base it on a dark shade of blue ❸. We also pass the base_style argument to use the LightColorizedStyle class (alias LCS). We then use Bar() to make a simple bar chart and pass it my_style ❹. We pass two more style arguments: we set the rotation of the labels along the x-axis to 45 degrees (x_label_rotation=45), and we hide the legend, because we're plotting only one series on the chart (show_legend=False). We then give the chart a title and set the x_labels attribute to the list names.

Because we don't need this data series to be labeled, we pass an empty string for the label when we add the data at ❺. The resulting chart is shown in Figure 17-1. We can see that the first few projects are significantly more popular than the rest, but all of them are important projects in the Python ecosystem.

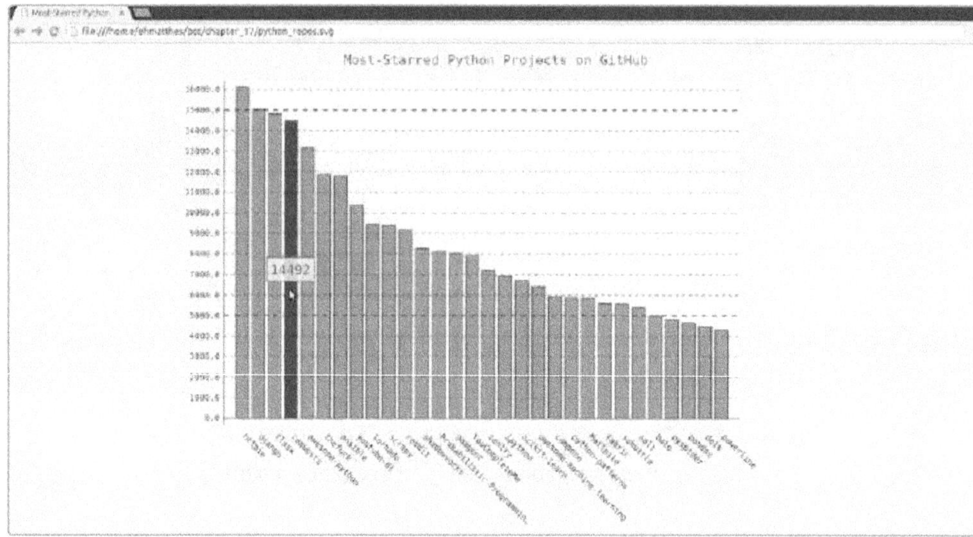

Figure 17-1: The most-starred Python projects on GitHub

Refining Pygal Charts

Let's refine the styling of our chart. We'll be making a few different customizations, so first restructure the code slightly by creating a configuration object that contains all of our customizations to pass to `Bar()`:

python_repos.py

```
--snip--

# Make visualization.
my_style = LS('#333366', base_style=LCS)

❶ my_config = pygal.Config()
❷ my_config.x_label_rotation = 45
  my_config.show_legend = False
❸ my_config.title_font_size = 24
  my_config.label_font_size = 14
  my_config.major_label_font_size = 18
❹ my_config.truncate_label = 15
❺ my_config.show_y_guides = False
❻ my_config.width = 1000

❼ chart = pygal.Bar(my_config, style=my_style)
  chart.title = 'Most-Starred Python Projects on GitHub'
  chart.x_labels = names

  chart.add('', stars)
  chart.render_to_file('python_repos.svg')
```

At ❶ we make an instance of Pygal's `Config` class, called `my_config`; modifying the attributes of `my_config` will customize the appearance of the chart. We set the two attributes `x_label_rotation` and `show_legend` ❷, originally passed as keyword arguments when we made an instance of `Bar`. At ❸ we set the font size for the chart's title, minor labels, and major labels. The minor labels in this chart are the project names along the x-axis and most of the numbers along the y-axis. The major labels are just the labels on the y-axis that mark off increments of 5000 stars. These labels will be larger, which is why we differentiate between the two. At ❹ we use `truncate_label` to shorten the longer project names to 15 characters. (When you hover over a truncated project name on your screen, the full name will pop up.) Next, we hide the horizontal lines on the graph by setting `show_y_guides` to `False` ❺. Finally, at ❻ we set a custom width so the chart will use more of the available space in the browser.

Now when we make an instance of `Bar` at ❼, we pass `my_config` as the first argument, and it sends all of our configuration settings in one argument. We can make as many style and configuration changes as we want through `my_config`, and the line at ❼ won't change. Figure 17-2 shows the restyled chart.

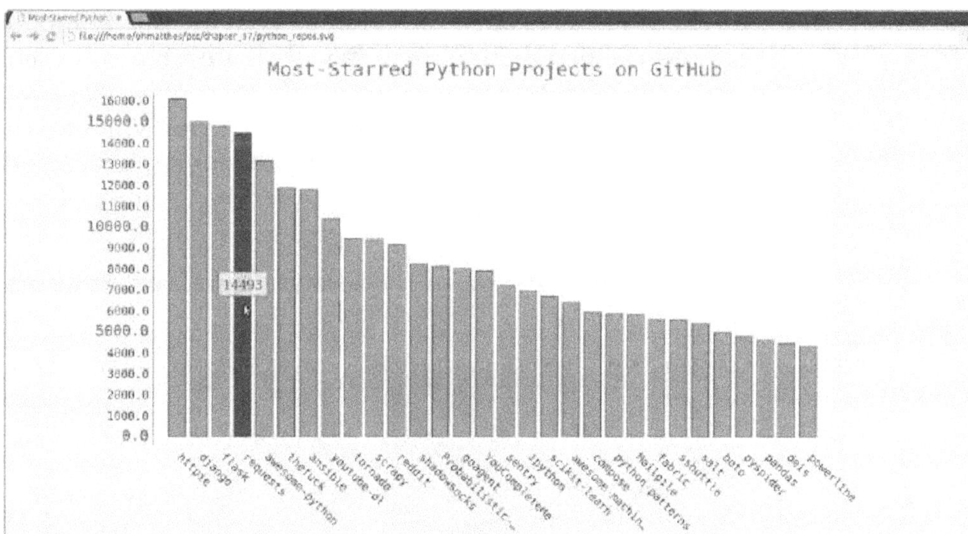

Figure 17-2: The styling for the chart has been refined.

Adding Custom Tooltips

In Pygal, hovering the cursor over an individual bar shows the information that the bar represents. This is commonly called a *tooltip*, and in this case it currently shows the number of stars a project has. Let's create a custom tooltip to show each project's description as well.

Let's look at a short example using the first three projects plotted individually with custom labels passed for each bar. To do this, we'll pass a list of dictionaries to `add()` instead of a list of values:

bar_descriptions.py

```
import pygal
from pygal.style import LightColorizedStyle as LCS, LightenStyle as LS

my_style = LS('#333366', base_style=LCS)
chart = pygal.Bar(style=my_style, x_label_rotation=45, show_legend=False)
```

```
  chart.title = 'Python Projects'
  chart.x_labels = ['httpie', 'django', 'flask']

❶ plot_dicts = [
❷     {'value': 16101, 'label': 'Description of httpie.'},
      {'value': 15028, 'label': 'Description of django.'},
      {'value': 14798, 'label': 'Description of flask.'},
      ]

❸ chart.add('', plot_dicts)
  chart.render_to_file('bar_descriptions.svg')
```

At ❶ we define a list called `plot_dicts` that contains three dictionaries: one for the HTTPie project, one for the Django project, and one for Flask. Each dictionary has two keys: `'value'` and `'label'`. Pygal uses the number associated with `'value'` to figure out how tall each bar should be, and it uses the string associated with `'label'` to create the tooltip for each bar. For example, the first dictionary at ❷ will create a bar representing a project with 16,101 stars, and its tooltip will say *Description of httpie.*

The `add()` method needs a string and a list. When we call `add()`, we pass in the list of dictionaries representing the bars (`plot_dicts`) ❸. Figure 17-3 shows one of the tooltips. Pygal includes the number of stars as a default tooltip in addition to the custom tooltip we passed it.

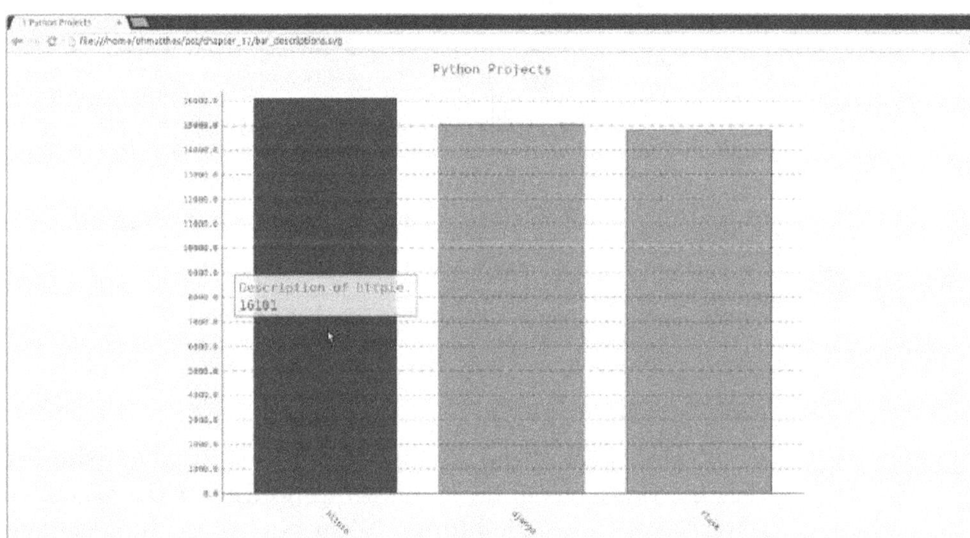

Figure 17-3: Each bar has a customized tooltip label.

Plotting the Data

To plot our data, we'll generate `plot_dicts` automatically for the 30 projects returned by the API call.

Here's the code to do this:

python_repos.py

```
--snip--
# Explore information about the repositories.
repo_dicts = response_dict['items']
print("Number of items:", len(repo_dicts))

❶ names, plot_dicts = [], []
for repo_dict in repo_dicts:
    names.append(repo_dict['name'])

❷     plot_dict = {
        'value': repo_dict['stargazers_count'],
        'label': repo_dict['description'],
        }
❸     plot_dicts.append(plot_dict)

# Make visualization.
my_style = LS('#333366', base_style=LCS)
--snip--

❹ chart.add('', plot_dicts)
chart.render_to_file('python_repos.svg')
```

At ❶ we make an empty list for `names` and an empty list for `plot_dicts`. We still need the `names` list in order to generate the labels for the x-axis.

Inside the loop we create the dictionary `plot_dict` for each project ❷. We store the number of stars with the key `'value'` and the project description with the key `'label'` in each `plot_dict`. We then append each project's `plot_dict` to `plot_dicts` ❸. At ❹ we pass the list `plot_dicts` to `add()`. Figure 17-4 shows the resulting chart.

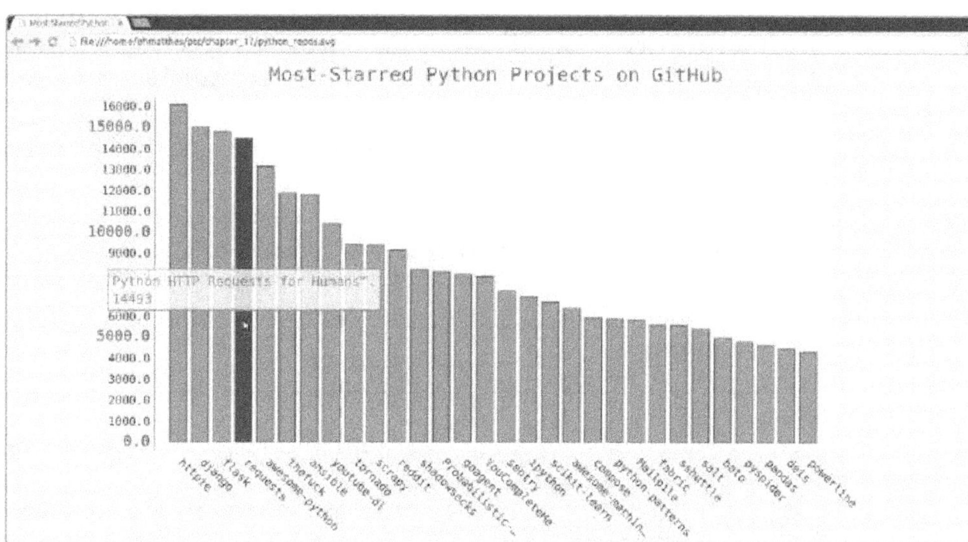

Figure 17-4: Hovering over a bar shows the project's description.

Adding Clickable Links to Our Graph

Pygal also allows you to use each bar in the chart as a link to a website. To add this capability, we just add one line to our code, leveraging the dictionary we've set up for each project. We add a new key-value pair to each project's `plot_dict` using the key `'xlink'`:

python_repos.py

```
--snip--
names, plot_dicts = [], []
for repo_dict in repo_dicts:
    names.append(repo_dict['name'])

    plot_dict = {
        'value': repo_dict['stargazers_count'],
        'label': repo_dict['description'],
        'xlink': repo_dict['html_url'],
        }
    plot_dicts.append(plot_dict)
--snip--
```

Pygal uses the URL associated with `'xlink'` to turn each bar into an active link. You can click any of the bars in the chart, and the GitHub page for that project will automatically open in a new tab in your browser. Now you have an interactive, informative visualization of data retrieved through an API!

The Hacker News API

To explore how you would use API calls on other sites, we'll look at Hacker News (*http://news.ycombinator.com/*). On Hacker News people share articles about programming and technology, and engage in lively discussions about those articles. Hacker News' API provides access to data about all submissions and comments on the site, which is available without having to register for a key.

The following call returns information about the current top article as of this writing:

```
https://hacker-news.firebaseio.com/v0/item/9884165.json
```

The response is a dictionary of information about the article with the ID 9884165:

```
{
❶    'url': 'http://www.bbc.co.uk/news/science-environment-33524589',
     'type': 'story',
❷    'title': 'New Horizons: Nasa spacecraft speeds past Pluto',
❸    'descendants': 141,
     'score': 230,
     'time': 1436875181,
     'text': '',
```

```
    'by': 'nns',
    'id': 9884165,
❹   'kids': [9884723, 9885099, 9884789, 9885604, 9885844]
}
```

The dictionary contains a number of keys we can work with, such as 'url' ❶ and 'title' ❷. The key 'descendants' contains the number of comments an article has received ❸. The key 'kids' provides the IDs of all comments made directly in response to this submission ❹. Each of these comments may have kids of their own as well, so the number of descendants a submission has can be greater than its number of kids.

Let's make an API call that returns the IDs of the current top articles on Hacker News, and then examine each of the top articles:

hn_submissions.py

```
import requests

from operator import itemgetter

# Make an API call and store the response.
❶ url = 'https://hacker-news.firebaseio.com/v0/topstories.json'
r = requests.get(url)
print("Status code:", r.status_code)

# Process information about each submission.
❷ submission_ids = r.json()
❸ submission_dicts = []
for submission_id in submission_ids[:30]:
    # Make a separate API call for each submission.
❹   url = ('https://hacker-news.firebaseio.com/v0/item/' +
            str(submission_id) + '.json')
    submission_r = requests.get(url)
    print(submission_r.status_code)
    response_dict = submission_r.json()

❺   submission_dict = {
        'title': response_dict['title'],
        'link': 'http://news.ycombinator.com/item?id=' + str(submission_id),
❻       'comments': response_dict.get('descendants', 0)
        }
    submission_dicts.append(submission_dict)

❼ submission_dicts = sorted(submission_dicts, key=itemgetter('comments'),
                            reverse=True)

❽ for submission_dict in submission_dicts:
    print("\nTitle:", submission_dict['title'])
    print("Discussion link:", submission_dict['link'])
    print("Comments:", submission_dict['comments'])
```

First, we make the API call and print the status of the response ❶. This API call returns a list containing the IDs of the 500 most popular articles on Hacker News at the time the call is issued. We then convert the response text to a Python list at ❷, which we store in `submission_ids`. We'll use these IDs to build a set of dictionaries that each store information about one of the current submissions.

We set up an empty list called `submission_dicts` at ❸ to store these dictionaries. We then loop through the IDs of the top 30 submissions. We make a new API call for each submission by generating a URL that includes the current value of `submission_id` ❹. We print the status of each request so we can see whether it is successful.

At ❺ we create a dictionary for the submission currently being processed, where we store the title of the submission and a link to the discussion page for that item. At ❻ we store the number of comments in the dictionary. If an article has no comments yet, the key `'descendants'` will not be present. When you're not sure if a key exists in a dictionary, use the `dict.get()` method, which returns the value associated with the given key if it exists or the value you provide if the key doesn't exist (0 in this example). Finally, we append each `submission_dict` to the list `submission_dicts`.

Submissions on Hacker News are ranked according to an overall score, based on a number of factors including how many times it's been voted up, how many comments it's received, and how recent the submission is. We want to sort the list of dictionaries by the number of comments. To do this, we use a function called `itemgetter()` ❼, which comes from the `operator` module. We pass this function the key `'comments'`, and it pulls the value associated with that key from each dictionary in the list. The `sorted()` function then uses this value as its basis for sorting the list. We sort the list in reverse order to place the most-commented stories first.

Once the list is sorted, we loop through the list at ❽ and print out three pieces of information about each of the top submissions: the title, a link to the discussion page, and the number of comments the submission currently has:

```
Status code: 200
200
200
200
--snip--

Title: Firefox deactivates Flash by default
Discussion link: http://news.ycombinator.com/item?id=9883246
Comments: 231

Title: New Horizons: Nasa spacecraft speeds past Pluto
Discussion link: http://news.ycombinator.com/item?id=9884165
Comments: 142

Title: Iran Nuclear Deal Is Reached With World Powers
Discussion link: http://news.ycombinator.com/item?id=9884005
Comments: 141
```

```
Title: Match Group Buys PlentyOfFish for $575M
Discussion link: http://news.ycombinator.com/item?id=9884417
Comments: 75

Title: Our Nexus 4 devices are about to explode
Discussion link: http://news.ycombinator.com/item?id=9885625
Comments: 14

--snip--
```

You would use a similar process to access and analyze information with any API. With this data, you could make a visualization showing which submissions have inspired the most active recent discussions.

TRY IT YOURSELF

17-1. Other Languages: Modify the API call in *python_repos.py* so it generates a chart showing the most popular projects in other languages. Try languages such as *JavaScript, Ruby, C, Java, Perl, Haskell,* and *Go.*

17-2. Active Discussions: Using the data from *hn_submissions.py,* make a bar chart showing the most active discussions currently happening on Hacker News. The height of each bar should correspond to the number of comments each submission has. The label for each bar should include the submission's title, and each bar should act as a link to the discussion page for that submission.

17-3. Testing *python_repos.py*: In *python_repos.py,* we printed the value of `status_code` to make sure the API call was successful. Write a program called *test_python_repos.py,* which uses `unittest` to assert that the value of `status_code` is 200. Figure out some other assertions you can make—for example, that the number of items returned is expected and that the total number of repositories is greater than a certain amount.

Summary

In this chapter you learned how to use APIs to write self-contained programs that automatically gather the data they need and use that data to create a visualization. We used the GitHub API to explore the most-starred Python projects on GitHub, and we looked briefly at the Hacker News API as well. You learned how to use the requests package to automatically issue an API call to GitHub and how to process the results of that call. We also introduced some Pygal settings that further customize the appearance of the charts you generate.

In the final project we'll use Django to build a web application.

PROJECT 3

WEB APPLICATIONS

18

GETTING STARTED WITH DJANGO

Behind the scenes, today's websites are actually rich applications that act like fully developed desktop applications. Python has a great set of tools for building web applications. In this chapter you'll learn how to use Django (*http://djangoproject.com/*) to build a project called Learning Log—an online journal system that lets you keep track of information you've learned about particular topics.

We'll write a specification for this project, and then we'll define models for the data the app will work with. We'll use Django's admin system to enter some initial data and then learn to write views and templates so Django can build the pages of our site.

Django is a *web framework*—a set of tools designed to help you build interactive websites. Django can respond to page requests and make it easier to read and write to a database, manage users, and much more. In Chapters 19 and 20 we'll refine the Learning Log project and then deploy it to a live server so you (and your friends) can use it.

Setting Up a Project

When beginning a project, you first need to describe the project in a specification, or *spec*. Then you'll set up a virtual environment to build the project in.

Writing a Spec

A full spec details the project goals, describes the project's functionality, and discusses its appearance and user interface. Like any good project or business plan, a spec should keep you focused and help keep your project on track. We won't write a full project spec here, but we'll lay out a few clear goals to keep our development process focused. Here's the spec we'll use:

> We'll write a web app called Learning Log that allows users to log the topics they're interested in and to make journal entries as they learn about each topic. The Learning Log home page should describe the site and invite users to either register or log in. Once logged in, a user should be able to create new topics, add new entries, and read and edit existing entries.

When you learn about a new topic, keeping a journal of what you've learned can be helpful in tracking and revisiting information. A good app makes this process efficient.

Creating a Virtual Environment

To work with Django, we'll first set up a virtual environment to work in. A *virtual environment* is a place on your system where you can install packages and isolate them from all other Python packages. Separating one project's libraries from other projects is beneficial and will be necessary when we deploy Learning Log to a server in Chapter 20.

Create a new directory for your project called *learning_log*, switch to that directory in a terminal, and create a virtual environment. If you're using Python 3, you should be able to create a virtual environment with the following command:

```
learning_log$ python -m venv ll_env
learning_log$
```

Here we're running the venv module and using it to create a virtual environment named *ll_env*. If this works, move on to "Activating the Virtual Environment" on page 399. If it doesn't work, read the next section, "Installing virtualenv."

Installing virtualenv

If you're using an earlier version of Python or if your system isn't set up to use the venv module correctly, you can install the virtualenv package. To install virtualenv, enter the following:

```
$ pip install --user virtualenv
```

Keep in mind that you might need to use a slightly different version of this command. (If you haven't used pip yet, see "Installing Python Packages with pip" on page 237.)

NOTE *If you're using Linux and this still doesn't work, you can install virtualenv through your system's package manager. On Ubuntu, for example, the command* `sudo apt-get install python-virtualenv` *will install virtualenv.*

Change to the *learning_log* directory in a terminal, and create a virtual environment like this:

```
learning_log$ virtualenv ll_env
New python executable in ll_env/bin/python
Installing setuptools, pip...done.
learning_log$
```

NOTE *If you have more than one version of Python installed on your system, you should specify the version for virtualenv to use. For example, the command* `virtualenv ll_env --python=python3` *will create a virtual environment that uses Python 3.*

Activating the Virtual Environment

Now that we have a virtual environment set up, we need to activate it with the following command:

```
  learning_log$ source ll_env/bin/activate
❶ (ll_env)learning_log$
```

This command runs the script *activate* in *ll_env/bin*. When the environment is active, you'll see the name of the environment in parentheses, as shown at ❶; then you can install packages to the environment and use packages that have already been installed. Packages you install in *ll_env* will be available only while the environment is active.

NOTE *If you're using Windows, use the command* `ll_env\Scripts\activate` *(without the word* `source`*) to activate the virtual environment.*

To stop using a virtual environment, enter deactivate:

```
(ll_env)learning_log$ deactivate
learning_log$
```

The environment will also become inactive if you close the terminal it's running in.

Installing Django

Once you've created your virtual environment and activated it, install Django:

```
(ll_env)learning_log$ pip install Django
Installing collected packages: Django
Successfully installed Django
Cleaning up...
(ll_env)learning_log$
```

Because we're working in a virtual environment, this command is the same on all systems. There's no need to use the `--user` flag, and there's no need to use longer commands like `python -m pip install` *package_name*.

Keep in mind that Django will be available only when the environment is active.

Creating a Project in Django

Without leaving the active virtual environment (remember to look for *ll_env* in parentheses), enter the following commands to create a new project:

```
❶ (ll_env)learning_log$ django-admin.py startproject learning_log .
❷ (ll_env)learning_log$ ls
learning_log ll_env manage.py
❸ (ll_env)learning_log$ ls learning_log
__init__.py  settings.py  urls.py  wsgi.py
```

The command at ❶ tells Django to set up a new project called *learning_log*. The dot at the end of the command creates the new project with a directory structure that will make it easy to deploy the app to a server when we're finished developing it.

NOTE *Don't forget this dot, or you may run into some configuration issues when we deploy the app. If you forget the dot, delete the files and folders that were created (except* ll_env*), and run the command again.*

Running the `ls` command (`dir` on Windows) ❷ shows that Django has created a new directory called *learning_log*. It also created a file called *manage.py*, which is a short program that takes in commands and feeds them to the relevant part of Django to run them. We'll use these commands to manage tasks like working with databases and running servers.

The *learning_log* directory contains four files ❸, the most important of which are *settings.py*, *urls.py*, and *wsgi.py*. The *settings.py* file controls how Django interacts with your system and manages your project. We'll modify a few of these settings and add some settings of our own as the project evolves. The *urls.py* file tells Django which pages to build in response to browser requests. The *wsgi.py* file helps Django serve the files it creates. The filename is an acronym for *web server gateway interface.*

Creating the Database

Because Django stores most of the information related to a project in a database, we need to create a database that Django can work with. To create the database for the Learning Log project, enter the following command (still in an active environment):

```
  (ll_env)learning_log$ python manage.py migrate
❶ Operations to perform:
    Synchronize unmigrated apps: messages, staticfiles
    Apply all migrations: contenttypes, sessions, auth, admin
    --snip--
    Applying sessions.0001_initial... OK
❷ (ll_env)learning_log$ ls
  db.sqlite3  learning_log  ll_env  manage.py
```

Any time we modify a database, we say we're *migrating* the database. Issuing the migrate command for the first time tells Django to make sure the database matches the current state of the project. The first time we run this command in a new project using SQLite (more about SQLite in a moment), Django will create a new database for us. At ❶ Django reports that it will make the database tables needed to store the information we'll use in this project (*Synchronize unmigrated apps*), and then make sure the database structure matches the current code (*Apply all migrations*).

Running the ls command shows that Django created another file called *db.sqlite3* ❷. SQLite is a database that runs off a single file; it's ideal for writing simple apps because you won't have to pay much attention to managing the database.

Viewing the Project

Let's make sure that Django has set up the project properly. Enter the runserver command as follows:

```
  (ll_env)learning_log$ python manage.py runserver
  Performing system checks...

❶ System check identified no issues (0 silenced).
  July 15, 2015 - 06:23:51
❷ Django version 1.8.4, using settings 'learning_log.settings'
❸ Starting development server at http://127.0.0.1:8000/
  Quit the server with CONTROL-C.
```

Django starts a server so you can view the project on your system to see how well it works. When you request a page by entering a URL in a browser, the Django server responds to that request by building the appropriate page and sending that page to the browser.

At ❶ Django checks to make sure the project is set up properly; at ❷ it reports the version of Django in use and the name of the settings file being used; and at ❸ it reports the URL where the project is being served. The URL *http://127.0.0.1:8000/* indicates that the project is listening for requests on port 8000 on your computer—called a localhost. The term *localhost* refers to a server that only processes requests on your system; it doesn't allow anyone else to see the pages you're developing.

Now open a web browser and enter the URL *http://localhost:8000/*, or *http://127.0.0.1:8000/* if the first one doesn't work. You should see something like Figure 18-1, a page that Django creates to let you know all is working properly so far. Keep the server running for now, but when you want to stop the server you can do so by pressing CTRL-C.

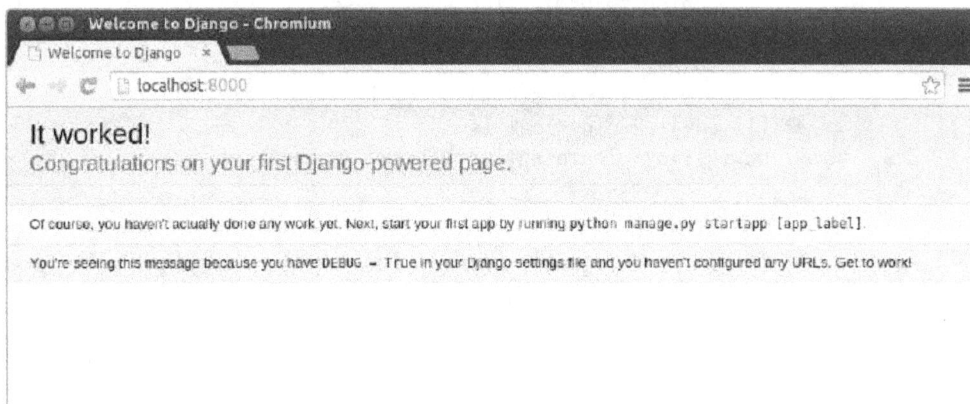

Figure 18-1: Everything is working so far.

NOTE *If you receive the error message* That port is already in use, *tell Django to use a different port by entering* `python manage.py runserver 8001` *and cycle through higher numbers until you find an open port.*

TRY IT YOURSELF

18-1. New Projects: To get a better idea of what Django does, build a couple of empty projects and look at what it creates. Make a new folder with a simple name, like *InstaBook* or *FaceGram* (outside of your *learning_log* directory), navigate to that folder in a terminal, and create a virtual environment. Install Django, and run the command `django-admin.py startproject instabook .` (make sure you include the dot at the end of the command).

Look at the files and folders this command creates, and compare them to Learning Log. Do this a few times until you're familiar with what Django creates when starting a new project. Then delete the project directories if you wish.

Starting an App

A Django *project* is organized as a group of individual *apps* that work together to make the project work as a whole. For now, we'll create just one app to do most of the work for our project. We'll add another app to manage user accounts in Chapter 19.

You should still be running `runserver` in the terminal window you opened earlier. Open a new terminal window (or tab) and navigate to the directory that contains *manage.py*. Activate the virtual environment, and then run the `startapp` command:

```
learning_log$ source ll_env/bin/activate
(ll_env)learning_log$ python manage.py startapp learning_logs
❶ (ll_env)learning_log$ ls
db.sqlite3  learning_log  learning_logs  ll_env  manage.py
❷ (ll_env)learning_log$ ls learning_logs/
admin.py  __init__.py  migrations  models.py  tests.py  views.py
```

The command `startapp` *appname* tells Django to create the infrastructure needed to build an app. If you look in the project directory now, you'll see a new folder called *learning_logs* ❶. Open that folder to see what Django has created ❷. The most important files are *models.py*, *admin.py*, and *views.py*. We'll use *models.py* to define the data we want to manage in our app. We'll get to *admin.py* and *views.py* a little later.

Defining Models

Let's think about our data for a moment. Each user will need to create a number of topics in their learning log. Each entry they make will be tied to a topic, and these entries will be displayed as text. We'll also need to store the timestamp of each entry so we can show users when they made each entry.

Open the file *models.py*, and look at its existing content:

models.py

```
from django.db import models

# Create your models here.
```

A module called `models` is being imported for us, and we're being invited to create models of our own. A model tells Django how to work with the data that will be stored in the app. Code-wise, a model is just a class; it has attributes and methods, just like every class we've discussed. Here's the model for the topics users will store:

```
from django.db import models

class Topic(models.Model):
    """A topic the user is learning about"""
❶    text = models.CharField(max_length=200)
❷    date_added = models.DateTimeField(auto_now_add=True)
```

```
❸     def __str__(self):
          """Return a string representation of the model."""
          return self.text
```

We've created a class called `Topic`, which inherits from `Model`—a parent class included in Django that defines the basic functionality of a model. Only two attributes are in the `Topic` class: `text` and `date_added`.

The `text` attribute is a `CharField`—a piece of data that's made up of characters, or text ❶. You use `CharField` when you want to store a small amount of text, such as a name, a title, or a city. When we define a `CharField` attribute, we have to tell Django how much space it should reserve in the database. Here we give it a `max_length` of 200 characters, which should be enough to hold most topic names.

The `date_added` attribute is a `DateTimeField`—a piece of data that will record a date and time ❷. We pass the argument `auto_add_now=True`, which tells Django to automatically set this attribute to the current date and time whenever the user creates a new topic.

NOTE *To see the different kinds of fields you can use in a model, see the* Django Model Field Reference *at* https://docs.djangoproject.com/en/1.8/ref/models/fields/. *You won't need all the information right now, but it will be extremely useful when you're developing your own apps.*

We need to tell Django which attribute to use by default when it displays information about a topic. Django calls a `__str__()` method to display a simple representation of a model. Here we've written a `__str__()` method that returns the string stored in the `text` attribute ❸.

NOTE *If you're using Python 2.7, you should call the* `__str__()` *method* `__unicode__()` *instead. The body of the method is identical.*

Activating Models

To use our models, we have to tell Django to include our app in the overall project. Open *settings.py* (in the *learning_log/learning_log* directory), and you'll see a section that tells Django which apps are installed in the project:

settings.py

```
--snip--
INSTALLED_APPS = (
    'django.contrib.admin',
    'django.contrib.auth',
    'django.contrib.contenttypes',
    'django.contrib.sessions',
    'django.contrib.messages',
    'django.contrib.staticfiles',
)
--snip--
```

This is just a tuple, telling Django which apps work together to make up the project. Add our app to this tuple by modifying `INSTALLED_APPS` so it looks like this:

```
--snip--
INSTALLED_APPS = (
    --snip--
    'django.contrib.staticfiles',

    # My apps
    'learning_logs',
)
--snip--
```

Grouping apps together in a project helps to keep track of them as the project grows to include more apps. Here we start a section caled *My apps*, which includes only `learning_logs` for now.

Next, we need to tell Django to modify the database so it can store information related to the model `Topic`. From the terminal, run the following command:

```
(ll_env)learning_log$ python manage.py makemigrations learning_logs
Migrations for 'learning_logs':
  0001_initial.py:
    - Create model Topic
(ll_env)learning_log$
```

The command `makemigrations` tells Django to figure out how to modify the database so it can store the data associated with any new models we've defined. The output here shows that Django has created a migration file called *0001_initial.py*. This migration will create a table for the model `Topic` in the database.

Now we'll apply this migration and have Django modify the database for us:

```
(ll_env)learning_log$ python manage.py migrate
--snip--
Running migrations:
  Rendering model states... DONE
❶ Applying learning_logs.0001_initial... OK
```

Most of the output from this command is identical to the output from the first time we issued the `migrate` command. The line we need to check appears at ❶, where Django confirms that everything worked `OK` when it applied the migration for `learning_logs`.

Whenever we want to modify the data that Learning Log manages, we'll follow these three steps: modify *models.py*, call `makemigrations` on `learning_logs`, and tell Django to `migrate` the project.

The Django Admin Site

When you define models for an app, Django makes it easy for you to work with your models through the *admin site*. A site's administrators use the admin site, not a site's general users. In this section, we'll set up the admin site and use it to add some topics through the Topic model.

Setting Up a Superuser

Django allows you to create a user who has all privileges available on the site, called a *superuser*. A *privilege* controls the actions a user can take. The most restrictive privilege settings allow a user to only read public information on the site. Registered users typically have the privilege of reading their own private data and some selected information available only to members. To effectively administer a web application, the site owner usually needs access to all information stored on the site. A good administrator is careful with their users' sensitive information, because users put a lot of trust into the apps they access.

To create a superuser in Django, enter the following command and respond to the prompts:

```
   (ll_env)learning_log$ python manage.py createsuperuser
❶ Username (leave blank to use 'ehmatthes'): ll_admin
❷ Email address:
❸ Password:
   Password (again):
   Superuser created successfully.
   (ll_env)learning_log$
```

When you issue the command createsuperuser, Django prompts you to enter a username for the superuser ❶. Here we're using *ll_admin*, but you can enter any username you want. You can enter an email address if you want or just leave this field blank ❷. You'll need to enter your password twice ❸.

NOTE *Some sensitive information can be hidden from a site's administrators. For example, Django doesn't actually store the password you enter; instead, it stores a string derived from the password, called a* hash. *Each time you enter your password, Django hashes your entry and compares it to the stored hash. If the two hashes match, you're authenticated. By requiring hashes to match, if an attacker gains access to a site's database, they'll be able to read its stored hashes but not the passwords. When a site is set up properly, it's almost impossible to get the original passwords from the hashes.*

Registering a Model with the Admin Site

Django includes some models in the admin site automatically, such as User and Group, but the models we create need to be registered manually.

When we started the `learning_logs` app, Django created a file called *admin.py* in the same directory as *models.py*:

admin.py

```
from django.contrib import admin

# Register your models here.
```

To register `Topic` with the admin site, enter:

```
from django.contrib import admin

❶ from learning_logs.models import Topic

❷ admin.site.register(Topic)
```

This code imports the model we want to register, `Topic` ❶, and then uses `admin.site.register()` ❷ to tell Django to manage our model through the admin site.

Now use the superuser account to access the admin site. Go to *http://localhost:8000/admin/*, enter the username and password for the superuser you just created, and you should see a screen like the one in Figure 18-2. This page allows you to add new users and groups and change existing ones. We can also work with data related to the `Topic` model that we just defined.

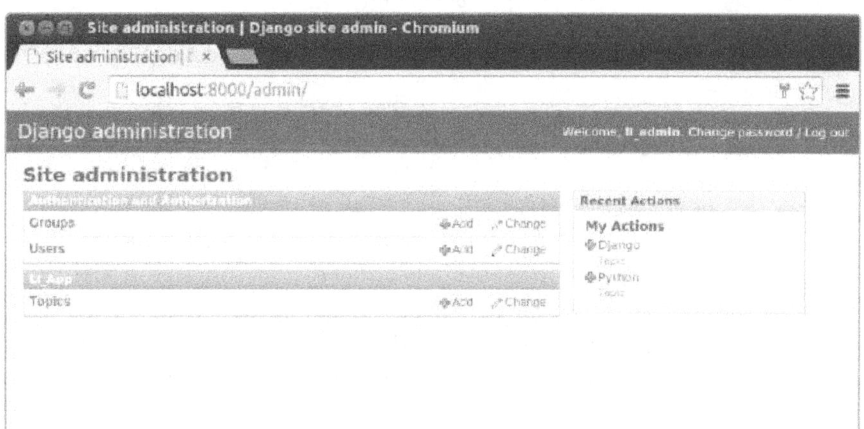

Figure 18-2: The admin site with `Topic` included

NOTE *If you see a message in your browser that the web page is not available, make sure you still have the Django server running in a terminal window. If you don't, activate a virtual environment and reissue the command* `python manage.py runserver`.

Adding Topics

Now that `Topic` has been registered with the admin site, let's add our first topic. Click **Topics** to go to the Topics page, which is mostly empty, because we have no topics to manage yet. Click **Add**, and you'll see a form for adding a new topic. Enter **Chess** in the first box and click **Save**. You'll be sent back to the Topics admin page, and you'll see the topic you just created.

Let's create a second topic so we'll have more data to work with. Click **Add** again, and create a second topic, **Rock Climbing**. When you click **Save**, you'll be sent back to the main Topics page again, and you'll see both Chess and Rock Climbing listed.

Defining the Entry Model

To record what we've been learning about chess and rock climbing, we need to define a model for the kinds of entries users can make in their learning logs. Each entry needs to be associated with a particular topic. This relationship is called a *many-to-one relationship*, meaning many entries can be associated with one topic.

Here's the code for the `Entry` model:

models.py

```
from django.db import models

class Topic(models.Model):
    --snip--

❶ class Entry(models.Model):
    """Something specific learned about a topic"""
❷     topic = models.ForeignKey(Topic)
❸     text = models.TextField()
    date_added = models.DateTimeField(auto_now_add=True)

❹     class Meta:
        verbose_name_plural = 'entries'

    def __str__(self):
        """Return a string representation of the model."""
❺         return self.text[:50] + "..."
```

The `Entry` class inherits from Django's base `Model` class, just as `Topic` did ❶. The first attribute, `topic`, is a `ForeignKey` instance ❷. A *foreign key* is a database term; it's a reference to another record in the database. This is the code that connects each entry to a specific topic. Each topic is assigned a key, or ID, when it's created. When Django needs to establish a connection between two pieces of data, it uses the key associated with each piece of information. We'll use these connections shortly to retrieve all the entries associated with a certain topic.

Next is an attribute called `text`, which is an instance of `TextField` ❸. This kind of field doesn't need a size limit, because we don't want to limit the size of individual entries. The `date_added` attribute allows us to present entries in the order they were created and to place a timestamp next to each entry.

At ❹ we nest the `Meta` class inside our `Entry` class. `Meta` holds extra information for managing a model; here it allows us to set a special attribute telling Django to use *Entries* when it needs to refer to more than one entry.

(Without this, Django would refer to multiple entries as *Entrys*.) Finally, the __str__() method tells Django which information to show when it refers to individual entries. Because an entry can be a long body of text, we tell Django to show just the first 50 characters of text ❺. We also add an ellipsis to clarify that we're not always displaying the entire entry.

Migrating the Entry Model

Because we've added a new model, we need to migrate the database again. This process will become quite familiar: you modify *models.py*, run the command python manage.py makemigrations *app_name*, and then run the command python manage.py migrate.

Migrate the database and check the output:

```
(ll_env)learning_log$ python manage.py makemigrations learning_logs
Migrations for 'learning_logs':
❶   0002_entry.py:
     - Create model Entry
(ll_env)learning_log$ python manage.py migrate
Operations to perform:
   --snip--
❷   Applying learning_logs.0002_entry... OK
```

A new migration called *0002_entry.py* is generated, which tells Django how to modify the database to store information related to the model Entry ❶. When we issue the migrate command, we see that Django applied this migration, and everything was okay ❷.

Registering Entry with the Admin Site

We also need to register the Entry model. Here's what *admin.py* should look like now:

admin.py

```
from django.contrib import admin

from learning_logs.models import Topic, Entry

admin.site.register(Topic)
admin.site.register(Entry)
```

Go back to *http://localhost/admin/*, and you should see *Entries* listed under *learning_logs*. Click the **Add** link for Entries, or click **Entries**, and then choose **Add entry**. You should see a drop-down list to select the topic you're creating an entry for and a text box for adding an entry. Select **Chess** from the drop-down list, and add an entry. Here's the first entry I made:

> The opening is the first part of the game, roughly the first ten moves or so. In the opening, it's a good idea to do three things—bring out your bishops and knights, try to control the center of the board, and castle your king.

> Of course, these are just guidelines. It will be important to learn when to follow these guidelines and when to disregard these suggestions.

When you click **Save**, you'll be brought back to the main admin page for entries. Here you'll see the benefit of using `text[:50]` as the string representation for each entry; it's much easier to work with multiple entries in the admin interface if you see only the first part of an entry rather than the entire text of each entry.

Make a second entry for Chess and one entry for Rock Climbing so we have some initial data. Here's a second entry for Chess:

> In the opening phase of the game, it's important to bring out your bishops and knights. These pieces are powerful and maneuverable enough to play a significant role in the beginning moves of a game.

And here's a first entry for Rock Climbing:

> One of the most important concepts in climbing is to keep your weight on your feet as much as possible. There's a myth that climbers can hang all day on their arms. In reality, good climbers have practiced specific ways of keeping their weight over their feet whenever possible.

These three entries will give us something to work with as we continue to develop Learning Log.

The Django Shell

Now that we've entered some data, we can examine that data programmatically through an interactive terminal session. This interactive environment is called the Django *shell*, and it's a great environment for testing and troubleshooting your project. Here's an example of an interactive shell session:

```
(ll_env)learning_log$ python manage.py shell
❶ >>> from learning_logs.models import Topic
>>> Topic.objects.all()
[<Topic: Chess>, <Topic: Rock Climbing>]
```

The command `python manage.py shell` (run in an active virtual environment) launches a Python interpreter that you can use to explore the data stored in your project's database. Here we import the model `Topic` from the `learning_logs.models` module ❶. We then use the method `Topic.objects.all()` to get all of the instances of the model `Topic`; the list that's returned is called a *queryset*.

We can loop over a queryset just as we'd loop over a list. Here's how you can see the ID that's been assigned to each topic object:

```
>>> topics = Topic.objects.all()
>>> for topic in topics:
```

```
...     print(topic.id, topic)
...
1 Chess
2 Rock Climbing
```

We store the queryset in `topics`, and then print each topic's `id` attribute and the string representation of each topic. We can see that Chess has an ID of 1, and Rock Climbing has an ID of 2.

If you know the ID of a particular object, you can get that object and examine any attribute the object has. Let's look at the `text` and `date_added` values for Chess:

```
>>> t = Topic.objects.get(id=1)
>>> t.text
'Chess'
>>> t.date_added
datetime.datetime(2015, 5, 28, 4, 39, 11, 989446, tzinfo=<UTC>)
```

We can also look at the entries related to a certain topic. Earlier we defined the `topic` attribute for the `Entry` model. This was a `ForeignKey`, a connection between each entry and a topic. Django can use this connection to get every entry related to a certain topic, like this:

```
❶ >>> t.entry_set.all()
[<Entry: The opening is the first part of the game, roughly...>, <Entry: In
the opening phase of the game, it's important t...>]
```

To get data through a foreign key relationship, you use the lowercase name of the related model followed by an underscore and the word `set` ❶. For example, say you have the models `Pizza` and `Topping`, and `Topping` is related to `Pizza` through a foreign key. If your object is called `my_pizza`, representing a single pizza, you can get all of the pizza's toppings using the code `my_pizza.topping_set.all()`.

We'll use this kind of syntax when we begin to code the pages users can request. The shell is very useful for making sure your code retrieves the data you want it to. If your code works as you expect it to in the shell, you can expect it to work properly in the files you write within your project. If your code generates errors or doesn't retrieve the data you expect it to, it's much easier to troubleshoot your code in the simple shell environment than it is within the files that generate web pages. We won't refer to the shell much, but you should continue using it to practice working with Django's syntax for accessing the data stored in the project.

NOTE *Each time you modify your models, you'll need to restart the shell to see the effects of those changes. To exit a shell session, enter* CTRL-D*; on Windows enter* CTRL-Z *and then press* ENTER.

TRY IT YOURSELF

18-2. Short Entries: The `__str__()` method in the `Entry` model currently appends an ellipsis to every instance of `Entry` when Django shows it in the admin site or the shell. Add an `if` statement to the `__str__()` method that adds an ellipsis only if the entry is more than 50 characters long. Use the admin site to add an entry that's fewer than 50 characters in length, and check that it doesn't have an ellipsis when viewed.

18-3. The Django API: When you write code to access the data in your project, you're writing a *query*. Skim through the documentation for querying your data at *https://docs.djangoproject.com/en/1.8/topics/db/queries/*. Much of what you see will look new to you, but it will be quite useful as you start to work on your own projects.

18-4. Pizzeria: Start a new project called `pizzeria` with an app called `pizzas`. Define a model `Pizza` with a field called `name`, which will hold name values such as `Hawaiian` and `Meat Lovers`. Define a model called `Topping` with fields called `pizza` and `name`. The `pizza` field should be a foreign key to `Pizza`, and `name` should be able to hold values such as `pineapple`, `Canadian bacon`, and `sausage`.

Register both models with the admin site, and use the site to enter some pizza names and toppings. Use the shell to explore the data you entered.

Making Pages: The Learning Log Home Page

Usually, making web pages with Django consists of three stages: defining URLs, writing views, and writing templates. First, you must define patterns for URLs. A URL pattern describes the way the URL is laid out and tells Django what to look for when matching a browser request with a site URL so it knows which page to return.

Each URL then maps to a particular *view*—the view function retrieves and processes the data needed for that page. The view function often calls a *template*, which builds a page that a browser can read. To see how this works, let's make the home page for Learning Log. We'll define the URL for the home page, write its view function, and create a simple template.

Because all we're doing is making sure Learning Log works as it's supposed to, we'll keep the page simple for now. A functioning web app is fun to style when it's complete; an app that looks good but doesn't work well is pointless. For now, the home page will display only a title and a brief description.

Mapping a URL

Users request pages by entering URLs into a browser and clicking links, so we'll need to decide what URLs are needed in our project. The home page URL is first: it's the base URL people use to access the project. At the moment, the base URL, *http://localhost:8000/*, returns the default Django site that lets us know the project was set up correctly. We'll change this by mapping the base URL to Learning Log's home page.

In the main *learning_log* project folder, open the file *urls.py*. Here's the code you'll see:

urls.py

```
❶ from django.conf.urls import include, url
  from django.contrib import admin

❷ urlpatterns = [
❸     url(r'^admin/', include(admin.site.urls)),
  ]
```

The first two lines import the functions and modules that manage URLs for the project and admin site ❶. The body of the file defines the `urlpatterns` variable ❷. In this *urls.py* file, which represents the project as a whole, the `urlpatterns` variable includes sets of URLs from the apps in the project. The code at ❸ includes the module `admin.site.urls`, which defines all the URLs that can be requested from the admin site.

We need to include the URLs for `learning_logs`:

```
  from django.conf.urls import include, url
  from django.contrib import admin

  urlpatterns = [
      url(r'^admin/', include(admin.site.urls)),
❶     url(r'', include('learning_logs.urls', namespace='learning_logs')),
  ]
```

We've added a line to include the module `learning_logs.urls` at ❶. This line includes a `namespace` argument, which allows us to distinguish `learning_logs`'s URLs from other URLs that might appear in the project, which can be very helpful as your project starts to grow.

The default *urls.py* is in the *learning_log* folder; now we need to make a second *urls.py* file in the *learning_logs* folder:

urls.py

```
❶ """Defines URL patterns for learning_logs."""

❷ from django.conf.urls import url

❸ from . import views

❹ urlpatterns = [
      # Home page
❺     url(r'^$', views.index, name='index'),
  ]
```

To make it clear which *urls.py* we're working in, we add a docstring at the beginning of the file ❶. We then import the `url` function, which is needed when mapping URLs to views ❷. We also import the `views` module ❸; the dot tells Python to import views from the same directory as the current *urls.py* module. The variable `urlpatterns` in this module is a list of individual pages that can be requested from the `learning_logs` app ❹.

The actual URL pattern is a call to the `url()` function, which takes three arguments ❺. The first is a regular expression. Django will look for a regular expression in `urlpatterns` that matches the requested URL string. Therefore, a regular expression will define the pattern that Django can look for.

Let's look at the regular expression `r'^$'`. The `r` tells Python to interpret the following string as a raw string, and the quotes tell Python where the regular expression begins and ends. The caret (`^`) tells Python to find the beginning of the string, and the dollar sign tells Python to look for the end of the string. In its entirety, this expression tells Python to look for a URL with nothing between the beginning and end of the URL. Python ignores the base URL for the project (*http://localhost:8000/*), so an empty regular expression matches the base URL. Any other URL will not match this expression, and Django will return an error page if the URL requested doesn't match any existing URL patterns.

The second argument in `url()` at ❺ specifies which view function to call. When a requested URL matches the regular expression, Django will call `views.index` (we'll write this view function in the next section). The third argument provides the name `index` for this URL pattern so we can refer to it in other sections of the code. Whenever we want to provide a link to the home page, we'll use this name instead of writing out a URL.

NOTE *Regular expressions, often called* regexes, *are used in almost every programming language. They're incredibly useful, but they take some practice to get used to. If you didn't follow all of this, don't worry; you'll see plenty of examples as you work through this project.*

Writing a View

A view function takes in information from a request, prepares the data needed to generate a page, and then sends the data back to the browser, often by using a template that defines what the page will look like.

The file *views.py* in *learning_logs* was generated automatically when we ran the command `python manage.py startapp`. Here's what's in *views.py* right now:

views.py

```
from django.shortcuts import render

# Create your views here.
```

Currently, this file just imports the render() function, which renders the response based on the data provided by views. The following code is how the view for the home page should be written:

```
from django.shortcuts import render

def index(request):
    """The home page for Learning Log"""
    return render(request, 'learning_logs/index.html')
```

When a URL request matches the pattern we just defined, Django will look for a function called index() in the *views.py* file. Django then passes the request object to this view function. In this case, we don't need to process any data for the page, so the only code in the function is a call to render(). The render() function here uses two arguments—the original request object and a template it can use to build the page. Let's write this template.

Writing a Template

A template sets up the structure for a web page. The template defines what the page should look like, and Django fills in the relevant data each time the page is requested. A template allows you to access any data provided by the view. Because our view for the home page provided no data, this template is fairly simple.

Inside the *learning_logs* folder, make a new folder called *templates*. Inside the *templates* folder, make another folder called *learning_logs*. This might seem a little redundant (we have a folder named *learning_logs* inside a folder named *templates* inside a folder named *learning_logs*), but it sets up a structure that Django can interpret unambiguously, even in the context of a large project containing many individual apps. Inside the inner *learning_logs* folder, make a new file called *index.html*. Write the following into that file:

index.html

```
<p>Learning Log</p>

<p>Learning Log helps you keep track of your learning, for any topic you're
learning about.</p>
```

This is a very simple file. If you're not familiar with HTML, the <p></p> tags signify paragraphs. The <p> tag opens a paragraph, and the </p> tag closes a paragraph. We have two paragraphs: the first acts as a title, and the second describes what users can do with Learning Log.

Now when we request the project's base URL, *http://localhost:8000/*, we'll see the page we just built instead of the default Django page. Django will take the requested URL, and that URL will match the pattern r'^$'; then Django will call the function views.index(), and this will render the page using the template contained in *index.html*. The resulting page is shown in Figure 18-3.

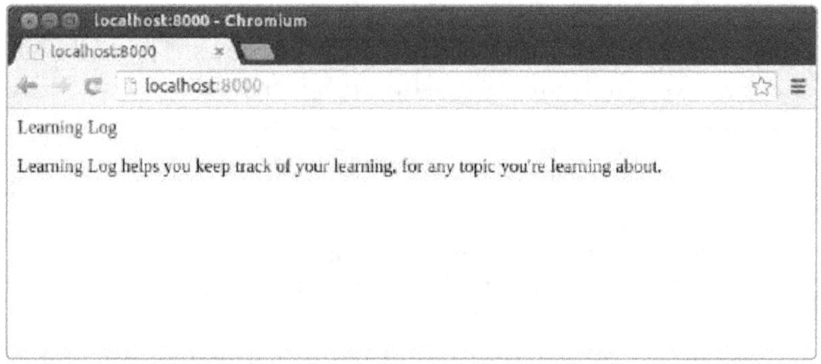

Figure 18-3: The home page for Learning Log

Although it may seem a complicated process for creating one page, this separation between URLs, views, and templates actually works well. It allows you to think about each aspect of a project separately, and in larger projects it allows individuals to focus on the areas in which they're strongest. For example, a database specialist can focus on the models, a programmer can focus on the view code, and a web designer can focus on the templates.

TRY IT YOURSELF

18-5. Meal Planner: Consider an app that helps people plan their meals throughout the week. Make a new folder called *meal_planner*, and start a new Django project inside this folder. Then make a new app called `meal_plans`. Make a simple home page for this project.

18-6. Pizzeria Home Page: Add a home page to the *Pizzeria* project you started in Exercise 18-4 (page 412).

Building Additional Pages

Now that we've established a routine for building a page, we can start to build out the Learning Log project. We'll build two pages that display data: a page that lists all topics and a page that shows all the entries for a particular topic. For each of these pages, we'll specify a URL pattern, write a view function, and write a template. But before we do this, we'll create a base template that all templates in the project can inherit from.

Template Inheritance

When building a website, you'll almost always require some elements to be repeated on each page. Rather than writing these elements directly into each page, you can write a base template containing the repeated elements and then have each page inherit from the template. This approach lets you focus on developing the unique aspects of each page and makes it much easier to change the overall look and feel of the project.

The Parent Template

We'll start by creating a template called *base.html* in the same directory as *index.html*. This file will contain elements common to all pages; every other template will inherit from *base.html*. The only element we want to repeat on each page right now is the title at the top. Because we'll include this template on every page, let's make the title a link to the home page:

base.html

```
<p>
❶  <a href="{% url 'learning_logs:index' %}">Learning Log</a>
</p>

❷ {% block content %}{% endblock content %}
```

The first part of this file creates a paragraph containing the name of the project, which also acts as a link to the home page. To generate a link, we use a *template tag*, indicated by braces and percent signs `{% %}`. A template tag is a bit of code that generates information to be displayed on a page. In this example, the template tag `{% url 'learning_logs:index' %}` generates a URL matching the URL pattern defined in *learning_logs/urls.py* with the name `'index'` ❶. In this example, `learning_logs` is the *namespace* and `index` is a uniquely named URL pattern in that namespace.

In a simple HTML page, a link is surrounded by the *anchor* tag:

```
<a href="link_url">link text</a>
```

Having the template tag generate the URL for us makes it much easier to keep our links up to date. To change a URL in our project, we only need to change the URL pattern in *urls.py*, and Django will automatically insert the updated URL the next time the page is requested. Every page in our project will inherit from *base.html*, so from now on every page will have a link back to the home page.

At ❷ we insert a pair of `block` tags. This block, named `content`, is a placeholder; the child template will define the kind of information that goes in the `content` block.

A child template doesn't have to define every block from its parent, so you can reserve space in parent templates for as many blocks as you like, and the child template uses only as many as it requires.

NOTE *In Python code, we almost always indent four spaces. Template files tend to have more levels of nesting than Python files, so it's common to use only two spaces for each indentation level.*

The Child Template

Now we need to rewrite *index.html* to inherit from *base.html*. Here's *index.html*:

index.html

```
❶ {% extends "learning_logs/base.html" %}

❷ {% block content %}
    <p>Learning Log helps you keep track of your learning, for any topic you're
    learning about.</p>
❸ {% endblock content %}
```

If you compare this to the original *index.html*, you can see that we've replaced the Learning Log title with the code for inheriting from a parent template ❶. A child template must have an `{% extends %}` tag on the first line to tell Django which parent template to inherit from. The file *base.html* is part of `learning_logs`, so we include *learning_logs* in the path to the parent template. This line pulls in everything contained in the *base.html* template and allows *index.html* to define what goes in the space reserved by the `content` block.

We define the content block at ❷ by inserting a `{% block %}` tag with the name `content`. Everything that we aren't inheriting from the parent template goes inside a `content` block. Here, that's the paragraph describing the Learning Log project. At ❸ we indicate that we're finished defining the content by using an `{% endblock content %}` tag.

You can start to see the benefit of template inheritance: in a child template we only need to include content that's unique to that page. This not only simplifies each template, but also makes it much easier to modify the site. To modify an element common to many pages, you only need to modify the element in the parent template. Your changes are then carried over to every page that inherits from that template. In a project that includes tens or hundreds of pages, this structure can make it much easier and faster to improve your site.

NOTE *In a large project, it's common to have one parent template called* base.html *for the entire site and parent templates for each major section of the site. All the section templates inherit from* base.html, *and each page in the site inherits from a section template. This way you can easily modify the look and feel of the site as a whole, any section in the site, or any individual page. This configuration provides a very efficient way to work, and it encourages you to steadily update your site over time.*

The Topics Page

Now that we have an efficient approach to building pages, we can focus on our next two pages: the general topics page and the page to display entries for a single topic. The topics page will show all topics that users have created, and it's the first page that will involve working with data.

The Topics URL Pattern

First, we define the URL for the topics page. It's common to choose a simple URL fragment that reflects the kind of information presented on the page. We'll use the word *topics*, so the URL *http://localhost:8000/topics/* will return this page. Here's how we modify *learning_logs/urls.py*:

urls.py

```
"""Defines URL patterns for learning_logs."""
--snip--
urlpatterns = [
    # Home page
    url(r'^$', views.index, name='index'),

    # Show all topics.
❶   url(r'^topics/$', views.topics, name='topics'),
]
```

We've simply added `topics/` into the regular expression argument used for the home page URL ❶. When Django examines a requested URL, this pattern will match any URL that has the base URL followed by *topics*. You can include or omit a forward slash at the end, but there can't be anything else after the word *topics*, or the pattern won't match. Any request with a URL that matches this pattern will then be passed to the function `topics()` in *views.py*.

The Topics View

The `topics()` function needs to get some data from the database and send it to the template. Here's what we need to add to *views.py*:

views.py

```
from django.shortcuts import render

❶ from .models import Topic

def index(request):
    --snip--

❷ def topics(request):
    """Show all topics."""
❸   topics = Topic.objects.order_by('date_added')
❹   context = {'topics': topics}
❺   return render(request, 'learning_logs/topics.html', context)
```

We first import the model associated with the data we need ❶. The `topics()` function needs one parameter: the `request` object Django received from the server ❷. At ❸ we query the database by asking for the `Topic` objects, sorted by the `date_added` attribute. We store the resulting queryset in `topics`.

At ❹ we define a context that we'll send to the template. A *context* is a dictionary in which the keys are names we'll use in the template to access the data and the values are the data we need to send to the template. In this case, there's one key-value pair, which contains the set of topics we'll display on the page. When building a page that uses data, we pass the `context` variable to `render()` as well as the `request` object and the path to the template ❺.

The Topics Template

The template for the topics page receives the `context` dictionary so the template can use the data that `topics()` provides. Make a file called *topics.html* in the same directory as *index.html*. Here's how we can display the topics in the template:

topics.html

```
{% extends "learning_logs/base.html" %}

{% block content %}

  <p>Topics</p>

❶  <ul>
❷    {% for topic in topics %}
❸      <li>{{ topic }}</li>
❹    {% empty %}
      <li>No topics have been added yet.</li>
❺    {% endfor %}
❻  </ul>

{% endblock content %}
```

We start by using the `{% extends %}` tag to inherit from *base.html*, just as the index template does, and then open a `content` block. The body of this page contains a bulleted list of the topics that have been entered. In standard HTML, a bulleted list is called an *unordered list*, indicated by the tags <ul></ul>. We begin the bulleted list of topics at ❶.

At ❷ we have another template tag equivalent to a `for` loop, which loops through the list `topics` from the `context` dictionary. The code used in templates differs from Python in some important ways. Python uses indentation to indicate which lines of a `for` statement are part of a loop. In a template, every `for` loop needs an explicit `{% endfor %}` tag indicating where the end of the loop occurs. So in a template, you'll see loops written like this:

```
{% for item in list %}
    do something with each item
{% endfor %}
```

Inside the loop, we want to turn each topic into an item in the bulleted list. To print a variable in a template, wrap the variable name in double braces. The code `{{ topic }}` at ❸ will be replaced by the value of `topic` on each pass through the loop. The braces won't appear on the page; they just indicate to Django that we're using a template variable. The HTML tag `<li></li>` indicates a list item. Anything between these tags, inside a pair of `<ul></ul>` tags, will appear as a bulleted item in the list.

At ❹ we use the `{% empty %}` template tag, which tells Django what to do if there are no items in the list. In this case, we print a message informing the user that no topics have been added yet. The last two lines close out the `for` loop ❺ and then close out the bulleted list ❻.

Now we need to modify the base template to include a link to the topics page:

base.html

```
   <p>
❶    <a href="{% url 'learning_logs:index' %}">Learning Log</a> -
❷    <a href="{% url 'learning_logs:topics' %}">Topics</a>
   </p>

   {% block content %}{% endblock content %}
```

We add a dash after the link to the home page ❶, and then we add a link to the topics page, using the URL template tag again ❷. This line tells Django to generate a link matching the URL pattern with the name `'topics'` in *learning_logs/urls.py*.

Now when you refresh the home page in your browser, you'll see a *Topics* link. When you click the link, you'll see a page that looks similar to Figure 18-4.

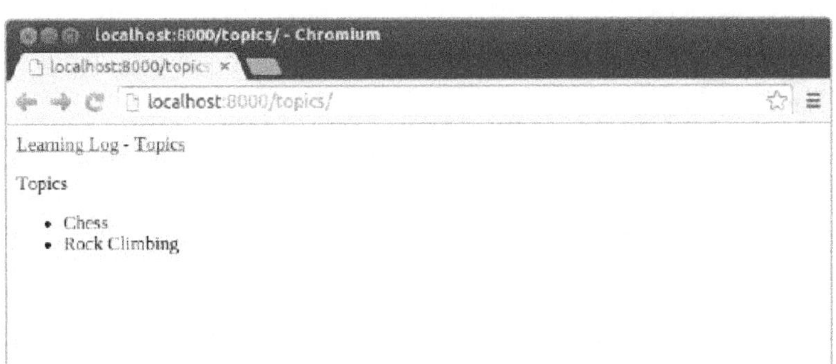

Figure 18-4: The topics page

Individual Topic Pages

Next, we need to create a page that can focus on a single topic, showing the topic name and all the entries for that topic. We'll again define a new URL pattern, write a view, and create a template. We'll also modify the topics page so each item in the bulleted list links to its corresponding topic page.

The Topic URL Pattern

The URL pattern for the topic page is a little different than the other URL patterns we've seen so far because it will use the topic's id attribute to indicate which topic was requested. For example, if the user wants to see the detail page for the topic Chess, where the id is 1, the URL will be *http://localhost:8000/topics/1/*. Here's a pattern to match this URL, which goes in *learning_logs/urls.py*:

urls.py

```
--snip--
urlpatterns = [
    --snip--
    # Detail page for a single topic
    url(r'^topics/(?P<topic_id>\d+)/$', views.topic, name='topic'),
]
```

Let's examine the regular expression in this URL pattern, r'^topics/(?P<topic_id>\d+)/$'. The r tells Django to interpret the string as a raw string, and the expression is contained in quotes. The second part of the expression, /(?P<topic_id>\d+)/, matches an integer between two forward slashes and stores the integer value in an argument called topic_id. The parentheses surrounding this part of the expression captures the value stored in the URL; the ?P<topic_id> part stores the matched value in topic_id; and the expression \d+ matches any number of digits that appear between the forward slashes.

When Django finds a URL that matches this pattern, it calls the view function topic() with the value stored in topic_id as an argument. We'll use the value of topic_id to get the correct topic inside the function.

The Topic View

The topic() function needs to get the topic and all associated entries from the database, as shown here:

views.py

```
   --snip--
❶ def topic(request, topic_id):
       """Show a single topic and all its entries."""
❷      topic = Topic.objects.get(id=topic_id)
❸      entries = topic.entry_set.order_by('-date_added')
❹      context = {'topic': topic, 'entries': entries}
❺      return render(request, 'learning_logs/topic.html', context)
```

This is the first view function that requires a parameter other than the request object. The function accepts the value captured by the expression (?P<topic_id>\d+) and stores it in topic_id ❶. At ❷ we use get() to retrieve the topic, just as we did in the Django shell. At ❸ we get the entries associated with this topic, and we order them according to date_added: the minus sign in front of date_added sorts the results in reverse order, which will display the most recent entries first. We store the topic and entries in the context dictionary ❹ and send context to the template *topic.html* ❺.

NOTE *The code phrases at ❷ and ❸ are called* queries, *because they query the database for specific information. When you're writing queries like these in your own projects, it's very helpful to try them out in the Django shell first. You'll get much quicker feedback in the shell than you will by writing a view and template and then checking the results in a browser.*

The Topic Template

The template needs to display the name of the topic and the entries. We also need to inform the user if no entries have been made yet for this topic:

topic.html

```
{% extends 'learning_logs/base.html' %}

{% block content %}

❶   <p>Topic: {{ topic }}</p>

    <p>Entries:</p>
❷   <ul>
❸   {% for entry in entries %}
      <li>
❹       <p>{{ entry.date_added|date:'M d, Y H:i' }}</p>
❺       <p>{{ entry.text|linebreaks }}</p>
      </li>
❻   {% empty %}
      <li>
        There are no entries for this topic yet.
      </li>
    {% endfor %}
    </ul>

{% endblock content %}
```

We extend *base.html*, as we do for all pages in the project. Next, we show the topic that's currently being displayed ❶, which is stored in the template variable `{{ topic }}`. The variable `topic` is available because it's included in the `context` dictionary. We then start a bulleted list to show each of the entries ❷ and loop through them as we did the topics earlier ❸.

Each bullet will list two pieces of information: the timestamp and the full text of each entry. For the timestamp ❹, we display the value of the attribute `date_added`. In Django templates, a vertical line (|) represents a template *filter*—a function that modifies the value in a template variable. The filter `date:'M d, Y H:i'` displays timestamps in the format *January 1, 2015 23:00*. The next line displays the full value of `text` rather than just the first 50 characters from `entry`. The filter `linebreaks` ❺ ensures that long text entries include line breaks in a format understood by browsers rather than showing a block of uninterrupted text. At ❻ we use the `{% empty %}` template tag to print a message informing the user that no entries have been made.

Links from the Topics Page

Before we look at the topic page in a browser, we need to modify the topics template so each topic links to the appropriate page. Here's the change to *topics.html*:

topics.html

```
--snip--
    {% for topic in topics %}
      <li>
        <a href="{% url 'learning_logs:topic' topic.id %}">{{ topic }}</a>
      </li>
    {% empty %}
--snip--
```

We use the URL template tag to generate the proper link, based on the URL pattern in `learning_logs` with the name `'topic'`. This URL pattern requires a `topic_id` argument, so we add the attribute `topic.id` to the URL template tag. Now each topic in the list of topics is a link to a topic page, such as *http://localhost:8000/topics/1/*.

If you refresh the topics page and click a topic, you should see a page that looks like Figure 18-5.

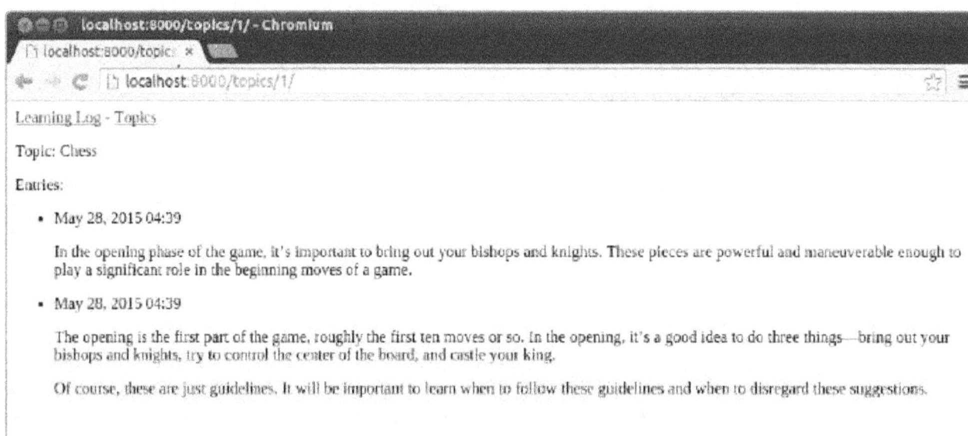

Figure 18-5: The detail page for a single topic, showing all entries for a topic

> **TRY IT YOURSELF**
>
> **18-7. Template Documentation:** Skim the Django template documentation at *https://docs.djangoproject.com/en/1.8/ref/templates/*. You can refer back to it when you're working on your own projects.
>
> **18-8. Pizzeria Pages:** Add a page to the *Pizzeria* project from Exercise 18-6 (page 416) that shows the names of available pizzas. Then link each pizza name to a page displaying the pizza's toppings. Make sure you use template inheritance to build your pages efficiently.

Summary

In this chapter you started learning how to build web applications using the Django framework. You wrote a brief project spec, installed Django to a virtual environment, learned to set up a project, and checked that the project was set up correctly. You learned to set up an app and defined models to represent the data for your app. You learned about databases and how Django helps you migrate your database after you make a change to your models. You learned how to create a superuser for the admin site, and you used the admin site to enter some initial data.

You also explored the Django shell, which allows you to work with your project's data in a terminal session. You learned to define URLs, create view functions, and write templates to make pages for your site. Finally, you used template inheritance to simplify the structure of individual templates and to make it easier to modify the site as the project evolves.

In Chapter 19 we'll make intuitive, user-friendly pages that allow users to add new topics and entries and edit existing entries without going through the admin site. We'll also add a user registration system, allowing users to create an account and to make their own learning log. This is the heart of a web app—the ability to create something that any number of users can interact with.

19

USER ACCOUNTS

At the heart of a web application is the ability for any user, anywhere in the world, to register an account with your app and start using it. In this chapter you'll build forms so users can add their own topics and entries, and edit existing entries. You'll also learn how Django guards against common attacks to form-based pages so you don't have to spend too much time thinking about securing your apps.

We'll then implement a user authentication system. You'll build a registration page for users to create accounts, and then restrict access to certain pages to logged-in users only. We'll then modify some of the view functions so users can only see their own data. You'll learn to keep your users' data safe and secure.

Allowing Users to Enter Data

Before we build an authentication system for creating accounts, we'll first add some pages that allow users to enter their own data. We'll give users the ability to add a new topic, add a new entry, and edit their previous entries.

Currently, only a superuser can enter data through the admin site. We don't want users to interact with the admin site, so we'll use Django's form-building tools to build pages that allow users to enter data.

Adding New Topics

Let's start by giving users the ability to add a new topic. Adding a form-based page works in much the same way as the pages we've already built: we define a URL, write a view function, and write a template. The one major difference is the addition of a new module called *forms.py*, which will contain the forms.

The Topic ModelForm

Any page that lets a user enter and submit information on a web page is a *form*, even if it doesn't look like one. When users enter information, we need to *validate* that the information provided is the right kind of data and not anything malicious, such as code to interrupt our server. We then need to process and save valid information to the appropriate place in the database. Django automates much of this work.

The simplest way to build a form in Django is to use a *ModelForm*, which uses the information from the models we defined in Chapter 18 to automatically build a form. Write your first form in the file *forms.py*, which you should create in the same directory as *models.py*:

forms.py

```
from django import forms

from .models import Topic

❶ class TopicForm(forms.ModelForm):
      class Meta:
❷         model = Topic
❸         fields = ['text']
❹         labels = {'text': ''}
```

We first import the forms module and the model we'll work with, Topic. At ❶ we define a class called TopicForm, which inherits from forms.ModelForm.

The simplest version of a ModelForm consists of a nested Meta class telling Django which model to base the form on and which fields to include in the form. At ❷ we build a form from the Topic model and include only the text field ❸. The code at ❹ tells Django not to generate a label for the text field.

The new_topic URL

The URL for a new page should be short and descriptive, so when the user wants to add a new topic, we'll send them to *http://localhost:8000/new_topic/*. Here's the URL pattern for the new_topic page, which we add to *learning_logs/urls.py*:

urls.py

```
--snip--
urlpatterns = [
    --snip--
    # Page for adding a new topic
    url(r'^new_topic/$', views.new_topic, name='new_topic'),
]
```

This URL pattern will send requests to the view function new_topic(), which we'll write next.

The new_topic() View Function

The new_topic() function needs to handle two different situations: initial requests for the new_topic page (in which case it should show a blank form) and the processing of any data submitted in the form. It then needs to redirect the user back to the topics page:

views.py

```
from django.shortcuts import render
from django.http import HttpResponseRedirect
from django.core.urlresolvers import reverse

from .models import Topic
from .forms import TopicForm

--snip--
def new_topic(request):
    """Add a new topic."""
❶    if request.method != 'POST':
        # No data submitted; create a blank form.
❷        form = TopicForm()
    else:
        # POST data submitted; process data.
❸        form = TopicForm(request.POST)
❹        if form.is_valid():
❺            form.save()
❻            return HttpResponseRedirect(reverse('learning_logs:topics'))

❼    context = {'form': form}
    return render(request, 'learning_logs/new_topic.html', context)
```

We import the class HttpResponseRedirect, which we'll use to redirect the reader back to the topics page after they submit their topic. The reverse() function determines the URL from a named URL pattern, meaning that Django will generate the URL when the page is requested. We also import the form we just wrote, TopicForm.

GET and POST Requests

The two main types of request you'll use when building web apps are GET requests and POST requests. You use *GET* requests for pages that only read data from the server. You usually use *POST* requests when the user needs to submit information through a form. We'll be specifying the POST method for processing all of our forms. (A few other kinds of requests exist, but we won't be using them in this project.)

The function `new_topic()` takes in the request object as a parameter. When the user initially requests this page, their browser will send a GET request. When the user has filled out and submitted the form, their browser will submit a POST request. Depending on the request, we'll know whether the user is requesting a blank form (a GET request) or asking us to process a completed form (a POST request).

The test at ❶ determines whether the request method is GET or POST. If the request method is not POST, the request is probably GET, so we need to return a blank form (if it's another kind of request, it's still safe to return a blank form). We make an instance of `TopicForm` ❷, store it in the variable `form`, and send the form to the template in the context dictionary ❼. Because we included no arguments when instantiating `TopicForm`, Django creates a blank form that the user can fill out.

If the request method is POST, the `else` block runs and processes the data submitted in the form. We make an instance of `TopicForm` ❸ and pass it the data entered by the user, stored in `request.POST`. The `form` object that's returned contains the information submitted by the user.

We can't save the submitted information in the database until we've checked that it's valid ❹. The `is_valid()` function checks that all required fields have been filled in (all fields in a form are required by default) and that the data entered matches the field types expected—for example, that the length of `text` is less than 200 characters, as we specified in *models.py* in Chapter 18. This automatic validation saves us a lot of work. If everything is valid, we can call `save()` ❺, which writes the data from the form to the database. Once we've saved the data, we can leave this page. We use `reverse()` to get the URL for the `topics` page and pass the URL to `HttpResponseRedirect()` ❻, which redirects the user's browser to the `topics` page. On the `topics` page, the user should see the topic they just entered in the list of topics.

The new_topic Template

Now we make a new template called *new_topic.html* to display the form we just created:

new_topic.html

```
{% extends "learning_logs/base.html" %}

{% block content %}
  <p>Add a new topic:</p>
```

```
❶ <form action="{% url 'learning_logs:new_topic' %}" method='post'>
❷   {% csrf_token %}
❸   {{ form.as_p }}
❹   <button name="submit">add topic</button>
  </form>

{% endblock content %}
```

This template extends *base.html*, so it has the same base structure as the rest of the pages in Learning Log. At ❶ we define an HTML form. The `action` argument tells the server where to send the data submitted in the form; in this case, we send it back to the view function `new_topic()`. The `method` argument tells the browser to submit the data as a POST request.

Django uses the template tag `{% csrf_token %}` ❷ to prevent attackers from using the form to gain unauthorized access to the server (this kind of attack is called a *cross-site request forgery*). At ❸ we display the form; here you see how simple Django can make tasks such as displaying a form. We only need to include the template variable `{{ form.as_p }}` for Django to create all the fields necessary to display the form automatically. The `as_p` modifier tells Django to render all the form elements in paragraph format, which is a simple way to display the form neatly.

Django doesn't create a submit button for forms, so we define one at ❹.

Linking to the new_topic Page

Next, we include a link to the `new_topic` page on the `topics` page:

topics.html

```
{% extends "learning_logs/base.html" %}

{% block content %}

  <p>Topics</p>

  <ul>
    --snip--
  </ul>

  <a href="{% url 'learning_logs:new_topic' %}">Add a new topic:</a>

{% endblock content %}
```

Place the link after the list of existing topics. Figure 19-1 shows the resulting form. Go ahead and use the form to add a few new topics of your own.

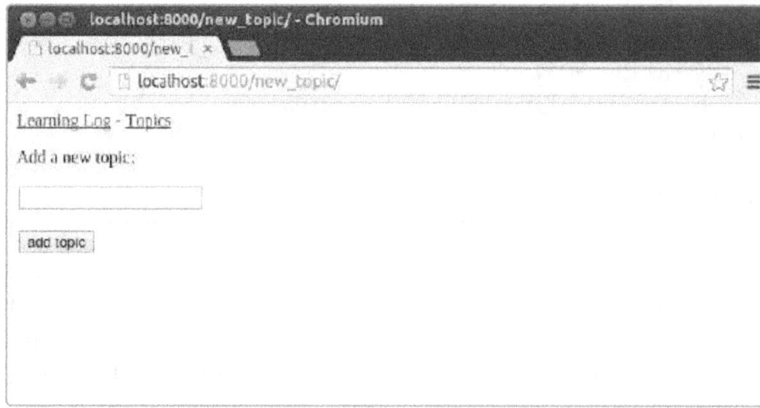

Figure 19-1: The page for adding a new topic

Adding New Entries

Now that the user can add a new topic, they'll want to add new entries too. We'll again define a URL, write a view function and a template, and link to the page. But first we'll add another class to *forms.py*.

The Entry ModelForm

We need to create a form associated with the `Entry` model, but this time with a little more customization than `TopicForm`:

forms.py

```
from django import forms

from .models import Topic, Entry

class TopicForm(forms.ModelForm):
    --snip--

class EntryForm(forms.ModelForm):
    class Meta:
        model = Entry
        fields = ['text']
❶       labels = {'text': ''}
❷       widgets = {'text': forms.Textarea(attrs={'cols': 80})}
```

We first update the `import` statement to include `Entry` as well as `Topic`. The new class `EntryForm` inherits from `forms.ModelForm` and has a nested `Meta` class listing the model it's based on and the field to include in the form. We again give the field `'text'` a blank label ❶.

At ❷ we include the `widgets` attribute. A *widget* is an HTML form element, such as a single-line text box, multi-line text area, or drop-down list. By including the `widgets` attribute you can override Django's default widget choices. By telling Django to use a `forms.Textarea` element, we're customizing the input widget for the field `'text'` so the text area will be 80 columns wide instead of the default 40. This will give users enough room to write a meaningful entry.

The new_entry URL

We need to include a topic_id argument in the URL for adding a new entry, because the entry must be associated with a particular topic. Here's the URL, which we add to *learning_logs/urls.py*:

urls.py

```
--snip--
urlpatterns = [
    --snip--
    # Page for adding a new entry
    url(r'^new_entry/(?P<topic_id>\d+)/$', views.new_entry, name='new_entry'),
]
```

This URL pattern matches any URL with the form http://localhost:8000/new_entry/*id*/, where *id* is a number matching the topic ID. The code (?P<topic_id>\d+) captures a numerical value and stores it in the variable topic_id. When a URL matching this pattern is requested, Django sends the request and the ID of the topic to the new_entry() view function.

The new_entry() View Function

The view function for new_entry is much like the function for adding a new topic:

views.py

```
from django.shortcuts import render
--snip--

from .models import Topic
from .forms import TopicForm, EntryForm

--snip--
def new_entry(request, topic_id):
    """Add a new entry for a particular topic."""
❶   topic = Topic.objects.get(id=topic_id)

❷   if request.method != 'POST':
        # No data submitted; create a blank form.
❸       form = EntryForm()
    else:
        # POST data submitted; process data.
❹       form = EntryForm(data=request.POST)
        if form.is_valid():
❺           new_entry = form.save(commit=False)
❻           new_entry.topic = topic
            new_entry.save()
❼           return HttpResponseRedirect(reverse('learning_logs:topic',
                                        args=[topic_id]))

    context = {'topic': topic, 'form': form}
    return render(request, 'learning_logs/new_entry.html', context)
```

We update the import statement to include the EntryForm we just made. The definition of new_entry() has a topic_id parameter to store the value it receives from the URL. We'll need the topic to render the page and process the form's data, so we use topic_id to get the correct topic object at ❶.

At ❷ we check if the request method is POST or GET. The if block executes if it's a GET request, and we create a blank instance of EntryForm ❸. If the request method is POST, we process the data by making an instance of EntryForm, populated with the POST data from the request object ❹. We then check if the form is valid. If it is, we need to set the entry object's topic attribute before saving it to the database.

When we call save(), we include the argument commit=False ❺ to tell Django to create a new entry object and store it in new_entry without saving it to the database yet. We set new_entry's topic attribute to the topic we pulled from the database at the beginning of the function ❻, and then we call save() with no arguments. This saves the entry to the database with the correct associated topic.

At ❼ we redirect the user to the topic page. The reverse() call requires two arguments—the name of the URL pattern we want to generate a URL for and an args list containing any arguments that need to be included in the URL. The args list has one item in it, topic_id. The HttpResponseRedirect() call then redirects the user to the topic page they made an entry for, and they should see their new entry in the list of entries.

The new_entry Template

As you can see in the following code, the template for new_entry is similar to the template for new_topic:

new_entry.html

```
{% extends "learning_logs/base.html" %}

{% block content %}

❶ <p><a href="{% url 'learning_logs:topic' topic.id %}">{{ topic }}</a></p>

  <p>Add a new entry:</p>
❷ <form action="{% url 'learning_logs:new_entry' topic.id %}" method='post'>
    {% csrf_token %}
    {{ form.as_p }}
    <button name='submit'>add entry</button>
  </form>

{% endblock content %}
```

We show the topic at the top of the page ❶, so the user can see which topic they're adding an entry to. This also acts as a link back to the main page for that topic.

The form's action argument includes the topic_id value in the URL, so the view function can associate the new entry with the correct topic ❷. Other than that, this template looks just like *new_topic.html.*

Linking to the new_entry Page

Next, we need to include a link to the new_entry page from each topic page:

topic.html

```
{% extends "learning_logs/base.html" %}

{% block content %}

  <p>Topic: {{ topic }}</p>

  <p>Entries:</p>
  <p>
    <a href="{% url 'learning_logs:new_entry' topic.id %}">add new entry</a>
  </p>
  <ul>
  --snip--
  </ul>

{% endblock content %}
```

We add the link just before showing the entries, because adding a new entry will be the most common action on this page. Figure 19-2 shows the new_entry page. Now users can add new topics and as many entries as they want for each topic. Try out the new_entry page by adding a few entries to some of the topics you've created.

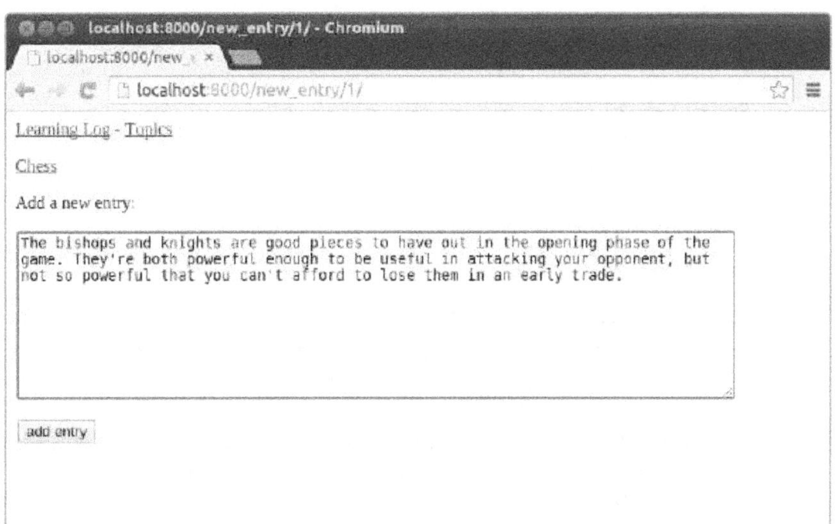

Figure 19-2: The new_entry page

Editing Entries

Now we'll make a page to allow users to edit the entries they've already added.

The edit_entry URL

The URL for the page needs to pass the ID of the entry to be edited. Here's *learning_logs/urls.py*:

urls.py

```
--snip--
urlpatterns = [
    --snip--
    # Page for editing an entry
    url(r'^edit_entry/(?P<entry_id>\d+)/$', views.edit_entry,
        name='edit_entry'),
]
```

The ID passed in the URL (for example, *http://localhost:8000/edit_entry/1/)* is stored in the parameter `entry_id`. The URL pattern sends requests that match this format to the view function `edit_entry()`.

The edit_entry() View Function

When the `edit_entry` page receives a GET request, `edit_entry()` will return a form for editing the entry. When the page receives a POST request with revised entry text, it will save the modified text into the database:

views.py

```
from django.shortcuts import render
--snip--

from .models import Topic, Entry
from .forms import TopicForm, EntryForm
--snip--

def edit_entry(request, entry_id):
    """Edit an existing entry."""
❶   entry = Entry.objects.get(id=entry_id)
    topic = entry.topic

    if request.method != 'POST':
        # Initial request; pre-fill form with the current entry.
❷       form = EntryForm(instance=entry)
    else:
        # POST data submitted; process data.
❸       form = EntryForm(instance=entry, data=request.POST)
        if form.is_valid():
❹           form.save()
❺           return HttpResponseRedirect(reverse('learning_logs:topic',
                                        args=[topic.id]))

    context = {'entry': entry, 'topic': topic, 'form': form}
    return render(request, 'learning_logs/edit_entry.html', context)
```

We first need to import the `Entry` model. At ❶ we get the entry object that the user wants to edit and the topic associated with this entry. In the `if` block, which runs for a GET request, we make an instance of `EntryForm` with the argument `instance=entry` ❷. This argument tells Django to create the form prefilled with information from the existing entry object. The user will see their existing data and be able to edit that data.

When processing a POST request, we pass the `instance=entry` argument and the `data=request.POST` argument ❸ to tell Django to create a form instance based on the information associated with the existing entry object, updated with any relevant data from `request.POST`. We then check if the form is valid; if it is, we call `save()` with no arguments ❹. We then redirect to the `topic` page ❺, where the user should see the updated version of the entry they edited.

The edit_entry Template

Here's *edit_entry.html*, which is similar to *new_entry.html*:

edit_entry.html

```
{% extends "learning_logs/base.html" %}

{% block content %}

  <p><a href="{% url 'learning_logs:topic' topic.id %}">{{ topic }}</a></p>

  <p>Edit entry:</p>

❶ <form action="{% url 'learning_logs:edit_entry' entry.id %}" method='post'>
    {% csrf_token %}
    {{ form.as_p }}
❷   <button name="submit">save changes</button>
  </form>

{% endblock content %}
```

At ❶ the `action` argument sends the form back to the `edit_entry()` function for processing. We include the entry ID as an argument in the `{% url %}` tag, so the view function can modify the correct entry object. We label the submit button as *save changes* to remind the user they're saving edits, not creating a new entry ❷.

Linking to the edit_entry Page

Now we need to include a link to the `edit_entry` page for each entry on the topic page:

topic.html

```
--snip--
  {% for entry in entries %}
    <li>
      <p>{{ entry.date_added|date:'M d, Y H:i' }}</p>
      <p>{{ entry.text|linebreaks }}</p>
      <p>
        <a href="{% url 'learning_logs:edit_entry' entry.id %}">edit entry</a>
      </p>
    </li>
--snip--
```

We include the edit link after each entry's date and text has been displayed. We use the {% url %} template tag to determine the URL for the named URL pattern edit_entry, along with the ID attribute of the current entry in the loop (entry.id). The link text "edit entry" appears after each entry on the page. Figure 19-3 shows what the topic page looks like with these links.

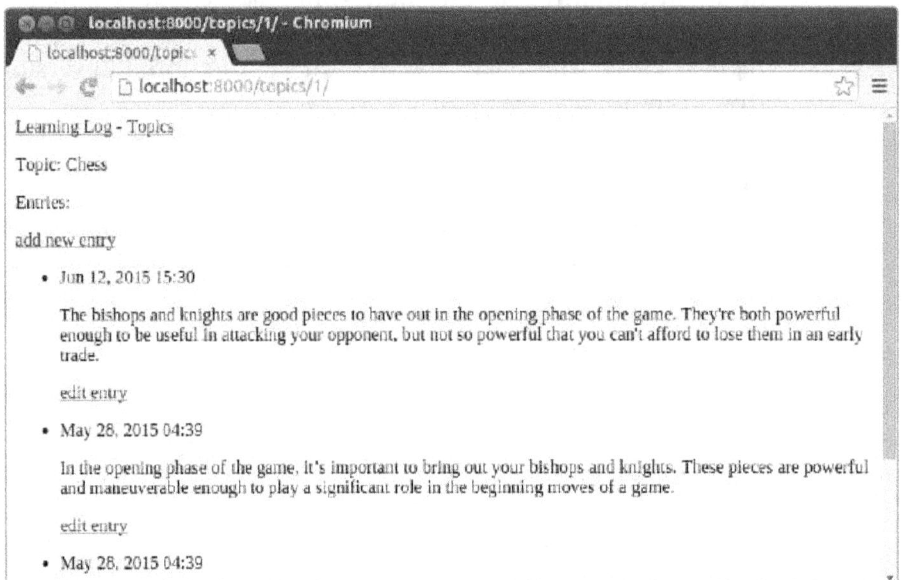

Figure 19-3: Each entry now has a link for editing that entry.

Learning Log now has most of the functionality it needs. Users can add topics and entries, and read through any set of entries they want. In the next section, we'll implement a user registration system so anyone can make an account with Learning Log and create their own set of topics and entries.

TRY IT YOURSELF

19-1. Blog: Start a new Django project called *Blog*. Create an app called *blogs* in the project, with a model called BlogPost. The model should have fields like title, text, and date_added. Create a superuser for the project, and use the admin site to make a couple of short posts. Make a home page that shows all posts in chronological order.

Create a form for making new posts and another for editing existing posts. Fill in your forms to make sure they work.

Setting Up User Accounts

In this section we'll set up a user registration and authorization system to allow people to register an account and log in and out. We'll create a new app to contain all the functionality related to working with users. We'll also modify the Topic model slightly so every topic belongs to a certain user.

The users App

We'll start by creating a new app called users, using the startapp command:

```
(ll_env)learning_log$ python manage.py startapp users
(ll_env)learning_log$ ls
❶ db.sqlite3  learning_log  learning_logs  ll_env  manage.py  users
(ll_env)learning_log$ ls users
❷ admin.py __init__.py migrations models.py tests.py views.py
```

This command makes a new directory called *users* ❶ with a structure identical to the learning_logs app ❷.

Adding users to settings.py

We need to add our new app to INSTALLED_APPS in *settings.py*, like so:

settings.py

```
--snip--
INSTALLED_APPS = (
    --snip--
    # My apps
    'learning_logs',
    'users',
)
--snip--
```

Now Django will include the users app in the overall project.

Including the URLs from users

Next, we need to modify the root *urls.py* so it includes the URLs we'll write for the users app:

urls.py

```
from django.conf.urls import include, url
from django.contrib import admin

urlpatterns = [
    url(r'^admin/', include(admin.site.urls)),
    url(r'^users/', include('users.urls', namespace='users')),
    url(r'', include('learning_logs.urls', namespace='learning_logs')),
]
```

We add a line to include the file *urls.py* from users. This line will match any URL that starts with the word *users*, such as *http://localhost:8000/users/*

login/. We also create the namespace 'users' so we'll be able to distinguish URLs that belong to the learning_logs app from URLs that belong to the users app.

The Login Page

We'll first implement a login page. We'll use the default login view Django provides, so the URL pattern looks a little different. Make a new *urls.py* file in the directory *learning_log/users/*, and add the following to it:

urls.py

```
"""Defines URL patterns for users"""

from django.conf.urls import url
❶ from django.contrib.auth.views import login

from . import views

urlpatterns = [
    # Login page
❷   url(r'^login/$', login, {'template_name': 'users/login.html'},
        name='login'),
]
```

We first import the default login view ❶. The login page's pattern matches the URL *http://localhost:8000/users/login/* ❷. When Django reads this URL, the word *users* tells Django to look in *users/urls.py*, and *login* tells it to send requests to Django's default login view (notice the view argument is login, not views.login). Because we're not writing our own view function, we pass a dictionary telling Django where to find the template we're about to write. This template will be part of the users app, not the learning_logs app.

The login Template

When the user requests the login page, Django will use its default login view, but we still need to provide a template for the page. Inside the *learning_log/users/* directory, make a directory called *templates*; inside that, make another directory called *users*. Here's the *login.html* template, which you should save in *learning_log/users/templates/users/*:

login.html

```
{% extends "learning_logs/base.html" %}

{% block content %}

❶ {% if form.errors %}
  <p>Your username and password didn't match. Please try again.</p>
  {% endif %}

❷ <form method="post" action="{% url 'users:login' %}">
  {% csrf_token %}
❸ {{ form.as_p }}

❹ <button name="submit">log in</button>
```

```
❺ <input type="hidden" name="next" value="{% url 'learning_logs:index' %}" />
  </form>

{% endblock content %}
```

This template extends *base.html* to ensure that the login page will have the same look and feel as the rest of the site. Note that a template in one app can extend a template from another app.

If the form's `errors` attribute is set, we display an error message ❶, reporting that the username and password combination don't match anything stored in the database.

We want the login view to process the form, so we set the `action` argument as the URL of the login page ❷. The login view sends a form to the template, and it's up to us to display the form ❸ and add a submit button ❹. At ❺ we include a hidden form element, `'next'`; the `value` argument tells Django where to redirect the user after they've logged in successfully. In this case, we send the user back to the home page.

Linking to the Login Page

Let's add the login link to *base.html* so it appears on every page. We don't want the link to display when the user is already logged in, so we nest it inside an `{% if %}` tag:

base.html

```
  <p>
    <a href="{% url 'learning_logs:index' %}">Learning Log</a> -
    <a href="{% url 'learning_logs:topics' %}">Topics</a> -
❶   {% if user.is_authenticated %}
❷     Hello, {{ user.username }}.
    {% else %}
❸     <a href="{% url 'users:login' %}">log in</a>
    {% endif %}
  </p>

  {% block content %}{% endblock content %}
```

In Django's authentication system, every template has a `user` variable available, which always has an `is_authenticated` attribute set: the attribute is `True` if the user is logged in and `False` if they aren't. This allows you to display one message to authenticated users and another to unauthenticated users.

Here we display a greeting to users currently logged in ❶. Authenticated users have an additional `username` attribute set, which we use to personalize the greeting and remind the user they're logged in ❷. At ❸ we display a link to the login page for users who haven't been authenticated.

Using the Login Page

We've already set up a user account, so let's log in to see if the page works. Go to *http://localhost:8000/admin/*. If you're still logged in as an admin, look for a logout link in the header and click it.

When you're logged out, go to *http://localhost:8000/users/login/*. You should see a login page similar to the one shown in Figure 19-4. Enter the username and password you set up earlier, and you should be brought back to the index page. The header on the home page should display a greeting personalized with your username.

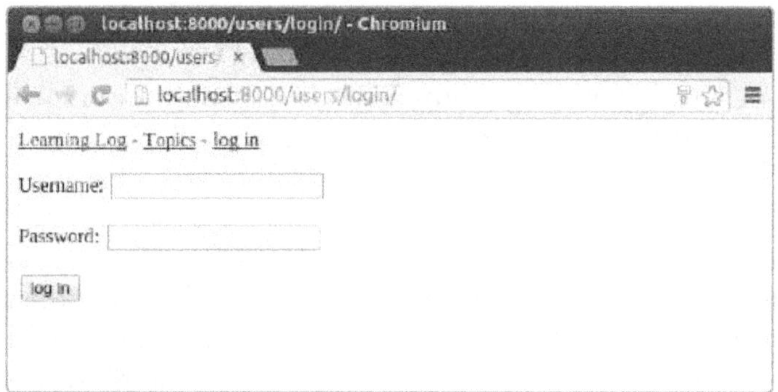

Figure 19-4: The login page

Logging Out

Now we need to provide a way for users to log out. We won't build a page for logging out; users will just click a link and be sent back to the home page. We'll define a URL pattern for the logout link, write a view function, and provide a logout link in *base.html*.

The logout URL

The following code defines the URL pattern for logging out, matching the URL *http://localhost:8000/users/logout/*. Here's *users/urls.py*:

urls.py

```
--snip--
urlpatterns = [
    # Login page
    --snip--
    # Logout page
    url(r'^logout/$', views.logout_view, name='logout'),
]
```

The URL pattern sends the request to the `logout_view()` function, which is named as such to distinguish it from the `logout()` function we'll call from within the view. (Make sure you're modifying *users/urls.py*, not *learning_log/urls.py*.)

The logout_view() View Function

The `logout_view()` function is straightforward: we just import Django's `logout()` function, call it, and then redirect back to the home page. Open *users/views.py*, and enter the following code.

views.py

```
  from django.http import HttpResponseRedirect
  from django.core.urlresolvers import reverse
❶ from django.contrib.auth import logout

  def logout_view(request):
      """Log the user out."""
❷     logout(request)
❸     return HttpResponseRedirect(reverse('learning_logs:index'))
```

We import the `logout()` function from `django.contrib.auth` ❶. In the function, we call `logout()` ❷, which requires the `request` object as an argument. We then redirect to the home page ❸.

Linking to the logout View

Now we need a logout link. We'll include it as part of *base.html* so it's available on every page and include it in the `{% if user.is_authenticated %}` portion so only users who are already logged in can see it:

base.html

```
--snip--
  {% if user.is_authenticated %}
    Hello, {{ user.username }}.
    <a href="{% url 'users:logout' %}">log out</a>
  {% else %}
    <a href="{% url 'users:login' %}">log in</a>
  {% endif %}
--snip--
```

Figure 19-5 shows the current home page as it appears to a logged-in user. The styling is minimal because we're focusing on building a site that works properly. When the required set of features works, we'll style the site to look more professional.

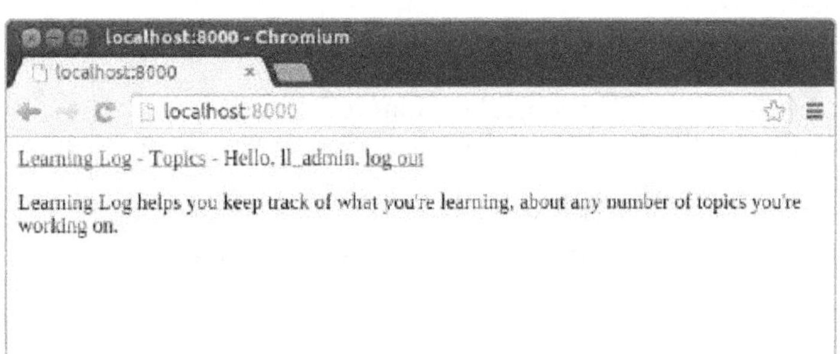

Figure 19-5: The home page with a personalized greeting and a logout link

The Registration Page

Next, we'll build a page to allow new users to register. We'll use Django's default `UserCreationForm` but write our own view function and template.

The register URL

The following code provides the URL pattern for the registration page, again in *users/urls.py*:

urls.py

```
--snip--
urlpatterns = [
    # Login page
    --snip--
    # Registration page
    url(r'^register/$', views.register, name='register'),
]
```

This pattern matches the URL *http://localhost:8000/users/register/* and sends requests to the register() function we're about to write.

The register() View Function

The register() view function needs to display a blank registration form when the registration page is first requested and then process completed registration forms when they're submitted. When a registration is successful, the function also needs to log in the new user. Add the following code to *users/views.py*:

views.py

```
from django.shortcuts import render
from django.http import HttpResponseRedirect
from django.core.urlresolvers import reverse
from django.contrib.auth import login, logout, authenticate
from django.contrib.auth.forms import UserCreationForm

def logout_view(request):
--snip--

def register(request):
    """Register a new user."""
    if request.method != 'POST':
        # Display blank registration form.
❶       form = UserCreationForm()
    else:
        # Process completed form.
❷       form = UserCreationForm(data=request.POST)

❸       if form.is_valid():
❹           new_user = form.save()
            # Log the user in and then redirect to home page.
❺           authenticated_user = authenticate(username=new_user.username,
                password=request.POST['password1'])
❻           login(request, authenticated_user)
❼           return HttpResponseRedirect(reverse('learning_logs:index'))

    context = {'form': form}
    return render(request, 'users/register.html', context)
```

We first import the render() function. We then import the login() and authenticate() functions to log in the user if their registration information is correct. We also import the default UserCreationForm. In the register() function, we check whether or not we're responding to a POST request. If we're not, we make an instance of UserCreationForm with no initial data ❶.

If we're responding to a POST request, we make an instance of UserCreationForm based on the submitted data ❷. We check that the data is valid ❸—in this case, that the username has the appropriate characters, the passwords match, and the user isn't trying to do anything malicious in their submission.

If the submitted data is valid, we call the form's save() method to save the username and the hash of the password to the database ❹. The save() method returns the newly created user object, which we store in new_user.

When the user's information is saved, we log them in, which is a two-step process: we call authenticate() with the arguments new_user.username and their password ❺. When they register, the user is asked to enter two matching passwords, and because the form is valid, we know the passwords match so we can use either one. Here we get the value associated with the 'password1' key in the form's POST data. If the username and password are correct, the method returns an authenticated user object, which we store in authenticated_user. We then call the login() function with the request and authenticated_user objects ❻, which creates a valid session for the new user. Finally, we redirect the user to the home page ❼ where a personalized greeting in the header tells them their registration was successful.

The register Template

The template for the registration page is similar to the login page. Be sure to save it in the same directory as *login.html*:

register.html

```
{% extends "learning_logs/base.html" %}

{% block content %}

  <form method="post" action="{% url 'users:register' %}">
    {% csrf_token %}
    {{ form.as_p }}

    <button name="submit">register</button>
    <input type="hidden" name="next" value="{% url 'learning_logs:index' %}" />
  </form>

{% endblock content %}
```

We use the as_p method again so Django will display all the fields in the form appropriately, including any error messages if the form is not filled out correctly.

Linking to the Registration Page

Next, we'll add the code to show the registration page link to any user who is not currently logged in:

base.html

```
--snip--
  {% if user.is_authenticated %}
    Hello, {{ user.username }}.
    <a href="{% url 'users:logout' %}">log out</a>
  {% else %}
    <a href="{% url 'users:register' %}">register</a> -
    <a href="{% url 'users:login' %}">log in</a>
  {% endif %}
--snip--
```

Now users who are logged in see a personalized greeting and a logout link. Users not logged in see a registration page link and a login link. Try out the registration page by making several user accounts with different usernames.

In the next section, we'll restrict some of the pages so they're available only to registered users, and we'll make sure every topic belongs to a specific user.

NOTE *The registration system we've set up allows anyone to make any number of accounts for Learning Log. But some systems require users to confirm their identity by sending a confirmation email the user must reply to. By doing so, the system generates fewer spam accounts than the simple system we're using here. However, when you're learning to build apps, it's perfectly appropriate to practice with a simple user registration system like the one we're using.*

TRY IT YOURSELF

19-2. Blog Accounts: Add a user authentication and registration system to the Blog project you started in Exercise 19-1 (page 438). Make sure logged-in users see their username somewhere on the screen and unregistered users see a link to the registration page.

Allowing Users to Own Their Data

Users should be able to enter data exclusive to them, so we'll create a system to figure out which data belongs to which user, and then we'll restrict access to certain pages so users can work with only their own data.

In this section, we'll modify the `Topic` model so every topic belongs to a specific user. This will also take care of entries, because every entry belongs to a specific topic. We'll start by restricting access to certain pages.

Restricting Access with @login_required

Django makes it easy to restrict access to certain pages to logged-in users through the `@login_required` decorator. A *decorator* is a directive placed just before a function definition that Python applies to the function before it runs to alter how the function code behaves. Let's look at an example.

Restricting Access to the Topics Page

Each topic will be owned by a user, so only registered users should be able to request the topics page. Add the following code to *learning_logs/views.py*:

views.py

```
--snip--
from django.core.urlresolvers import reverse
from django.contrib.auth.decorators import login_required

from .models import Topic, Entry
--snip--

@login_required
def topics(request):
    """Show all topics."""
    --snip--
```

We first import the `login_required()` function. We apply `login_required()` as a decorator to the `topics()` view function by prepending `login_required` with the `@` symbol so Python knows to run the code in `login_required()` before the code in `topics()`.

The code in `login_required()` checks to see if a user is logged in, and Django will run the code in `topics()` only if they are. If the user is not logged in, they're redirected to the login page.

To make this redirect work, we need to modify *settings.py* so Django knows where to find the login page. Add the following at the very end of *settings.py*:

settings.py

```
"""
Django settings for learning_log project
--snip--

# My settings
LOGIN_URL = '/users/login/'
```

Now when an unauthenticated user requests a page protected by the `@login_required` decorator, Django will send the user to the URL defined by `LOGIN_URL` in *settings.py*.

You can test this setting by logging out of any user accounts and going to the home page. Next, click the Topics link, which should redirect you to the login page. Then log in to any of your accounts, and from the home page click the Topics link again. You should be able to reach the topics page.

Restricting Access Throughout Learning Log

Django makes it easy to restrict access to pages, but you have to decide which pages to protect. It's better to think about which pages need to be unrestricted first and then restrict all the other pages in the project. You can easily correct overrestricting access, and it's less dangerous than leaving sensitive pages unrestricted.

In Learning Log, we'll keep the home page, the registration page, and logout unrestricted. We'll restrict access to every other page.

Here's *learning_logs/views.py* with `@login_required` decorators applied to every view except `index()`:

views.py

```
--snip--
@login_required
def topics(request):
    --snip--

@login_required
def topic(request, topic_id):
    --snip--

@login_required
def new_topic(request):
    --snip--

@login_required
def new_entry(request, topic_id):
    --snip--

@login_required
def edit_entry(request, entry_id):
    --snip--
```

Try accessing each of these pages while logged out: you'll be redirected back to the login page. You'll also be unable to click links to pages such as `new_topic`. But if you enter the URL *http://localhost:8000/new_topic/*, you'll be redirected to the login page. You should restrict access to any URL that's publicly accessible and relates to private user data.

Connecting Data to Certain Users

Now we need to connect the data submitted to the user who submitted it. We need to connect only the data highest in the hierarchy to a user, and the lower-level data will follow. For example, in Learning Log, topics are the highest level of data in the app, and all entries are connected to a topic. As long as each topic belongs to a specific user, we'll be able to trace the ownership of each entry in the database.

We'll modify the `Topic` model by adding a foreign key relationship to a user. We'll then have to migrate the database. Finally, we'll have to modify some of the views so they only show the data associated with the currently logged-in user.

Modifying the Topic Model

The modification to *models.py* is just two lines:

models.py

```
from django.db import models
from django.contrib.auth.models import User

class Topic(models.Model):
    """A topic the user is learning about"""
    text = models.CharField(max_length=200)
    date_added = models.DateTimeField(auto_now_add=True)
    owner = models.ForeignKey(User)

    def __str__(self):
        """Return a string representation of the model."""
        return self.text

class Entry(models.Model):
    --snip--
```

We first import the User model from django.contrib.auth. We then add an owner field to Topic, which establishes a foreign key relationship to the User model.

Identifying Existing Users

When we migrate the database, Django will modify the database so it can store a connection between each topic and a user. To make the migration, Django needs to know which user to associate with each existing topic. The simplest approach is to give all existing topics to one user—for example, the superuser. First, we need to know the ID of that user.

Let's look at the IDs of all users created so far. Start a Django shell session and issue the following commands:

```
(venv)learning_log$ python manage.py shell
❶ >>> from django.contrib.auth.models import User
❷ >>> User.objects.all()
[<User: ll_admin>, <User: eric>, <User: willie>]
❸ >>> for user in User.objects.all():
...     print(user.username, user.id)
...
ll_admin 1
eric 2
willie 3
>>>
```

At ❶ we import the User model into the shell session. We then look at all the users that have been created so far ❷. The output shows three users: *ll_admin*, *eric*, and *willie*.

At ❸ we loop through the list of users and print each user's username and ID. When Django asks which user to associate the existing topics with, we'll use one of these ID values.

Migrating the Database

Now that we know the IDs, we can migrate the database.

```
❶ (venv)learning_log$ python manage.py makemigrations learning_logs
❷ You are trying to add a non-nullable field 'owner' to topic without a default;
  we can't do that (the database needs something to populate existing rows).
❸ Please select a fix:
   1) Provide a one-off default now (will be set on all existing rows)
   2) Quit, and let me add a default in models.py
❹ Select an option: 1
❺ Please enter the default value now, as valid Python
  The datetime and django.utils.timezone modules are available, so you can do
  e.g. timezone.now()
❻ >>> 1
  Migrations for 'learning_logs':
    0003_topic_owner.py:
      - Add field owner to topic
```

We start by issuing the makemigrations command ❶. In the output at ❷, Django indicates that we're trying to add a required (non-nullable) field to an existing model (topic) with no default value specified. Django gives us two options at ❸: we can provide a default right now, or we can quit and add a default value in *models.py*. At ❹ we've chosen the first option. Django then asks us to enter the default value ❺.

To associate all existing topics with the original admin user, *ll_admin*, I entered the user ID of 1 at ❻. You can use the ID of any user you've created; it doesn't have to be a superuser. Django then migrates the database using this value and generates the migration file *0003_topic_owner.py*, which adds the field owner to the Topic model.

Now we can carry out the migration. Enter the following in an active virtual environment:

```
  (venv)learning_log$ python manage.py migrate
  Operations to perform:
    Synchronize unmigrated apps: messages, staticfiles
    Apply all migrations: learning_logs, contenttypes, sessions, admin, auth
  --snip--
  Running migrations:
    Rendering model states... DONE
❶   Applying learning_logs.0003_topic_owner... OK
  (venv)learning_log$
```

Django applies the new migration, and the result is OK ❶.

We can verify that the migration worked as expected in the shell session, like this:

```
❶ >>> from learning_logs.models import Topic
❷ >>> for topic in Topic.objects.all():
  ...     print(topic, topic.owner)
```

```
...
Chess ll_admin
Rock Climbing ll_admin
>>>
```

We import `Topic` from `learning_logs.models` ❶ and then loop through all existing topics, printing each topic and the user it belongs to ❷. You can see that each topic now belongs to the user *ll_admin*.

NOTE *You can simply reset the database instead of migrating, but that will lose all existing data. It's good practice to learn how to migrate a database while maintaining the integrity of users' data. If you do want to start with a fresh database, issue the command* `python manage.py flush` *to rebuild the database structure. You'll have to create a new superuser, and all of your data will be gone.*

Restricting Topics Access to Appropriate Users

Currently, if you're logged in, you'll be able to see all the topics, no matter which user you're logged in as. We'll change that by showing users only the topics that belong to them.

Make the following change to the `topics()` function in *views.py*:

views.py

```
--snip--
@login_required
def topics(request):
    """Show all topics."""
    topics = Topic.objects.filter(owner=request.user).order_by('date_added')
    context = {'topics': topics}
    return render(request, 'learning_logs/topics.html', context)
--snip--
```

When a user is logged in, the request object has a `request.user` attribute set that stores information about the user. The code fragment `Topic.objects.filter(owner=request.user)` tells Django to retrieve only the `Topic` objects from the database whose `owner` attribute matches the current user. Because we're not changing how the topics are displayed, we don't need to change the template for the topics page at all.

To see if this works, log in as the user you connected all existing topics to, and go to the topics page. You should see all the topics. Now log out, and log back in as a different user. The topics page should list no topics.

Protecting a User's Topics

We haven't actually restricted access to the topic pages yet, so any registered user could try a bunch of URLs, like *http://localhost:8000/topics/1/*, and retrieve topic pages that happen to match.

Try it yourself. While logged in as the user that owns all topics, copy the URL or note the ID in the URL of a topic, and then log out and log back in as a different user. Enter the URL of that topic. You should be able to read the entries, even though you're logged in as a different user.

We'll fix this now by performing a check before retrieving the requested entries in the topic() view function:

views.py

```
  from django.shortcuts import render
❶ from django.http import HttpResponseRedirect, Http404
  from django.core.urlresolvers import reverse
  --snip--

  @login_required
  def topic(request, topic_id):
      """Show a single topic and all its entries."""
      topic = Topic.objects.get(id=topic_id)
      # Make sure the topic belongs to the current user.
❷     if topic.owner != request.user:
          raise Http404

      entries = topic.entry_set.order_by('-date_added')
      context = {'topic': topic, 'entries': entries}
      return render(request, 'learning_logs/topic.html', context)
  --snip--
```

A 404 response is a standard error response that's returned when a requested resource doesn't exist on a server. Here we import the Http404 exception ❶, which we'll raise if the user requests a topic they shouldn't see. After receiving a topic request, we make sure the topic's user matches the currently logged-in user before rendering the page. If the current user doesn't own the requested topic, we raise the Http404 exception ❷, and Django returns a 404 error page.

Now if you try to view another user's topic entries, you'll see a *Page Not Found* message from Django. In Chapter 20, we'll configure the project so users will see a proper error page.

Protecting the edit_entry Page

The edit_entry pages have URLs in the form http://localhost:8000/edit_entry/*entry_id*/, where the *entry_id* is a number. Let's protect this page so no one can use the URL to gain access to someone else's entries:

views.py

```
--snip--
@login_required
def edit_entry(request, entry_id):
    """Edit an existing entry."""
    entry = Entry.objects.get(id=entry_id)
    topic = entry.topic
    if topic.owner != request.user:
        raise Http404
```

```
    if request.method != 'POST':
        # Initial request; pre-fill form with the current entry.
        --snip--
```

We retrieve the entry and the topic associated with this entry. We then check if the owner of the topic matches the currently logged-in user; if they don't match, we raise an `Http404` exception.

Associating New Topics with the Current User

Currently, our page for adding new topics is broken, because it doesn't associate new topics with any particular user. If you try adding a new topic, you'll see the error message `IntegrityError` along with `learning_logs_topic.user_id may not be NULL`. Django's saying you can't create a new topic without specifying a value for the topic's `owner` field.

There's a straightforward fix for this problem, because we have access to the current user through the `request` object. Add the following code, which associates the new topic with the current user:

views.py

```
--snip--
@login_required
def new_topic(request):
    """Add a new topic."""
    if request.method != 'POST':
        # No data submitted; create a blank form.
        form = TopicForm()
    else:
        # POST data submitted; process data.
        form = TopicForm(request.POST)
        if form.is_valid():
❶           new_topic = form.save(commit=False)
❷           new_topic.owner = request.user
❸           new_topic.save()
            return HttpResponseRedirect(reverse('learning_logs:topics'))

    context = {'form': form}
    return render(request, 'learning_logs/new_topic.html', context)
 --snip--
```

When we first call `form.save()`, we pass the `commit=False` argument because we need to modify the new topic before saving it to the database ❶. We then set the new topic's `owner` attribute to the current user ❷. Finally, we call `save()` on the topic instance just defined ❸. Now the topic has all the required data and will save successfully.

You should be able to add as many new topics as you want for as many different users as you want. Each user will have access only to their own data, whether they're viewing data, entering new data, or modifying old data.

> **TRY IT YOURSELF**
>
> **19-3. Refactoring:** There are two places in *views.py* where we make sure the user associated with a topic matches the currently logged-in user. Put the code for this check in a function called `check_topic_owner()`, and call this function where appropriate.
>
> **19-4. Protecting new_entry:** A user can add a new entry to another user's learning log by entering a URL with the ID of a topic belonging to another user. Prevent this attack by checking that the current user owns the entry's topic before saving the new entry.
>
> **19-5. Protected Blog:** In your Blog project, make sure each blog post is connected to a particular user. Make sure all posts are publicly accessible but only registered users can add posts and edit existing posts. In the view that allows users to edit their posts, make sure the user is editing their own post before processing the form.

Summary

In this chapter you learned to use forms to allow users to add new topics and entries, and edit existing entries. You then learned how to implement user accounts. You allowed existing users to log in and out, and you learned how to use Django's default `UserCreationForm` to let people create new accounts.

After building a simple user authentication and registration system, you restricted access to logged-in users for certain pages using the `@login_required` decorator. You then attributed data to specific users through a foreign key relationship. You also learned to migrate the database when the migration requires you to specify some default data.

Finally, you learned how to make sure a user can see only data that belongs to them by modifying the view functions. You retrieved appropriate data using the `filter()` method, and you learned to compare the owner of the requested data to the currently logged-in user.

It may not always be immediately obvious what data you should make available and what data you should protect, but this skill will come with practice. The decisions we've made in this chapter to secure our users' data illustrate why working with others is a good idea when building a project: having someone else look over your project makes it more likely that you'll spot vulnerable areas.

We now have a fully functioning project running on our local machine. In the final chapter we'll style Learning Log to make it visually appealing, and we'll deploy the project to a server so anyone with Internet access can register and make an account.

20

STYLING AND DEPLOYING AN APP

Learning Log is fully functional now, but it has no styling and runs only on your local machine. In this chapter we'll style the project in a simple but professional manner and then deploy it to a live server so anyone in the world can make an account.

For the styling we'll use the Bootstrap library, a collection of tools for styling web applications so they look professional on all modern devices, from a large flat-screen monitor to a smartphone. To do this, we'll use the django-bootstrap3 app, which will also give you practice using apps made by other Django developers.

We'll deploy Learning Log using Heroku, a site that lets you push your project to one of its servers, making it available to anyone with an Internet connection. We'll also start using a version control system called Git to track changes to the project.

When you're finished with Learning Log, you'll be able to develop simple web applications, make them look good, and deploy them to a live server. You'll also be able to use more advanced learning resources as you develop your skills.

Styling Learning Log

We've purposely ignored styling until now to focus on Learning Log's functionality first. This is a good way to approach development, because an app is useful only if it works. Of course, once it's working, appearance is critical so people will want to use it.

In this section I'll introduce the django-bootstrap3 app and show you how to integrate it into a project to make it ready for live deployment.

The django-bootstrap3 App

We'll use django-bootstrap3 to integrate Bootstrap into our project. This app downloads the required Bootstrap files, places them in an appropriate location in your project, and makes the styling directives available in your project's templates.

To install django-bootstrap3, issue the following command in an active virtual environment:

```
(ll_env)learning_log$ pip install django-bootstrap3
--snip--
Successfully installed django-bootstrap3
```

Next, we need to add the following code to include django-boostrap3 in `INSTALLED_APPS` in *settings.py*:

settings.py

```
--snip--
INSTALLED_APPS = (
    --snip--
    'django.contrib.staticfiles',

    # Third party apps
    'bootstrap3',

    # My apps
    'learning_logs',
    'users',
)
--snip--
```

Start a new section called *Third party apps* for apps created by other developers and add `'bootstrap3'` to this section. Most apps need to be included in `INSTALLED_APPS`, but to be sure, read the setup instructions for the particular app you're using.

We need django-bootstrap3 to include jQuery, a JavaScript library that enables some of the interactive elements that the Bootstrap template provides. Add this code to the end of *settings.py*:

settings.py

```
--snip--
# My settings
LOGIN_URL = '/users/login/'

# Settings for django-bootstrap3
BOOTSTRAP3 = {
    'include_jquery': True,
    }
```

This code spares us from having to download jQuery and place it in the correct location manually.

Using Bootstrap to Style Learning Log

Bootstrap is basically a large collection of styling tools. It also has a number of templates you can apply to your project to create a particular overall style. If you're just starting out, it's much easier to use these templates than it is to use individual styling tools. To see the templates Bootstrap offers, go to the *Getting Started* section at *http://getbootstrap.com/*; then scroll down to the *Examples* heading, and look for the *Navbars in action* section. We'll use the *Static top navbar* template, which provides a simple top navigation bar, a page header, and a container for the content of the page.

Figure 20-1 shows what the home page will look like after we apply Bootstrap's template to *base.html* and modify *index.html* slightly.

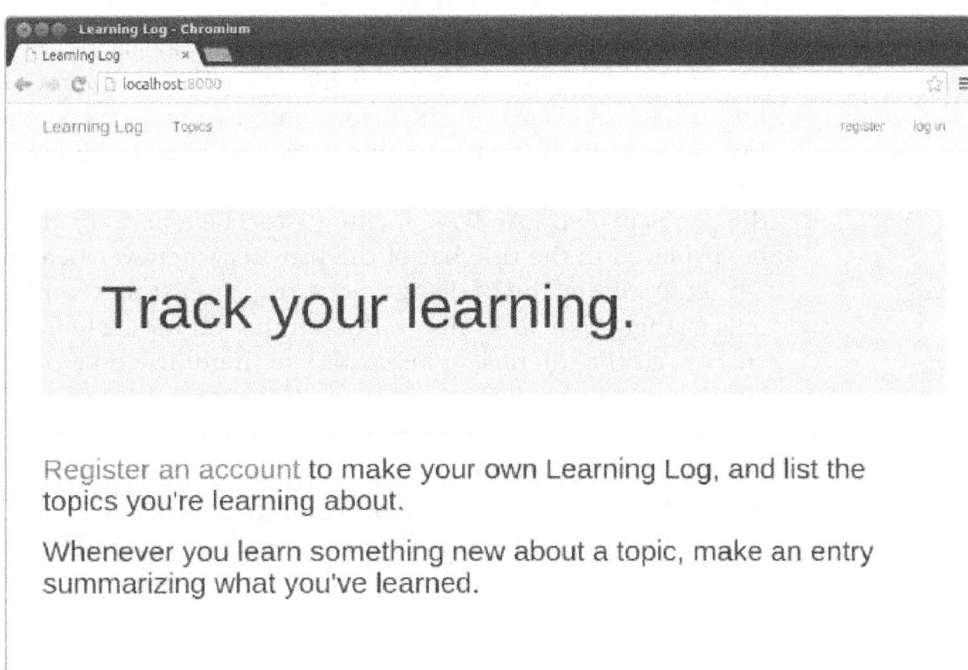

Figure 20-1: The Learning Log home page using Bootstrap

Now that you know the result we're after, the sections that follow will be easier to understand.

Modifying base.html

We need to modify the *base.html* template to accommodate the Bootstrap template. I'll introduce the new *base.html* in parts.

Defining the HTML Headers

The first change to *base.html* defines the HTML headers in the file so whenever a Learning Log page is open, the browser title bar displays the site name. We'll also add some requirements for using Bootstrap in our templates. Delete everything in *base.html* and replace it with the following code:

base.html

```
❶ {% load bootstrap3 %}

❷ <!DOCTYPE html>
❸ <html lang="en">
❹   <head>
      <meta charset="utf-8">
      <meta http-equiv="X-UA-Compatible" content="IE=edge">
      <meta name="viewport" content="width=device-width, initial-scale=1">

❺     <title>Learning Log</title>

❻     {% bootstrap_css %}
      {% bootstrap_javascript %}

❼   </head>
```

At ❶ we load the collection of template tags available in django-bootstrap3. Next, we declare this file as an HTML document ❷ written in English ❸. An HTML file is divided into two main parts, the *head* and the *body*—the head of the file begins at ❹. The head of an HTML file doesn't contain any content: it just tells the browser what it needs to know to display the page correctly. At ❺ we include a `title` element for the page, which will be displayed in the title bar of the browser whenever Learning Log is open.

At ❻ we use one of django-bootstrap3's custom template tags, which tells Django to include all the Bootstrap style files. The tag that follows enables all the interactive behavior you might use on a page, such as collapsible navigation bars. At ❼ is the closing `</head>` tag.

Defining the Navigation Bar

Now we'll define the navigation bar at the top of the page:

```
--snip--
  </head>

  <body>

    <!-- Static navbar -->
```

```
❶     <nav class="navbar navbar-default navbar-static-top">
        <div class="container">

          <div class="navbar-header">
❷           <button type="button" class="navbar-toggle collapsed"
                data-toggle="collapse" data-target="#navbar"
                aria-expanded="false" aria-controls="navbar">
            </button>
❸           <a class="navbar-brand" href="{% url 'learning_logs:index' %}">
                Learning Log</a>
          </div>

❹         <div id="navbar" class="navbar-collapse collapse">
❺           <ul class="nav navbar-nav">
❻             <li><a href="{% url 'learning_logs:topics' %}">Topics</a></li>
            </ul>

❼           <ul class="nav navbar-nav navbar-right">
              {% if user.is_authenticated %}
                <li><a>Hello, {{ user.username }}.</a></li>
                <li><a href="{% url 'users:logout' %}">log out</a></li>
              {% else %}
                <li><a href="{% url 'users:register' %}">register</a></li>
                <li><a href="{% url 'users:login' %}">log in</a></li>
              {% endif %}
❽           </ul>
          </div><!--/.nav-collapse -->

        </div>
      </nav>
```

The first element is the opening `<body>` tag. The body of an HTML file contains the content users will see on a page. At ❶ is a `<nav>` element that indicates the navigation links section of the page. Everything contained in this element is styled according to the Bootstrap style rules defined by the selectors `navbar`, `navbar-default`, and `navbar-static-top`. A *selector* determines which elements on a page a certain style rule applies to.

At ❷ the template defines a button that will appear if the browser window is too narrow to display the whole navigation bar horizontally. When the user clicks the button, the navigation elements will appear in a drop-down list. The `collapse` reference causes the navigation bar to collapse when the user shrinks the browser window or when the site is displayed on mobile devices with small screens.

At ❸ we set the project's name to appear at the far left of the navigation bar and make it a link to the home page, because it will appear on every page in the project.

At ❹ we define a set of links that lets users navigate the site. A navigation bar is basically a list that starts with `<ul>` ❺, and each link is an item in this list (`<li>`) ❻. To add more links, insert more lines using the following structure:

```
<li><a href="{% url 'learning_logs:title' %}">Title</a></li>
```

This line represents a single link in the navigation bar. The link is taken directly from the previous version of *base.html*.

At ❼ we place a second list of navigation links, this time using the selector `navbar-right`. The `navbar-right` selector styles the set of links so it appears at the right edge of the navigation bar where you typically see login and registration links. Here we'll display the user greeting and logout link or links to register or log in. The rest of the code in this section closes out the elements that contain the navigation bar ❽.

Defining the Main Part of the Page

The rest of *base.html* contains the main part of the page:

```
--snip--
    </nav>

❶   <div class="container">

      <div class="page-header">
❷       {% block header %}{% endblock header %}
      </div>
      <div>
❸       {% block content %}{% endblock content %}
      </div>

    </div> <!-- /container -->

  </body>
</html>
```

At ❶ is an opening div with the class `container`. A *div* is a section of a web page that can be used for any purpose and can be styled with a border, space around the element (margins), space between the contents and the border (padding), background colors, and other style rules. This particular div acts as a container into which we place two elements: a new block called `header` ❷ and the `content` block we used in Chapter 18 ❸. The header block contains information telling the user what kind of information the page holds and what they can do on a page. It has the class `page-header`, which applies a set of style rules to the block. The content block is in a separate div with no specific style classes.

When you load the home page of Learning Log in a browser, you should see a professional-looking navigation bar that matches the one shown in Figure 20-1. Try resizing the window so it's really narrow; the navigation bar should be replaced by a button. Click the button, and all the links should appear in a drop-down list.

NOTE *This simplified version of the Bootstrap template should work on most recent browsers. Earlier browsers may not render some styles correctly. The full template, available at* http://getbootstrap.com/getting-started/#examples/, *will work on almost all available browsers.*

Styling the Home Page Using a Jumbotron

Let's update the home page using the newly defined header block and another Bootstrap element called a *jumbotron*—a large box that will stand out from the rest of the page and can contain anything you want. It's typically used on home pages to hold a brief description of the overall project. While we're at it, we'll update the message on the home page as well. Here's *index.html*:

index.html

```
{% extends "learning_logs/base.html" %}

❶ {% block header %}
❷   <div class='jumbotron'>
      <h1>Track your learning.</h1>
    </div>
  {% endblock header %}

  {% block content %}
❸   <h2>
      <a href="{% url 'users:register' %}">Register an account</a> to make
      your own Learning Log, and list the topics you're learning about.
    </h2>
    <h2>
      Whenever you learn something new about a topic, make an entry
      summarizing what you've learned.
    </h2>
  {% endblock content %}
```

At ❶ we tell Django that we're about to define what goes in the header block. Inside a jumbotron element ❷ we place a short tagline, *Track your learning*, to give first-time visitors a sense of what Learning Log does.

At ❸ we add text to provide a little more direction. We invite people to make an account, and we describe the two main actions—add new topics and make topic entries. The index page now looks like Figure 20-1 and is a significant improvement over our unstyled project.

Styling the Login Page

We've refined the overall appearance of the login page but not the login form yet, so let's make the form look consistent with the rest of the page:

login.html

```
  {% extends "learning_logs/base.html" %}
❶ {% load bootstrap3 %}

❷ {% block header %}
    <h2>Log in to your account.</h2>
  {% endblock header %}

  {% block content %}

❸   <form method="post" action="{% url 'users:login' %}" class="form">
      {% csrf_token %}
```

```
❹       {% bootstrap_form form %}

❺       {% buttons %}
          <button name="submit" class="btn btn-primary">log in</button>
        {% endbuttons %}

        <input type="hidden" name="next" value="{% url 'learning_logs:index' %}" />
      </form>

    {% endblock content %}
```

At ❶ we load the bootstrap3 template tags into this template. At ❷ we define the `header` block, which describes what the page is for. Notice that we've removed the `{% if form.errors %}` block from the template; django-bootstrap3 manages form errors automatically.

At ❸ we add a `class="form"` attribute, and then we use the template tag `{% bootstrap_form %}` when we display the form ❹; this replaces the `{{ form.as_p }}` tag we were using in Chapter 19. The `{% boostsrap_form %}` template tag inserts Bootstrap style rules into the individual elements of the form as it's rendered. At ❺ we open a bootstrap3 template tag `{% buttons %}`, which adds Bootstrap styling to buttons.

Figure 20-2 shows the login form as it's rendered now. The page is much cleaner and has consistent styling and a clear purpose. Try logging in with an incorrect username or password; you'll see that even the error messages are styled consistently and integrate well with the overall site.

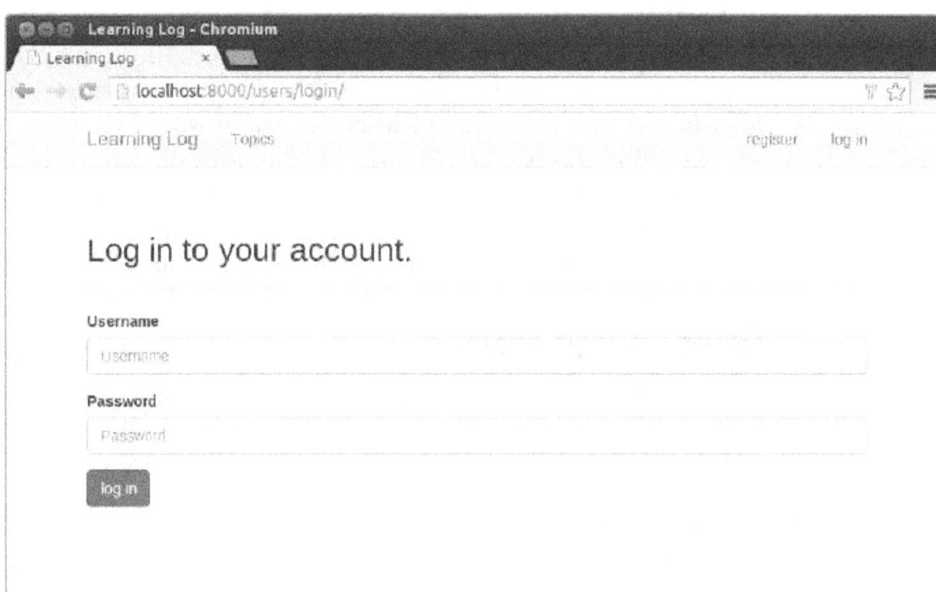

Figure 20-2: The login page styled with Bootstrap

Styling the new_topic Page

Let's make the rest of the pages look consistent as well. We'll update the new_topic page next:

new_topic.html

```
{% extends "learning_logs/base.html" %}
{% load bootstrap3 %}

❶ {% block header %}
    <h2>Add a new topic:</h2>
  {% endblock header %}

  {% block content %}

❷   <form action="{% url 'learning_logs:new_topic' %}" method='post'
        class="form">

      {% csrf_token %}
❸     {% bootstrap_form form %}

❹     {% buttons %}
        <button name="submit" class="btn btn-primary">add topic</button>
      {% endbuttons %}

    </form>

  {% endblock content %}
```

Most of the changes here are similar to those applied in *login.html*: we load bootstrap3 and add the header block with an appropriate message at ❶. Then we add the class="form" attribute to the <form> tag ❷, use the {% bootstrap_form %} template tag instead of {{ form.as_p }} ❸, and use the bootstrap3 structure for the submit button ❹. Log in and navigate to the new_topic page; it should look similar to the login page now.

Styling the Topics Page

Now let's make sure the pages for viewing information are styled appropriately as well, starting with the topics page:

topics.html

```
{% extends "learning_logs/base.html" %}

❶ {% block header %}
    <h1>Topics</h1>
  {% endblock header %}

  {% block content %}

    <ul>
      {% for topic in topics %}
        <li>
```

```
❷         <h3>
            <a href="{% url 'learning_logs:topic' topic.id %}">{{ topic }}</a>
          </h3>
        </li>
      {% empty %}
        <li>No topics have been added yet.</li>
      {% endfor %}
    </ul>

❸   <h3><a href="{% url 'learning_logs:new_topic' %}">Add new topic</h3>

  {% endblock content %}
```

We don't need the `{% load bootstrap3 %}` tag, because we're not using any custom bootstrap3 template tags in this file. We add the heading *Topics* inside the `header` block ❶. We style each topic as an `<h3>` element to make them a little larger on the page ❷ and do the same for the link to add a new topic ❸.

Styling the Entries on the Topic Page

The topic page has more content than most pages, so it needs a bit more work. We'll use Bootstrap's panels to make each entry stand out. A *panel* is a div with predefined styling and is perfect for displaying a topic's entries:

topic.html

```
  {% extends 'learning_logs/base.html' %}

❶ {% block header %}
    <h2>{{ topic }}</h2>
  {% endblock header %}

  {% block content %}
    <p>
      <a href="{% url 'learning_logs:new_entry' topic.id %}">add new entry</a>
    </p>

    {% for entry in entries %}
❷     <div class="panel panel-default">
❸       <div class="panel-heading">
❹         <h3>
            {{ entry.date_added|date:'M d, Y H:i' }}
❺           <small>
              <a href="{% url 'learning_logs:edit_entry' entry.id %}">
                edit entry</a>
            </small>
          </h3>
        </div>
❻       <div class="panel-body">
          {{ entry.text|linebreaks }}
        </div>
      </div> <!-- panel -->
```

```
  {% empty %}
    There are no entries for this topic yet.
  {% endfor %}

{% endblock content %}
```

We first place the topic in the `header` block ❶. We then delete the unordered list structure previously used in this template. Instead of making each entry a list item, we create a `panel` div element at ❷, which contains two more nested divs: a `panel-heading` div ❸ and a `panel-body` div ❻. The `panel-heading` div contains the date for the entry and the link to edit the entry. Both are styled as `<h3>` elements ❹, but we add `<small>` tags around the `edit_entry` link to make it a little smaller than the timestamp ❺.

At ❻ is the `panel-body` div, which contains the actual text of the entry. Notice that the Django code for including the information on the page hasn't changed at all; only the elements that affect the appearance of the page have changed.

Figure 20-3 shows the topic page with its new look. The functionality of Learning Log hasn't changed, but it looks more professional and inviting to users.

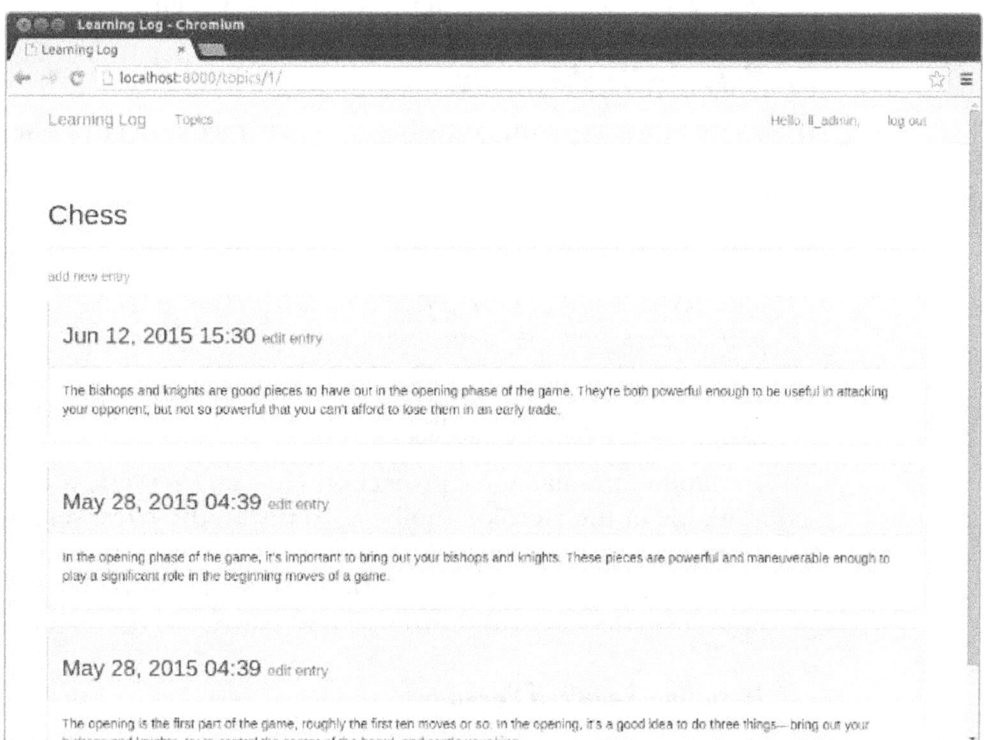

Figure 20-3: The topic page with Bootstrap styling

NOTE *If you want to use a different Bootstrap template, follow a similar process to what we've done so far in this chapter. Copy the template into* base.html*, and modify the elements that contain actual content so the template displays your project's information. Then use Bootstrap's individual styling tools to style the content on each page.*

TRY IT YOURSELF

20-1. Other Forms: We've applied Bootstrap's styles to the `login` and `add_topic` pages. Make similar changes to the rest of the form-based pages: `new_entry` and `edit_entry`, and `register`.

20-2. Stylish Blog: Use Bootstrap to style the Blog project you created in Chapter 19.

Deploying Learning Log

Now that we have a professional-looking project, let's deploy it to a live server so anyone with an internet connection can use it. We'll use Heroku, a web-based platform that allows you to manage the deployment of web applications. We'll get Learning Log up and running on Heroku.

The process is slightly different on Windows than it is on Linux and OS X. If you're using Windows, check for notes in each section that specify what you'll need to do differently on your system.

Making a Heroku Account

To make an account, go to *https://heroku.com/* and click one of the signup links. It's free to make an account, and Heroku has a free tier that allows you to test your projects in live deployment.

NOTE *Heroku's free tier has limits, such as the number of apps you can deploy and how often people can visit your app. But these limits are generous enough to let you practice deploying apps without any cost.*

Installing the Heroku Toolbelt

To deploy and manage a project on Heroku's servers, you'll need the tools available in the Heroku Toolbelt. To install the latest version of the Heroku Toolbelt, visit *https://toolbelt.heroku.com/* and follow the directions for your operating system, which will include either a one-line terminal command or an installer you can download and run.

Installing Required Packages

You'll also need to install a number of packages that help serve Django projects on a live server. In an active virtual environment, issue the following commands:

```
(ll_env)learning_log$ pip install dj-database-url
(ll_env)learning_log$ pip install dj-static
(ll_env)learning_log$ pip install static3
(ll_env)learning_log$ pip install gunicorn
```

Make sure you issue the commands one at a time so you know if any package fails to install correctly. The package `dj-database-url` helps Django communicate with the database Heroku uses, `dj-static` and `static3` help Django manage static files correctly, and `gunicorn` is a server capable of serving apps in a live environment. (*Static files* contain style rules and JavaScript files.)

NOTE *Some of the required packages may not install on Windows, so don't be concerned if you get an error message when you try to install some of them. What matters is getting Heroku to install the packages on the live deployment, and we'll do that in the next section.*

Creating a Packages List with a requirements.txt File

Heroku needs to know which packages our project depends on, so we'll use pip to generate a file listing them. Again, from an active virtual environment, issue the following command:

```
(ll_env)learning_log$ pip freeze > requirements.txt
```

The `freeze` command tells pip to write the names of all the packages currently installed in the project into the file *requirements.txt*. Open *requirements.txt* to see the packages and version numbers installed in your project (Windows users might not see all of these lines):

requirements.txt

```
Django==1.8.4
dj-database-url==0.3.0
dj-static==0.0.6
django-bootstrap3==6.2.2
gunicorn==19.3.0
static3==0.6.1
```

Learning Log already depends on six different packages with specific version numbers, so it requires a specific environment to run properly. When we deploy Learning Log, Heroku will install all the packages listed in *requirements.txt*, creating an environment with the same packages we're using locally. For this reason, we can be confident the deployed project will behave the same as it does on our local system. This is a huge advantage as you start to build and maintain various projects on your system.

Next, we need to add `psycopg2`, which helps Heroku manage the live database, to the list of packages. Open *requirements.txt* and add the line `psycopg2>=2.6.1`. This will install version 2.6.1 of `psycopg2`, or a newer version if it's available:

requirements.txt

```
Django==1.8.4
dj-database-url==0.3.0
dj-static==0.0.6
django-bootstrap3==6.2.2
gunicorn==19.3.0
```

```
static3==0.6.1
psycopg2>=2.6.1
```

If any of the packages didn't install on your system, add those as well. When you're finished, your *requirements.txt* file should include each of the packages shown above. If a package is listed on your system but the version number differs from what's shown here, keep the version you have on your system.

NOTE *If you're using Windows, make sure your version of* requirements.txt *matches the list shown here regardless of which packages you were able to install on your system.*

Specifying the Python Runtime

Unless you specify a Python version, Heroku will use its own current default version of Python. Let's make sure Heroku uses the same version of Python we're using. In an active virtual environment, issue the command `python --version`:

```
(ll_env)learning_log$ python --version
Python 3.5.0
```

In this example I'm running Python 3.5.0. Make a new file called *runtime.txt* in the same directory as *manage.py*, and enter the following:

runtime.txt

```
python-3.5.0
```

This file should contain one line with your Python version specified in the format shown; make sure you enter `python` in lowercase, followed by a hyphen, followed by the three-part version number.

NOTE *If you get an error reporting that the Python runtime you requested is not available, go to* https://devcenter.heroku.com/ *and click* ***Python****; then look for a link to* Specifying a Python Runtime. *Scan through the article to find the available runtimes, and use the one that most closely matches your Python version.*

Modifying settings.py for Heroku

Now we need to add a section at the end of *settings.py* to define some settings specifically for the Heroku environment:

settings.py

```
--snip--
# Settings for django-bootstrap3
BOOTSTRAP3 = {
    'include_jquery': True,
    }
```

```
  # Heroku settings
❶ if os.getcwd() == '/app':
❷     import dj_database_url
      DATABASES = {
          'default': dj_database_url.config(default='postgres://localhost')
      }

      # Honor the 'X-Forwarded-Proto' header for request.is_secure().
❸     SECURE_PROXY_SSL_HEADER = ('HTTP_X_FORWARDED_PROTO', 'https')

      # Allow all host headers.
❹     ALLOWED_HOSTS = ['*']

      # Static asset configuration
❺     BASE_DIR = os.path.dirname(os.path.abspath(__file__))
      STATIC_ROOT = 'staticfiles'
      STATICFILES_DIRS = (
          os.path.join(BASE_DIR, 'static'),
      )
```

At ❶ we use the function `getcwd()`, which gets the *current working directory* the file is running from. In a Heroku deployment, the directory is always */app*. In a local deployment, the directory is usually the name of the project folder (*learning_log* in our case). The `if` test ensures that the settings in this block apply only when the project is deployed on Heroku. This structure allows us to have one settings file that works for our local development environment as well as the live server.

At ❷ we import `dj_database_url` to help configure the database on Heroku. Heroku uses PostgreSQL (also called Postgres), a more advanced database than SQLite, and these settings configure the project to use Postgres on Heroku. The rest of the settings support HTTPS requests ❸, ensure that Django will serve the project from Heroku's URL ❹, and set up the project to serve static files correctly on Heroku ❺.

Making a Procfile to Start Processes

A *Procfile* tells Heroku which processes to start in order to serve the project properly. This is a one-line file that you should save as *Procfile*, with an uppercase *P* and no file extension, in the same directory as *manage.py*.

Here's what goes in *Procfile*:

Procfile

```
web: gunicorn learning_log.wsgi --log-file -
```

This line tells Heroku to use gunicorn as a server and to use the settings in *learning_log/wsgi.py* to launch the app. The `log-file` flag tells Heroku the kinds of events to log.

Modifying wsgi.py for Heroku

We also need to modify *wsgi.py* for Heroku, because Heroku needs a slightly different setup than what we've been using:

wsgi.py

```
--snip--
import os

from django.core.wsgi import get_wsgi_application
from dj_static import Cling

os.environ.setdefault("DJANGO_SETTINGS_MODULE", "learning_log.settings")
application = Cling(get_wsgi_application())
```

We import Cling, which helps serve static files correctly, and use it to launch the application. This code will work locally as well, so we don't need to put it in an `if` block.

Making a Directory for Static Files

On Heroku, Django collects all the static files and places them in one place so it can manage them efficiently. We'll create a directory for these static files. Inside the *learning_log* folder we've been working from is another folder called *learning_log*. In this nested folder, make a new folder called *static* with the path *learning_log/learning_log/static/*. We also need to make a placeholder file to store in this directory for now, because empty directories won't be included in the project when it's pushed to Heroku. In the *static/* directory, make a file called *placeholder.txt*:

placeholder.txt

```
This file ensures that learning_log/static/ will be added to the project.
Django will collect static files and place them in learning_log/static/.
```

There's nothing special about this text; it just reminds us why we included this file in the project.

Using the gunicorn Server Locally

If you're using Linux or OS X, you can try using the gunicorn server locally before deploying to Heroku. From an active virtual environment, run the command `heroku local` to start the processes defined in *Procfile*:

```
(ll_env)learning_log$ heroku local
Installing Heroku Toolbelt v4... done
--snip--
forego | starting web.1 on port 5000
❶ web.1  | [2015-08-13 22:00:45 -0800] [12875] [INFO] Starting gunicorn 19.3.0
❷ web.1  | [2015-08-13 22:00:45 -0800] [12875] [INFO] Listening at:
    http://0.0.0.0:5000 (12875)
❸ web.1  | [2015-08-13 22:00:45 -0800] [12878] [INFO] Booting worker with pid: 12878
```

The first time you run `heroku local`, a number of packages from the Heroku Toolbelt will be installed. The output shows that gunicorn has been started with a process id of 12875 in this example ❶. At ❷ gunicorn is listening for requests on port 5000. In addition, gunicorn has started a *worker* process (12878) to help it serve requests ❸.

Visit *http://localhost:5000/* to make sure everything is working; you should see the Learning Log home page, just as it appears when you use the Django server (`runserver`). Press CTRL-C to stop the processes started by `heroku local`. You should continue to use `runserver` for local development.

NOTE *gunicorn won't run on Windows, so skip this step if you're using Windows. This won't affect your ability to deploy the project to Heroku.*

Using Git to Track the Project's Files

If you completed Chapter 17, you'll know that Git is a version control program that allows you to take a snapshot of the code in your project each time you implement a new feature successfully. This allows you to easily return to the last working snapshot of your project if anything goes wrong; for example, if you accidentally introduce a bug while working on a new feature. Each of these snapshots is called a *commit.*

Using Git means you can try implementing new features without worrying about breaking your project. When you're deploying to a live server, you need to make sure you're deploying a working version of your project. If you want to read more about Git and version control, see Appendix D.

Installing Git

The Heroku Toolbelt includes Git, so it should already be installed on your system. But terminal windows that were open before you installed the Heroku Toolbelt won't have access to Git, so open a new terminal window and issue the command `git --version`:

```
(ll_env)learning_log$ git --version
git version 2.5.0
```

If you get an error message for some reason, see the instructions in Appendix D for installing Git.

Configuring Git

Git keeps track of who makes changes to a project, even in cases like this when there's only one person working on the project. To do this, Git needs to know your username and email. You have to provide a username, but feel free to make up an email for your practice projects:

```
(ll_env)learning_log$ git config --global user.name "ehmatthes"
(ll_env)learning_log$ git config --global user.email "eric@example.com"
```

If you forget this step, Git will prompt you for this information when you make your first commit.

Ignoring Files

We don't need Git to track every file in the project, so we'll tell Git to ignore some files. Make a file called *.gitignore* in the folder that contains *manage.py*. Notice that this filename begins with a dot and has no file extension. Here's what goes in *.gitignore*:

.gitignore

```
ll_env/
__pycache__/
*.sqlite3
```

We tell Git to ignore the entire directory *ll_env*, because we can re-create it automatically at any time. We also don't track the *__pycache__* directory, which contains the *.pyc* files that are created automatically when Django runs the *.py* files. We don't track changes to the local database, because it's a bad habit: if you're ever using SQLite on a server, you might accidentally overwrite the live database with your local test database when you push the project to the server.

NOTE *If you're using Python 2.7, replace* `__pycache__` *with* `*.pyc` *because Python 2.7 doesn't create a* __pycache__ *directory.*

Committing the Project

We need to initialize a Git repository for Learning Log, add all the necessary files to the repository, and commit the initial state of the project. Here's how we do that:

```
❶ (ll_env)learning_log$ git init
Initialized empty Git repository in /home/ehmatthes/pcc/learning_log/.git/
❷ (ll_env)learning_log$ git add .
❸ (ll_env)learning_log$ git commit -am "Ready for deployment to heroku."
[master (root-commit) dbc1d99] Ready for deployment to heroku.
 43 files changed, 746 insertions(+)
 create mode 100644 .gitignore
 create mode 100644 Procfile
 --snip--
 create mode 100644 users/views.py
❹ (ll_env)learning_log$ git status
# On branch master
nothing to commit, working directory clean
(ll_env)learning_log$
```

At ❶ we issue the `git init` command to initialize an empty repository in the directory containing Learning Log. At ❷ we use the `git add .` command, which adds all the files that aren't being ignored to the repository. (Don't forget the dot.) At ❸ we issue the command `git commit -am` *`commit message`*: the `-a` flag tells Git to include all changed files in this commit, and the `-m` flag tells Git to record a log message.

Issuing the git status command ❹ indicates that we're on the *master* branch and that our working directory is *clean*. This is the status you'll want to see any time you push your project to Heroku.

Pushing to Heroku

We're finally ready to push the project to Heroku. In an active terminal session, issue the following commands:

```
❶ (ll_env)learning_log$ heroku login
  Enter your Heroku credentials.
  Email: eric@example.com
  Password (typing will be hidden):
  Logged in as eric@example.com
❷ (ll_env)learning_log$ heroku create
  Creating afternoon-meadow-2775... done, stack is cedar-14
  https://afternoon-meadow-2775.herokuapp.com/ |
      https://git.heroku.com/afternoon-meadow-2775.git
  Git remote heroku added
❸ (ll_env)learning_log$ git push heroku master
  --snip--
  remote: -----> Launching... done, v6
❹ remote:        https://afternoon-meadow-2775.herokuapp.com/ deployed to Heroku
  remote: Verifying deploy.... done.
  To https://git.heroku.com/afternoon-meadow-2775.git
     bdb2a35..62d711d  master -> master
  (ll_env)learning_log$
```

First, log in to Heroku in the terminal session with the username and password you used to create an account at *https://heroku.com/* ❶. Then tell Heroku to build an empty project ❷. Heroku generates a name made up of two words and a number; you can change this later on. We then issue the command git push heroku master ❸, which tells Git to push the master branch of the project to the repository Heroku just created. Heroku then builds the project on its servers using these files. At ❹ is the URL we'll use to access the live project.

When you've issued these commands, the project is deployed but not fully configured. To check that the server process started correctly, use the heroku ps command:

```
  (ll_env)learning_log$ heroku ps
❶ Free quota left: 17h 40m
❷ === web (Free): `gunicorn learning_log.wsgi __log-file -`
  web.1: up 2015/08/14 07:08:51 (~ 10m ago)
  (ll_env)learning_log$
```

The output shows how much more time the project can be active in the next 24 hours ❶. At the time of this writing, Heroku allows free deployments to be active for up to 18 hours in any 24-hour period. If a project exceeds these limits, a standard server error page will be displayed; we'll customize this error page shortly. At ❷ we see that the process defined in *Procfile* has been started.

Now we can open the app in a browser using the command `heroku open`:

```
(ll_env)learning_log$ heroku open
Opening afternoon-meadow-2775... done
```

This command spares you from opening a browser and entering the URL Heroku showed you, but that's another way to open the site. You should see the home page for Learning Log, styled correctly. However, you can't use the app yet because we haven't set up the database.

NOTE *Heroku's deployment process changes from time to time. If you have any issues you can't resolve, look at Heroku's documentation for help. Go to* https://devcenter.heroku.com/, *click* ***Python****, and look for a link to* Getting Started with Django. *If you can't understand what you see there, check out the suggestions in Appendix C.*

Setting Up the Database on Heroku

We need to run `migrate` once to set up the live database and apply all the migrations we generated during development. You can run Django and Python commands on a Heroku project using the command `heroku run`. Here's how to run `migrate` on the Heroku deployment:

```
❶ (ll_env)learning_log$ heroku run python manage.py migrate
❷ Running `python manage.py migrate` on afternoon-meadow-2775... up, run.2435
    --snip--
❸ Running migrations:
    --snip--
    Applying learning_logs.0001_initial... OK
    Applying learning_logs.0002_entry... OK
    Applying learning_logs.0003_topic_user... OK
    Applying sessions.0001_initial... OK
  (ll_env)learning_log$
```

We first issue the command `heroku run python manage.py migrate` ❶. Heroku then creates a terminal session to run the `migrate` command ❷. At ❸ Django applies the default migrations and the migrations we generated during the development of Learning Log.

Now when you visit your deployed app, you should be able to use it just as you did on your local system. However, you won't see any of the data you entered on your local deployment, because we didn't copy the data to the live server. This is normal practice: you don't usually copy local data to a live deployment because the local data is usually test data.

You can share your Heroku link to let anyone use your version of Learning Log. In the next section we'll complete a few more tasks to finish the deployment process and set you up to continue developing Learning Log.

Refining the Heroku Deployment

In this section we'll refine the deployment by creating a superuser, just as we did locally. We'll also make the project more secure by changing the setting `DEBUG` to `False`, so users won't see any extra information in error messages that they could use to attack the server.

Creating a Superuser on Heroku

You've already seen that we can run one-off commands using the `heroku run` command. But you can also run commands by opening a Bash terminal session while connected to the Heroku server using the command `heroku run bash`. *Bash* is the language that runs in many Linux terminals. We'll use the Bash terminal session to create a superuser so we can access the admin site on the live app:

```
(ll_env)learning_log$ heroku run bash
Running `bash` on afternoon-meadow-2775... up, run.6244
❶ ~ $ ls
learning_log learning_logs manage.py Procfile requirements.txt runtime.txt
users
staticfiles
❷ ~ $ python manage.py createsuperuser
Username (leave blank to use 'u41907'): ll_admin
Email address:
Password:
Password (again):
Superuser created successfully.
❸ ~ $ exit
exit
(ll_env)learning_log$
```

At ❶ we run `ls` to see which files and directories exist on the server, which should be the same files we have on our local system. You can navigate this file system like any other.

NOTE *Windows users will use the same commands shown here (such as* `ls` *instead of* `dir`*), because you're running a Linux terminal through a remote connection.*

At ❷ we run the command to create a superuser, which outputs the same prompts we saw on our local system when we created a superuser in Chapter 18. When you're finished creating the superuser in this terminal session, use the `exit` command to return to your local system's terminal session ❸.

Now you can add */admin/* to the end of the URL for the live app and log in to the admin site. For me, the URL is *https://afternoon-meadow-2775.herokuapp.com/admin/*.

If other people have already started using your project, be aware that you'll have access to all of their data! Don't take this lightly, and users will continue to trust you with their data.

Creating a User-Friendly URL on Heroku

You'll probably want your URL to be friendlier and more memorable than *https://afternoon-meadow-2775.herokuapp.com/*. You can rename the app using a single command:

```
(ll_env)learning_log$ heroku apps:rename learning-log
Renaming afternoon-meadow-2775 to learning-log... done
https://learning-log.herokuapp.com/ | https://git.heroku.com/learning-log.git
Git remote heroku updated
(ll_env)learning_log$
```

You can use letters, numbers, and dashes when naming your app, and call it whatever you want, as long as no one else has claimed the name. This deployment now lives at *https://learning-log.herokuapp.com/*. The project is no longer available at the previous URL; the `apps:rename` command completely moves the project to the new URL.

NOTE *When you deploy your project using Heroku's free service, Heroku puts your deployment to sleep if it hasn't received any requests after a certain amount of time or if it's been too active for the free tier. The first time a user accesses the site after it's been sleeping, it will take longer to load, but the server will respond to subsequent requests more quickly. This is how Heroku can afford to offer free deployments.*

Securing the Live Project

One glaring security issue exists in the way our project is currently deployed: the setting `DEBUG=True` in *settings.py*, which provides debug messages when errors occur. Django's error pages give you vital debugging information when you're developing a project, but they give way too much information to attackers if you leave them enabled on a live server. We also need to make sure no one can get information or redirect requests by pretending to be the project's host.

Let's modify *settings.py* so we can see error messages locally but not on the live deployment:

settings.py

```
--snip--
# Heroku settings
if os.getcwd() == '/app':
    --snip--
    # Honor the 'X-Forwarded-Proto' header for request.is_secure().
    SECURE_PROXY_SSL_HEADER = ('HTTP_X_FORWARDED_PROTO', 'https')

    # Allow only Heroku to host the project.
❶   ALLOWED_HOSTS = ['learning-log.herokuapp.com']

❷   DEBUG = False

    # Static asset configuration
    --snip--
```

We need to make only two changes: at ❶ we modify ALLOWED_HOSTS, so the only server allowed to host the project is Heroku. You need to use the name of your app, whether it's the name Heroku provided, such as *afternoon-meadow-2775.herokuapp.com*, or the name you chose. At ❷ we set DEBUG to False, so Django won't share sensitive information when an error occurs.

Committing and Pushing Changes

Now we need to commit the changes made to *settings.py* to the Git repository, and then push the changes to Heroku. Here's a terminal session showing this process:

```
❶ (ll_env)learning_log$ git commit -am "Set DEBUG=False for Heroku."
  [master 081f635] Set DEBUG=False for Heroku.
   1 file changed, 4 insertions(+), 2 deletions(-)
❷ (ll_env)learning_log$ git status
  # On branch master
  nothing to commit, working directory clean
  (ll_env)learning_log$
```

We issue the git commit command with a short but descriptive commit message ❶. Remember that the -am flag makes sure Git commits all the files that have changed and records the log message. Git recognizes that one file has changed and commits this change to the repository.

At ❷ the status shows that we're working on the master branch of the repository and that there are now no new changes to commit. It's essential that you check the status for this message before pushing to Heroku. If you don't see this message, some changes haven't been committed, and those changes won't be pushed to the server. You can try issuing the commit command again, but if you're not sure how to resolve the issue, read through Appendix D to better understand how to work with Git.

Now let's push the updated repository to Heroku:

```
(ll_env)learning_log$ git push heroku master
--snip--
remote: -----> Python app detected
remote: -----> Installing dependencies with pip
--snip--
remote: -----> Launching... done, v8
remote:        https://learning-log.herokuapp.com/ deployed to Heroku
remote: Verifying deploy.... done.
To https://git.heroku.com/learning-log.git
   4c9d111..ef65d2b  master -> master
(ll_env)learning_log$
```

Heroku recognizes that the repository has been updated, and it rebuilds the project to make sure all the changes have been taken into account. It doesn't rebuild the database, so we won't have to run migrate for this update.

To check that the deployment is more secure now, enter the URL of your project with an extension we haven't defined. For example, try to visit *http://learning-log.herokuapp.com/letmein/*. You should see a generic error page on your live deployment that doesn't give away any specific information about the project. If you try the same request on the local version of Learning Log at *http://localhost:8000/letmein/*, you should see the full Django error page. The result is perfect: you'll see informative error messages when you're developing the project further, but users won't see critical information about the project's code.

Creating Custom Error Pages

In Chapter 19, we configured Learning Log to return a 404 error if the user requests a topic or entry that doesn't belong to them. You've probably seen some 500 server errors (internal errors) by this point as well. A 404 error usually means your Django code is correct, but the object being requested doesn't exist; a 500 error usually means there's an error in the code you've written, such as an error in a function in *views.py*. Currently, Django returns the same generic error page in both situations, but we can write our own 404 and 500 error page templates that match the overall appearance of Learning Log. These templates must go in the root template directory.

Making Custom Templates

In the *learning_log/learning_log* folder, make a new folder called *templates*. Then make a new file called *404.html* using the following code:

404.html

```
{% extends "learning_logs/base.html" %}

{% block header %}
    <h2>The item you requested is not available. (404)</h2>
{% endblock header %}
```

This simple template provides the generic 404 error page information but is styled to match the rest of the site.

Make another file called *500.html* using the following code:

500.html

```
{% extends "learning_logs/base.html" %}

{% block header %}
    <h2>There has been an internal error. (500)</h2>
{% endblock header %}
```

These new files require a slight change to *settings.py*.

settings.py

```
--snip--
TEMPLATES = [
    {
        'BACKEND': 'django.template.backends.django.DjangoTemplates',
        'DIRS': [os.path.join(BASE_DIR, 'learning_log/templates')],
```

```
        'APP_DIRS': True,
        --snip--
    },
]
--snip--
```

This change tells Django to look in the root template directory for the error page templates.

Viewing the Error Pages Locally

If you want to see what the error pages look like on your system before pushing them to Heroku, you'll first need to set `Debug=False` on your local settings to suppress the default Django debug pages. To do so, make the following changes to *settings.py* (make sure you're working in the part of *settings.py* that applies to the local environment, not the part that applies to Heroku):

settings.py

```
--snip--
# SECURITY WARNING: don't run with debug turned on in production!
DEBUG = False

ALLOWED_HOSTS = ['localhost']
--snip--
```

You must have at least one host specified in `ALLOWED_HOSTS` when `DEBUG` is set to `False`. Now request a topic or entry that doesn't belong to you to see the 404 error page, and request a URL that doesn't exist (such as *localhost:8000/letmein/*) to see the 500 error page.

When you're finished checking the error pages, set `DEBUG` back to `True` to further develop Learning Log. (Make sure `DEBUG` is still set to `False` in the section of *settings.py* that applies to the Heroku deployment.)

NOTE *The 500 error page won't show any information about the user who's logged in, because Django doesn't send any context information in the response when there's a server error.*

Pushing the Changes to Heroku

Now we need to commit the template changes and push them live to Heroku:

```
❶ (ll_env)learning_log$ git add .
❷ (ll_env)learning_log$ git commit -am "Added custom 404 and 500 error pages."
   3 files changed, 15 insertions(+), 10 deletions(-)
   create mode 100644 learning_log/templates/404.html
   create mode 100644 learning_log/templates/500.html
❸ (ll_env)learning_log$ git push heroku master
  --snip--
  remote: Verifying deploy.... done.
```

```
To https://git.heroku.com/learning-log.git
   2b34ca1..a64d8d3  master -> master
(ll_env)learning_log$
```

We issue the git add . command at ❶ because we created some new files in the project, so we need to tell Git to start tracking these files. Then we commit the changes ❷ and push the updated project to Heroku ❸.

Now when an error page appears, it should have the same styling as the rest of the site, making for a smoother user experience when errors arise.

Using the get_object_or_404() Method

At this point, if a user manually requests a topic or entry that doesn't exist, they'll get a 500 server error. Django tries to render the page but it doesn't have enough information to do so, and the result is a 500 error. This situation is more accurately handled as a 404 error, and we can implement this behavior with the Django shortcut function get_object_or_404(). This function tries to get the requested object from the database, but if that object doesn't exist, it raises a 404 exception. We'll import this function into *views.py* and use it in place of get():

views.py

```
--snip--
from django.shortcuts import render, get_object_or_404
from django.http import HttpResponseRedirect, Http404
--snip--
@login_required
def topic(request, topic_id):
    """Show a single topic and all its entries."""
    topic = get_object_or_404(Topic, id=topic_id)
    # Make sure the topic belongs to the current user.
    --snip--
```

Now when you request a topic that doesn't exist (for example, *http://localhost:8000/topics/999999/*), you'll see a 404 error page. To deploy this change, make a new commit, and then push the project to Heroku.

Ongoing Development

You might want to further develop Learning Log after your initial push to a live server or develop your own projects to deploy. There's a fairly consistent process for updating projects.

First, you'll make any changes needed to your local project. If your changes result in any new files, add those files to the Git repository using the command git add . (be sure to include the dot at the end of the command). Any change that requires a database migration will need this command, because each migration generates a new migration file.

Then commit the changes to your repository using git commit -am "*commit message*". Thereafter, push your changes to Heroku using the command git push heroku master. If you migrated your database locally, you'll need to migrate the live database as well. You can either use the one-off command heroku run python manage.py migrate, or open a remote terminal session with heroku run bash and run the command python manage.py migrate. Then visit your live project, and make sure the changes you expect to see have taken effect.

It's easy to make mistakes during this process, so don't be surprised when something goes wrong. If the code doesn't work, review what you've done and try to spot the mistake. If you can't find the mistake or you can't figure out how to undo the mistake, refer to the suggestions for getting help in Appendix C. Don't be shy about asking for help: everyone else learned to build projects by asking the same questions you're likely to ask, so someone will be happy to help you. Solving each problem that arises helps you steadily develop your skills until you're building meaningful, reliable projects and you're answering other people's questions as well.

The SECRET_KEY Setting

Django uses the value of the SECRET_KEY setting in *settings.py* to implement a number of security protocols. In this project, we've committed our settings file to the repository with the SECRET_KEY setting included. This is fine for a practice project, but the SECRET_KEY setting should be handled more carefully for a production site. If you build a project that's getting meaningful use, make sure you research how to handle your SECRET_KEY setting more securely.

Deleting a Project on Heroku

It's great practice to run through the deployment process a number of times with the same project or with a series of small projects to get the hang of deployment. But you'll need to know how to delete a project that's been deployed. Heroku might also limit the number of projects you can host for free, and you don't want to clutter your account with practice projects.

Log in to the Heroku website (*https://heroku.com/*), and you'll be redirected to a page showing a list of your projects. Click the project you want to delete, and you'll see a new page with information about the project. Click the **Settings** link, and scroll down until you see a link to delete the project. This action can't be reversed, so Heroku will ask you to confirm the request for deletion by manually entering the project's name.

If you prefer working from a terminal, you can also delete a project by issuing the destroy command:

```
(ll_env)learning_log$ heroku apps:destroy --app appname
```

Here *appname* is the name of your project, which is either something like afternoon-meadow-2775 or learning-log if you've renamed the project. You'll be prompted to reenter the project name to confirm the deletion.

NOTE *Deleting a project on Heroku does nothing to your local version of the project. If no one has used your deployed project and you're just practicing the deployment process, it's perfectly reasonable to delete your project on Heroku and redeploy it.*

> **TRY IT YOURSELF**
>
> **20-3. Live Blog:** Deploy the Blog project you've been working on to Heroku. Make sure you set `DEBUG` to `False` and change the `ALLOWED_HOSTS` setting, so your deployment is reasonably secure.
>
> **20-4. More 404s:** The `get_object_or_404()` function should also be used in the `new_entry()` and `edit_entry()` views. Make this change, test it by entering a URL like *http://localhost:8000/new_entry/99999/*, and check that you see a 404 error.
>
> **20-5. Extended Learning Log:** Add one feature to Learning Log, and push the change to your live deployment. Try a simple change, such as writing more about the project on the home page. Then try adding a more advanced feature, such as giving users the option of making a topic public. This would require an attribute called `public` as part of the `Topic` model (this should be set to `False` by default) and a form element on the new_topic page that allows the user to change a topic from private to public. You'd then need to migrate the project and revise *views.py* so any topic that's public is visible to unauthenticated users as well. Remember to migrate the live database after you've pushed your changes to Heroku.

Summary

In this chapter you learned to give your projects a simple but professional appearance using the Bootstrap library and the django-bootstrap3 app. Using Bootstrap means the styles you choose will work consistently on almost any device people use to access your project.

You learned about Bootstrap's templates, and we used the *Static top navbar* template to create a simple look and feel for Learning Log. You learned how to use a jumbotron to make a home page's message stand out, and you learned to style all the pages in a site consistently.

In the final part of the project, you learned how to deploy a project to Heroku's servers so anyone can access it. You made a Heroku account and installed some tools that help manage the deployment process. You used Git to commit the working project to a repository and then pushed the repository to Heroku's servers. Finally, you learned to secure your app by setting `DEBUG=False` on the live server.

Now that you've finished Learning Log, you can start building your own projects. Start simple, and make sure the project works before adding complexity. Enjoy your learning, and good luck with your projects!

www.ingramcontent.com/pod-product-compliance
Lightning Source LLC
LaVergne TN
LVHW082027200926
848481LV00010B/2937